Law-Making in the Global Community

CONTRIBUTORS

Antony D'Amato, *Professor, Northwestern University School of Law*

Richard A. Falk, *Albert G. Milbank Professor of International Law and Practice, Department of Politics and Woodrow Wilson School of Public and International Affairs, Princeton University*

Gidon Gottlieb, *Leo Spitz Professor of Law and International Diplomacy, The Law School, The University of Chicago*

Charles W. Kegley, Jr., *Professor, Department of Government and International Studies, University of South Carolina*

Nicholas Greenwood Onuf, *Associate Professor, School of International Service, The American University*

Zdenek J. Slouka, *Professor, Department of International Relations, and Director, International Studies Program, Center for Social Research, Lehigh University*

This book was written under the auspices of the
Center of International Studies,
Princeton University

Law-Making in the Global Community

edited by

Nicholas Greenwood Onuf

CAROLINA ACADEMIC PRESS

DURHAM, NORTH CAROLINA

International Standard Book Number: 0-89089-169-9
Library of Congress Catalog Card Number: 80-68078
Printed in the United States of America

Carolina Academic Press
P.O. Box 8795, Forest Hills Station
Durham, North Carolina 27707

Contents

Foreword

RICHARD FALK

Law-making is necessarily fundamental for a world order system dominated by territorial states. Indeed, the whole enterprise of law without government or governance taxes the jurisprudential imagination of each generation of international lawyers. Our shaping image of law is associated, if not with commands and centralized enforcement, at least with centralized institutions of authority possessing the competence to specify, as necessary, legal rights and duties. On these grounds, international law remains, especially on issues of war and peace, a disappointing endeavor.

International law as a legal order is, as a consequence, both confusing in its character and controversial in its effects. It is confusing because the explanation of its validity under varying circumstances is in many respects a subjective matter. For instance, whether we endow General Assembly resolutions with law-making potential reflects an underlying disposition as to whether "law" is an expression of natural rights and duties, emergent customary practice, or remains tied to the consent of governments. This underlying disposition can be rationalized in a number of coherent ways incorporating, presumably, some unacknowledged ideological biases. For instance, someone eager to promote the growth of supranationalism or convinced that the General Assembly majority is mostly on the side of "justice" is inclined to endow such resolutions with legal effect. On the contrary, someone who believes in the validity and viability of the state system or is of the opinion that the General Assembly majority is "irresponsible" is likely to dismiss the law-making claims of such resolutions with scorn.

Because there is no convincing way to resolve the confusion, especially given the degree to which it reflects differing values and assessments of what is necessary and possible, controversy is inevitable. Proponents of each position marshall their precedents and doctrinal justifications, argue against or, what is worse, ignore opposing positions, and appeal to a variety of audiences, some of which are overtly partisan (as in political arenas), others of which are covertly partisan (as in professional arenas, for instance, international law societies). The predominant reality, however, is the subjectivity that attaches to an appraisal of all features of the international legal order, including even the actions of its own most juridical of institutions (International Court of Justice, International Commission of Jurists).

Such subjectivity is an unavoidable feature of a political order composed of actors with diverse, often antagonistic, interests and normative traditions. At times, this subjectivity can be disguised or minimized, as was the case in the eighteenth and nineteenth century, when international society was dominated by a group of state actors who generally shared a common set of interests and normative traditions. It is also true that if the role of law is specified in marginal ways—to set the rules of the game, as by requiring declarations of war, peace treaties, and the like—then the participants are more likely to be willing to respect its constraints than if it attempts more ambitious matters such as recourse to force or limiting the means by which war is waged.

What has been happening in recent decades is for the subjectivity of the international legal order to grow more evident and troublesome. For one thing, the decolonization process has made the diversity among states more manifest as participants in the world system clash on the basis of opposed interests and ideals. For another, the march of normative evolution, catalyzed by public pressures, has crowded in on the practice of geopolitics and sovereign rights. We have in this century the growth of legal restraints on the use of force, even including the radical Nuremberg claim to impose criminal standards of accountability on governmental leaders, and an emergent human rights law prohibiting gross abuses of citizens within their own sovereign states. This growth of law, however has neither bent state practice to its will, nor established means by which to deal with flagrant violations. As a consequence, there is prevalent a phenomenon of "soft law," rules that possess formal validity but engender virtually no respect. For instance, after years of effort, a definition of aggression was finally endorsed in 1974 by all governments as an authoritative guideline to the United Nations Charter, and yet, as was quite predictable, it is virtually ignored in the formation of state policy. Governments do not even take the trouble to make out a case that a given use of force is compatible with the agreed renunciation of aggression.

And yet, on other levels, the pressures for more ambitious law-making are getting stronger. The complexity and interdependence of the present world system means that it is much costlier to leave certain kinds of interaction either to chance or the self-interest of particular states, or to rely upon the crude, uncrystallized guidelines of customary international law. Whether the matter is allocation of radio or TV frequencies, protecting endangered species of whales or birds, or guarding against the adverse effects of oil spillage, the shared, global need for a regulatory framework is evident. The long struggle to negotiate a new law of the seas is illustrative of these various pushes and pulls. The diversities among actors make the negotiating process more arduous, perhaps even problematic. The complexities establish the incentive to establish as much "hard law" as possible. Hence, the negotiating ordeal tests the limits of bargaining as a law-making energy in international life. Whatever emerges from these massive negotiations in the end, it will provide an invaluable insight into the adaptive potential of law-making approaches to international order.

A central challenge for law-making efforts is to identify widely endorsed images of "reasonableness." The voluntarist character of the present system (lacking sanctions, police capabilities) requires its rules to seem beneficial and fair for all, thereby minimizing the incentive to violate. Whenever diversities are too acute or interests too intense, the validity of a legal rule will not engender much respect if incentives to violate emerge in a strong form. Embodying a bargain on specifics in treaty form is one way to test whether a given set of rule is likely to serve as a basis of effective constraint on state behavior.

But a treaty format is not necessarily sufficient, as is evident in the setting of the November 1979 seizure of diplomatic premises and personnel at the United States Embassy in Teheran by student militants. The Vienna Convention on Diplomatic Relations (1961) contains evidently unambiguous, authoritative rules that serve the common, reciprocal interests of governments in unconditional immunity. These interests received full endorsement after the Iranian hostage seizure by both the International Court of Justice and the Security Council. And yet there was something lacking besides the refusal of Ayatollah Khomeini to urge compliance with international law in this instance.

This "something lacking" has to do with the perceived one-sidedness of international law by many actors, especially Third World governments. Why should the rules against using embassy premises to subvert the constitutional order of the host state be conditional under international law while the immunity of diplomats and their facilities be unconditional? Why should it be so comparatively easy to extradite those who commit crimes of resistance (called *terrorism*) and so difficult to extradite or even assess the accountability of those who commit crimes of state (exempted as *political crimes*)? These questions suggest that "reasonableness" is a political fact, shifting with the consciousness of the actors who compose the world system. Responses must acknowledge in the first instance *the hegemonial structure* of the state system (that is, prevailing international law inhibits inequalities of power more ambiguouly than it sets common rules of the statist game) and in the second instance *the statist character* of the present world order system (that is, prevailing international law achieves far greater cooperation to protect the state against its enemies than to apprehend those power-wielders who abuse state power). Law-making procedures that maintain a stiff-necked disdain for these political facts will seem artificial, and will aggravate the tensions of diversity. The path to maximum legal effectiveness includes validating the dynamic of accommodation as between law and political setting, and not insisting upon the permanent durability of old rules and standards just because they are formally binding.

Of course, some balance is desirable. The agreement process so crucial to law-making among governments is worth the trouble only if it tends to guide and orient behavior over a reasonable period of time. It is costly, also, to cast aside legal constraints. The objections, to be consistent with a viable international legal order, need to be principled claims based on the arbitrariness or unfairness of the old legal regime. Mere inconvenience is not enough to justify a refusal by a government to obey applicable rules.

In contrast, legal controversies about the testing of nuclear weapons on the high seas in the 1950s or the establishment of a quarantine on international shipping during the Cuban Missile Crisis of 1962 are framed in an enlarged context. In each instance, the United States claim to act, although based on some wider world order justifications, would appear dubious from the point of view of prior law. The plausibility of these legal claims seemed mainly to reflect the availability of superior military force. Yet, in the Iran hostage crisis, a stalemate resulted because the availability of superior military force could not be translated into the effective assertion of the American legal claim. The rescue mission fiasco of April 1980 was an attempt of sorts to reinforce the United States claim that the hostages were being held illegally in Iran, but it was an effort that was blocked decisively by logistical difficulties, and by a realization that any more intense reliance on military force would hurt national interests even wider than those at stake in relation to the hostage seizure. As a consequence, the Iranian resistance to the claims of the old law was not overcome. The eventual negotiated resolution failed to shed much light on the status of the respective legal positions.

What is evident, however, is the connection between law-making and power in any controversial setting. The Western approach to Iran was influenced by interests in Persian Gulf oil and by the Iranian options to shift diplomatic alignment, including seeking support from the Soviet Union. That is, as Ali Mazrui has vividly shown, at this stage in history, power comes as readily, perhaps more readily, from a barrel of oil than it does from the barrel of a gun. It is this interplay of coercive capabilities among contending actors that provides the background of compliance and violation, but its an interplay vastly more complicated than drawing out the implications of whatever ratio of military forces exists in the situation.

The law-making potential here extends beyond whether a country can succeed in widening the context of claim to include its grievances about the United States role. It extends to whether governmental grants of asylum for deposed leaders accused of state crimes are unconditional and discretionary. It also extends to whether the abuse of diplomatic privileges by recourse to covert operations or through complicity in state crimes (for instance, training foreign state policy in torture techniques) gives rise to certain rights of retaliation by the territorial sovereign beyond declaring diplomatic personnel to be *personae non gratae*.

We have in these settings the elusive outer margins of customary international law. That is, a continuous flow of legal expectations whose shifting course reshape the riverbed of obligation in ways that are often difficult for even experts to agree upon.

There are, of course, many other settings that seem challenging from theoretical and practical law-making perspectives. The momentum of technological innovation, both in relation to scale and type of concern, create pressures for international legal arrangements. One haunting question concerns the allocation of rights and duties in advance of explicit agreement on the legal treatment of "a new fact" in international life. Nothing illustrates this concern more powerfully than the fitful debate that has swirled around the legal status of nuclear weapons since their initial use in 1945. One this momentous matter it remains controversial as to whether law has been "made" since the Hiroshima blast. One side invokes the *Lotus* principle that everything is permitted unless prohibited, the other contending that the general principles of the law of war based on discrimination and humanity (i.e., the avoidance of cruel effects) are applicable to new weapons and tactics, an applicability confirmed by a Japanese domestic court in the *Shimoda* decision of 1963. In any event, there exists a law-making gap, possibly inevitable in an international legal order that is divided between a few powerful nuclear weapon states and a large number of non-nuclear countries.

One way of filling such a gap, at least provisionally, consists of the multifarious international law activities of domestic courts. There is an enormous potential here to the extent that domestic courts conceive of their identity as shaped, in part at least, by their functions as agents of the international legal order rather than as judicial branches of a particula national government. Such roles are likely to be unevenly enacted from country to country and from issue-area to issue-area for some time to come. For instance, United States courts are prepared to pronounce upon the law-at-stake more easily on behalf of property rights than of human rights. However, in a recent American case, *Filartiga v Pena-Irala*, 630 BF. 2d 876 (2d. Cir. 1980), a domestic court held that an international legal rule prohibiting torture could be invoked in a tort action against foreign government officials who acted in a foreign country. That is, a domestic court "created" an international law criterion for the protection of human rights. It will be important to discover whether this salutary initiative will be sustained in the American judicial order and extended to other contexts.

What seems evident, however, is the importance of law-making processes to the evolution of tolerable forms of order in international life. Despite the elusiveness of these processes at the international level, the conjoining of claim with justification gives the legal approach to international order definite advantages over either reliance on naked force or empty moralism. At least it seems that law-making provides a framework within which to balance a concern with stability against the pressure for change.

These potential contributions will not amount to much unless there is a widespread realization that "law" is mainly helpful as a strategy of participation in international life. Given the largely voluntaristic character of world order, as matters now stand, various actors must become aware that their aspirations and interests can be promoted by creative uses of international law. In this regard, if international law is experienced mainly as a legacy from the past, then it will be resisted by actors who possess sweeping demands for change. Law-making potential enables post-colonial adjustments, provided enough flexibility exists. Again, a balance is sought. Excessive flexibility would undermine any tendency to accord respect to obligations that exerted a constraining impact on discretion.

Given the persistence of international turmoil it becomes crucial to reconsider law-making potential. In part, such reassessment is needed to discover whether the balance between flexibility and stability is adequate in the present would order system, and if not, how it might be improved in a variety of procedural and substantive settings. In part, also, the purpose of this inquiry is to encourage awareness, especially conveying actual and potential roles for law in relation to even reform-oriented leadership of state actors. It is possible to shake the mystique that law is *necessarily* holding back pressures for change; creative use of various law-making arenas, contrary to the conservative image, will include principled demands to satisfy these pressures. The progressive prospects for international law require more than complaints and critique. It depends on a flow of law-making efforts, including the reorientation of law-making around the quest for widely affirmed world order values.

Preface

Between 1969 and 1972 the Center of International Studies at Princeton University published in four volumes a comprehensive survey, several years in preparation, on *The Future of the International Legal Order*. Scholars contributed forty substantial essays to the project under the editorial direction of Richard A. Falk and Cyril E. Black. Each volume in turn aroused considerable interest within the scholarly community, cumulatively encouraging the Center's leadership to plan a second phase for the project. Again volumes of original essays were to be the format, but each volume would be devoted to a well-defined topic. Because of its obvious importance to the unfolding of a just and durable global order, law-making was one topic designated for early attention.

The Center prepared for work on global law-making by holding a day-long planning conference in March 1973. Participants agreed that a project under Center auspices was well warranted. Soon thereafter, I was invited to become a Visiting Research Fellow at the Center during the Spring of 1974 and assume responsibility for directing the project. More specifically I was to prepare a working paper on law-making, invite other interested scholars to develop appropriate additional essays, and organize a two-day conference to discuss my paper and a number of outlines, with an eye to the eventual publication of a volume of essays. Prospective contributors and other interested specialists attended this second conference in May 1974.

A generous grant from the Rockefeller Foundation allowed me to return to the Center in the Spring of 1975 in order to organize a third and final conference on law-making. Several major papers were circulated prior to the two days of discussions in May, and they along with my own much expanded and revised essay were projected as the core of a volume systematically treating global law-making in all its major dimensions.

My efforts to fill gaps and order materials into a comprehensive and coherent whole met with a variety of difficulties during the 1975-1976 academic year, which was spent only part-time at the Center. Eventually an alternative strategy prevailed, namely, one that traded any pretense of a comprehensive treatment of the subject for a volume consisting of even fewer essays whose complementary character allowed the volume an unforced coherence. All of the essays retained for publication shared an additional attribute. They presented summaries of existing scholarship only incidentally. Instead they concentrated on fresh conceptualizations of a subject dominated by centuries-old intellectual traditions. Consequently the volume shows a marked tendency toward abstract formulation. Finally all of these essays shared a concern for law-making that draws on the conceptual and empirical arsenals of legal scholarship and the social sciences. While lawyers and political scientists, which we are in equal number, rarely trouble to communicate with each other, these essays were united in the willingness of their authors to range across allied but not always congenial realms of discourse.

Finding a publisher and securing revised essays from busy contributors who had long since turned to other endeavors occupied my intermittent attention long after my relation to Princeton had come to a formal close. Assistance from Professors Falk and Black continued. Keith Sipe on behalf of Carolina Academic Press provided needed encouragement, and all contributors, I among them, revised their essays. I made no effort to pressure my collaborators to touch on stated themes or develop particular points: the harmony of the whole proceeds from a shared desire to penetrate beneath the surface of conventional ideas about law-making rather than from the presentation of an integrated facade. There are no doubt times in which our respective efforts to avoid the stifling effects of received categories and conceptions run at cross-purposes. But there are many more times in which these essays unconsciously resonate with each other more than they do with the available literature on the subject.

Of course, the fact that we all discussed these papers at Princeton promotes such concordance as may exist. Common influences are also at work. Page after page in this book offers proof of Professor Richard Falk's impact on contemporary scholarship. Standing behind Falk and in some measure all of us is Myres S. McDougal. Professor McDougal's example inspires a commitment found everywhere in this volume to demystify legal processes. Both the grounds and means for doing so are eclectically drawn from pragmatism, legal and political realism, functional approaches in several fields, political behavioralism, and scientific positivism. These are characteristic, but not always reconcilable, ingredients of a distinctively American brew. For the contributors, all of whom work in the United States, this brew is seasoned with one other ingredient, which is American only, by reputation, in its most naive expression. This is a commitment to a just and humane planetary order.

None of us mix these ingredients in the same proportion or to the same effect. For the most part their relevance is acknowledged only implicitly, so that their presence, though uneven, is no basis for editorial intervention and embellishment in the form of an introductory essay. The order of presentation is determined, without further comment, by the specificity of the problem area addressed by each essay. Each defines its compass more narrowly than the one before. This is not to say that the chapters are ordered from abstract to concrete in content. They vary even within themselves in their concern for applied empirics, but all are devoted in the first instance in rethinking the foundations of the problem area identified for consideration in that essay.

The substantive results of the law-making project stand as presented, the responsibility of their several authors. Whether they stand together is my responsibility, not theirs. Without the assistance of the late Mrs. Jane G. McDowall and her staff at the Center of International Studies, and energetic discussions at the three conferences held at Princeton, there would be no results to report. The participants in the three conferences, and the years of their attendance, are given below as grateful acknowledgement of their help and support in bringing this project to its present conclusion.

Participants, Conferences on Law-Making in the Global Community, Center of International Studies, Princeton University, and years attending

Fouad Ajami	1974,5
Richard R. Baxter	1974
Cyril E. Black	1973,4,5
Samuel A. Bleicher	1973
Nam-Yearl Chai	1974,5
Jerome A. Cohen	1974,5
Percy E. Corbett	1973
Anthony D'Amato	1975
Richard A. Falk	1973,4,5
Thomas M. Franck	1973
Robert L. Friedheim	1974,5
Gerald Garvey	1973,4

L. F. E. Goldie	1973
Leon Gordenker	1974,5
Gidon Gottlieb	1973,5
Charles W. Kegley, Jr.	1974,5
Jan Kolasa	1975
Richard B. Lillich	1973
Lennart Lundqvist	1974
Donald W. McNemar	1974,5
N. G. Onuf	1973,4,5
Chris Osakwe	1974,5
Arvid Pardo	1974
Arthur W. Rovine	1974
James P. Sewell	1974,5
Zdenek J. Slouka	1973,4,5
John Stremlau	1974
John R. Stevenson	1973
Oran R. Young	1975

Global Law-Making and Legal Thought

NICHOLAS GREENWOOD ONUF

THE PROVINCE OF JURISPRUDENCE CONSIDERED: DISCIPLINED THOUGHT ABOUT LAW AND LAW-MAKING

Positivism: Pure and Simple

Legal thought is a term used in these pages, for lack of a better but equally convenient formulation, to comprehend any tradition of disciplined social thought as it relates to law and law-making. Legal thought normally refers to intellectual traditions directly concerned with the connection between law and order. The larger use of the term employed here requires us to supply in some instances the relation of law to an otherwise well-developed body of thought about social order and its origins.

An encompassing definition risks loss of discipline and a shapeless text. A measure of formality in the organization of work, a format more like that of a treatise than an essay, reduces that risk. The gain from such a definition comes in the form of a challenge, necessarily informal and occasionally speculative, to deeply entrenched patterns of legal thought narrowly defined. By no means does this challenge imply a blanket repudiation of the great traditions of legal thought, whose makers are drawn from freely and whose main works are acknowledged, even echoed in some of the essay's major headings.

All the more because of our inclusive definition, we cannot hope to survey the entire landscape of disciplined legal thought in limited space. We shall confine ourselves to two respects: first, to legal thought bearing on the normative order said to operate at the global level—the international legal order, as it has increasingly come to be called[1]— and, second, to the contemporary reality of a globalized state system of distinctly Western origins. Thus we begin with the development of positivist doctrine.

Historically and conceptually positivism, more than any other system of legal

In addition to the 1974 and 1975 Conference participants listed in the Preface, Kenneth D. Auerbach, Michael Barkun, Catherine L. Bruno, Roger Congress, David P. Forsythe, Jeffrey Hart, Fritz Kratochwil, Larman C. Wilson, and Kathryn Wittneben read and commented on drafts of this essay. I thank them all. Hereinafter "I" becomes the formal or impersonal "we" but never the committee "we," attributing or assuming concurrence on the part of fellow contributors or other friendly critics.

1. On the evolution of the international legal order as an idea, with particular attention to the problem of order in Western political thought, see Nicholas Greenwood Onuf, "International Legal Order as an Idea," *American Journal of International Law*, Vol. 73, No. 2 (April 1979), pp. 244-266. If the present essay slights a major intellectual tradition devoted to the problem of social order, it is that associated with Western political thought. This essay and the one cited may thus be taken as complementary attacks on one of the greatest of all intellectual puzzles—the nature and origins of social order.

thought, is identified with the Western state system. The central positivist tenet, developed presently, that law is made by men and, by extension, human collectivities called states, is the dominant jurisprudential stance of our own time. As with the state system itself, we can decry positivism in specifics without affecting the way it colors our vision of social reality. Positivism and behind it Western liberal rationalism stand in symbiotic relation to the Western state system and its normative order. As long as the system succeeds in dominating the globe, positivism as a way of thinking about law contributes to the system's legitimacy and so to its success. In turn positivism is legitimized by the system as a global reality. One might even say that through the state system positivism confers legitimacy upon itself.

As the Western state system globalized in the years following World War II, some wondered whether newly independent states would challenge the validity of the international legal order. The Soviet Union and the People's Republic of China provided ample precedent with their own challenges to Western institutions and ideas. Nevertheless, evidence was soon forthcoming to assure the West that new states would not, or could not, renounce the order receiving them.[2] The price of acceptance in the system was to accept the system on its own terms. With nothing to bargain with, no other terms were possible. Accepting the system, however, new states found opportunities to pool an asset derived from participation, namely, their votes in the United Nations. They vote for changes in the normative order (whether real or apparent is another matter) on the assumption that this changes the system itself.[3]

The circumstances of their piecemeal entry into the system have forced new states into a strategy that might be described as revolution from within. The interesting feature of most such revolutions is the extent to which revolutionary zeal is tempered both by day-to-day participation in the system's affairs and by gradual assimilation of the system's underlying assumptions. While there is no assurance that the revolution from within will not tear the system apart, we may suppose that the longer the system survives the more likely it is to subdue restive members than be subverted by them.

Positivism will survive to the extent the system does. As the system changes, however, so does the normative order and supporting doctrine.[4] Changes in the system, like most social change, make the system more complex. Gone with the simplicity of the classical system is the purity of positivist doctrine expressed in its most classical form.

---

2.   The literature on new states in the international legal order is too large to be cited at length. Some major sympathetic treatments are: Richard A. Falk, "The New States and the International Legal Order," Academie de Droit International, *Recueil des cours*, Vol. 118 (1966/II), pp. 7-102; A. A. Fatouros, "The Participation of the 'New' States in the International Legal Order," in Richard A. Falk and Cyril E. Black, eds., *The Future of the International Legal Order. Vol. I, Trends and Patterns* (Princeton: Princeton University Press, 1969), pp. 317-371; R. P. Anand, *New States and International Law* (Delhi: Vikas Pub., 1972). On new states accepting the order as such, see respectively pp. 31-37, 336-346, 62-70.

3.   See the second section of this chapter, under "New Sources," for more on this controversial matter.

4.   The term *doctrine* is generally used in preference to *theory* throughout this essay for two reasons. While there is considerable overlap, the former clearly includes any general system of explanation, including explanations about things that are observed, supposed, or even imagined. Whether the latter term is this inclusive is a matter of some controversy. The term *doctrine* also connotes a significant level of acceptance, be it the product of faith or observation, which need not accompany theory. Obviously a general theory that appears to explain what it purports to is indistinguishable from doctrine. The transformation of apparently good theory into doctrine helps to explain the resistance to discarding or amending theory once it becomes less tenable in light of new observations, especially those that are the direct result of theory testing. Testing theories and renovating them accordingly is at the heart of the scientific enterprise. This kind of activity has not really penetrated the realm of legal thought, only partly because of procedural difficulties (what lawyers might call evidentiary considerations). Consequently, some philosophers of science might hesitate to call legal theory theory as such, though doctrine it surely is.

Confronted by an increasingly chaotic empirical reality, received doctrine cannot sustain the burden of baroque embellishment. Instead its formal elegance is slowly dissolving in a sea of competing critiques and alternative formulations. What survives is not altogether dissimilar from the rude features of nascent positivism: less a doctrine about law than a procedure for ascertaining laws.[5]

A generally accepted doctrinal accommodation to the globalization of the Western state system may yet emerge. Such a time may be decades off, however, if we are to judge from the history of positivist legal thought. Doctrine has always lagged behind changes in the system and their cumulative effects, all the more obviously when cumulative effects snowball into a change of system, such as took place several centuries ago in "the long century" (1450-1640).[6] If we are now in the midst of a sea-change in the world system comparable to the transition from the medieval to the modern world, then a long time may pass before the normative order settles down enough for the elaboration of an appropriately comprehensive doctrine to begin. Such a doctrine would surely be as different from positivism as positivism is from its predecessor, the doctrine called naturalism, that law is found in nature and reflects a higher order of things.[7]

The real challenge to the world system is not simply or even primarily the challenge posed by its newer members. It is the convergence of factors brought on as much as anything by the system's success—success we recognize in its globalization and even more in the explosive rates of growth characterizing almost anything touched by the West. If the system changes enough to meet the challenge,[8] positivism will be with us as long as states, or anything resembling them, are. If the system and its normative order succumb or change so fundamentally that states no longer exist, the present disarray of

---

5. Related to this argument is Alexandrowicz' interesting assertion that "the concept of a *European* law of nations emerged only in the second half of the eighteenth century." Prior to that time European states dealt widely with Asian and African political entities later absorbed as colonial entities. Their reappearance correlates with the reappearance of rude, or "empirical" postivism, to use Alexandrowicz' term. C. H. Alexandrowicz, "Empirical and Doctrinal Positivism in International Law," *British Year Book of International Law*, Vol. 47 (1974-1975), pp. 286-289, quoting p. 288 with original emphasis. In an earlier work, "The Afro-Asian World and the Law of Nations (Historical Aspects)," Academie de Droit International, *Recueil des cours*, Vol. 123 (1968/I), pp. 123-127, Alexandrowicz confused empirical positivism with natural law doctrine because of the latter's universalizing tendencies. Such tendencies are equally attributable to positivism before its doctrinal ossification.

6. This phrase is Immanuel Wallerstein's. His book, *The Modern World-System, Capitalist Agriculture and the Origins of the European World-Economy in the Sixteenth Century* (New York: Academic Press, 1974), is a striking appreciation of the magnitude of change involved. By emphasizing the socioeconomic foundations of such change, Wallerstein casts doubt on the proposition that the last several centuries have seen a succession of systems whose essential attributes we might call political. The most notable example of this orientation is Richard Rosecrance, *Action and Reaction in World Politics* (Boston: Little, Brown, 1963), in which nine distinct systems spanning the years 1740-1960 are identified.

7. The position taken here is quite at odds with Richard A. Falk's in "A New Paradigm for International Legal Studies: Prospects and Proposals," *Yale Law Journal*, Vol. 84, No.5 (April 1975), pp. 975-992. Falk sees the emergence of the new system (the Peace of Westphalia) and the emergence of supporting doctrine as virtually simultaneous. This view is doubly defective. As noted, the present system began to emerge two centuries before Westphalia. And though he may be the father of international law, Grotius could hardly be said to have launched those elements of doctrine most essential to the system's support, which we now know as positivism. Falk's view of the "modern statist paradigm" (to use his words) as having emerged rather rapidly, contribute to his sanguine view that a postmodern juridical paradigm can also emerge rapidly, indeed as a revolutionary force. See pp. 1009-1021.

8. The Club of Rome has made the world familiar with this as the *problematique humaine*. For a systematic consideration of the problems and prospects of engineering a change from the present to a preferred world in the future, see Richard A. Falk, *A Study of Future World* (New York: The Free Press, 1975).

doctrine is merely a prelude to the decline and disappearance of even the simplest kind of positivism.[9]

*   *   *   *   *   *

The Western state system took at least two centuries to emerge fully from the medieval order in Europe. The medieval view of the world as a natural order was never discredited by rapid change in socioeconomic and political circumstances. Through gradual secularization natural law doctrine was stretched to the point of becoming transparently thin. Emerich de Vattel's famous treatise, *Le droit des gens* (1758), illustrates this trend perfectly. Deferential to but undirected by natural law doctrine, Vattel was forced to rely on his limited diplomatic experience and Enlightenment sensibilities in describing the substantive law among nations. Unmatched in its influence for a hundred years, Vattel's work epitomizes the misguiding light thrown by that era.[10]

Positivism emerged in the late eighteenth century, contemporaneously with Vattel (1714-1767) and at least a hundred, possibly two or three hundred, years after circumstances ordained its arrival. When it finally came, positivism was unencumbered with any but the simplest doctrine: The law among states was made by states among themselves. Early positivism, as in the hands of Johann Jakob Moser (1701-1785) and Georg Friedrich von Martens (1756-1821), was dedicated to finding out what the law actually was by looking at what states did and how they construed what they did. As a practical matter, this simple mandate presented the legal scholar with an enormous challenge, for the evidence of state practice, as it was called, was anything but uniformly accessible. This challenge perhaps delayed for a time the raising of a number of interpretative questions. For example, was all practice to be weighed equally? How much practice was enough? The response to these questions was piecemeal and pragmatic. Each writer made his own judgments, more or less consistently with the judgment of his fellows.

The appearance of a substantial doctrinal edifice, beginning in the early nineteenth century was an event quite independent of the accretion of evidence about state practice and the development of criteria for interpreting that evidence. Instead the study of domestic legal orders faced a lesser, or at least a different, empirical challenge than that posed by relations among states and fostered the growth of positivist doctrine, in due course brought to bear on the international legal order. Abstract propositions about the nature of law were advanced in the context of general philosophical systems and defended in deductive terms. First with Jeremy Bentham (1748-1832), then John Austin (1790-1859),

---

9.   For some observations on the kind of world system likely to arise from the ashes of the present system, should it succumb, see N. G. Onuf and Fouad Ajami, "Feudalism—The Normative Side of Dominance and Dependence," presented at the 1975 Meeting of the American Political Science Association.

10.   Consistent with his view on the rapid emergence of doctrine buttressing the state system, Falk sees Vattel as consolidating the juridical revolution begun by Grotius. Falk (fn. 7), pp. 977,990. While Vattel was undeniably influential, especially in the United States, we may attribute this to the persistence of secular-naturalist ideas of the Enlightment by virtue of being sanctified as revolutionary ideals. While Enlightenment ideas may be said to have deeply affected the nature of domestic institutions within many states, they have proven to be basically irrelevant to the system of relations between states. Thus the principle of equality is incidental to the principle of sovereignty in positivist doctrine and has no autonomous significance, as Enlightenment-inspired doctrine would dictate, despite its operational importance.

See Arthur Nussbaum, *A Concise History of the Law of Nations* (New York: Macmillan, rev. ed., 1954), pp. 156-164, on Vattel's stature and relation to the emergence of positivist doctrine. The position taken here and in the following paragraph is guided by Nussbaum's treatment of the period from Westphalia to the Napoleonic Wars (ch. 5).

and eventually to our century with German and English language variants on positivism, doctrinal considerations have received continuous attention, albeit with only ephemeral relation to ongoing compilation and analysis of the actual (positive) law.

We could even say that positivism has developed distinct branches of macro- and micro-analysis, one a purely formal construction of what law is, the other a simple prescription for painstaking research into what states do in the name of law. Simple positivism is reflected in the production of major treatises, digests of state practice, and codes of alleged rules. In short, it has become a major enterprise, involving the activities of private individuals and increasingly public bodies.[11] Pure positivism, by contrast, has always been the preserve of a few great masters. Despite the modest wave of current interest in theoretical matters, the great masters of doctrine, intent on capturing the essence of law and stating it as pure theory, have all but disappeared.[12] Their passing is little mourned, but their influence persists to a degree that suggests their work was basically finished. Most accurately, they came in their work to the doctrine's logical limits. Positivist logic continues to appeal within its limits even as it has defied masterful attempts to move beyond them.

By the end of the nineteenth century, pure positivism had already come under severe criticism for its excessively formalistic, analytical qualities.[13] This was part of a larger revolt against formalism which took place most conspicuously in American intellectual life but was felt elsewhere, at least in legal thought.[14] The movement against positivist doctrine has come to be known as sociological jurisprudence.[15] Despite this title, it has very little to do with the development of systematic sociology then underway in Europe.[16] Rather it was influenced most markedly by the well-known American penchant

---

11.   See the second section of this chapter, under "New Sources," for further observations on this kind of activity.

12.   *Pure theory* is a term identified especially with Hans Kelsen, perhaps the most prominent master of positivist doctrine in this century. The current wave of interest in theory is almost entirely what McDougal and associates call "limited factor analyses," instead of general theoretical constructs capable of doctrinal service. Myres S. McDougal, Harold D. Lasswell, and W. Michael Reisman, "Theories about International Law: Prologue to a Configurative Jurisprudence," *Virginia Journal of International Law*, Vol. 8, No. 2 (April 1968), pp. 188-299. See also Richard A. Falk, "Some New Approaches to the Study of International Law," in Falk, *The Status of Law in International Society* (Princeton: Princeton University Press, 1970), pp. 447-469.

Although the configurative jurisprudence of McDougal and associate may yet prove to be the major exception they claim, so far it must he regarded as a limited factor approach couched in an ambitious but largely unrealized framework. It is as if doctrinal elaboration has outpaced the development of ideas with explanatory potential (theory).

13.   Pure positivist doctrine is widely known by the name *analytical jurisprudence* because of its deductive orientation.

14.   This phrase is Morton White's subtitle to *Social Thought in America* (Boston: Beacon Press, rev. ed., 1957). White identifies legal scholar Oliver Wendell Holmes, Jr., as a major figure in a revolt that extended to most aspects of social inquiry.

15.   The title *sociological jurisprudence* was quite possibly Roscoe Pound's inspiration, and certainly it was Pound who popularized it. More than Holmes or any other figure, Pound must be called the father of sociological jurisprudence and its most dedicated exponent. See his famous series of essays in the *Harvard Law Review* entitled, "The Scope and Purpose of Sociological Jurisprudence," Vol. 24, No. 8 (June 1911), pp. 591-619, Vol. 25, No. 2 (December 1911), pp. 140-168, and Vol. 25, No. 6 (April 1912), pp. 489-516; and see his reaffirmation of the scope and purpose of sociological jurisprudence in light of subsequent scholarship in Roscoe Pound, *Jurisprudence*, Vol. I (St. Paul, Minn.: West Pub., 1959), ch. 6. See also Alan Hunt, *The Sociological Movement in Law* (Philadelphia: Temple University Press, 1978), Ch. 2, for a critical assessment of Pound's contribution to legal thought.

16.   See the third section of this chapter under "Law as Solutions and Law as Artifacts," for the parallel but largely unrelated development of a sociology of law integral to the sociology then flowering in France and Germany. It should be said of Pound that he was intimately aware of this development and counted it as part

for applied knowledge, which by then had acquired philosophical standing and the altogether appropriate name of Pragmatism.

Sociological jurisprudence eschewed the elaboration of doctrine. Its one tenet, that law is a means of social control, delimited the scope of sociological jurisprudence and led to the espousal of an ambitious program to insure practical consequences of legal study.[17] Having damned the doctrinal edifice of positivism, members of the sociological movement were content to ignore rather than dismantle that edifice because of its patent irrelevance to their principal concern, which was the actual workings of a given legal order. The practical experience of lawyers and judges was more valued than any philosopher's constructions, although specific insights and formulations might be borrowed from allied disciplines. The interdisciplinary proclivities of sociological jurisprudence were more a matter of rhetoric than practice, however, because the movement's members were for the most part lawyers, with little interest and background in the just developing social sciences.

Sociological jurisprudence developed a body of literature extolling its own importance and speculating rather informally on the relation of law to society and morality. As a school, sociological jurisprudence produced a mystique instead of a master. Its success was in some part because it encouraged doctrinal complacency and research pluralism. By the time a contemporary, systematically inclined scholar like Julius Stone attempted to develop a sustained doctrinal perspective, the sheer mass and diversity of material defeated his valiant effort. The master came too late. A monument to learning is hardly the same as a doctrinal edifice. The former is measured by what it includes, the latter by how much it explains.

The relation of law to varieties of social experience is not intrinsically unyielding to generalization and doctrinal elaboration. The Marxist perspective on law illustrates the possibility, despite the tendentious purposes to which the elaboration of Marxist doctrine are sometimes put.[19] The absence of a sociological doctrinal edifice less critically directed than the larxist is thus a product of the fragmentation of intellectual tendencies generally in post-Victorian life as well as the peculiar accidents of history we find in the sociological movement. Lacking a unifying edifice, sociological jurisprudence ultimately failed to dislodge positivist doctrine from its commanding position in legal training and legal thought.[20] Whatever its defects, the positivist reduction of virtually all societies to just one kind of order, legal in nature, is still with us. It coexists uneasily with recognition that social control, as an empirical matter, is an enormously complicated and infinitely varied process.

The Pillars of Positivist Doctrine: Subject, Sanction, and Source

To the contemporary legal mind, steeped in positivism, three words—subject, sanction, and source—instantly trigger a chain reaction of loosely associated ideas. Taken

---

of the rich early history of sociological jurisprudence. Nonetheless, the term *sociological* seems to have been chosen more to contrast the new school with historical and analytical branches of jurisprudence dominated by British and Continental writers than to ally it with sociology.

17.   Pound, (fn. 15), pp. 350-358.

18.   See his *Social Dimensions of Law and Justice* (Stanford: Stanford University Press, 1966).

19.   See the Fourth section of this chapter, under "Law and Order."

20.   This is even more the case with Socialist legal doctrine which, though rooted in Marx's system of socioeconomic explanation, is nonetheless supremely positivistic in its conception of the international legal order. Of course positivist principles have been a major asset for Socialist states wishing to secure their place in a hostile world.

together, they may fairly be said to embody most lawyers' theoretical appreciation of law, as opposed to their infinitely richer and more complex working knowledge of the law. Of the three, the term subject is central to the positivist conception of a distinctive and clearly delimited international order. The other two terms tell us the international order is a legal one.

Positivist doctrine interprets the fact that the order is international to mean that the subjects are and can only be independent and fully sovereign nation states. Minor anomalies in the form of partially sovereign principalities left over from the medieval order were explained away with the fiction that ultimate sovereignty could always be located. Since the anomalous entities were themselves disappearing over the years as major states rounded out their territories, there was little pressure on the premise that the subjects of the order were states alone.

After World War II the trend was clearly reversed. Both international organizations and private persons, corporate and individual, were treated for some purposes as subjects of the order. This posed a problem for positivist doctrine, the response to which has been a subtle and sometimes unacknowledged shift of emphasis from states as subjects to the system itself. In this view the decisive feature of the international legal order is its relation to a system which is more than a collection of states but less than the totality of human relations across state frontiers. Some writers see the system dominated by the relations of states, even though the system includes other entities and relations whose status is ultimately determined by states.[21] For others, who are growing in number, new actors are gradually encroaching on matters once the preserve of states in such a way as to enlarge the domain of transnational public order at the expense of both the international legal order and domestic orders.[22] A few others go further and argue that states are already moribund or rapidly deteriorating in their capacity to engender order in the system. The system's disarray has reached the point that new actors are not just encroaching on the system but are in the midst of reconstituting it from the inside out.[23]

The common theme in these apparently diverse trends is an attempt to accommodate what is happening in the system by de-emphasizing state actors as fully independent sovereigns. General agreement that the emerging order differs fundamentally from the postulated order is one thing. Agreement on exactly how it is different is quite another. Nonetheless there is considerable willingness to treat the question, How much different?

---

21. See as important examples: P. E. Corbett, *Law and Society in the Relations of State* (New York: Harcourt, Brace and Co., 1951); Charles DeVisscher, *Theory and Reality in Public International Law* (Princeton: Princeton University Press, rev. ed. trans. P. E. Corbett. 1968, first pub. 1953); and more overtly systemic, being influenced by trends in the social sciences, Stanley Hoffmann, "International Law and International Systems," *World Politics*, Vol. 14, No. 1 (October 1961), pp. 205-237; Morton A. Kaplan and Nicholas DeB. Katzenbach, *The Political Foundations of International Law* (New York: John Wiley and Sons, 1961).

22. Philip C. Jessup, *A Modern Law of Nations* (New York: Macmillan, 1948), ch. 2; Philip C. Jessup, *Transnational Law* (New Haven: Yale University Press, 1956); Wolfgang Friedmann, *The Changing Structure of International Law* (New York: Columbia University Press, 1964). Curiously, while the systems motif appeared first in sociology and political science and was imported to the study of international law, the transnational motif was well established in the latter before it was "discovered" by the former. See Robert Cooley Angell, *Peace on the March, Transnational Participation* (New York: Van Nostrand Reinhold, 1969); Robert O. Keohane and Joseph S. Nye, Jr., eds., "Transnational Relations and World Politics," *International Organization*, Vol. 25, No. 3 (Summer 1971).

23. Falk's work (fn. 7, pp. 993-1021, for example) dominates scholarly literature espousing this view, without neglecting to document the resistance of states to system transformation. On such resistance see also Richard A. Falk, *A Global Approach to National Policy* (Cambridge, Mass.: Harvard University Press, 1975), ch. 1.

as an empirical matter. Going out and looking at what is happening in the system is consistent with simple positivism which, in its earliest traditions, concerned itself with what was happening with the actors. The difference is one of focus. The system itself can no longer be taken for granted as merely framing the positivist field of vision. Now the researcher must establish what the system is before he can ascertain the content of norms ordering the system.

Furthermore, concern for the system is entirely in keeping with the research tradition of sociological jurisprudence. Without denying an intrinsically legal character to the international system, the sociological tradition encourages the researcher to explore the complexities of the present-day system and attunes him to the accompanying complexities of social control in such a system. Sociological jurisprudence may have made its greatest gift to international legal studies by tempering the positivist mind-set with a sensitivity to the rapidly changing nature of international reality, as manifested in the proliferation of unfamiliar types of actors which are nonetheless integral to the legal order of the system. By absorbing the system view, positivism has absorbed what sociological jurisprudence has to offer in bringing positivism, including its doctrine, closer to contemporary intellectual taste.

*   *   *   *   *   *

In positivist doctrine the terms *sanction* and *source* are shorthand statements about the essential and defining features of all law, truly so-called. The question, What counts as law?[24] is subject to categorical answer because terms, *sanction* and *source,* provide us with (in principle) a sharply defined conceptual domain, law, against which the empirical domain, what, can be assessed. What fits, counts. Positivism gives us a counting technique. Note that counting here is a strictly utilitarian device to establish what falls within a stipulated category called law and what does not. It cannot decide what is important—what really counts, or what one can count on, to use everyday language.

Counting in a proper utilitarian sense implies that all pertinent phenomena can be reduced to individual items which can be tagged, grouped, and rearranged at will. This assumption, so much at the heart of philosophical and scientific positivism generally, surely helps to account for positivism's hold on the modern Western mind. If we turn to international legal scholarship, we find an almost obsessive concern with one question —Is international law truly law? Asked another way, Should we count it as law? Inevitably the answer is structured around the terms *sanction* and *source,* which become the principal categories for dealing with the problem of what is legal about, or in, the international order.

Consider the matter of sanction. Following in Hobbes' footsteps, Bentham and most memorably Austin identified the application of a sanction in the event of violative behavior as the singularly decisive property that law must have to be law. Austin concluded that international law in particular could not be law because no centralized enforcement procedure existed. Writing nearly a century later, Max Weber (1864-1920) could say that international law was a marginal case of law, while his near contemporary Hans Kelsen (1881-1973) could defend the view that international law was indeed law. Since all three conclusions started with the same Austinian premise, we infer that an

---

24.   As framed the question is borrowed from Anthony A. D'Amato. See his essay below. See also Ronald Dworkin, "A Model of Rules," *University of Chicago Law Review* Vol. 35, No. 1 (August 1967), p. 18, in which counting is referred to in the same manner.

extraordinary amount of doctrinal manipulation is possible. For Austin the critical factor is the absence of centralized sanctioning procedures, for Weber external guarantee of law by an independent and professional staff is crucial, and for Kelsen the existence of self-help through reprisals is sufficient for the purpose of proving sanctions exist in the instance of international law.[25]

The notion of sanction is an article of faith in positivist doctrine. The precise meaning of the term, however, is anything but a matter of common agreement, at least when it is applied to the problem of international law as law. Impurities in the notion are apparently inevitable, as is disquiet over the resulting doctrinal incongruities. In recent years especially sanctions thinking has received a certain amount of critical scrutiny,[26] but the effect on positivist thought is negligible (as yet) compared to the widespread grass-roots ferment over the old positivist position on subjects of the international legal order. Perhaps the failure of sociological jurisprudence to confront the essence of positivist doctrine head-on helps to account for the persistence of sanctions thinking in connection with the international legal order.

The notion of source is second only to sanction as a property of legal orders. Less discomfort arises when international law is under scrutiny because the international legal order does not differ visibly from domestic orders with respect to this property. While the existence of an authentic sanctioning procedure at the international level is a fiercely contested proposition, there is near universal agreement that the international order does possess identifiable sources of its law. Fears about the status of international law as law, raised by the sanctions problem, can be allayed by invoking its sources as a property of law discernibly fulfilled. Any difficulties with this idea apply generally to whatever might count as law and thus do not constitute a basis for singling out international law as defective.

Sources thinking is less an invention of positivist thought than sanctions thinking is. Rather it is an importation from Roman law, which became a subject of immense interest in the nineteenth century. Revived largely as a vehicle for systematic and comparative thinking about law, Roman law does not make sources a logical requirement of law. Instead, having something called sources is a convenient organizing tool. It can be modified as needed to give a designated legal order a classification of the particular means by which its rules are elaborated. No such classification itself makes the way (or ways) law comes forth proper or valid. There must be an independent basis for validity. Yet positivist thought has inextricably associated sources, as a taxonomic convenience, with the separable question of the ultimate source of validity as if the former were somehow, implicitly, an answer to the latter.

The presence of sources hardly answers the question of validity. At best it provides clues to the first causes of legal order, as we note in a later section. If source and validity are not logically connected, then we cannot assume that sources are intrinsic to legal orders. Whether we can ever answer the question of validity, we can always inquire into

---

25. John Austin, *The Province of Jurisprudence Determined* (1832 and many later ed.), Lecture V; *Max Weber on Law in Economy and Society* (New York: The Free Press, 1954), pp. 5-7; Hans Kelsen, *Principles of International Law* (New York: Rinehart and Co., 1952), pp. 18-25.

26. Michael Barkun, *Law without Sanction* (New Haven: Yale University Press, 1968); Gidon Gottlieb, "The Nature of International Law: Toward a Second Concept of Law," in Richard A. Falk and Cyril E. Black, eds., *The Future of the International Legal Order, Vol. IV, The Structure of the International Environment* (Princeton: Princeton University Press, 1972), pp. 331-383; Nicholas Greenwood Onuf, *Reprisals Rituals, Rules, Rationales*, Research Monograph No. 42, Center of International Studies, Princeton University (1974).

the utility of a particular classification of sources. We can retain the Roman law classification, update it, or cast it aside for an alternative conceptualization better suited to the empirical reality of a particular legal order.

The term *source* is itself easily jettisoned. Law-making, for example, has a contemporary ring to it, and it is somewhat less deterministic in implication. The change in terminology from *sources of law* to *modes of law-making* aptly suggests that over time in most legal orders the active control over the production of law (legislation, treaties) seems to have gained relative to the emergence of law as the unpremeditated consequence of other activities (precedent, custom). Despite the shift in emphasis, substitution of the term *law-making* for *sources* is frequently cosmetic. Modes of law-making and particular sources of law match closely.[27] Else the term *law-making*, or such terms as *normative processes*, may be used generically in place of a classificatory scheme.[28]

It might be argued that any classification uses incidental differences to make artificial categories, dividing that which is integral, and imposing structure on that which flows as a process. Used generically, terms like *law-making* and *normative processes* cut through thickets of overrefined and unhelpful distinctions to expedite the investigation of how law happens.[29] Carried to an extreme, however, the refusal to impose analytical order on a complicated reality, simply because distortions result, is ultimately a refusal to engage in intellectual activity as understood in the rationalist-positivist tradition of the West. A holistic orientation toward law-making is thus a methodological choice made in its extreme form as a matter of principle and in moderate form as a substantive judgment about the nature of law.

Pure positivism is, as we know, analytical in temper. Most positivist doctrinalists undoubtedly prefer a differentiating construct to murkily holistic substitutes like *law-making*. This is not to say that source is the best conceivable construct. Quite to the contrary, H. L. A. Hart, who is possibly the most formidable of contemporary pure positivists, has elaborated an alternative conceptualization that has attracted considerable attention.

According to Hart, a legal order consists in a union of primary rules imposing obligations and secondary rules conferring powers. A simple society may have rules only of the former type, sometimes called custom, which apparently make the order pre-legal.[30] International law is an exception. While it possesses only primary rules, at least

---

27.   Carleton Kemp Allen's major treatise, *Law in the Making* (Oxford University Press, 1927 and many later ed.), pioneered the cosmetic use of the term *law-making* while dealing with the standard sources. Citing Allen, Jenks wrote of "law-making processes of the international community—a topic which corresponds to national discussions of the respective roles of custom, judicial precedent, doctrinal discussion and legislation in legal evolution." C. Wilfred Jenks, *The Common Law of Mankind* (London: Stevens and Sons, 1958), pp. 28-35, quoting from pp. 28-29. G. I. Tunkin, *Theory of International Law* (Cambridge, Mass.: Harvard University Press, trans. William E. Butler, 1974), Part II, also abandons sources terminology, although his list of "processes of forming norms" repeats the usual sources of international law. Alice B. Haemmerli prefers "international norm-creation," as in "International Norm-Creation for a Divided Society: A Reappraisal of Some Perennial Problems," *Orbis*, Vol. 20. No. 3 (Summer 1976), pp. 315-341.

28.   See Slouka's essay in this volume for the phrase *normative processes* used generically in place of specified sources. See also J. S. Nye, 'Ocean Rule-Making from a World Politics Perspective," in *Perspectives on Ocean Policy*, NSF 75-17 (Washington, D.C.: Government Printing Office, 1975), pp. 221-144, in which the phrase *rule-making processes* is preferred.

29.   As the title of this volume suggests, most of its contributors are chary of reliance on sources terminology. This is in keeping with our collective goal of identifying patterns in the way law comes into being, and of course trends in these patterns, without assuming conformity with conventional descriptions of sources.

30.   H. L. A. Hart, *The Concept of Law* (Oxford: Oxford University Press, 1961), p. 91.

according to Hart, it deserves to be called law because in content "no other social rules are as close to municipal law as those of international law."[31]

Secondary rules are, as Hart says, rules about the primary rules. "They specify the way in which the primary rules may be conclusively ascertained, introduced, eliminated, varied, and the fact of their violation conclusively determined."[32] Secondary rules are of three types: recognition, change, and adjudication. The first, augmented by the others, tells us how the law is known; the second, augmented by the others, how it is managed; and the third, again augmented, how it is used. What a given legal order calls sources is merely a particular configuration of secondary rules.

We know that primary rules are valid by reference to secondary rules. How do we know the validity of secondary rules? Hart treats this question with a subtle change of terminology. The rule of recognition (now in the singular) is indeed "a supreme criterion and ultimate rule," and a validating referent for all other rules.[33] Validity is dependent on no higher rule, for there is none, but rather on the fact of its general acceptance (just as the validity of primary rules in simple orders, lacking secondary rules, comes from general acceptance of each such rule individually).

The problem of sources has become the problem of validity. Actually Hart has introduced without acknowledgment a tertiary rule which is the validating rule. If there is no immediately evident tertiary rule, such as a formal constitution, then we suppose that rule is collapsed into a secondary rule, as in the case of British parliamentary enactments. Analytically a tertiary rule exists if, as positivist doctrine insists, law must have a pedigree.[34]

International law has no evident validating rule, so Hart mistakenly says that it has no rules of recognition.[35] Clearly it has secondary rules, called sources, which are indispensable for determining the status of primary rules. As with the British constitution, the tertiary rule in international law is not in evidence because that rule is indistinguishable from a secondary rule, or source, so being by virtue of general acceptance. This is custom.

There is, of course, another, deeper question lurking here, namely, How can general acceptance give rise to a tertiary rule? We turn to this problem below. For the moment, however, note that Hart's confusion over the sources of law and the source of validity is no different from the confusion displayed by many positivist doctrinalists in their pursuit of law as a pure construct. Hart is not saved by his innovative terminology. If anything he is misled by it.

Of the three pillars of positivist doctrine, *source* is least developed, quite plausibly because it is external to the edifice of doctrine—an ornamental pillar. Doctrine aside, most positivists, whether analytically or sociologically inclined, seem to agree that the immediate material circumstances associated with the origin of specific legal norms are to be called the sources of law. They also agree that there are several distinctive sources, or

---

31.   Ibid., p. 231.

32.   Ibid., p. 92.

33.   Ibid., p. 103.

34.   Dworkin (fn. 24), pp. 17-18. While Dworkin uses the term *pedigree* in reference to source, clearly he would be concerned with the pedigree of those who grant pedigrees. Dworkin criticizes Hart's treatment of custom along lines that converge with the critique presented here (pp. 42-44).

35.   See also D'Amato's critique of Hart on this point. Anthony A. D'Amato, "The Neo-Positivist Conception of International Law," *American Journal of International Law*, Vol. 59, No. 2 (April 1965), pp. 321-324.

categories, into which material conditions can be grouped. There is less agreement on the actual identification of sources. Legislation, judicial action, the opinion of authorities, and custom are on virtually everybody's list. Equity is also a common item on such lists, although it presents a doctrinal problem which is all the more obvious when morality and religion are mentioned as sources in their own right.[36] Naturalist sentiments accompanied by the vaguest of empirical support are found side by side with propositions that have been inductively established in the best positivist tradition.

British jurisprudence conventionally distinguishes material from formal sources.[37] The latter specifically refers to the agency by which a substantive statement about conduct gains authority, and the former therefore refers to the agency through which a substantive statement is formulated. Thus legislation as a process is the material source of legislation which as a product is a formal source of law. Legislation is one form of law, and we note that what are widely called the forms of law are simply categories of law distinguished according to their formal sources.

As long as the problem of validity does not intrude on the task of identifying laws in accordance with their immediate source, positivists are little troubled by the absence of supporting doctrine. The problem of validity is clearly secondary when the empirical thrust of positivism is most easily honored, as it is when the focus of attention is legislation. Judicial action, and expert opinion and custom even more so, brings the positivist closer to the problem of validity and away from the protection afforded his empirical activities by the umbrella of positivist doctrine. If he concerns himself with anything else in the name of sources, he is beset with the problem of validity, whether acknowledged or not, and his only doctrinal recourse is a naturalist one.

Positivist writers have usually been able to skirt the problem of validity without so much as a sideward glance. This has been possible because they possess a working ideology often called *legal science,* which supports their activities even when doctrinal questions should give them pause. Legal science should not be confused with the science associated with the employment of the scientific method. Legal science has nothing to do with measurement, replication, or verification. Rather, it is a mandate for ordering and systematizing what is already known or readily determined through simple investigation.[38] The chief objectives of legal science are to establish the content of the law and make it accessible. Legal science is therefore generally inductive and strongly taxonomic. The important tasks are the proper ordering of available materials and the discovery of new material to be fit in with the rest. The typical products of legal science are major treatises whose frameworks endure for numerous editions and are widely borrowed. These same frameworks come to describe the curriculum of law faculties and dominate teaching materials.[39]

---

36.   Roscoe Pound in particular includes "religion" and moral and philosophical ideas in his list. Pound (fn. 15), III, pp. 384-385.

37.   Pound traces the distinction to the first edition of J. A. Salmond's *Jurisprudence* (1902). Ibid., p. 381.

38.   This is in keeping with the original Enlightenment meaning of science as rational inquiry and is what was meant by political science, for example, when that designation gained popularity. The phrase *legal science* is attributable to Blackstone, whose *Commentaries* (1765) was intended to free from religious mystification by reducing it to rational principles. See Daniel J. Boorstin, *The Mysterious Science of Law* (Cambridge, Mass.: Harvard University Press, 1941), Ch. I; and see generally Huntington Cairns, *Theory of Legal Science* (Chapel Hill: University of North Carolina Press, 1941).

39.   The casebook method of teaching in Americal law schools arose from the conviction that law as a science had to be studied in printed materials which embodied all legal knowledge and thus were the

Even after the more stringent methods of inquiry developed in the natural sciences began to penetrate social inquiry, legal science was largely unaffected.[40] Legal science is learned as craft by lawyers who tend to feel they have no real difficulty explaining how a rule of law comes into being or is used. Instead, they want to be clear on what the rule says, whether it is compatible with other rules, and how to find it again conveniently. Obviously the craft orientation of legal science enables writers of all persuasions to agree on an apparently reasonable and descriptive (common sense) ordering of the categories by which rules of law definitively come into being. That these categories—sources of law—are accepted uncritically by most writers even today attests to the powerful grip that legal science has had on the working legal mind and thus legal thought itself.[41]

Evidence grows that these categories miss or distort the complex processes of law-making. Yet writers continue to invest their time, energy, and ingenuity in reformulating known sources and, when desperate enough, postulating new ones.[42] They cope with an existing framework. Rarely do they admit to the possibility that the framework itself is the problem and might better be abandoned altogether.[43] In the instance of the natural sciences we are told that the norm—normal science—is ongoing empirically directed research within guidelines provided by accepted theory. Normal science implies an integral relation between accepted theory and successful applications.[44] Mounting evidence of a theory's unworthiness in the form of unsatisfactory applications eventually gives rise to theoretical reassessment. Legal science is not normal science even if we put the matter of method aside. Legal science does not purport to evaluate explanations advanced by theory. Nor does it provide an incentive to revise theoretical constructs, even those at the primitive level of categorization schemes, no matter how much damaging evidence accumulates.

---

equivalent of a laboratory. Case books ordered the original sources of material which a lawyer was obliged to study in the name of science. A continental lawyer found his raw material already ordered in code form and was not obliged to have recourse to case books. This view of legal education was the law-in-books orientation that Roscoe Pound juxtaposed against law-in-action. Pound was not rejecting legal science nor the view of legal education it implied. Rather, he was warning his fellows about the tendency to assume that the law is frozen in the form found in books.

See William Twining, *Karl Llewellyn and the Realist Movement* (London: Weidenfeld and Nicholson, 1973), Ch. 1; Roscoe Pound, "Law in Books and Law in Action," *American Law Review*, Vol. 44, No. 1 (Jan.-Feb. 1910), 12-36.

40. See the Fifth section of this chapter, under "Law-Making as Law-Doing," on the relation of legal realism, as a revolt against formalistic tendencies in legal science, to the rising interest in scientific method in other areas of social inquiry.

41. In American sholarship the term *legal science* has largely disappeared, although the practices associated with it prosper. Continental scholarship continues to use the term, with Socialist writers still insisting that there is bourgeois legal science and the true science derived from Marxist-Leninist principles. See, for example, Tunkin (fn. 27), Ch. 9.

42. As will be evident in the next section, this statement is deliberately confessional. The third section sould be understood as an abandonment of the writer's earlier work within the sources framework. The fourth section attempts explanations for the hold of the sources framework on the legal mind.

43. Myres S. McDougal and his associates stand apart by having self-consciously rid themselves of received frameworks, including the sources scheme, but in the process have engaged in a gigantic effort to reorganize legal knowledge in terms of generally stated principles. What could be better evidence that the spirit of legal science lives than this effort?

44. Thomas S. Kuhn, *The Structure of Scientific Revolution* (Chicago: University of Chicago Press, 2nd ed. enl., 1970), p. 10.

LEGAL SCIENCE AND GLOBAL LAW-MAKING: SOURCES OF INTERNATIONAL LAW

Traditional Sources: Custom, Courts, and Writers; Treaties

The peculiar nature of international law has created for legal thought some of its greatest problems. And the matter of sources is one of the least developed areas of legal doctrine. Taking these conditions together, the matter of sources in international law has understandably been the source of great confusion.[45] The confusion begins with the importance of custom in the international legal order. Customary law is widely considered the hallmark of primitive orders.[46] Yet, if international law is merely primitive, then why are there so many additional sources? For each writer has a list of sources which bears a more than coincidental resemblance to the standard list of sources said to characterize the legal orders of socioeconomically advanced states. The one significant difference between the usual sources of international law and those of complex domestic orders is the presence of treaties but not legislation among the former and of legislation but not treaties among the latter. Apparently impressed by the parallels in all such lists, many writers have minimized this one difference or explained it away.[47] For them what distinguishes sources of international law and of domestic law is the relative frequency sources are resorted to and not the nature of the sources themselves.

There is of course a school of thought which identifies international law as primitive law, but in doing so fixes attention more on the absence of enforcement machinery than on the rudimentary character of the international legal order's law-making machinery.[48] Decentralization is as much a feature of law-making as law-using in the contemporary global order. In a later section we expand on what should be a commonplace observation, namely, that law-making and law-using tend to be aspects of the same phenomenon.

---

45. For a brief review of this confusion, see Clive Parry, *The Sources and Evidences of International Law* Manchester: Manchester University Press. 1965). In addition to Parry's, major recent treatments of the sources of international law include the following: Michel Virally, "The Sources of International Law," in Max Sørensen, ed., *A Manual of Public International Law* (New York: St. Martin's, 1968), pp. 116-174; Tunkin (fn. 27), Part II; T. O. Elias, "Modern Sources of International Law," in Wolfgang Friedmann, Louis Henkin, and Oliver Lissitzyn, eds., *Transnational Law in a Changing Society* (New York: Columbia University Press, 1972), pp. 34-69. Though utterly different in their doctrinal stances, Robert W. Tucker and Richard A. Falk have most influenced the writer's thinking about sources. See in particular Hans Kelsen, *Principles of International Law*, Second Edition Revised and Edited by Robert W. Tucker (New York: Holt, Rinehart and Winston, 1966), pp. 420-508; Richard A. Falk, *The Status of Law in International Society* (Princeton: Princeton University Press, 1970), Ch. V-VII.

46. A useful treatment of custom in a variety of legal orders is Pound's (fn. 15) III, pp. 389-410. The usual view, most closely associated with Savigny and the historical school is that customary law arises from the genius of the people expressed in habitual popular action. Sir Henry Maine in *Ancient Law* (1861 and many later ed.) took an alternative view to the effect that a "personal agent" makes individual judgments which by being generalized are no longer "mere commands" but custom having the quality of law. Custom is still the source of law in this interpretation, although custom itself is taken to be more complicated in nature that the usual historicalist view admits. See also fn. 96 below.

47. Hence the strong tendency to label multilateral treaties and the process of making them "international legislation." See prominently Manley O. Hudson, *International Legislation*, Vol. I (Washington: Carnegie Endownment of International Peace, 1931), pp. xiii-xix. An alternative, less influential view denied that treaties can be a source of international law in any case and that the development of new customary law might properly be called international legislation. Torsten Gihl, *International Legislation* (London: Oxford University Press, 1937), p. 151.

48. Kelsen in particular developed the primitive law analogy, (fn. 25), pp. 3-25. See also Barkun (fn. 26) for a systematic study of international law as primitive in nature and use. And see the fourth section of this chapter, under "Law and Community," for a discussion of the legal mind as "savage" and the international legal community as "primitive" in a special sense.

Separating aspects of things is analytically legitimate as long as the separation does not come to signify something more fundamental than it really is. Unfortunately the habit of separating law-making from law-using is so deeply ingrained, and the construction of a list of sources so dependent on such a separation, that writers have made a convenient fiction into an ersatz reality, similar to the reality they impute to domestic legal orders.[49]

If international legal order is unlike the simple, structurally and functionally undifferentiated model associated with primitive orders, its complexity need not resemble that ascribed to advanced domestic orders. The fact that law-minded scholars and statesmen see the global order as complex in the manner of domestic orders is to a degree self-fulfilling—after all, the order does appear to have sources formally stated as law (see below) and conforming to everyone's list. Clearly differentiated modes of law-making (separate sources) are nonetheless a superficial reality. It is not sustained by a deeper reality in which the customary distinction between law-making and law-using is meaningful.

Arguably the civilized veneer of separated sources overlays an amorphous and exceedingly plastic order that approaches the truly primitive. Or, more likely, there is underlying that veneer a differently organized complexity the deep structures of which do not underpin, and give deeper reality to, the shallow surface structure of separate sources.[50] The discovery and description of these deeper structures would seem to be the task of scholars capable of detaching themselves from the superficial and self-created reality of sources resembling the sources of complex orders.[51]

*   *   *   *   *   *

Because legal science has prevailed and the same several sources have always been discussed, we cannot ignore them. Whether and in what sense these sources really exist, they assuredly do exist in and for the purposes of legal science. Most writers agree, as they have for generations, that there are two primary sources—custom and treaties—and two secondary sources— judicial decisions and scholarly writing. The latter pair are treated separately from custom only as a matter of convention. The twentieth century has seen the addition of a new source—general principles of law recognized by civilized nations—which first gained expression in the famous recitation of sources found in the Statute of the World Court. Since 1919, when the Court's Statute was drafted, there has been widespread acceptance not only of the list of sources but the specific language used to describe them. A signal exception is the description of custom as a source, perhaps reflecting the particularly unsettled state of doctrine in this area.[52] For the rest, the

---

49. One of the great achievements of the legal realist movement is to have raised serious doubt as to the validity of a firm distinction between law-making and law-using even in complex legal orders. See the fifth section of this chapter, under "Law-Making as Law-Doing." It may be part of McDougal's realist heritage that, more than anyone else in the study of international law, he and his associates insist on using language free from the assumption that law-making and law-using are necessarily different.

50. The terms *organized complexity* and *deep structure* are borrowed from the social sciences, where they are widely used. Their use here is intended to suggest that once conventional legal notions are cast aside, inquiry must be guided by other branches of social inquiry. See generally the fourth and fifth sections of this chapter.

51. This argument is presented in somewhat fuller form in N. G. Onuf, "The Scholar in the International Legal Order," *SAIS Review*, Vol. 15, No. 4 (Fall, 1971), pp. 15-20. See below, this section, for more on the tasks of scholars, and the third section of this chapter, under "Standardizing Solutions," for an effort to identify some of the global order's underlying structure.

52. What appears to be a consensus among the critics is described by Karol Wolfke, *Custom in Present International Law* (Wroclaw: Polskiej Akademii Nauk, 1964), pp. 26-28.

Statute's language is sufficiently generalized that an air of acceptance hardly signifies a dissipation of the historic controversies associated with sources doctrine.

Still, law is a matter of language, and we would be well advised to have such widely received language before us. Article 38 of the Statute of the International Court of Justice reads as follows:

> 1. The Court, whose function is to decide in accordance with international law such disputes as are submitted to it, shall apply:
>
> a. international conventions, whether general or particular, establishing rules expressly recognized by the consenting state;
>
> b. international custom, as evidence of a general practice accepted as law;
>
> c. the general principles of law recognized by civilized nations;
>
> d. subject to the provisions of Article 59, judicial decisions and the teachings of the most highly qualified publicists of the various nations, as subsidiary means for the determination of rules of law.
>
> 2. This provision shall not prejudice the power of the Court to decide a case *ex aequo et bono,* if the parties agree thereto.[53]

Only the ordering of items in Article 38 is commonly ignored by writers, who generally prefer to begin their discussions with custom, the more basic and historically the more important of the two main sources. We shall do the same. Custom is invariably seen as having two uneasily coupled components, one behavioral and quantitative, the other attitudinal and qualitative.[54]

Each component presents a significant problem for writers. In the instance of the behavioral, quantitative component, the problem is obvious: How much of the behavior of state actors which is typically called practice makes a custom "accepted as law"?[55] The problem must be pursued in three dimensions simultaneously, these being temporal, spatial, and distributional dimensions. A legal custom requires the passage of time almost by definition. How much time is impossible to say in the abstract, although there appears to be an inverse relationship between the amount of time and amount of behavior required for a given pattern of behavior to become a legal custom. The greater the volume of behavior, the less time must pass. Similarly, to gain legal character a custom must be widespread. But how widespread? We can only say that the more widespread a practice, the less volume as a function of time is required. This distribution of behaviors affirming and denying the relevance of a custom must be seen the same way. The higher the ratio of affirmative to negative behavior, the less volume as a function of time and space is required.

Altogether, we achieve a general proposition that the volume of practice necessary to constitute a custom as law is a function of its duration, extent, and consistency.[56] The

---

53. Article 59 reads: The decision of the Court has no binding force except between the parties and in respect of that particular case.

54. For a lucid and much fuller discussion, see Anthony A. D'Amato, *The Concept of Custom in International Law* (Ithaca: Cornell University Press, 1971). D'Amato's effect on the following discussion will be apparent to any reader of both. See also Michael Akehurst, "Custom as a Source of International Law," *British Year Book of International Law,* Vol. 47 (1974–1975), pp. 1-53, much of which appears to be a running commentary on D'Amato's book.

55. Equally obvious is the problem writers have with the wording of Article 38. It is practice which is seen as evidence of custom accepted as law and not the contrary suggested by the Statute. We take this to be a matter of faulty drafting and nothing more. Hereinafter we will denote custom accepted as law, on the evidence of general practice, as *legal custom.*

56. We advance this proposition merely as a summary of the preceding discussion and not as an equation capable of solution. It would be the latter only if we could standardize scoring, i.e., express values assigned to each variable on a common scale, which assumes that the relative importance or weight of each

limiting cases are: *One point in time,* requiring overwhelmingly generalized and consistent practice and establishing instantaneous custom; *two actors,* requiring overwhelmingly consistent and durable practice confined to the actors and establishing special or local custom; and *unilateral acts,* requiring the indefinite passage of time free from inconsistent and contesting acts and establishing a prescriptive exception to generally valid law.[57]

Notice that unilateral acts involve a large number of actors, all but one of which refrain from acting. Logically speaking, not acting is a tacit form of acting. The important quality here is consistency of acts, which is contributed to by the fact that virtually all of them require no action. The position taken by the World Court in the Nuclear Test Cases (1974) "that declarations made by way of unilateral acts, concerning legal or factual situations, may have the effect of creating legal obligations" is quite different from the one taken here.[58] The Court supposes that a state is unilaterally bound by its declarations when it is its intention to be so bound. Such legal obligation will not disappear with a change of intention. Inasmuch as unilateral acts as understood here require perfect consistency, a change of heart by the initiating state immediately violates that requirement and creates instead a sequence of inconsistent acts without particular legal consequence. Other grounds for holding states bound by unilateral acts later repudiated, such as good faith (intelligible only in the context of agreements between two or more actors), are simply not persuasive.[59]

The limiting cases are intrinsically interesting and even have an occasional application. But they do not solve the quantitative problem for the vast number of situations in which practice of some duration, extent, and consistency may or may not be a legal custom. Writers frequently display a tendency to state arbitrary but demanding criteria for establishing the existence of legal custom in the abstract and in particular situations relax these criteria without admitting to having done so. In fact they must relax their criteria or they would find that very few rules of customary international law could be said to exist at all.[60]

---

variable is known and that the variable relationships are linear. We would also have to know or be able to fix on that scale some value for the volume of practice representing a threshold for the existence of a customary rule. Such a threshold may itself vary with the specificity of the rule being superseded: a specific exception to a general and permissive rule (one that proscribes no particular kind of behavior) demands less practice to create it as a rule than is necessary to dismantle a specific rule which is then to be replaced. See similarly Akehurst (fn. 54), pp. 18-19. Considering the difficulties posed, any effort to devise and employ an equation expressing the conditions for the existence of a customary rule is ill advised. For one such attempt, and its perils, see Irving L. White, "A Framework for Analyzing International Law-in-Action: A Preliminary Proposal," *International Studies Quarterly*, Vol. 13, No. 1 (March 1969), pp. 46-69, and N. G. Onuf, "International Law-in-Action and the Numbers Game: A Comment," *International Studies Quarterly*, Vol. 14, No. 3 (September 1970), pp 325-333.

57.   As to instantaneous custom, see Bin Cheng, "United Nations Resolutions on Outer Space: Instant International Customary Law?" *Indian Journal of International Law*, Vol. 5, No. 1 (January 1965), pp. 23-48; as to special custom, see D'Amato (fn. 54), Ch. 8; as to unilateral acts, see Erik Suy, *Les actes juridiques unilateraux en droit international public* (Paris: Pichon, 1962). As to whether unilateral acts can create general law see Zdenek J. Slouka, *International Custom and the Continental Shelf* (The Hague: Nijhoff, 1968), and D'Amato, Ch. 7.

58.   *I.C.J. Reports, 1974*, pp. 253, 457. Rubin demonstrates that only six judges actively concurred in the paragraphs of the Judgments bearing the argument from which the quotation is taken. Alfred P. Rubin, "The International Legal Effects of Unilateral Declarations," *American Journal of International Law*, Vol. 71 No. 1 (January 1977), p. 1, fn. 3.

59.   See Rubin's devastating critique, ibid., pp. 1-30.

60.   An orderly relaxation of these criteria would relate their stringency to the specificity of preexisting rules. See fn. 56. In the instance of a gap in the law, Akehurst contends that "a very small number of acts," perhaps involving as few as one state acting and one or two others (not) reacting, would suffice to create a

The problem with the qualitative, attitudinal component of legal custom is no less evident. Some kinds of behavior are voluminous, durable, widespread, and uniform, and yet they are not regarded as binding. They are seen and always referred to as courtesies but not as law. Obviously what differentiates this kind of behavior from law-generative behavior is how the actors feel about it and their willingness to say how they feel about it. Anthony D'Amato would say that there must be articulated recognition that behavior has legal consequences for those consequences to take place. We find the notion of articulation a great advance over the historic but hopelessly circular notion of *opinio juris,* namely, of behavior being undertaken in "conscious accordance with law preexisting the action."[61] Nonetheless, D'Amato's position is a restrictive one, taken in light of his observation that articulation must be visible. By employing the articulation criterion we would again have to conclude that there are very few customary rules (excepting those coextensive with treaties—see below), particularly if articulations are to be evaluated by their volume, duration, extent, and consistency. The problem generally resembles the difficulty with the constitutive theory of recognition.[62] How many acts of recognition, or articulation, are required for a legal condition to be constituted: one, all that are possible, or some arbitrary number in between? As an alternative to articulation as a necessary ingredient for customary law, we suggest that articulation is required to establish only that a custom is *not* law. Thus, a courtesy remains a courtesy as long as there are periodic statements by actors to the effect that they continue to see the matter as one of simple custom.

Such articulations are indeed commonplace and that is precisely how we know that courtesies are not binding. In the absence of statements disavowing legal consequences of particular customs, we may assume that when quantitative criteria, whatever they are, have been fulfilled, then law does exist in customary form. This position would seem to be consistent both with contemporary, more flexible conceptions of the nature of international law, which this writer shares, and with the practice of states, which involves a good deal of inarticulated acceptance of legal consequences, as we shall see below.[63]

A sharp distinction between behavior and articulated attitudes is hardly manifested, after all, in the concrete emanations we call practice. While we have interchanged the terms *behavior* and *practice* in these pages, practice is the generic description of everything that state actors do, individually and collectively, and what they do involves indeterminate proportions of verbal and non-verbal behavior, and verbal as well as non-verbal demonstrations of what they take to be the significance of that behavior. What then is the point of separating behavior from attitude as components of practice? For our purposes what matters is the intensity of practice as it relates inversely to volume. The more intensely expressed an act, the fewer such acts are required for a legal custom to emerge. Articulation as formalization may be the best measure of intensity.[64] Articula-

---

legal custom. Akehurst (fn. 57). pp. 16, 18. This we would treat as a prescriptive exception to a general and permissive rule, supported by subsequent lack of inconsistent acts and therefore approaching the limiting case of unilateral acts as a source of legal custom.

61. D'Amato (fn. 54). p. 66. On the circularity of *opinio juris,* see pp. 66-7; on articulation, pp. 73-87.

62. For a cogent presentation and assessment of this theory. see Kelsen-Tucker, (fn. 45), pp. 389-395.

63. Rebutting this position and its supporting contentions is D'Amato's essay in this volume.

64. There is some evidence though that in small groups the most intensely held rules are least articulated, that articulation can invalidate such rules, and consequently a prime, if inarticulated, rule

tion may thus be instrumental to intensity, which is what makes the practice count more heavily. By itself though, articulation has no consistent meaning and significance, except in the special case of articulations to the effect that customary practices are without legal effect. We may now expand our general proposition to read: the volume of practice necessary to constitute a custom as law is a function of the product of its duration, extent, consistency, and intensity.

*   *   *   *   *   *

A discussion of articulation is obviously incomplete without taking into account the place court decisions and writers occupy in customary law formation. As is well known, the decisions of international tribunals do not set precedents, for customary law is fundamentally different from common law. Such decisions are seen as evidence of the existence of customary law and, in the very process of providing evidence of such law, are items of practice further substantiating the evident practice. Decisions of national courts may be of comparable value to the international legal order. Indeed, if the value of such decisions is in the evidence they provide of state practice, then the decisions of domestic courts can be more important than those of international tribunals, Richard A. Falk has argued, because they more authoritatively capture the practice of states. In many domestic legal orders such decisions are indistinguishable from actual practice of states.[65] By the same reasoning the arguments of litigants before an international tribunal would be more valuable than the judgment itself. Only insofar as decisions of international tribunals receive subsequent affirmation in state practice can they be classified as practice, or more properly, evident practice and not merely evidence of practice.

In order to avoid the logical implications of Falk's position, we could assume that the practice that creates custom goes beyond practice of states. We suspect that this is a common assumption but, being unarticulated, contains no guidelines on the extent of relevant practice. Nevertheless, we can imagine informal criteria of prestige and quality operating. The higher the prestige of the tribunal and the individuals who sit on it, and the more craftsmanlike their opinions, the greater the value of such opinions as practice. Thus by assuming that law-generating practice does not necessarily refer exclusively to what states do, it is possible to erect an especially prominent position for the decisions and minority opinions emanating from the World Court and, correlatively, to explain the great interest that so frequently attends the drafting of decisions and opinions.

Simply by giving voice to this assumption, most positivists would see it as unsound in its assertion that states do not necessarily make the law between states. But can we disavow it and still explain the esteem with which the practice of the Court is held?[66]

"states" that rules are not to be articulated. See Walter O. Weyrauch, "The 'Basic Law' or 'Constitution' of a Small Group," *Journal of Social Issues*, Vol. 27, No. 2 (1971), pp. 49-63. Gidon Gottlieb, in surveying emergent trends below in his essay, inversely relates "formality and legal effect of international engagements." Gottlieb's illustrations suggest that the most striking cases of informal but effective rules are those created by a small group of states(men) in the course of protracted bargaining. The intensity of such intimate situations overwhelms the discriminatory power of a measure like relative articulation. These situations also differ substantially from the model situation of generalized, episodic practice. See also the third section of this chapter, under "Standardizing Solutions," on practice and treating.

65. Richard A. Falk, *The Role of Domestic Courts in the International Legal Order* (Syracuse: Syracuse University Press, 1964), pp. 19-20.

66. We disavow the assertion that law-making need not be confined exclusively to the activities of states only for the sake of argument. See the third section of this chapter, under "Standardizing Solutions,"

Implied here is a further question: Does esteem for the Court and its work bear any relation to the generation of legal custom? There are two answers to these questions, both correct. On occasion the Court is a generator of practice, in a very important but nonetheless indirect sense. By means of the visibility, salience, and reasonableness of its judgments, it can prompt immediate and widespread supportive behavior from states. In effect certain decisions of the Court have a near oracular impact on community opinion, catalyzing the necessary practice for the rapid emergence of a customary norm.[67] To give an example, the Court's judgment in the *Anglo-Norwegian Fisheries Case* is frequently cited as a landmark in the emergence of a customary rule affirming the use of the straight baseline method for demarcating certain territorial waters.[68] In contrast is the Court's judgment in the *Nottebohm Case*. As in the Fisheries Case, the Court set forth a novel construction of the controlling law, but its argument is so muddled that it is little understood and, when understood, it is little respected.[69]

Considerations of timing, craftsmanship, and what, with Weber, we might call charisma are important factors in the catalytic effect. It has occurred just often enough that every decision is awaited with an air of expectation that it may be happening again. When these expectations are dashed, great criticism is voiced and the Court's prestige is eclipsed, only to be revived in anticipation of the next oracular event. Although the Court's light caseload is invariably bemoaned by its supporters, we might observe that the cycle of expectation and oracular event, whether followed by catalysis or catharsis, is immeasurably supported by the Court's leisurely pace. By contrast the oracular impact of the United States Supreme Court is diminished by the swamping effect of its vast number of decisions.

The other reason for the Court's prominence has less to do with a law-generative role for its practice. Legal scholars take the decisions of the Court with the utmost seriousness. They do so because the Court's work is highly visible and, at the same time, sufficiently modest in volume to be assimilated into scholarship.[70] Beyond this, legal scholars, particularly in the common law world, are trained to think in terms of cases and as teachers they characteristically use cases to illustrate the content and application of rules of law. The influence of the Anglo-American preoccupation with cases in interna-

---

on the empirical irrelevance of a distinction between public and private domains, the former defining the state in positivist terms, for contemporary law-making.

67. Compare Max Weber's discussion of the Anglo-American legal experience. The following discussion is much influenced by Weber (fn. 25), Ch. VII-XI.

68. The Court of course could not intend that its decisions be generalized to all comparable situations. On the contrary, the Court felt bound to show that in the situation at hand, it had merely found evidence of practice accepted as law. "The Court is thus led to conclude that the method of straight baselines, established in the Norwegian system, was imposed by the peculiar geography of the Norwegian coast; that even before the dispute arose this method had been consolidated by a constant and sufficiently long practice, in the face of which the attitude of governments bears witness to the fact that they did not consider it to be contrary to international law." *I.C.J. Reports, 1951, p.139.*

69. *I.C.J. Reports, 1955,* pp. 5-26. Properly understood the judgment deprives Nottebohm of any nationality at all and not, as is usually thought, of one of two nationalities to which the Court determined he was less effectively linked.

70. The opinions of judges, many of them separate or dissenting from the majority judgment, are typically scholarly in character and often lengthy. This is apparently partly attributable to the particulars of the Court's deliberative process, as described by Richard Lillich and G. Edward White, "The Deliberative Process of the International Court of Justice: A Preliminary Critique and Some Possible Reforms." *American Journal of International Law,* Vol. 70, No. 1 (January 1976), pp. 28-40, and, we think likely, partly attributable to some judges' personal interest in securing a place in subsequent scholarship. It is also attributable, given the Court's deliberative procedures, to the ample time available for each decision.

tional law extends far beyond the influence of the common law tradition generally. There are obviously reasons for this. Since customary law is so difficult to establish, all legal scholars are impressed with the Anglo-American procedure of looking at cases: it gets results. The signal importance of Britain and the United States in the development of international law has inevitably created an intense interest in case-oriented Anglo-American scholarship. Finally, the sheer volume of Anglo-American literature in international law has the effect of flooding out different perceptions of the Court's influence that might arise in other legal cultures.

The World Court's prestige is handsomely reinforced by the fact that its membership is drawn from the community of scholars and state practitioners who are generally given to emphasizing the importance of the Court's decisions. Not only do these individuals wish someday to crown their careers with election to the Court, but their friends and colleagues are sitting there already. The decisions of the Court receive the attention that the work of the most senior and respected scholars would receive in any discipline.

*   *   *   *   *   *

By viewing the World Court as the apex of the world of scholarship, we have moved into a consideration of the place of writers in the formation of customary law. Historically writers occupied a place very close to what we now attribute to courts. Writers have had a marked effect on the emergence of rules when their opinions were timely, reasonable, and well-crafted. Such writers acquired the prestige to have their opinions quoted and requoted almost as if they were oracular pronouncements, the oracle's name each time invoked with greater deference and awe.

It is generally assumed that landmark opinions of revered writers have decisively affected the emergence of legal custom by catalyzing supportive state behavior. While this was doubtless the case in some instances, writers rather more than statesmen felt the catalytic effect. The tendency for writers to seize on oracular pronouncements and reiterate them for generations can create an impression in the minds of those same writers that the rule exists simply because they are writing about it as if it exists. The relevant practice is largely the opinions of earlier writers, salted with the occasional instances of supportive state behavior that have come along. Instances of contrary behavior are dismissed in footnotes as irrelevant to the consensual view of scholars, if they are acknowledged at all.[71]

At least to a degree this is the history of the putative rule establishing the limit of the territorial sea at three miles.[72] Scholars were shocked when a substantial number of states resisted codification of the three-mile limit at the Hague Codification Conference in 1930. Subsequent state practice strongly suggests that many states had always prescinded from the prevailing scholarly view of the three-mile limit. The practices of these states

---

71. This process is brilliantly described by Schwarzenberger as "inductive mimicry." Georg Schwarzenberger, *The Inductive Approach to International Law* (London: Stevens and Sons, 1965), pp. 47-50.

72. The definitive history of the three-mile limit is Sayre A. Swarztrauber, *The Three-Mile Limit of Territorial Seas* (Annapolis: Naval Institute Press, 1972). Swartztrauber affirms the conventional view that the existence of a rule limiting the territorial sea to three miles "scarcely needs proving," while its demise must be determined with care (p. 2). To this writer the contrary is closer to the truth: While careful research succeeds in casting doubt on the existence of such a rule, its rejection by states has been so massive and open that its demise may be taken for granted.

could be ignored as long as scholars represented a significant element in the connective structures of the international system. With the bureaucratization of foreign policy in the nineteenth century, diplomat-bureaucrats replaced writers as an integrative feature of the system, very much as a jurists began to replace writers as law-making catalysts. Legal order became progressively detached from the system, a structure unto itself, tended by writers with strong preferences for order and coherence.

Codification is virtually synonymous with the quest for a detached, almost mechanical orderliness. The promotion of codification and systematic improvement of the law was a characteristic activity of the nineteenth century legal order and the special province of writers. Yet codification is also highly susceptible to bureaucratization. One can almost guess what happened over a period of decades. Codification was first undertaken through private initiative, then by scientific societies, and finally in coordination with public bureaucracies. At first codification resembled compilations of oracular pronouncements, then elaborately organized scholarly systems, and finally practice-sensitive draft treaties for state signature.[73]

Only when the last stage was reached were scholars able to test their status as agents in law-making. As the 1930 Hague Conference eloquently testified, scholars found not only that they could no longer make oracular law but that the oracular pronouncements of earlier centuries were not nearly so much cherished by states as they were by successive generations of scholars.[74]

In recent decades the bureaucratization of codification is nearly complete, with the role of scholars now close to nominal. Thus scholars are superseded by the World Court in catalyzing law-making *and* superseded by public officials in codification. Only by being jurist or state bureaucrat can the scholar occupy his traditional place. The greater number of scholars who are simply private persons can contribute to the development of law only in a general way through their efforts to comprehend and rationalize state behavior played out against the backdrop of existing but frequently ignored rules of law. Such activity is important because its cumulative effect is to anchor the legal order in the international system without fully sacrificing the scholarly community's normative preferences. After a century of the legal order being detached from the system, these are hardly trivial activities, but they are not directly related to law-making.[75]

*   *   *   *   *   *

Treaties are a good deal easier to discuss than custom, for there is only one major controversy about them as a source that commands our attention. While most writers

---

73. The history of international codification is thoroughly described in R. P. Dhokalia, *The Codification of Public International Law* (Manchester: Manchester University Press, 1970); Nicholas Greenwood Onuf, "International Codification: Interpreting the Last Half Century," forthcoming in Fritz Kratochwil, Richard Falk and Saul Mendlovitz, eds., *Toward a Just World Order, Vol. II, International Law* (Boulder: Westview, 1981).

74. We do not wish to suggest that no other factors contributed to the failure of the Hague Codification Conference. Most obvious among them was the decline of Anglo-American maritime dominance. Note, however, that English language scholarship dominated nineteenth and early twentieth century consideration of the law of the sea. Maritime and scholarly dominance were probably reciprocally reinforcing. See also remarks above in this section on the Anglo-American preoccupation with cases and legal opinions, inevitably drawn mostly from the English speaking world and providing the bulk of evidence on state practice.

75. This position is more fully developed in Onuf (fn. 26).

simply state that properly concluded treaties are a source of law, some British writers have argued that such treaties are demonstrably a source of obligation, but that the source of law is a customary rule, *pacta sunt servanda,* which grants an obligatory character to properly concluded treaties.[76] In effect, an analogy is drawn between a treaty and a contract in municipal law. In advanced municipal orders obligations are clearly differentiated from the law by virtue of which the discharge of certain obligations is guaranteed. In primitive orders legal obligations are undifferentiated, meaning that every rule bears a potential obligation but no obligation exists without a rule. The legal order treats every obligation individually, and not as a class, by endowing each with individual legality. The demands on a primitive order are sufficiently slight to allow individuation. The demands for special law through treaty-making may well be reaching an intolerable magnitude in the international legal order, but that in itself does not make a contract regime operative.[77]

There would seem to be little substantive difference in viewing treaties as a source of law or as a source of obligation if what results is a legal obligation on a par with the legal obligations that result from the operation of custom. The latter of course are general, the former specific to the parties, but they are treated by states as comparable kinds of obligations. Thus it is widely agreed that a treaty obligation supersedes a prior customary obligation between the parties.[78] A contract in a municipal order, however, cannot supplant generally binding law but instead must be consistent with it. Moreover, an emergent customary legal obligation supersedes a prior treaty obligation of the same content. If a treaty obligation has the same content as a customary obligation, whichever came first, both continue to be obligations in their own right.

As D'Amato has taken pains to show, the relationship between legal custom and treaties is really organic. Perhaps the most visible index of a state's practice in the present day is its treaty obligations. Multilateral treaties in particular show a considerable tendency to have significantly prompted the emergence of coextensive customary norms. D'Amato is inclined to see treaties as the principal means by which states articulate their acceptance of the legal consequences of their practice. Since he regards such articulation as a necessary component of a legal custom, the effect is to make custom nearly synonymous with treaties.[79]

---

76. First stated by Sir Gerald G. Fitzmaurice, "Some Problems Regarding the Formal Sources of International Law," *Symbolae Verzijl* (The Hague: Nijhoff, 1958), pp. 153-176, the argument is intended to be a concrete application of the characteristically British doctrine distinguishing formal from material sources. See the First section of this chapter, under "The Pillars of Positivist Doctrine." The Norwegian writer Gihl (fn. 47) argued to the same effect without this doctrinal support.

77. For a sense of the magnitude, see Peter H. Rohn, *Institutions in Treaties: A Global Survey of Magnitudes and Trends from 1945 to 1965* (Syracuse: The Maxwell School of Citizenship and Public Affairs, Syracuse University, 1970), Annex.

78. "The maxim that 'particularistic law' . . . 'breaks' (i.e., takes precedence over) the 'law of the land' (i.e., the generally valid common law) was recognized almost universally and it obtains even today in almost all legal systems outside the Occident." Weber (fn. 25), p. 141.

79. Baxter has gone even further to observe "that if a treaty is declaratory or constitutive of customary international law, the customary international law dehors the treaty (but identical in terms with it) is frozen in the same pattern as the law of the treaty. To the extent that customary international law assimilates itself to the treaty, to that same extent the growth and further development of customary international law will be arrested. If a treaty is revised or amended, the customary international law will remain in the image of the treaty as it was before it was revised." R. R. Baxter, "Treaties and Custom," Academie de Droit International, *Recueil des cours*, Vol. 129 (1970/I), pp. 96-97. We do not see how the third sentence follows from the first two. Whether custom is frozen without treaty revision would seem to depend on interpretation

As stated already, we do not attach the same importance to articulation and would say that D'Amato does not go far enough. Not only is much of the vast volume of treaty law coextensive with customary law for which treaties, by virtue of their public and formal nature, are decisive practice, but there also exists a great deal of informal and unarticulated practice which is nonetheless treated as if it were law by those who are exposed to it.

We should note in closing this part of the discussion that D'Amato accepts the possibility that on a few occasions provisions of multilateral treaties can create general international law directly, apparently without the process of customary law creation coming into play at all. This position effectively asserts that a new source of international law, generally different from either custom or treaties, is operating. We will return this controversial assertion in the next section

New Sources: General Principles, Declarations

Ever since its hasty and rather unreflective drafting in 1919, the source called "general principles of international law recognized by civilized nations" has been the subject of furious but inconclusive debates. We do not propose to rehearse these debates at any length, because they do not seem to have affected the conclusion drawn by many writers that, whatever we might say about their source, very few such principles can be shown to exist. Those that do exist appear to be procedural guidelines for international tribunals substantially derived from the Western legal tradition. In these recurring debates, the school of thought with which we are most sympathetic merely claims that such guidelines are all we might reasonably expect to find as general principles of law.

The existence and utilization of procedural guidelines implies nothing about general principles as a source but does tell us a good deal about the training of jurists. Arguably, there is now something akin to a common law of international judicial procedure, created by judges and applying to them. The source of this specialized law, doubtfully international law at all, is international law in the form of Article 38 and its subsequent interpretation, through which states tolerate the recourse to procedural precedents in international tribunals under the guise of general principles. Only indirectly are states subject to the judges' common law of procedure, if this is what it is, but at least there are tangible rules to show for it. Otherwise, insofar as states are directly concerned, widely held principles and doctrines in various municipal orders can serve as fertile analogies in the hands of scholars and statesmen as well as jurists, who apply them to international law situations as they see fit. Though legally intangible in themselves, such principles can contribute to the catalytic success of oracular pronouncements by enhancing their saliency to practitioners.

The alternative school of thought treats general principles of law as truly the most important source of all. Thus we find references to general principles as the "common law" or "basic foundations" of the international legal order.[80] Some writers in this school are clearly making projections or stating preferences. They think that if there were, or will ever come to be, substantive rules emanating from this source, these rules would be fundamental in character. Other writers would appear to see general principles as part of the underlying structure of the international legal order, given formal expression in the

---

of the treaty and other informal practices; we see the circumstances described in the first two sentences as a distinct possibility but not a necessity.

80. For a brief critical review of the main positions on general principles, appropriately cited, see Tunkin (fn. 27), Ch. 7.

Statute of the World Court for reasons of recent history but nonetheless incidental to the matter of sources per se. This view is quite consistent with the position adduced above that prevalent municipal principles can give structure and thrust to landmark pronouncements in the formation of custom. Only when the substratum is called "law" simply by the authority of Article 38 are these irreconcilable views. We see no case in theory or in the behavior of states for the direct attribution of international legal validity to general principles of law.

*   *   *   *   *   *

The phrase *general principles of law recognized by civilized nations* has engendered confusion as well as controversy, for the language of international law has long known the phrase *general principles of international law.* Some writers have attempted a sleight of hand by trying to assimilate the two into a unified term *the general principles of national and international law.* Since general principles of international law are substantive in character, then there would be at least a superficial connection between general principles as a source and general principles as substantive law. But the connection is only superficial. The use of the phrase *general principles of international law* has been a casual means of denoting rules that are taken to be more notable than other rules. They are not generally seen as superior in the obligations they create, unless they are further set apart as peremptory norms. General principles of international law are undeniably important because of the depth and extent of affirmative practice but not different in legal quality for that reason. By the same token, they do not arise from a source of general principles which is the source of their importance as well.[81]

Informally designated as general principles because of their history and content, such rules of international law are rarely given sustained attention as a class for any reason. What little attention writers have granted general principles of international law has come only recently and without any relation to the concern for general principles of international law recognized by civilized nations. We have already alluded to the possibility that some multilateral treaty provisions may create general law directly. These provisions are best understood as general principles, set apart from the rest of the treaty's obligations in style and form. As D'Amato would have it, the world community has displayed a "manifest intent" to make these provisions general law directly. None of the traditional sources covers this law-generative process: it must be described as a new source. [82]

---

81.   This writer has taken issue with the common view that peremptory norms are superior in binding quality to other rules. Instead, peremptory norms are held to be a variant of general principles, which are set apart as a whole from other rules neither in source nor status but in function. See N. G. Onuf and Richard K. Birney, "Peremptory Norms of International Law: Their Source, Function and Future," *Denver Journal of International Law and Policy,* , Vol. 4, No. 2 (Fall 1974), pp. 187-198. See also Dworkin's argument (fn. 24). pp. 22-40, that principles should be regarded as a set of standards which are not (legal) rules and "have a dimension that rules do not—the dimension of weight or importance." (p. 27) Principles can thus be weighty *because* they are not rules, the latter being condemned to equal weight because they are equal in the obligations they create. Applying Dworkin's position to peremptory norms, if such norms are to be considered law, they cannot be superior in binding quality, only different in function. The alternative is not to consider them law at all—a view which finds support in Thomas R. Kearns' rebuttal of Dworkin's position in "Rules, Principles and the Law," *American Journal of Jurisprudence,* Vol. 18 (1973), pp. 114-135. Kearn views principles resorted to for purposes of judicial innovation as maxims justified by their "relation to what can reasonably be supposed to be a binding norm of some relevant ideal legal system." (p. 125). Hence their resemblance to law.

82.   Anthony A. D'Amato, "Manifest Intent and the Generation by Treaty of Customary Rules of International Law," *American Journal of International Law,* Vol. 64, No. 5 (October 1970), pp. 892-902; N.

This novel doctrine is not merely a matter of casual speculation on the part of a few writers. Ambiguous but intriguing passages in the World Court's 1969 Judgment on the *North Sea Continental Shelf Cases* encourage the belief that Articles 1-3 of the 1958 Geneva Convention on the Continental Shelf are set apart from the rest of that document (they alone could not have reservations attached to them by ratifying states) *and* currently have the status of general law. The Judgment is no help by itself in explaining how these provisions came to acquire general legal status. One minority Opinion, by well-known Danish publicist, Max Sørensen, forcefully argued the instantaneous custom explanation. But Vladimir Koretsky, a greatly respected Soviet jurist, offered an unambiguous opinion to the effect that the relevant provisions of the Continental Shelf Convention are general principles of international law, made so by the intent of the participants in the Geneva Conference.[83]

This writer has elsewhere observed that it is not the treaty so much as the conference at which it was adopted which warrants our attention. The Conference in 1958 can claim to have constituted a forum of the world community. The General Assembly of the United Nations represents a comparable forum but has at its disposal a different instrumentality—resolutions as opposed to a drafty treaty—with what is ordinarily a very different legal status.[84] But the status of the instrumentality is unimportant, for the instrumentality is being borrowed by the forum for the promulgation of a rule whose legal status is already assured. Such emanations from community forums are set apart in style, tone, and generality of language, taking the generic form of a declaration. They are adopted unanimously or nearly so, they are infrequent occasions, and they are patently a serious matter for the participants in the forum.

D'Amato has even suggested that some few overwhelmingly supported rules that are ordinarily taken to be customary are indeed general law emanating directly from community consensus and not custom at all.[85] There is a certain appeal to D'Amato's position since it gives a historical dimension to what we can see is a long-standing source only now recognized as such. Nonetheless, it requires us to employ the image of a decentralized forum of the world community. While the passage of time may well substitute for the collective aspect of the forum, the result is indistinguishable from customary law formation. D'Amato's position however was predicated on being able to distinguish between the ordinary run of customary rules and exceptional instances of consensus as a source of law.

Evidently declarations are general principles of international law notable for their formality as much as their content and readily altered in content only through community decisions of comparable formality. The provisions of such declarations are simultaneously potent organizing symbols and potential constitutive propositions for a world order that may be decades in emerging.[86] If declarations are understood in these terms, we can see that there is a great deal at stake in attributing legal status directly to

---

G. Onuf, "Further Thoughts on a New Source of International Law: Professor D'Amato's 'Manifest Intent'," *American Journal of International Law*, Vol. 65, No. 5 (October 1971), pp. 774-781. D'Amato fails to draw the conclusion that he is talking about a new source; this writer argues that it can be nothing else.

83.   *I.C.J. Reports, 1969*, pp. 41-44, 156-158 and 244-247 for the judgment, Koretsky and Sørensen respectively.

84.   Richard A. Falk, "On the Quasi-Legislative Competence of the General Assembly," *American Journal of International Law*, Vol. 60, No. 4 (October 1966), pp. 782-79; N. G. Onuf, "Professor Falk on the Quasi-Legislative Competence of the General Assembly," *American Journal of International Law*, Vol. 64, No. 2 (April 1970), pp. 349-355.

85.   D'Amato (fn. 54), pp. 41-42.

86.   These ideas are more fully developed in Onuf and Birney (fn. 81).

them. We can well guess that some states have far more to gain than others in the establishment of a new source giving legal consequence to the voice of community consensus. In fact, the resistance of Western states to the operation of a new source is notorious. Arrayed against the Western states are a modest number of Western scholars, including this writer, and a much larger number of statesmen from the non-Western world, who have sought in their diversely motivated and articulated ways to establish that a new source can, should, or does exist.

Disunited in their perceptions of the present situation, not to mention their strategies for changing it, proponents of a new source are united only in their belief that significant changes in the structure and substance of the received liberal-capitalist order of the West can be significantly abetted through the validation of a new source. Only a new source of international law can permit the direct and determinative participation of all peoples in the workings of an order which is now only nominally for all to share in.

Despite our sympathies, we find the unwillingness of Western states to accept a new source as an insurmountable obstacle to its actually existing. Before these attitudes are likely to change, the pervasive sense of stalemate and confrontation over the future development of the international legal order must dissipate.[87] Even in the unlikely event that Western states were to yield on this crucial point, suspicion remains that many non-Western states would be far less innovative in making these principles concrete than they are in sending them forth as resplendent rhetoric. Stripped of the convenient shelter of Western obstinacy, many of the leaders in these states could well realize the threatening implications of the social changes contemplated on a world-scale in the programmatic statements they now so heartily declare their support for.

Of course, it is the historic and enduring nature of international law that it supports the international order of structural violence so eloquently depicted by Johan Galtung.[88] We can only suggest that the transformation of the international legal order into an order so radically just as to eliminate structural violence is unlikely to be accomplished by the emergence of a new source of law which nonetheless keeps control over the law in the hands of entrenched and interlocking elites. While this truth should prompt moral concern, its dogmatic assertion would invalidate any consideration whatsoever of law-making in the context of the global community as we know it now.

The Source of Sources: Can Custom Be the Source of Custom as a Source?

The decisive obstacle to the emergence of declarations of general principles as a source of international law is the unwillingness of the world community to validate it as a source. The validating procedure would be accomplished by having the new source stated in legal form through the operation of an existing source. Thus general principles of law recognized by civilized nations are validated as a source because they are stated as such in the Statute of the World Court. In that form they are a source only for the Court, but may be considered as having generalized validity because of the emergence of customary

---

87.   Western states resist a new source even though they would be protected from its use against them by the requirement of overwhelming consensus. Recognition of this is apparently greater among some non-Western statesmen who now decry consensus for this very reason. Haemmerli (fn. 27), pp. 337-338. Their preferred alternative of a majoritarian decision rule would make a new source nothing other than legislation, which is under no conceivable circumstance acceptable to the West.

88.   See Johan Galtung, "Violence. Peace and Peace Research," *Journal of Peace Research*, Vol. 8 (1969), pp. 167-191, and "A Structural Theory of Imperialism," *Journal of Peace Research*, Vol. 8 (1971), pp. 81-117. See also Asborn Eide, "International Law, Dominance and the Use of Force," *Journal of Peace Research*, Vol. 11, No. 1 (1974), pp. 1-20, on the relation of structural violence to international law.

law precipitated by the universal acceptance of Article 38 and coextensive with it. Treaties are also affirmed as a source in Article 38, but this was merely declaratory of a legal condition long established in custom. Finally custom itself is affirmed as a source in Article 38, and again this may be taken as declaratory, for we have long known that custom is a source of law. But what is the source of the rule validating custom as a source? Unclear is how that source can be any of the known sources: Can custom be the source of custom as a source? Can a treaty be the source of custom when treaties gain their validity as a source from a legal custom?

The logical problem is so obvious but apparently unanswerable that it is as much ignored in the literature on the sources of international law as it is debated in legal and social philosophy. Three general positions on the basis of legal obligation are apparent, each of them taking the form of a familiar metalegal postulate. The basis of obligation for any system of law is said to be formal agreement (social contract) or spontaneous general agreement (consensus) or the instinct or need for order (social imperative). These are not mutually exclusive possibilities, even though they tend to be posed as such. Taken together in given mixes or combinations, they may tell us in very general terms how social orders begin or are fundamentally transformed.

In recent decades, there has been remarkably little opinion on, much less systematic consideration of, what might be called first causes in the international legal order. This is not to suggest that we are all too sophisticated for eighteenth century social philosophizing; it means only that we tend to be unwitting adherents to one position or another. Perhaps Kelsen has given the matter the most thought. He concluded that a social imperative ("states ought to behave as they customarily have behaved") was at the root of the international legal order (to which all domestic legal orders were formally subordinated). This was Kelsen's famous *Grundnorm,* which he took to be sociological in character and thus beyond appreciation in legal science.[89]

Kelsen's concern for formally validated hierarchies of legal orders distinguishes his work from conventional positivist thought. Positivism, by holding consent to be the decisive element for participation in the international legal order, suggests a voluntarist worldview that is unsympathetic if formally compatible with the Kelsenian *Grundnorm.* One might think that a consent-oriented view of international law would incline writers instead toward a contractual view of the international legal order's origins. Custom could be a source only to the extent that states so consented, very much as if they had agreed to a tacit treaty. While this position is latent in positivism, the emphasis in this school on the decentralized character of the international legal order yields a concern for what states do with respect to each other and not how the system of states came into being. The positivist doctrine of recognition provides a means of assimilating new entities into an existing system but begs more fundamental questions. Since positivists display so little interest in the tacit treaty that validates custom, they force us to identify it for them as a social contract, or validated by a social contract, which is to the same effect.[90]

Contract theories have receded from favor in the face of anthropological and historical evidence suggesting the unlikelihood of a formally constituted international order.[91] The idea of consensus is gradually supplanting the idea of contract, as the

---

89. See among his many works Kelsen (fn. 25), Part V.

90. In its underlying assumptions simple positivism is thus the unwitting recipient of a residue of Enlightenment thought despite appearing as a departure from the Enlightenment cast of mind. See the first section of this chapter, under "Positivism."

91. At least at its origins. It is quite plausible to argue that the international legal order was

progressive reinterpretation of Rousseau reveals.[92] Present-day apostles of the consensus position have generally been concerned to expose the anomalies in positivist assumptions.[93] By taking the battle to conventional positivists, the consensus school has tended to accept the positivist view of what the war is all about. The focus is always on whether custom as a source requires or implies literal consent or something less demanding in the formation of *particular* rules. The question not being asked is whether consent, collectively yielding a tacit treaty or social contract, or consensus, as a concretization of the general will, is the constitutive source of custom as a source.

We find this the ultimate issue in the debate over consent and consensus, although only D'Amato has come to recognize it so far. D'Amato's first probings of the problem are intriguing but inconsistent. He has argued that the source of custom may well be provided for by consensus,[94] but he has separately argued in convincing fashion that consensus is not a "metarule" effectuating declarations as a source "but merely a definition of what we mean by the expression 'international law'."[95] If consensus is simply the latter, it is not immediately evident how it came to be the metarule creating custom as a source. The mechanics of consensus operating to this effect, which D'Amato elaborates so carefully in respect to declarations, cannot be taken for granted in the case of custom.

In short, how do we know that several hundred years ago mechanical requirements for the expression of a consensus of states necessary to constitute custom as a source of legally binding rules were properly fulfilled? If mechanical requirements are unnecessary because consensus is in reality nothing more than the spontaneous emanation of the general will, how do we know that kind of emanation when we see it?[96] Consensus seems to be little different from contract, as a postulated beginning of the legal order and of custom as a source, in specifying *how* things began. If the question of mechanics is to be answered with requisite specificity, such an answer will doubtless reconcile elements of the arguments invoking contract, consensus, or social imperative as source of sources.

We find in David Hume (1711-1776), nominally a contractarian, just such a reconciliation when he identified convention as the origin of orderly social behavior (for

---

reconstituted in formal terms at the San Francisco Conference in 1945, and perhaps had been previously at Westphalia (1648) and Vienna (1815). Article 38 could certainly be seen as part of the latest "constitution" of the legal order.

92. Roger D. Masters, *The Political Philosophy of Rousseau* (Princeton: Princeton University Press, 1968), Ch. VI and VII. While consent has always been a paramount concern of political theory, "consensus appears most often in theories sociologists advance to explain social order and cohesion." P. H. Partridge, *Consent and Consensus* (New York: Praeger, 1971), p. 71. See generally Ch. 4. Sociology through Durkheim is itself greatly in debt to Rousseau.

93. See prominently Falk (fn. 7).

94. D'Amato (fn. 54), pp. 41-44. D'Amato uses Hart's construction of primary and secondary rules (asserting as Hart did not that international law has secondary rules) and argues that the source of custom is a secondary rule. In the first section of this chapter, under "The Pillars of Positivist Doctrine," we argue that custom as a source is a secondary rule, thus making the source of custom a tertiary rule.

95. Anthony D'Amato, "On Consensus," *Canadian Yearbook of International Law*, Vol. 8 (1970), p. 122. Emphasis in original.

96. Generally following Maine (fn. 46) and Weber (fn. 25), we can see two closely related possibilities—identifying a charismatic or seemingly divine figure who is either a judgment giver or law finder. Individual judgments could precipitate a consensus, or a consensus might crystallize around a set of general commands which are found and appropriately formulated. In either event, the result must be a general command generally accepted, stating Kelsen's grundnorm or something equivalent. This would be the metarule creating custom as source. Whether this process of metarule formation actually describes the beginning of Ancient Greek, Hebraic, or Islamic legal order, to use familiar examples, it is difficult to see

Hume, tantamount to justice).[97] "It has been asserted by some that justice arises from human conventions and proceeds from the voluntary choice, consent, or combination of mankind. If by *convention* be here meant a *promise*—which is the most usual sense of the word—nothing can be more absurd than this position. . . . But if by convention be meant sense of common interest, . . . justice arises from human conventions."[98] Hume deliberately disallowed a contractual source of order without disavowing the usual contractarian premise that common interest must prevail over the pursuit of particular advantage for order to ensue. He departed most profoundly from the contract school by denormativizing this premise. The common interest prevails, not because it is right, rational, or required, but because it represents a characteristic accommodation of immediate circumstances, such as revealed in Hume's famous illustration of two men, each with an oar, attempting to row a boat. Through trial and error they learn to coordinate their efforts, enabling them to achieve their common interest of propelling the boat through the water. As their coordinative efforts pay off, expectations about each other's movements develop accordingly, and they recognize incentives not to deviate from their established pattern of coordinated rowing. A convention is established.[99]

"Thus two men pull the oars of a boat by common convention for common interest, without any promise or contract; thus gold and silver are made the measures of exchange; thus speech and words and language are fixed by human convention and agreement. Whatever is advantageous to two or more persons if all perform their part, but what loses all advantage if only one perform, can arise from no other principle."[100] Observe that while contracts are necessarily bilateral—between two parties—conventions are only illustratively so. Conventions come about through actions involving or extending readily to any number of individuals. Indeed, the larger a convention's compass, the more it seems to have a life of its own, independent of individual wills. This spontaneous, generalizing property of conventions avoids the impossible mechanics of formal agreement for an indeterminately large population and captures therefore the most attractive element in the consensus position. At the same time, conventions are not just spontaneous occurrences or diffuse emanations of an allegedly general will, lacking internal logic or structural integrity. Instead conventions arise through discernible mechanics, resembling custom in their accretional character but not custom's implicit mindlessness.

---

how it may have operated in the instance of the international legal order. Who was the judgment giver or law finder? Why is there no record of his commands or legend supporting his authority? Grotius came too late, and even he does not remotely resemble the charismatic figure called for.

97.   Hume's analysis "Of the Original Contract" is found in his *Essays Moral, Political and Literary* (1741-1742). It is a collateral rather than integral part of his conception "Of the Origin of Justice and Property," *A Treatise of Human Nature* (1738), Book III, Part II, Section II. Reprinted in Henry D. Aiken, ed., *Hume's Moral and Political Philosophy* (New York: Hafner Pub. Co., 1968), pp. 356-372, 55-69, respectively.

98.   David Hume, *An Enquiry concerning the Principles of Morals* (1751), Appendix III, "Some Further Reflections with Regard to Justice," in Aiken, p. 278. Emphasis in original. For the remainder of this section we use the terms *convention* and *contract* as Hume did, implying the adjective "social" rather than "legal" before each use.

99.   "Of the Origin of Justice and Property," Aiken, p. 60. For a careful treatment of convention along these lines, see David K. Lewis,*Convention* (Cambridge, Mass.: Harvard University Press, 1968), pp. 36-42 and throughout. See also Thomas C. Schelling, *The Strategy of Conflict* (Cambridge,Mass.: Harvard University Press, 1960), ch. 3, 4, on coordination in the absence of communication. Hume's illustration allows but does not require communication of any kind.

100.   Hume, "Some Further Reflections . . .," Aiken, p. 280.

Conventions create tangible and reciprocal expectations from which the makers of such conventions deduce equally tangible obligations. Gone is the need to infer specific obligation from a general will to be ruled by law, which is possibly the weakest feature of the consensus position.

Observe also that Hume's empirical approach to the problem of order avoids making conventional behavior a social imperative taking the form of a collective injunction. Parties to an order need not to be told that they ought to behave as they always have. They will for the most part behave that way anyway. They do so because of an individual imperative and not a social one. Should they fail to recognize such an imperative individually, then others will respond, as their needs dictate, either to have the imperiled convention honored or its terms adjusted to accord with the revised constellation of relevant behavior. The inherently conservative nature of law and order is thus acknowledged, but so are orderly processes of change and growth.

Another virtue of Hume's position is its avoidance of a narrow construction of any society's principal, conventionally fixed sources of order. Conventions are not just the source of rights and obligations but also of symbols to express or identify things, relations, ideas, or values. Language and economy thus join law as conventional sources of order. Not only did Hume reconcile competing postulates on how legal order begins, he provided an equally simple and appealing model of social order's origins in a more general form than his competition managed. Hume's model is exceptionally well-suited to the decentralized but hardly diffuse order represented by the Western state system. Agreements, institutions, and coordinative arrangements of all kinds fit loosely together in a web of relations distinctly Humean both in origins and proportions.[101]

THE SOCIOLOGY OF LAW AND LAW-MAKING: SPECIES OF INTERNATIONAL LAW

Law as Solutions and Law as Artifacts: Durkheim and Weber

In his famous lectures on jurisprudence John Austin announced that laws "are a *species* of commands" distinguished from the other species of commands, "occasional or particular commands," by their general applicability to a class of acts. Commands are defined as a signification of desire accompanied by the means to compel its fulfillment. Obedience is secured through enforcement (sanction) and may be supported by habit.[102] This is the command theory of law, which forms the basis of pure positivist doctrine. The typical positivist critique of the command theory is that it misses the other distinctive attribute of law, namely, that it takes the form of rules which derive their binding status from yet other rules and not from the specific attribute of being accompanied by the means of enforcement. In other words, the duty to obey individual rules arises from their

---

101. Fritz Kratochwil, "The Humean Perspective in International Relations," presented at 1980 Meeting of the International Studies Association, also makes this case. Hume wrote briefly on international law and the balance of power but presented no general view of the international, or any decentralized, order.

102. John Austin, *The Province of Jurisprudence Determined* and *The Uses of the Study of Jurisprudence*, with an Introduction by H. L. A. Hart (London: Weidenfeld and Nicolson, 1954), pp. 13, 19. See generally Lecture I. Gidon Gottlieb, *The Logic of Choice* (New York: Macmillan, 1968), pp. 37–39, identifies nine "prominent species of normative sentences," or rules, possessing "functional kinship" and "constant structural characteristics." Only one of these species of rules can be called commands as Austin used the term. Unlike Austin, Gottlieb does not attempt to develop a closed system of species-candidates by varying an attribute like degree of generality. Instead he produces an experientially derived, open-ended list of species.

status in a hierarchy of rules and not from the existence of individual sanctions. Instead, the enforcement capacity is attached to the legal order as a whole and the presence of a sanction is an attribute generally of all rules therein.[103]

Positivist legal thought after Austin has thus concerned itself with two quite related things. The first is the validity of laws formally and properly promulgated as rules. The second is the generic properties of enforcement in the legal order. What has been ignored by comparison is the apparent specificity of some rules and some sanctions, which respectively deny Austin's requirement that law is generally applicable and the requirement of Austin's critics that enforcement is a general condition of legal order. Nowhere are these anomalies more apparent than in the instance of international law.

International law preeminently poses a problem for any assumption that a general sanction exists, as we noted earlier. While writers have proven to be adept at constructing hierarchies of rules of international law, the resulting structure is not a legal order complete with a general sanctioning competence. The latter must be achieved independently. Consequently the process of validating a given rule by reference to its source cannot have the effect of bringing to bear a generally available sanction. Individually available sanctions are attached not just to individual rules but are separately attached to each use of the rule. That the same or similar sanctions may be used recurringly permits descriptive generalization but not the inference that a generalization about sanctions is the same thing as a general sanction. Furthermore, the validity of a rule is inferred from its apparent enforcement, at least in the instance of legal custom, which means that logically a rule cannot depend on validation for bindingness. Validation merely confirms a pattern of compliance such that a general sanction, or individual sanctions, or indeed any mix of factors are at work.

International law perhaps more than any other kind of law directs attention to the vital place of habit and other factors unrelated to enforcement in explaining obedience. It illustrates the empirical reality of law abidingness in the absence of meaningful sanctions acting as external means of enforcement. Thus the example of international law should raise questions about the adequacy of the Austinian model and its variations for all those who balk at Austin's conclusion that international law is simply not law properly so-called. As the sorriest, or at least the murkiest example of law to be dealt with, international law almost demands a conceptual leap beyond the constraints of the model of law as commands.

Dissatisfaction with Austin's model, as applied to international law, is abundantly evident in the contemporary literature. It remained for Gidon Gottlieb to present an alternative with full attention to doctrinal questions. Gottlieb's alternative is an "acceptance model" of law.[104] In brief he puts the habit element ahead of the command element in the Austinian equation and argues that principled decisions, guided by "public considerations," have the nature of law; other decisions do not. By framing his arguments in terms of decisions, Gottlieb has significantly but only tacitly abandoned Austin's belief that laws populate the species of commands held apart because they are general in

---

103. Hart's Introduction (fn. 102), pp. xi-xiii. While Austin used the term *rule* to describe legal commands, he did so without concern for validity, which Hart takes to be the decisive feature of the "rule-dependent notion." Like Gottlieb, we see rules as norms, but sufficiently precise in content that both the expected behavior and the basis for demanding it are clear to the intended target. A clear statement of expected behavior is a necessary but not a sufficient condition for a rule to be a command; a clear statement of where it comes from, or what it is based on, is a necessary but not a sufficient condition for its validity.

104. Gottlieb (fn. 26), pp. 362-374.

scope.[105] Discounting the difference between general and particular commands frees Gottlieb from undue concern for formal validity and hierarchical arrangements of rules.[106] That which is accepted as law includes but is not restricted to that which is formally derived from other law. Law includes that which is generally or specifically accepted, formally or otherwise. The acceptance model simultaneously enlarges the idea of command to refer to a command-compliance nexus and the idea of rule to mean principled decision.

Gottlieb's radical reformulation of Austin's position while partially returning to the Austinian frame of reference permits us to conceive of law itself as having different species. These would be: (1) decisions that are both enforced and general in scope; (2) decisions that are specific but nonetheless enforced; (3) decisions that are not enforced, but still obeyed, and general in scope; and (4) decisions that are neither general nor enforced, but still obeyed.[107] The first is the species of law commonly found in advanced Western orders. The second is special law, a species mostly to be found in relatively primitive, usually non-Western orders.[108] The third makes principles and standards a species of law.[109] The fourth is a species set apart from other decisions by being principled, guided by public considerations, and thus regarded as having applicability that reaches beyond their specific terms. If the two concepts of law yield four species of law, only two of them—the third and fourth identified here—are species of international law. This is because only the second concept of law spelled out in the acceptance model meaningfully describes what we normally call international law. Neither species resembles the typical positivist view of international law as a homogeneous entity not so very different from domestic law.

If we accept the conclusion that law is the conventional term for a family of social forms which together contribute decisively to social order, we must also conclude that *legal order* as understood in positivist doctrine is not the necessary foundation of all social orders. Legal order is merely the collection of species of law, however distributed, which operate separately and only sometimes interactively in the direction of ordering a given social unit. Much else operates with species of law to the same effect, although the relative importance of all such factors is beyond the province of positivist legal thought. If legal order is not defined as the root source of a social order, then we may ask without prejudice (or at least without *that* prejudice) how particular social orders, and types of orders, actually work. We become sociologists.

Sociology began in continental Europe basically to provide a frame of reference for

---

105.   In his earlier work (fn. 102), p. 42, Gottlieb held the view that commands "addressed *ad hominem*" do not qualify even as rules, much less as law. It may be possible to retain Austin's classifying attribute of degree of generality and at the same time count most ad hominem commands out of the family of rule-species by distinguishing between impersonal and personal commands. The latter are exclusively ad hominem and therefore not rules by any definition. The former may be specific as enunciated but indifferent with respect to subsequent use. They would qualify as rules much as precedents would seem to. Thus principled decision could mean a specific decision which by being impersonal encourages an appreciation of its wider implications.

106.   The fact that treaties as special international law can nonetheless be placed in a validating hierarchy demonstrates that specificity and validity are compatible attributes of law. The point is that Gottlieb's scheme is *not dependent* on validation as a device either to make laws general or to bring a general sanction to bear.

107.   Each of the first two species has two subspecies within it: decisions enforced through a general sanction, and decisions enforced through a specific sanction. Clearly Austin's two species of commands are really the first two species of law insofar as they are principled in character. Commands not law are thus unprincipled enforced decisions, presumably in parallel species and subspecies.

108.   See above (fn. 78).

109.   Compare Dworkin (fn. 24).

making sense of the stupendous and unprecedented growth of nineteenth century industrial society. In the hands of such towering figures as Karl Marx (1818-1883), Emile Durkheim (1858-1917), and Max Weber, systematic and comparative study of advanced social economies developed. Economics was freed from the need to be concerned with social setting and grew in the highly technical and formal direction so familiar in the United States, while the heritage of the social-economic systematizers expanded substantively to become sociology as we now know it. Though inevitably attenuated by the widening scope of sociology, the original link between society and economy nonetheless continues to be crucial for organizing explanations on the working of social orders. Such a link represents a direct alternative to the long-standing presumption of legal-political thought that the crucial relationship for explaining the operation of social orders is between law and order. Apparently, legal thought and classical sociology offer a choice of approaches to the problem of social order that can be captured in their characteristic terminology. Sociologists seize on the *social* as the critical factor and find it substantially dependent on economy, while most legal scholars treat *order* as the critical factor substantially dependent on law.

Durkheim and Weber may be considered the fathers of the sociology of law, at one in detaching law from some simple idea of order. Instead they tie law in with other organized activities making up social economy. Yet their different treatments of the general problem of social order provide us with two quite different ways of looking at law. In fact, they provide basic descriptions of the two species of law which, though unacknowledged in positivist doctrine, we have already defined as best fitting international law.[110]

*   *   *   *   *   *

Durkheim's ideas about the place of law in society are an integral part of his famous early treatise, *De la division du travail social,* first published in 1893.[111] He identified two major forms of social order: those we would call primitive, which he described in terms of "mechanical solidarity," and those we would call complex or modern, which he described in terms of "organic solidarity." Organic solidarity takes place through the division of labor. Fundamentally different types of law characterize the two kinds of solidarity. Mechanical solidarity yields, and uses, repressive law, meaning law possessing a repressive sanction in response to deviancy, which describes criminal law even today. Organic solidarity yields, and uses, restitutive law, meaning law the sanction of which "consists of a simple *return in state.*"[112] Restitutive law is thus roughly analogous to civil law and, most eminently, contract law. It performs "special tasks," largely unrelated to "transcendental authority which, when offended, demands expiation."[113] As social orders grow more complex, labor is further and further divided, and special tasks, along with their regulation, increase as an overlayer on the formerly dominant substratum of repressive law. In an organically solidary social order, restitutive law vastly outweighs the law for which forcible sanctions are normally brought to bear, with significant institutional

---

110.   The inspiration. though little of the substantive detail, for the following comparative treatment of Durkheim and Weber as the founders of the sociology of law comes from B. C. Cartwright and R. D. Schwartz, "The Invocation of Legal Norms: An Empirical Investigation of Durkheim and Weber," *American Sociological Review*, Vol. 38, No. 3 (June 1973), pp. 340-354.

111.   Emile Durkheim, *The Division of Labor in Society*, trans. George Simpson (New York: Macmillan, 1933; Free Press, 1964). A recent, useful treatment of Durkheim's sociology of law is Hunt's (fn. 15), Ch. 4.

112.   Ibid., p. 111. Emphasis in original.

113.   Ibid., p. 127.

consequences. "While repressive law tends to remain diffuse within society, restitutive law creates organs which are more and more specialized: consular tribunals, councils of arbitration, administrative tribunals of every sort. Even in its most general part, that which pertains to civil law, it is exercised only through particular functionaries; magistrates, lawyers, etc., who have become apt in this role because of very special training."[114]

Durkheim has given us a comprehensive description of social orders acting as legal orders without assuming the dependence of social orders in general on a particular species of law. To what extent does the international legal order resemble the social order types presented by Durkheim? Mechanical solidarity is notoriously absent, as are effective repressive sanctions. Laws that depend on such sanctions exist in a rhetorical but otherwise unrealized sense. Yet organic solidarity is as much a reality of contemporary international life as modern social orders are, for no other reason than that such orders are in constant and interpenetrating relations with each other.[115] Following Durkheim, the advanced condition of the division of labor in the international social order compels the utilization of an extensive body of restitutive laws. These laws need not come from a legislative fount; they do not come exclusively from such a fount in any order. They do come from the formal agreements or treaties, comparable in function to contracts in municipal orders, and the myriad practices on which all functionaries and administrative organs performing innumerable specialized tasks are forced to rely in the process of generating further practice.

There is a singular resemblance between Durkheim's conceptions of social order types applied to the contemporary international legal order and Wolfgang Friedmann's notable schematization in his book, *The Changing Structure of International Law.*[116] Friedmann (1907-1972) confirmed the rapid growth of what he called the law of cooperation in the international legal order, very much as Durkheim would have predicted. Durkheim might nonetheless have been surprised at the vigor of an organic order underlain only by the rudest kind of mechanical order, embodied for Friedmann in the law of coexistence. Although he was sensitive to abnormal forms, Durkheim's frame of reference was almost exclusively Western European experience, and even there his sense of history is defective.[117] As Bronislaw Malinowski (1884-1942) demonstrated so brilliantly in *Crime and Custom in Savage Society,* civil law based on economic relationships is an integral and important part of many apparently primitive orders.[118] Furthermore, with Malinowski, Durkheim simply imputed a repressive sanction to primitive orders without demonstrating its existence. The international legal order may well resemble a multitude of orders, including those of Europe, which were well developed organically

---

114. Ibid., p. 113.

115. That interdependence is rapidly increasing in recent years is a popular article of faith, although scholars debate the matter sharply. For a thorough assessment, see Edward L. Morse, *Foreign Policy and Interdependence in Gaullist France* (Princeton: Princeton University Press, 1973), Ch. 2. Interdependence and organized complexity (fn. 50) are conceptually related by Ernst B. Haas, "Is There a Hole in the Whole? Knowledge, Technology, Interdependence and the Construction of International Regimes," *International Organization,* Vol. 29, No. 3 (Summer 1975), pp. 852-859. The notion of "complex interdependence" informs Robert O. Keohane and Joseph S. Nye's recent, influential textbook, *Power and Interdependence* (Boston: Little, Brown, 1977).

116. Friedmann (fn. 22).

117. See further Robert Nisbet, *The Sociology of Emile Durkheim* (New York: Oxford University Press, 1974), pp. 128-132. Apparently realizing the historical limitations of his typology of social orders, Durkheim never returned to it in his later work. We do not feel the typology's analytic value has been effectively challenged; indeed we feel that it has been enhanced by reading history as we have here.

118. Bronislaw Malinowski, *Crime and Custom in Savage Society* (London: Routledge, 1926).

long before the emergence of a coercive apparatus of any consequence.[119]

If law and law-relevant institutions in an organically solidary order arise in response to the division of labor, it is because they solve, through available instrumentalities, the particular kinds of problems that arise for participants in a very much divided society. Standard solutions are supplied in diverse situations. Standard operating procedures are employed. Contract law, as the most characteristic form of organic law, "has for its function much less the creation of new rules than the diversification in particular of pre-established rules."[120] Since the international legal order is decentralized in its law-making procedures, that very diversification is simultaneously the particularization of new rules incidental to particular solutions.

The foregoing raises an issue which Durkheim himself addressed, although in the instance of the international legal order it appears in aggravated form. If law is nothing more than solutions to problems created by the division of labor, then is not each solution constructed from the particulars of the situation, representing nothing more than a balance of private interests? Each solution is a law, one that lives only for that solution. Durkheim argued that "law is, above all, a social thing and has a totally different object than the interest of its pleaders."[121] This is actually a definition of law that requires the solutions to be made by reference to some external standard. Not all problems generated by the division of labor are dealt with by reference to law. And although law can be seen in terms of solutions, all solutions are not law. Those solutions using law as an external standard, whether legislated, created by agreement, or divined from prior solutions, are the solutions in which the social order has a direct role.

Law is the aggregate of solutions, but more especially of solutions connected to other solutions by reference to each other or common, objectively stated standards for handling problems. In the international legal order more than in centralized orders, solutions are likely to be obtained by reference to comparable solutions, the first of which was not legal, or nearly as legal as the latest, rather than by reference to objective standards. In due course standard solutions are seen as objective standards.[122] For our purposes, legality is a relative condition. Standardization is the empirical measure of relative legality. To speak of standard solutions is to employ a convention meaning only: standard enough to be called law.[123]

*   *   *   *   *   *

Weber's work on law is perhaps even more extensive than Durkheim's; at any rate, it is more systematically presented and set apart from the rest of his sociology. Though

---

119.   The coercive apparatus so essential to the systematic employment of repressive sanctions over a territorially defined population developed in European states only after 1500. Particularly important was the creation of efficient methods of taxation to pay the costs of national security. Prior to this European states possessed extensive decentralized political structures deriving from innumerable corporate and deliberative bodies. This feudal inheritance displayed the complexity and restitutive legal forms of organic orders. See Charles Tilly, "Reflections on the History of European State-Making," in Tilly, ed., *The Formation of National States in Western Europe* (Princeton: Princeton University Press, 1975), pp. 17-25, 71-76, summarizing contributors' pertinent findings.

120.   Durkheim (fn. 111), p. 215.

121.   Ibid., p. 113.

122.   Such standards resemble what Pound saw as administrative law grown from a "customary course of administrative action." (fn. 15) III, p. 396.

123.   One objective threshold of standardization such that we may speak of law is suggested by Thomas M. Franck, *The Structure of Impartiality* (New York: Macmillan, 1968). A standard may be called law

only one part of Weber's monumental unfinished treatise *Wirtschaft und Gesellschaft* (1922),[124] the work on law begins with a tightly related set of definitions and proceeds to a comparative and developmental systematization of legal orders and legal thought. However much our reading of Durkheim's thought was selective, the complexity and richness of Weber's contribution compels even greater selectivity.[125] Picking and choosing as we must, we should note from the very beginning that we do not find Weber's formal definition of law to be of any great service by itself. It is recognizably in the Austinian tradition but avoids Austin's necessary link between law and political authority or the state: "An order will be called *law* if it is externally guaranteed by the probability that coercion (physical or psychological), to bring about conformity or avenge violation, will be applied by a *staff* of people holding themselves specially ready for that purpose."[126] Weber countenanced a greater variety of ordered situations as being legal than did Austin, while doubting that international law is truly law.[127]

Weber's background in the pandectist, or Germanic ultra-positivist school, is evident in his definition of law, yet his subsequent sociology of law is not really dependent on this definition. Weber is justly famous for his interest in bureaucracy, which can be inferred even from his definition of law—sanctions are applied by a staff—and is a constant theme in his review of legal orders. But his concern is not simply or even primarily for that single class or group of persons called bureaucrats. Rather he is interested in any distinguishable group involved in the operation of legal orders. Weber determined that most such groups in all but the most primitive social orders are composed of lawyers, that is, persons trained in and having scarce or possibly even exclusive knowledge about how law works.[128]

Lawyers' groups in different orders tend to be organized differently, and Weber took pains to show that the organization of lawyers and of legal thought is a complex phenomenon only generally connected with socioeconomic developments. Social orders have distinctive legal systems reflecting separate developmental experiences for their specialists in legal knowledge. For Weber this turned out to be a good deal more revealing than the definitional presence of enforcement staffs. Weber saw a social order as dependent on a legal order, but only as a standard item that all advanced orders possess without its decisively affecting the direction of socioeconomic development. Furthermore, the existence of a legal order gives rise to the distinctive organization of legal knowledge and activity which accompanies the developing social economy without either the organization of legal knowledge or the social economy being decisively affected by or

---

insofar as it is discerned by an impartial third party as appropriate for his use in finding a workable solution to a disagreement between two parties. The difficulty with this is the necessary link between law and adversary situations. Such situations no doubt punctuate some customary courses of administrative action but hardly define their essence.

124. The whole work is only recently available in English: *Economy and Society*, Guenther Roth and Claus Wittich, eds. (New York: Bedminister Press, 1968), 3 vol. The segment on law has been available longer (fn. 25).

125. For a more comprehensive treatment of Weber's sociology of law, which corrects any impression of simplicity inadvertently produced by selectivity in the following discussion, see Hunt (fn. 15), Ch. 5.

126. Weber (fn. 25), p. 5. Emphasis in original.

127. Ibid., p. 6.

128. Richard D. Schwartz and James C. Miller report in a study of mediation in pre- or nonmodern societies that only a few employed counsel as a specialized vocation. They conclude that lawyers are found only at a late stage of legal evolution, typically in "urbanized, literate societies." "Legal Evolution and Societal Complexity," *American Journal of Sociology*, Vol. 70, No. 2 (September 1964), p. 167.

dependent on the other. This parallel development is Weber's rationale for treating the sociology of law apart from the rest of his sociology of advanced orders and is simultaneously his critique of more deterministic treatments of economy, society, and law.

What does this have to do with international law? Weber stipulated that enforcement staffs are decisive for legal orders but demonstrated that the organization of legal knowledge is the more dominant feature of the social orders that he considered legal. Conceivably foreign office legal advisers and their staffs are "an organized coercive apparatus for the nonviolent exercise of legal coercion," possessing "such power that there is in fact a significant probability" that norms will be respected.[129] Whether legal advisers are indeed enforcement staffs, they are only a small part of the organization of legal knowledge and activity at the international level. Just as with municipal orders, the more dominant feature is the substantial presence of lawyers organized in a distinctive fashion. Obviously, the presence of lawyers is not a consequence of the creation of an international legal order. The creation of that legal order is only now and only possibly taking place, and it is very much lawyers' doing. In fact, lawyers have been supplied by the domestic orders where they exist in abundance.

It is one of the ironies of history that the Austinian tradition should dominate so much of twentieth century legal thought and yet lawyers should persist in viewing international law as an appropriate subject for training, scholarship, and career. The fact that they do means that a substantial, well-organized legal community exists on a world scale. Following Weber, this does not mean that we have an international legal order. What would appear to be the legal organization of the international order does not make the latter a legal order, for there are good reasons why lawyers would undertake to organize themselves as if they were the instrumentalities of an advanced legal order, even a state. Most obviously, lawyers benefit psychologically from the collective conceit of organizing the way they do. Hence we have the World Court, made by lawyers for lawyers, legal committees of the General Assembly, and so on. Weber would not say that the way lawyers organized is inconsequential, but he would be inclined to see it as symptomatic of developments in advanced orders and not a signification of the existence of an international legal order.

We can proceed one last step to the inevitable if heretical conclusion that what international lawyers care to describe as international law is their own invention. Their invention supports the illusion that there is international legal order and that they are in charge of it. They see their rules of law as the specific, tangible instrumentalities by which states are made a part of that order and their behavior governed by it. The alternative is to say that lawyers exist in their currently organized form at the international level at the sufferance and for the convenience of states, and that order is achieved through circumstances and processes largely unrelated to the availability of law or laws created by lawyers. In this view law is little more than a set of artifacts. They appear to be germane to international life simply to fulfill their illusory function for lawyers. Lawyers make their artifacts as realistic as possible. Like popguns for children, international laws can look deceptively like real laws without working, because there is no legal order for them to work in.

International law can nonetheless have considerable utility without being operative. It can serve as a model of what the law in an operative international legal order would or

---

129. Weber (fn. 25), p. 14.

should look like, and thus may serve an educational function both for statesmen and publics. Negative educational effects are hardly unheard of, however, as when artifacts demonstrably fail to function as law in highly publicized situations or when swiftly changing circumstances make artifactual laws look irrelevant or outmoded. Such occasions, of course, give further employment to the international lawyers who are so well organized to refurbish and refine their artifacts.

We have derived from the sociologies of Durkheim and Weber two characterizations of law as different from each other as they are from Austinian law. Neither characterization excludes the other. Remember that these are not merely alternative conceptions. They are characterizations of laws typical of two different species of law. They fit international law especially and together account for much of the body of that law. Both species—law as standard solutions and law as lawyers' artifacts—command our attention.

Standardizing Solutions: The Role of Practice, Treating, and Codifying

The traditional sources of international law are conventionally understood to yield one kind of law. But if indeed there are two distinct species of international law, then there may also be two generically different kinds of sources. If we grant that sources are not intrinsic to law, but merely external descriptions of how law comes into being, it may be useful to align species and sources. Segregating a specific traditional source into one or the other class could be complicated or even confounded by the received content of that source. In this event we would have reason to reconceptualize the source at that level of specificity, and in the process we might remove some of the anomalies and ambiguities we have already noted in the traditional formulations.

Let us look first at custom as a source of law. Is it a source of law as solutions or as artifacts? The answer is unclear and the attempt to segregate it unhelpful. Reconceptualizing custom into customary state practices, on the one hand, and reiterations of legal principles, on the other, brings to the surface a latent distinction in the traditional idea of custom. The distinction remains latent because of the assumption that reiterated principles are abstracted from state practices. This assumption is of course made necessary by the definition of legal custom as practice recognized by states to have legal consequences. Yet the definition is too stringent for much customary law to exist apart from that which generalizes treaties.[130] If we discard the definition, we can exchange the assumption of a relationship between practice and principle for an assessment of the extent to which practice and principles are actually related. Short of a systematically empirical survey, which is extraordinarily difficult to perform, our assessment must be informal and inconclusive. Nonetheless, we judge that the overwhelming proportion of technical problem-solving, though standardized, is not subjected to principled restatement. There is no need to do so, it is costly to do so, and it can easily be embarrassing to do so. Nor is it unprincipled conduct, in the sense Gottlieb uses the term, to prefer not to state principles in the absence of clear need.

Legal advisers and other bureaucrats can and consistently do act in a way that is law-minded without couching all their conduct in legal principles.[131] Law-mindedness is being attentive to standard procedures and always selecting the most formal of available

---

130.   See the second section of this chapter, under "Traditional Sources."

131.   See also Roger Fisher's well-known discussion of bureaucratic law-mindedness in "Bringing Law to Bear on Government," *Harvard Law Review*, Vol. 74. No. 6 (April 1961), pp. 1130-1140. The debt to Weber's work on bureaucratic rationality goes without saying. At least nothing is said about it.

solutions consistent with desired outcomes. Law-minded behavior need not draw a firm distinction between legal and illegal possibilities. It merely presumes in favor of the solution most nearly articulated as principle when other considerations are roughly equal. Many circumstances permit behavior that is consistent with unstated principles and unaccompanied by principled statements. Other circumstances require some level of elaboration on how a particular solution can be said to be standard, but the argumentation never reaches the level of public visibility that is almost definitionally required for the reiteration of principles. Finally, in a few circumstances solutions must be sorted into the few publicly available possibilities and advanced as lawful in the fullest sense of being consistent with practice and its public articulation.

The practice of foreign office legal advisers is thus largely a matter of solutions whose standardization is for the most part subterranean. That solutions are cast in legal language is more a consequence of the lawyer's training and habits of mind than it is of his consideration of legal weight or merit per se. The standardization of solutions is surely expedited by the use of standard forms and terms in legal language, but this is hardly synonymous with articulation, which implies the identification of legal principles which are seen as determinative for the situation at hand (and any others like it).

For simplicity's sake, we have used the work of foreign office legal advisers to illustrate the nature of international law as standard solutions. This is unduly restrictive, however. There is no clear boundary between those in governments whose activities make up international law and those whose activities do not. Any time any public functionary has recourse to a standard solution to any kind of situation with an international component, it may be said that he is using international law. Whether he recognizes it to be international law or whether we could find written confirmation anywhere of the solution's legal status, is immaterial. Most such solutions are so specialized and their standard character appreciated by so few people that there is no conceivable way that all of them could be transcribed into the public record as "the law." Even if this were possible through vastly improved record collection and utilization systems, the very fact of making at least some of these solutions public would undermine their value, for they would be seen as private bargains by any number of interests not represented in their fashioning or previous use.

There is no reason why we should restrict our attention to governmental activity. Major governments formally defined are surrounded by a penumbra of institutions and agents, although granted varying degrees of public status, very much a part of the network of activity centered in the government. The boundaries between government and subgovernment are harder to find the closer one looks. As soon as we accept the relevance to international law of quasi-public governmental activity, there is little reason to hesitate about activity which is almost entirely centered in private governments like corporations, foundations, and universities. The only proviso is that private governmental activity must have public consequences. Such consequences may not be visible to the general public. They may arise from private concern for publicly defined intererests or they may attend the sheer size of some private institutions, however they define their concerns. In sum, we can limit our universe of standard solutions constituting a species of international law to all those solutions that are public. This includes solutions involving public bodies and those of private bodies which involve public considerations. We must keep in mind, however, that this boundary, perhaps even more than the one between formal and informal government, is more readily stipulated than ascertained.[132]

---

132. See Charles E. Merriam, *Public and Private Government* (New Haven: Yale University Press, 1944), Lecture I, on private governments and the distinction between public and private. Haas (fn. 115), pp. 849-852, has emphasized the importance of adversary processes among groups of experts in the identification

We can further confine our universe of standard solutions to those which are transnational in character.[133] Inasmuch as we are concerned with activity which is public in the widest sense, we must reach beyond the traditional domain of official interstate relations. Yet there must be some limit to our frame of reference. One limit is imposed by the existence of the state system, which clearly demarcates the world into more or less autonomous territorial units, each with its own system of public order. The alternative of dealing with everything social or finding and defending a less obvious cutoff point are less appealing. Therefore, to qualify for our attention the bundles of activity resulting in standard solutions must include specific sequences of activity which cross state frontiers.

Restricted even to this extent, the full range of standard solutions apparently constituting a species of international law is beyond assessment, perhaps beyond imagining. Except for the fact that a small proportion of all such solutions has always been called law, or said to be in conformity with law, we might not be inclined to use the term at all. Otherwise we should disclose what additional attribute we use to differentiate law from whatever is not law.

Two such attributes might be suggested. To qualify as law, standard solutions must be publicly acknowledged as legal (in which case, however, they may be exceptional rather than standard solutions, requiring the exceptional treatment implied by public acknowledgment). As we previously noted, this is the traditional way of establishing legal custom, and we return to it presently. The other possibility is less obvious but not completely unfamiliar. To qualify as law, standard solutions must result from the activities of lawyers.[134]

---

of the public interest. Adversary processes are thus one way private activities can enter the public realm and insofar as the result of such processes is consensually reached (becomes standard) or, following Franck (fn. 123), achieved with third party assistance, acquire legal status. Needless to say, there is no guarantee that the balance of private interests, even if it is adversarily reached, is in or the same as the public interest, substantively understood. For Haas, this is a procedural definition of the public interest; for our purposes, it is a partial definition of the terms *public* and *standard*, as in solutions which become both standard and public through adversary processes.

133. We should note that the term *transnational*, as developed by Jessup (fn. 22), included all public and private relations crossing state frontiers. Keohane and Nye specifically narrowed the meaning of the term to include only those relations not involving states exclusively (relations that are not international). They have also evolved a third term, *transgovernmental relations*, to account for situations in which governmental entities more or less autonomous from states are involved. Robert O. Keohane and Joseph S. Nye, "Transgovernmental Relations and International Organizations," *World Politics*, Vol. 27, No. 1 (October 1974), pp. 39-42. Keohane and Nye's attempt to divide the universe of relations across frontiers into three mutually exclusive categories—international, transnational, and transgovernmental—is no help at all in mixed cases involving actors from different categories. In this essay we will adhere to Jessup's usage, since we are concerned with the whole universe of relations without prejudice to their origins.

134. D'Amato has argued that law is but the prediction of official behavior. While anyone can (and does) make such predictions, their reliability is increased by seeking advice. With their training in materials that officials rely on and their understanding of official reasoning, lawyers offer the best advice. Basically D'Amato is saying that law is what lawyers advise us to expect from officials. In this reasoning standard solutions are past official behavior. Except in the simplest of situations, it is only with the advice of a lawyer that we are likely to be able to determine what standard solutions are and to predict their use. This is all the more the case when competing solutions offer themselves and the predictor must choose among them. Note that the latter situation is precisely the adversarial one discussed in fn. 132. While they are peculiarly identified with adversarial proceedings, lawyers are not indispensable to their conduct. Official behavior in highly specialized arenas, in which adversaries receive expert advice, may have all the attributes of a legal or judicial situation without a lawyer being present. D'Amato assumes but does not actually insist that lawyers are the predictors in situations of any complexity. We doubt that lawyers are present as a matter of course, but we would agree that the lawyerly activity of giving specialized advice is almost always present in such situations. See Anthony D'Amato, "The Limits of Legal Realism," *Yale Law Journal*, Vol. 87, No. 2 (January 1978), pp. 478-513.

There are some obvious difficulties in identifying law with what lawyers do. Simply in procedural terms the identification is ambiguous with respect to marginal situations in which lawyers are infrequent users of standard solutions. Are they legal solutions only when lawyers use them, or only when they are used by lawyers a certain proportion of the time, or any time after a lawyer has used them? Ambiguity on this score adds to the already vexing problem of imprecise boundaries for standard solutions as a species of international law. A more important, substantive difficulty is reflected in the uneven distribution of lawyers even among advanced industrial orders.[135] The likelihood that lawyers will be a part of the process of finding and using solutions to problems defined in specialized terms through the division of labor is greatest in United States. While this might encourage the American writer to overstate the importance of lawyers in institutional problem-solving, it also suggests that Americans play a disproportionate part in turning standard solutions that are both public and transnational into law. With these caveats in mind, we suggest that whenever lawyers are present in problem-solving situations, any use of standard solutions is a lawful use, making law of the solutions so used. The converse does not follow, however: the absence of lawyers does not necessarily prevent a standard solution from being legal.[136] (See Figure 1.1, p. 81.)

If we take the restrictive criteria that standard solutions must be public and transnational and the permissive criterion that such solutions must be law if lawyers are involved and may also be even if lawyers are not, we fix overlapping boundaries within which lies the domain of standard solutions as a species of international law.

The alternative to the mapping exercise just presented identifies as legal only those standard solutions that are publicly acknowledged as legal. Earlier we determined that public acknowledgment of legality *(opinio juris)*, or indeed public acknowledgment of any kind (articulation), is likely for a custom (and, by extension, a standard solution) only when it is incorporated in the provisions of a treaty. Treaties are manifestly public, transnational solutions to problems. They have the further advantage of being objective in character and are agreed to as such. Their formality makes them visible as solutions. Embodiment in a treaty thus provides a certain and simple answer to the question, "When is a standard solution legal?" Obviously all treaties are standard solutions that qualify as law. But are all solutions not embodied in treaties not law for that reason alone? Even if we say that treaties are the only standard solutions we can be sure are law, should we ignore subsequent interpretation, supporting documents, and patterns of use? If we stop looking at the treaty as a solution attaining a high level of formality and look instead at the treating process, is it so generically different from the processes by which solutions of lesser formality become standardized? The answer to this and all the other

---

135.   In the United States there are apparently 400,000 lawyers and an additional 100,000 law students, while Japan has only 10,000 lawyers. In 1956 China had 3500 lawyers, at present the legal profession as such does not even exist. See Frank Bray Gibney, "10,000 Lawyers vs. 350,000," *Center Report*, Vol. 8, No. 4 (October 1975), pp. 7-10; Victor Li, *Law Without Lawyers* (Boulder: Westview Press, 1978), pp. 9-10. Schwartz and Miller's conclusion (fn. 128), pp. 163-169, that societal complexity correlates with legal evolution and thus is related to the emergence of legal counsel therefore does not extend to modern societies and the density of legal roles. In other words, all modern societies appear to have a lawyerly class, but its size is ambiguously related to complexity and modernity.

136.   Thus a disinterested third party may sit in judgment in an adversary situation. Or, interested third parties may give advice to adversaries on the likely outcome of such situations. These roles are closely associated with law, or what is distinctive about law (compare Franck, fn. 123, and D'Amato, fn. 134). In effect law arises in situations in which lawyers characteristically but not necessarily participate.

questions is that treaties are less easily portrayed as the only law-solutions than might first appear to be the case.[137]

Treaties differ from practice in degree only, and most of the time the treating process is little different even in degree from the kinds of activity that go into less formal problem-solving.[138] It is probably fair to say that treating is more concerned with creating a new solution than applying available ones to a particular situation, but the distinction between old and new is so much manipulated from case to case that any generalization is not very useful. Thus when a particular solution is provided for a situation by treaty, the parties to the solution have an interest in seeing it as a new solution. When the solution is provided less formally, there is an interest in seeing it as well established. More often than not, any solution is a particularization of an earlier solution, so that it is specifically novel and generically familiar at one and the same time.[139]

The difficulty in identifying particular solutions as old and new is graphically illustrated by contemporary international codification. The statute of the United Nations International Law Commission (ILC), a subsidiary organ of the General Assembly, clearly differentiates between progressive development, meaning the drafting of new solutions, and codification, meaning the reproduction of old solutions. This distinction has been utterly unworkable in practice and long abandoned. In the deliberations of the ILC the bureaucrat-specialists who make up its membership (most are foreign office personnel presumed to function in an independent capacity) sort through the intricacies of state practice, which they render in standardized form.[140] Increasingly they perform these tasks without reference to, or need of, the abstract and generalized statements dominating legal treatises.[141] Effectively the ILC has superseded the scholar in sifting through state practice because it is in a better position to do so. Both the intricacy and immediacy of law-solutions defy capturing by individual scholars. Even teams of specialists systematically plumbing narrowly defined areas of such law are barely scratching its surface. Codification has become the visible surface of the vast network of activity whose full dimensions are beyond discernment. Endeavoring to standardize solutions to the chronic consequences of complexity is the present business of the ILC, just as it is with foreign office legal advisers, phalanxes of government lawyers, and private as well as public bureaucrats and managers in general. This is hardly the original intent of codification, however much it bears out Weber's judgment that codification is integrally related to bureaucratization.[142]

---

137. In our treatment of articulation in the second section of this chapter, under "Traditional Sources," we argued (contra D'Amato) that public acknowledgment that a custom (standard solution) was *not* law was necessary to prevent it from becoming law. Turning back to the alternative approach to the problem of defining which standard solutions are law, we could amend our list of criteria and say that standard solutions qualify as international law when they are public, transnational, involve lawyers or lawyerly roles, and are not publicly denied as having legal quality. The last of these operates infrequently to disqualify solutions as law because such denials are inconsistent with the temper of specialized problem-solving.

138. For a similar view, see Myres S. McDougal, Harold D. Lasswell, and James C. Miller, *The Interpretation of Agreements and World Public Order* (New Haven: Yale University Press, 1967), p. 5, fn. 5.

139. This recalls Durkheim's view of contract law quoted above. On "individualization" in international law, i.e., particularization, see also De Visscher (fn. 21), pp. 144-163.

140. On the ILC and its membership see Herbert W. Briggs, *The International Law Commission* (Ithaca: Cornell University Press, 1965); B. G. Ramcharan, *The International Law Commission* (The Hague: Nijhoff, 1977).

141. Concern for principles was last seen in the mid-1960's, when questions relating to peremptory norms and coercion in the conclusion of treaties received extraordinary attention.

142. See the second section of this chapter, under "Traditional Sources."

If we consider law as standard solutions, we find that we have very little access to the solutions themselves. These solutions are so many, so specialized, and standard in such a relative sense that we may well decide that there is little advantage to be gained from trying to investigate them directly. Instead we are drawn to the integral process of standardizing solutions and utilizing standard solutions. We become interested in the kinds of individuals whose activity fits this description and the kinds of situations in which such activity takes place. We conclude that international law in the image of Durkheim is a matter of how more than what, and that the former lends itself more fruitfully to inquiry than does the latter.

Artifacts and Functionaries: The Role of Scholars, Jurists, and the General Assembly

In its way the history of international codification is quite revealing. Codification at present is largely devoted to standardizing solutions, yet it had once offered scholars an opportunity to reiterate legal principles in as formal a manner as possible. Concern for state practice was frequently subordinated to the integrity of the principles. Codification became more disciplined in time and, as we have seen, the distinction between development and codification gained currency, only to disappear again as principles became less and less relevant to the bureaucratized codificatory process.

The transformation of codification tells most of the story of the changing status of scholars in the international legal order. Scholars were once significant agents for the articulation of the kind of law we have derived from Weber's work. Custom consists of practice *and* reiterated principles, which have been associated together as much by definition as anything else. The role of scholars in generating practice may have been more than nominal in the earliest days of the international system, when all roles were diffuse. As labor became divided and subdivided, the activities of legal scholars were fictionalized as integral to the law-making process, when in fact there were two such processes, not integrally related and with a place for scholars in only one of them. Even if scholars had little place in making and using standard solutions, they were paramount in publicizing general principles stated in the form of law. The best evidence of this is nineteenth century codification and the great treatises of that time.

Ostensibly scholars derived principles from the evidence provided by practice and treaties, thus making their texts the key link between standard solutions and reiterated principles as necessary components of international law. We do not mean to suggest that in those simpler days scholars were incapable of assessing practice and erecting principles consistent with it. We are skeptical that scholars were able to do these things often enough to justify the image that the international law depicted in their books is the same international law used by states in their daily intercourse. Yet this is the image that they have endowed us with. The geometric growth of foreign affairs bureaucracies and interstate acitivities over the last century has altogether outstripped the capacity of scholars to stay even nominally in touch with the burgeoning body of standard solutions. Statements of principles gained support from metalegal arguments and reciprocal citation. The legal order emerging in the nineteenth century was perforce detached from the law-patterns of the ever more institutionalized international system. The legal order was all the scholar saw around him, for it was an order of his own making, an artifactual order.

The chronic upheaval of the twentieth century has all but destroyed the credibility of the legal order invented by scholars. The world has come to doubt the value of international law even as the daily working of the world depends on law-solutions. Scholars have been the principal casualty in the demise of their creation. Literally, of course, international legal scholars survive and their number increases (though surely not in proportion to the growth in numbers of lawyers or intellectuals overall). Gone is the scholar's preeminent role in the articulation of a renewed legal order, in setting forth symbols systematically organized in relation to key principles yet dressed in the concrete language of law-solutions.[143] This does not mean, however, that the manufacture of legal artifacts and their assembly into legal order are activities no longer with us. On the contrary, scholars have been superseded by public functionaries.

Among the relics of the scholar's legal order is the principle that a truly legal order requires judicial machinery. The creation of the World Court stands as a memorial to the old order, although its activities are hardly those envisaged for it. The World Court has become the scholar's institutional equivalent. Though technically occupied with discrete situations, the Court and its audience quietly collude in treating judgments as something more than an adjunct to the processes of standardizing solutions. The Court's procedure for delivering extended judgments and minority opinions, the stature and independence of its members, and their weighty style all contribute to the position of the Court in producing artifacts for the legal order. To some extent this role is thrust upon the Court, and its members are unsure whether the principles they are supposed to articulate are representative of the nineteenth century legal order or some dawning order whose principles are more inchoate.[144] By its nature, the World Court is severely restricted in the range and volume of its activities. Frequently it has been denied the opportunity to expound principles relating to sensitive aspects of state relations and deeply contested values. The Court's necessary reliance on the multiple fictions of being a problem-solving institution further inhibit its venturing into areas beyond the purview of the nineteenth century legal order. Thus for a variety of reasons the Court's half-willing judges are pressed into service but found wanting as formulators of artifacts.

* * * * * *

Whatever the inadequacies of jurists, artifacts belong to the public sphere. Clearly there is a yearning for the artifacts of legal order even as there is dismay over their irrelevance. The symbolic and ultimately manipulative importance of artifactual law is widely recognized and control over production of artifacts is sought by statesmen with large stakes in the way the international system is ordered and, quite conceivably, with a sense of having lost control over routine problem-solving activities. Inevitably, a highly visible public forum, less constrained by considerations of decorum and legal sanctity, has become the locus of activity for making legal artifacts. The General Assembly is almost ideally suited for the purpose, in part because its outcomes can have a very formal but not strictly legal status. The decisive factor, though, is the General Assembly's view of itself

---

143. Perhaps the best current example of the effort to perform the scholar's historic role going unrewarded is the work of Myres S. McDougal and his associates. For a sense of the scale and scope of the New Haven effort, see Eisuke Suzuki, "The New Haven School of International Law: An Invitation to a Policy Oriented Jurisprudence," *Yale Studies in World Public Order*, Vol. 1, No. 1 (1974), pp. 1-48. An intriguing effort to revive the scholar's role is the work of Saul H. Mendlovitz, Richard A. Falk, and others in the World Order Models Project (WOMP). Despite its origins in the World Peace through World Law movement, WOMP has cast aside explicit reference to the legal order (as indeed McDougal and associates have done) and legally stated principles within a jurisprudentially couched framework (as McDougal and associates have not). In their place WOMP emphasizes a directly normative and decidedly futurist orientation. It would appear that WOMP has been liberated from law and legal discourse to enhance its credibility in articulating a preferred vision of the global order. For an overview of WOMP, see Saul Mendlovitz, ed., *On Creating a Just World Order* (New York: Free Press, 1975).

144. The Court's ambivalence is graphically illustrated in its infamous judgment in the South West Africa Case. *I. C. J. Reports*, 1966, pp. 4-51.

as a forum of world community, the only such body permanently constituted to deal with the full range of contemporary community concerns.

The General Assembly has as one of its seven main standing committees a legal committee (the Sixth Committee), which is populated by lawyers with a high annual rate of return to the Committee. And its agenda is usually less crowded than agendas of the other main standing committees. Under the circumstances it would be no great surprise if the Sixth Committee has carved out for itself a major role in making artifacts. In its earliest years, for example, the Sixth Committee prepared and adopted a series of draft resolutions affirming the Nuremberg Principles and the crime of genocide as principles of international law.[145] And in 1970 the Sixth Committee completed an intensive effort to formulate the so-called Principles of Friendly Relations and Co-operation among States.[146] Yet the 1960's and 70's may be remembered as the golden age for the General Assembly's production and promotion of artifacts, during which time the Sixth Committee was conspicuously not a participant in these activities. What are the reasons for this? One reason appears to have been the Sixth Committee's preoccupation with supervising the work of the International Law Commission. The energy and success of the ILC, combined with the fact that many of the ILC's members are Sixth Committee veterans, has engendered an intense, though hardly overbearing, interest in the Commission.[147]

The other reason for the Sixth Committee's failure to engage in the making of artifacts comes from the very fact of its competence in legal matters. The General Assembly as a whole recognized the need to extend and transform the traditional legal order. With its concern for legal niceties but without the substantive charge of the other main standing committees, the Sixth Committee could only be a hindrance in artifactual law-making. Declarations on Colonialism, Permanent Sovereignty over Natural Resources, Elimination of Racial Discrimination, Exploration and Use of Outer Space, Nonintervention, and the Establishment of a New International Economic Order, to use prominent examples, were drafted and adopted entirely without reference to the Sixth Committee.[148] After the initial burst of activity in which innovative as opposed to legal qualities of artifacts were emphasized, a period of consolidation has followed. At least it would appear to be consolidation such as one finds in customary law formation. The content of declarations of artifacts were reiterated in subsequent resolutions. All other resolutions even vaguely related in content make reference to such declarations in their preambulatory paragraphs. Having declared principles, the General Assembly makes them integral to its practice.[149]

If re-citation is a case of legal custom forming, then it must be a special case, in which the relevant practice need only be rhetorical since the rules being affirmed are only

---

145.   These resolutions are enumerated, as adopted in plenary, and their legal significance briefly discussed by Jorge Castaneda, *Legal Effects of United Nations Resolutions* (New York: Columbia University Press, 1969), pp. 191-193.

146.   Adopted by the General Assembly without a vote as a Declaration. Resolution 2625 (XXV), 24 October 1970. Work on the principles began in 1963.

147.   If anything the ILC dominated its parent organ during these years. See Briggs (fn. 140), pp. 316-361, on ILC-Sixth Committee relations.

148.   Respectively Resolutions 1514 (XV), 14 December 1960; 1803 (XVII), 14 December 1962; 1904 (XVIII), 20 November 1963; 1962 (XVIII), 13 December 1963; 2131 (XX), 21 December 1965; 3201 (S-VII), 1 May 1974. The last of these was the sole business of a special session of the General Assembly.

149.   For an important discussion and quantitative survey of the General Assembly's re-citative practice, see Samuel A. Bleicher, "The Legal Significance of Re-Citation of General Assembly Resolutions," *American Journal of International Law*, Vol. 63, No. 3 (July 1969), pp. 444-478.

artifacts.[150] We would prefer to avoid recourse to the language of custom altogether, because custom, unlike artifacts, needs consolidation. Once articulated at a requisite level of formality, subsequent activity, unless equally formal, does not decisively affect either content or status of the artifact. For an artifact, having legality is simply a level of formality, generality, and rhetorical acceptance that can be achieved in a variety of ways, but most easily and directly in a community forum. We call these artifacts law because lawyers provide the appropriate language and statesmen the rhetoric of acceptance. This results from a deep-seated cultural need to arrange many of our artifacts in what we prefer to call a legal order.

The generation of artifacts by the General Assembly does not in itself make a new legal order. If the old order were unchallenged, new artifacts would fit in easily. But we are faced instead with a situation in which numerous and possibly competing principles are promulgated as elements, or even pedestals, of a new order but are not assembled in an orderly way. Some of the subsequent re-citation has the effect of sorting out and ordering the host of new artifacts, while scholars and jurists contribute to envisioning the whole from the newly minted pieces. The Sixth Committee, however, may come to occupy the most important place of all in this process. The construction of a draft declaration on the Principles of Friendly Relations is precisely a major effort to restate and reconcile the most important of the new artifacts with each other and with the Charter of the United Nations. The result is the most formal and sustained delineation of an emerging, renovated legal order in existence.[151] The artifacts are endowed neither with greater legality nor with greater persuasiveness for problem-solvers; they are rendered in a form which illuminates the function of artifacts in providing us with a sense of systemic order and coherence consistent with changing ideas of what is just and fair on a world scale.

We have conceptualized the emergence of artifactual law in two stages. The first is the articulation of principles and the second is their assembly in a form recognizable as legal order. The Sixth Committee has recently assumed what could become the preeminent role in the second stage, just as it is precluded from the first because of its lack of substantive competence and because of its heritage of concern for law. As the new order becomes less new and necessary principles are already articulated, then it is likely that the highly visible role of the other main standing committees will recede. The Sixth Committee, on the other hand, virtually defines the legal community of public functionaries who will be custodians of the artifacts already existing. If the task of refining and ordering artifacts is shared at all, then it is only with a small circle of jurists and scholars, most of whom are Sixth Committee intimates.

$$*\quad*\quad*\quad*\quad*\quad*$$

The source of artifacts cannot be adequately described in the language of the traditional sources, any more than the source of standard solutions can be. We have reconceptualized custom into practice and reiterated principles and aligned the two components with standard solutions and artifacts respectively. These operations in turn

---

150. This is no different from the activity of scholars reaffirming artifactual statements originating in landmark form with either scholars or jurists.

151. It should be noted that the order delineated is not new in the sense of overturning the state system; it is only new in the sense of reordering characteristic state relations. For further comment, see Nicholas Greenwood Onuf, "The Principle of Nonintervention, the United Nations, and the International System," *International Organization*, Vol. 25, No. 2 (Spring 1971), pp. 209-227

suggested a connection between practice in general and treating in particular. And they suggested that the articulation of principles has progressed from scholars to jurists and finally to functionaries in the General Assembly. In a crude way it would seem that once custom is reconceptualized, the remaining sources (except the non-source, general principles of law) fall into place to give us distinctive sources for the two species of international law. The fit is not perfect, for some treaty forums are used to enunciate artifacts just as functionaries in the General Assembly use that forum for the kind of problem-solving that relies on standard solutions.

The real question is whether very much is gained by realigning sources in this fashion. To some extent the use of traditional categories of description, like practice, is a convenience, though it is hardly sufficient for our needs. Other categories, like treaties, are less satisfactory, and we prefer to speak of treating. Clearly, any label is just a label, to be used or passed over for another label depending on how much it helps us understand the phenomena in question. But the labels have nothing to do with the phenomena—they are artifacts of the observe's attempt to order what he sees. Accordingly the traditional conceptualization of the sources is artifactual as well. The traditional artifacts were made and used by many observers—scholars, jurists and statesmen— because these artifacts in particular complemented a collective vision of international legal order while they corresponded at least in a general way, given the state of social knowledge at the time, to actual processes of law-making in the system. The vision has faded, the characteristics of law-making have changed, knowledge has become more specialized, and the artifacts make less sense. New artifacts are needed, not to make things work better, but to make them look neater. If declarations become enshrined as a source because they are articulated as such in the most formal sense possible, it does not mean that declarations will suddenly be used to produce standard solutions. Declarations are not structured for this use. Instead, they will continue to embody artifacts, for which they are ideally suited.

Actual changes can be made in law-making processes, but not through the process of making artifacts. Promulgating a new source either confirms a change that has taken place or creates an illusion. If declarations become a source, that event will confirm the reality that the production of artifacts is now mostly in the hands of public functionaries using world community forums, and it will foster an illusion for those who wish to believe that declarations are a source of standard solutions. Promulgated or not, declarations are a source for those for whom it serves as a convenient label describing what has already come to pass with respect to production and organization of artifacts. The point remains: we could just as well use other labels, in greater or lesser harmony with what actually happens, without benefit or detriment to what happens. We could cease to speak of sources altogether, and speak only of making law-solutions and making law-artifacts, if we or anyone else found these artifactual categories useful. Even if they were to become dignified in due course as law, they would not be the *source* of anything that happens.

THE LEGAL MIND: WHY SOURCES PERSIST

Law and Order: Explanations, Institutions

The sources of international law are not as they seem.[152] This judgment follows reasonably enough from the realization that international law is not the single, homoge-

___

152. The second section of this chapter, being within the framework of received sources doctrine, is what some anthropologists would call an emic account of where law comes from. The third section, by

neous thing it is usually thought to be. We observe, however, that while legal minds differ greatly on essential properties of law, the more so when they consider international law, sources are invariably presented in the same, uniform way. How can sources doctrine have persisted, so little challenged or changed, for centuries? Changes in the real world of international relations have been accommodated by adding new sources as required, without affecting the status of older sources. Changes in legal thought discernible in major reconsiderations of particular sources, not to mention discussions of new sources, leave the classificatory scheme underlying all writing on sources untouched.

Such persistence can be made intelligible by noting some enduring features of the legal mind. Two stand out. One is the pervasive concern for, and consistency of assumptions about, social order and its relation to law and legal activity. The other resides in the fact that legal life is sustained by a community, elementary in organization and resistant to change, which in turn supplies the larger order with law and law-defined institutions. Locked within the legal mind's preoccupation with order and dependence on community are several conceivable explanations — perhaps competing, perhaps converging — for the remarkable durability of sources doctrine.

*   *   *   *   *   *

The legal mind consistently, and unsurprisingly, supposes that law and order are causally related. Without such an assumption there could be no domain for legal theory, which must always provide in general form an explanation for the relation of social items called law and social items called behavior, the latter collectively construed to take the form of order. The supposition that law and order are related rests, therefore, on the belief that all such social items tangibly exist. Though self-evident to the legal mind, and unchallenged for the most part in legal thought, law and order may not be so easy to defend as existential realities.

Granting the existence of social items that look like law and social items of behavior that constitute order, the two sets need not be causally related. Or causality may govern, but in reverse: certain kinds of (orderly) behavior appear lawlike, this being no more than a social construction of behavioral regularities.[153] Law provides such motifs abundantly in the name of producing order, when it could be that other, subjectively frivolous social needs are being met. If virtually all human cultures appear to engage in the decoration of useful material objects independently of their utility, merely to enhance their esthetic appeal or create for them a ritual or immaterial significance, then law may be a widespread phenomenon for this reason alone.

It is even possible that social items appearing to be law and clearly related to order are nothing more than sequences of random events resulting, with considerable probabili-

---

classifying species of law and law-making and describing their morphology would be an etic account. "In carrying out research in the emic mode, the observer attempts to acquire a knowledge of the categories and rules that one must know is order to think and act like a native." The natives in question are those of legal mind, typically lawyers. "Etic operations have as their hallmark the elevation of observers to the status of ultimate judges of the categories and concepts used in descriptions and analysis. . . . Rather than employ concepts that are necessarily real, meaningful, and appropriate from the native point of view, the observer is free to use other categories and rules derived form the data language of science." We proceed for the most part etically, observing the legal mind. Marvin Harris, *Cultural Materialism* (New York: Random House, 1979), p. 32. See generally Ch. 2.

153.   The phrase and point are adapted from Peter Berger and Thomas Luckmann, *The Social Construction of Reality* (Garden City, N.Y.: Doubleday, 1967). See also Friedrich V. Kratochwil, *International Order and Foreign Policy* (Boulder, Colo.: Westview Press, 1978), Ch. 3.

ty, in an objective condition which can only be called order. This possibility totally defies conventional assessments of social reality, because it accepts the relationship of law and order but relegates it to the realm of the unsocial—that is, the realm of human activity which is undirected by goals and unaffected by past choices. Social thought, and within it legal thought, depends on the belief that in the absence of the social, chaotic disorder will reign. We cannot know this with any certainty. We think we know by extrapolating from experience with what appears to be more or less order and the greater or lesser presence of law and other constraining social items. The assumption breaks down if a comparable correlation between law and order can come about randomly.

A deliberately random sequence can, and normally does, have a striking pattern to it. Such a sequence is generated by tossing a coin repeatedly. If a coin is perfectly balanced, each toss creates an equal chance that one or the other side will face up when the coin comes to rest. Given enough tosses, something approaching an equal number of heads and tails will be tallied. It would seem to follow from this fact that the lead, as between heads and tails, will change constantly. The fact is that the lead will change infrequently.[154]

Illustratively, in one experimental run of ten thousand tosses, the lead changed only eight times. Even more strikingly, 9930 tosses saw one side ahead in cumulative tosses. In other words, 99.3% of the time there were more tails, say, than heads tossed. Yet the odds are one in ten that a ten thousand toss sequence will be even more imbalanced than this. The results are stunning, even to most statisticians.[155]

The coin tossing model "may serve as a first approximation to many more complicated choice dependent processes in physics, economics and learning theory."[156] Arguably it fits the circumstances of law as a direct approximation. If we impute to law the quality of reducing choices to a simple either-or form, then we may regard the first instance in which normative significance is imputed to an act—either it is right or wrong—as a first coin toss. Every subsequent act reflecting the same structure of choice will be additional coin tosses. Suppose that no particular choice is affected by its predecessors, that is, each time the structure but not the content of the initial norm is recalled. Even then the cumulative effect of such choices, like tosses, will be to affirm one or the other of the choices. Notice that this affirmation has no causal meaning, since each choice, or toss, is a random, 50-50 event. Norms will appear to have long lives in which they are amply confirmed by cumulative affirmation but are still indispensable because there are frequent affirmations of the alternative choice, seen normatively as violative behavior. Eventually the accumulation of opposing choices may outweigh the earlier accumulation of affirmations—the lead changes—and a norm will appear to have fallen on hard times, only to be replaced by one also long lasting but of contrary content. Or it may be eclipsed for intervals but reappear before its absence comes to acquire much significance.

Not only does randomness appear to result in durable order, despite frequent acts contrary to established norms, but the order is defined precisely in terms of the solidity such norms have achieved over considerable periods of time. If the durability of norms

---

154. William Feller, *An Introduction to Probability Theory and Its Applications*, Vol. I (New York: John Wiley, 3rd. ed., 1968), Ch. 3. Feller appears to be the major figure in developing the implications of the coin tossing model.
155. Ibid., p. 88.
156. Ibid., p. 71.

yields a picture of a stable, gradually changing order, it is an order much stronger in perceptual than behavioral terms, inasmuch as fully half of all items of behavior will violate standing norms. The persistence of law despite gross violation appears to account for order. Curiously, behavior so massively inconsistent is seen by those engaging in it as rule-guided: "people have a rule for everything they do."[157] The subjective impression of scrupulous rule compliance, individual by individual, relieves the dissonance between random or rampantly unsocial behavior and stable order. It also explains the proliferation of new rules for constantly redefined situations of choice.[158] Stability and complexity come to be seen as interlocking attributes of an order that cannot be happenstance. It can.

Legal thought fails to acknowledge even the possibility that law serves to sanction random behavior—violative as often as not—while confirming order as a product of such randomness in sequence. Social thought at large does not know an unalloyed version of anarchism in which the complete absence of rule is no less orderly than orders men make for themselves. The principle of disorder in chaos is so thoroughgoing, at least to the Western mind, that the quest for order, not the results, dominates social thought. Even if this quest yields indifferent results, ones no different from randomly obtained results, the reality of order still promotes the perception that it could be achieved only through human endeavor, and the quest is justified. Law is a vehicle for order as a state of mind.

Legal thought has produced numerous explanations for what is taken to be a general relationship between law, however defined, and order as a real and preferred condition. Each such explanation assigns the existence of order to the presence of law, at least in part, and admits the possibility of explaining the persistence of law, and thus its sources, by reference to the prevalence of order.

Positivism has at its heart a simple first order explanation relating order causally to the presence of law, the absence of the latter resulting in the absence of the former.[159] $Y \rightarrow Z$; law yields order.[160] Sociological jurisprudence presents a special case of this simple explanation.[161] $Y,X \rightarrow Z$; law, other instruments of social control yield order.

A second order general form of explanation of the relation of law to order is conjunctive in character. Something conceived as subject to change and something else conceived as responsible for such change, that is, concepts taking the form of dependent and independent variables, are conjoined by an intervening variable which maps the

---

157.   Harris (fn. 152), p. 275. "Since we intuitively know that there is a rule for everything, we are easily mislead into believing that rules govern or cause behavior."

158.   Ambiguity in rules or situations to which they apply spawn "rules for breaking rules," ibid., also to be understood as rules for outfitting any fresh definition of a situation with its own rule.

159.   Recall from the first section of this chapter that positivism defines law as accompanied by sanctioning capacity, which makes order by enforcing law. Law is logically dispensable, however, because the sanction-bearer can make order merely by imposing his will. Law is then a rationale for willful behavior stated in the form of rules. On rules and rationales, see Onuf (fn. 26).

160. $Y \rightarrow Z$ is a common, convenient symbolic representation of a causal relationship. It is not to be confused with a mathematical expression taking the general form $Z = f(Y)$. The notational format used hereafter, and much of the following discussion, is influenced by Arthur L. Stinchcombe, *Constructing Social Theories* (New York: Harcourt, Brace and World, 1968). In principle the positivist rendition of the relation of law to order can be mathematically formulated because it expresses a causal relationship as variations in states of related things—in this case, law, no law; order, disorder—as a theory must. Because positivism is accepted as correct without the formalization, operationalization, and testing to which theories are normally subjected, it is preeminently doctrine, as defined in fn. 4.

161.   See also the first section of this chapter, under "Positivism."

relationship between the two.[162] In legal thought we find the example of historical jurisprudence.[163] Law maps the *Volkgeist* to yield order; $X \rightarrow Y \rightarrow Z$. Another second order form of explaining law's relation to order we might call complex. Functionalism in legal thought is an example.[164] Various forms of social control yield order revealed as law. Changes fed into the independent variable—instruments of social control—are needed to adjust for the effects of a disordering variable operating autonomously but revealed in its effects as a failure of law compliance;   Not only can law function to reveal the

$$X \rightarrow Z,Y$$
$$W$$

extent of order versus disorder and the need for adjustment in the means of social control, it may also be an instrument of control. In this case,

$$X,Y \rightarrow Z,Y$$
$$W$$

An interesting special case of the complex form of explanation is first order in the number of variables involved. Legal realism assumes a simple but sustained relationship between law as a device for distributing social values and order as a stable distribution of values favoring those who can take advantage of this device. Thus having order reinforces using law, which sustains order in a repeating fashion; $Y \leftrightarrows Z$. The repeating, or institutionalized, relationship uses power to protect and enhance values preferred by the powerful, including of course their power.[165] Explained in particular is the persistence of relationships despite changes in potential independent variables;

$$X \rightarrow Y \rightarrow Z \text{ or } Y \rightarrow Z$$
$$W$$

As a class these are institutional—historicist explanations, well-suited to the special, cordoned-off relationship of law and order.

Third order explanations are created merely by combining lower order forms. Combinatorial explanations exceed the explanatory ambitions of major schools in legal thought, but they are necessary if we are to find a place for sources integral to an established relationship between law and order. So we must devise explanation in general form, or theory, as needed. We begin by identifying a plausible independent variable, or provisional first cause. One good possibility would be (changes in) communications technology related to types of craft skills of lawyers, as a mapping variable, which become institutionalized in the form of characteristic sources of law, which in turn are vehicles for law and then, presumably, order. All such relationships would obviously be institutionalized in a large, interlocking system of persistent phenomena;

technology   skills   sources   law   order.

$V \rightarrow$ $W \rightarrow X \rightarrow$ $Y \rightarrow Z$

---

162.   Stinchcombe (fn. 160), p. 204. On law as "social mapping," see Kratochwil (fn. 153), pp. 45-48.

163.   See also fn. 46 above.

164.   On functionalist logic, see Stinchcombe (fn. 160), pp. 80-101; on functionalism in legal thought, see the fifth section of this chapter, under "Law-Making as Law-Doing."

165.   See as well the fifth section of this chapter, under "Law Making as Law-Doing," on legal realism. Stinchcombe defines institutionalization comparably. See generally ibid., pp. 101-127.

Historian Harold A. Innis (1894-1952) identified intriguing relationships between communications technologies, monopolies of knowledge, and instruments of social control, including law.[166] Pre-technological communications are embodied in the oral tradition, supremely expressed in classical Greece and especially suitable for organizing time. It is the ideal vehicle for custom, its Solonic tendencies (Grotius said . . .) a kind of heroic imagery well matched to the personalist social orders typified by the state-sovereigns of the early Western state system. The Romantic, nineteenth century discovery of folk and epic literature undoubtedly helped to save custom's place during the golden age of positivism, which emphasized consent over custom and ascendancy of the state as a territorial abstraction over the sovereign as a particular person.

Positivist preoccupation with consent and thus with treaties suggests the next stage in the evolution of communications technology, suited to the organization of space and expressed in the writing tradition of Rome. Early Western state sovereigns struck their agreements orally, but writing quickly came to prevail. Treaty compilations in the hands of centralizing state bureaucracies parallel the emergence of parchment codex as an instrument of control by imperial Roman bureaucracy.

It may be argued that the putative relationship between technology and legal craft fails to hold in the instance of the Western state system because printing had been invented in the system's early days to supersede earlier communication technologies for purposes of social control. If, however, we regard the international legal order as pre-modern but post-Renaissance—that is, not transformed in its political and cultural premises by scientific and industrial revolutions (even though its principal members were) but nevertheless decisively affected by the rediscovery of Greco-Roman social, political, and administrative practices—then it is possible to view modern technologies like printing, not as supplanting traditional sources originating in pre-modern technologies, but as facilitating their retention. They become nostalgic sources of law for an order that has remained stubbornly decentralized and traditionally organized through diplomatic collegiality.

Jurists and scholars as sources supporting custom fit nicely into the oral tradition because they retain oral roles in their particular legal crafts. Yet they find print a convenient medium to guarantee wide dissemination of such oral activities as giving judgment or instruction. Concluding treaties is also an oral activity which links legal craft with the diplomat's negotiating duties. More important to treating, at least from the point of view of law, is the demanding task of drafting texts to withstand the most intense scrutiny. Similarly, legal advisers occasionally provide their services orally but more characteristically through memoranda anticipating challenges to governmental decisions. Codification even more clearly may involve discussions among codifiers whose efforts nevertheless center on the precise wording of law made durable and accessible by being written down. Artifactual law derives from the oral tradition and, just as evidently, standard operating procedures depend on the written tradition.

As a failed source, general principles of law recognized by civilized nations represent an abortive effort to anchor international law in a printing tradition. Innis pointed out the relation of popular principles like self-determination to the ascendancy of printing.[167] That such principles are today often proclaimed as peremptory strongly suggests the

---

166.   Harold A. Innis, *The Bias of Communication* (Toronto: University of Toronto Press, 1951); *Empire and Communications*, Revised by Mary Q. Innis (Toronto: University of Toronto Press, 1972).

167.   *The Bias of Communication*, pp. 81-82.

power of printing to create the illusion that its products simultaneously organize time and space and in so doing, supersede lesser sources of social control. The price paid for this illusion is the absence of content for international law made in the printing tradition. This conclusion is further supported by the realization that in domestic orders the rise of printing has gone hand in hand with the ascendancy of law-making by legislation.

Legislation as a process uses talking and writing in an effort to organize time and space simultaneously, but legislation as a product is overwhelmingly dependent on printing to give form to legislative intent. The formalizing quality of the printed word detaches what is said from those who say it, thereby creating the appearance that what is said is objective and disinterested. Printed law, like general principles, seems to be peremptory and prompts a regard verging on reverence. Yet, unlike general principles, printing enables an extraordinary degree of specificity in the content of the law. While principles appear disembodied, printing allows law to differentiate categories and proliferate injunctions, combining individuation and abstraction. Impersonal in form and immensely personal in effect, printed law is doubly intimidating. Legislation may be the vehicle for popular expression, as print is generally, but it also creates an opportunity for the extension and centralization of technologies of social control.

Inasmuch as global legislation with its centralizing tendencies cannot be reconciled with a pervasively decentralized international legal order, it may seem entirely fanciful to discuss the communication technology to succeed printing. This of course is electronically assisted communication, which tends to dissolve time and space instead of organizing it.[168] Visions of an electromagnetically mediated global village notwithstanding, the pertinent feature of this new technology for global law-making is undoubtedly the storage and retrieval capacity of high speed computers. Bureaucracy and the writing tradition will be vastly augmented by the dispersion of these capabilities. Arguably printing has saved a place for law as lawyers' artifacts despite the dramatic growth of lawyer-sanctioned standard operating procedures. Electronic technology operates to different effect. Interlocking bureaucracies with an exponentially growing need to institutionalize their response to social complexity could even transform the international legal order from its recalcitrantly pre-modern current condition to one which is truly post-modern.

The explanation for persistence developed here puts legal order at the end of a long causal chain which is reinforced by repeating feedback loops. At the beginning of the chain, printing happened to support the institutionalization of Renaissance traditions in the global order. A technological revolution undercutting that support, however, may actually make it easier for a change to work its way through the causal chain. In other words, the emergence of electronic communication technology, by dissolving instead of organizing time and space, would not be so likely to support an existing order. But by no means can we be sure that the new technology will introduce change into the causal chain radical enough to overcome its dampening mechanisms.

*   *   *   *   *   *

To place legal order at the end of a long causal chain invites the view that legal order is a product, and conceivably even an externality, or unsought consequence, of

---

168.   This Innis failed to anticipate, as Marshall McLuhan points out in his Introduction to ibid., pp. xii-xiii. McLuhan is of course celebrated for spelling out time and space implications of electronic media.

social activities like communication rooted in an autonomous material order. So understood, legal order is little more than a tautology, law by its nature being orderly. The material order, on the other hand, arises from complex physical, demographic, and technological occurrences. Its major contours lend themselves most readily to socioeconomic description and encapsulation, much as we saw with Weber. But an unqualifiedly materialist orientation goes further to make all government, law, and social ideas superstructure: products therefore of socioeconomic formations fixed by material conditions unfolding from the previous epoch.[169]

The material order of capitalism correlates with republican and pluralist political institutions. It is preceded by feudalism, an order marked by rank and reward bestowing relations and descended from the ancient city-slave based societies with patrician assemblies, in turn descended from communal bands of hunters, gatherers, and barterers.[170] Also descending from primitive bands are Asiatic or hydraulic societies ruled by despotic bureaucracies.[171]

Each socioeconomic formation embodies a distinctive mode of material production and engenders an equally distinctive mode of superstructural production or source of legal and political practices. Custom is a characteristic source of the legal and political practices of primitive communalism. Imperial decrees are the source of order in Asiatic, despotic systems, while decrees emerging from patrician consensus are source for ancient systems. Special law, reciprocal in obligation but asymmetric in content, is source of feudal ranking. Legislation, which creates a plurality of general and restricted legal regimes, such as for contractual relations, dominates the capitalist era.

If we assume these correlations operate internationally as well as domestically, we must infer from the persistence of customary and conventional law-making categories that the international order is in some proportion primitive and feudal at the same time. Great power management techniques codified in Chapter VII of the United Nations Charter are reminiscent of the ancient mode, as despotic tendencies of the superpowers

---

169. Legal order does relate to the underlying material order through a long feedback loop, not to mention through lesser time-lagging loops along the chain.

material order   technology   legal craft   sources   law   legal order

$$U \xrightarrow{\quad} V \rightarrow W \rightarrow X \rightarrow Y \rightarrow Z$$

Obviously we move away from explanation in general form and toward explication of the unique. Theory gains in precision but loses in power.

170. This is Marx's familiar typology. See Karl Marx, *Pre-Capitalist Economic Formations*, Edited and with an Introduction by Eric J. Hobsbawm (New York: International Publishers. 1965). Of some interest also is Frederick Engels. *The Origin of the Family, Private Property and the State*, Edited, with an Introduction by Eleanor Burke Leacock (New York: International Publishers, 1972). Contemporary anthropology is hardly content with these coarse divisions, which are perhaps least adequate in capturing the variety of cultures which are more than simply communal and less than formally coercively organized for governance. They include tribes, chiefdoms, big men cultures, rank societies, and prestates. Marx himself noted a Germanic, tribal variation of communalism, and Hobsbawm observes that "it is possible that Marx and Engels also had in mind some sort of intermediate historical phase of communal disintegration, out of which ruling classes of different types might emerge." (p. 53) Undoubtedly mixed, transitional types are an important empirical reality, if not a conceptual complication.

171. Marx slighted the Asiatic mode of production and Engels was worse. (Harris, fn. 152, pp. 162-163; Leacock's Introduction to Engels. pp. 49-50) Shlomo Avineri admirably synthesizes what Marx did have to say in "Karl Marx on Colonialism and Modernization," in M. C. Howard and J. E. King, eds., *The Economics of Marx* (New York: Penguin Books, 1976), pp. 235-257. Karl Wittfogel's *Oriental Despotism* (New Haven: Yale University Press, 1957) filled the void with a vengeance. Hydraulic society is his coinage.

within spheres of influence are of the Asiatic mode. The international order appears to be an unparalleled mix of pre-capitalist socioeconomic formations.

There are two serious objections to this position. The first is that Marx, who furnished these categories initially, saw them as sequenced through a dialectical process, beginning with the primitive mode, advancing historically through capitalism, and thence to socialism and communism. Only the Asiatic mode appears to be set apart from this lock-step progression. Eric J. Hobsbawm argues that a close examination of Marxian texts undercuts the rigid determinism associated with this view.[172] Furthermore, a materialist need not be saddled with dialectical determinism at all, in which case it is admissible to say that whenever material conditions warrant, mandated socioeconomic formations emerge. A devolution from capitalism to feudalism is an altogether feasible consequence of overreaching limits to growth.[173]

The second objection to viewing international law's sources as correlates of pre-capitalist socioeconomic formations bears more directly on our consideration of why sources persist. If the international order's major members have become capitalist or possibly, in some instances, socialist, then one might ask why the order among them does not share superstructural attributes of capitalism. The answer lies in the fact that pre-capitalist international arrangements, of which sources doctrine is a small, fictive part, serve the modern state as well as or better than they did those same entities before capitalism transformed them. In other words, capitalism's very success within states was expedited by the retention of pre-capitalist relations between them.[174] The international order buffers states developing along divergent trajectories, and inhibits the catastrophic collisions Lenin forecast from uneven development.[175] At the same time pre-capitalist global superstructure enables societies ahead in development to exploit the human and physical resources of parts of the world that are behind. This system of "feudo-imperial" relations, or dependency, materially supports capitalist societies governed internally by more modern instruments of social control and distribution.[176] Thus we have a material-ist explanation for the persistence of superstructural phenomena in a world repeatedly convulsed by socioeconomic changes.

If the international order were to transform materially, or modernize, as some argue it is now doing, obstacles to the emergence of legislation as master source would soon disappear.[177] Superstructural adaptation might fulfill liberal-legalist dreams of a global

172. In his Introduction to Marx (fn. 170), pp. 36-38.

173. See Onuf and Ajami (fn. 9); N. G. Onuf with Kathryn Wittneben, "Reports to the Club of Rome," mimeo., American University, 1981.

174. "Capitalism has been able to flourish precisely because the world economy has had within its bounds not one but a multiplicity of political systems. . . . This gives capitalism a freedom of maneuver that is structurally based. It has made possible the constant economic expansion of the world-system, albeit a very skewed distribution of its rewards." Wallerstein (fn. 6) p. 230.

175. V. I. Lenin, Imperialism The Highest Stage of Capitalism (New York: International Publishers, 1939). See also Walter G. Seabold and N. G. Onuf, "Late Capitalism, Uneven Development and Foreign Policy Postures," forthcoming in The Political Economy of Foreign Policy, Sage International Yearbook of Foreign Policy Studies, Vol. 6 (1981), pp. 23-37.

176. Ali A. Mazrui uses the phrase feudo-imperial interdependence in "The New Interdependence," in Guy F. Erb and Valeriana Kallab, eds., Beyond Dependency (Washington: Overseas Development Council, 1975), p. 39. For impeccable scholarship see the special issue of International Organization devoted to "Dependence and Dependency in the Global System," Vol. 32, No. 1 (Winter 1978).

177. See Edward L. Morse, Modernization and the Transformation of International Relations (New York: The Free Press, 1976); Nicholas Greenwood Onuf, "Comparative International Politics," forthcoming in Year Book of World Affairs, Vol. 35 (1981).

order in which large scale violence and injustice were legislated away, though for reasons unrelated to those dreams. There is a more sinister interpretation of global legislation as master source, however. Alienating or fetishistic properties of the material order of capitalism may be seen as extending to superstructural phenomena.[178] Legislation is particularly vulnerable in this respect because of qualities printing imparts to it. Law made legislatively would thus resemble commodities as Marx saw them: their existence has "absolutely no connection with their physical properties and with the material relations arising therefrom. There it is a definite social relation among men, that assumes in their eyes, the fantastic form of a relation between things."[179]

Law and Community: Metaphors, Myths

Is legislation an event staged to impress or instruct some public, but still just an event, or is it a thing, or fixed relation of things, however fantastic? The same question extends to law (laws in aggregate) generally. Perhaps just to speak about rules of law is, as Hardy Dillard argues, "unwittingly to endow them with a kind of reality or existence, even a metaphysical existence, which is illusory. Rules of law do not 'exist' in the sense in which a tree or a stone or the planet Mars may be said to exist. True, they may be articulated and put on paper and in that form they exist, but . . . are merely signs mediating human subjectivities."[180] Are they not therefore events of a certain kind: events of the mind, or mental things, as real in the mind as any material thing is, since all things, physical and metaphysical, are mentally and thus socially mediated?[181] But even if laws, like the responses they elicit, are merely events, they are events detained in defiance of time, reduced to objective form, related to other things, collected and reproduced when needed. Everything about them exists.

The materialist would find the questions in this debate inconsequential if not unintelligible. They are debatable only in idealist intellectual traditions, to which we now turn.

We saw that law could be treated as a random sequence of events leading unexpectedly to order. We saw it as a decorative thing. It could be, and probably is, an ordered sequence of events, and just as well it could be a labile ensemble of useful and durable things, called laws, upon which order is imposed. Further abstraction does not lead to greater understanding. Metaphors may.

Events exist only as they take place. That they happen in a particular order gives a distinctive meaning to them not discernible from the events individually. Without means of preserving the sequence of events, that meaning is lost. Law is therefore very much like music, to borrow a provocative metaphor from C. A. W. Manning (1894-1978).[182]

Music can be found, as in the music of a bird's song, or made, as music usually is, by a variety of methods. It exists only at the moment of its performance, and it will be lost if it is not remembered or recorded. It can be performed again, but then it is a different if very similar event. If it is remembered faithfully it may indeed be performed

---

178. Alienation and fetishism in the production of commodities (goods produced for exchange in the capitalist mode) is one of Marx's larger themes. See Karl Marx, excerpts 7-11, in Howard and King (fn.171).

179. Ibid., p. 99. The translation is clumsy but the meaning clear.

180. Hardy Cross Dillard, "The Policy-Oriented Approach to Law," *Virginia Quarterly Review*, Vol. 40, No. 4 (Autumn 1964), p. 629, quoted by McDougal, Lasswell and Reisman (fn. 12), p. 251.

181. See further Berger and Luckmann (fn. 153).

182. C. A. W. Manning, *The Nature of International Society* (New York: John Wiley and Sons, 1962), pp. 108-109.

over and over in a form which is little changed and which begins to stand in for the music itself. This too is the nature of law. Notice that what music does is the least important question. We may presume that it pleases someone, although who we need not know. It may please no one, but distract, inspire, infuriate, or intimidate someone. The list of things music may do is obviously open-ended and can never define the nature of the musical event. More interesting than the functions of music are all the activities that allow music to happen, and happen over and over again. These collectively take the form of what in these pages we call an order.

There is something important to be learned from treating law as an event. What law is need not be approached from the point of view of what it does. In fact we might better approach it by considering what makes it happen and what makes it memorable. Even if law is a thing, we may ask as we did with music whether it is found or made, how it is conserved, and, in this large context, what its uses may be and what effects follow.

To illustrate, in legal orders dominated by legislation, codes, or regulations, it is fair to think of law as made—the product of conscious activity. But in the international order, law tends not to be made in this sense.[183] Rather it is made use of and, to the extent anyone is aware of its independent existence, it is found. So conceived, law less resembles music, which is usually a man-made event, than it does water, which is a naturally occurring thing available for human use. Water is not found in uniform abundance, however. In some environments it is scarce or irregular in supply and must be managed and conserved. The need for it is basic, but the amount needed varies greatly with the physical economy of any given community.[184]

Unless water is available, no activity relevant to physical economy is possible. In the absence of law we cannot imagine activity relevant to what we might call the political or social economy of a given community. Whatever law does, nothing else is done unless there is law to make it possible. Like water, law is preliminary to all other activity and the question of its availability primary. As with water, the answer to this question varies with the circumstances a community finds itself in and with its inventiveness. In other words, different circumstances and different minds at work yield different solutions to the kind of problem posed by the need both for water and law.

One of the most striking properties of water is its formless state, at least when normally put to human use. Water takes the shape of its container, as does law. The latter's form is nothing other than the way it is made available. Water is found in nature and conserved by man in several forms—streams, springs, and lakes are natural forms, while wells, channels, and reservoirs are man-made. Law also takes several forms, revealingly called sources, which roughly parallel the forms water takes or is given. Customary law takes a form analogous to streams, which after all result from the accumulation and flow of water made available in the generalized form of rain. Judges' decisions (precedents) resemble springs and contribute to customary streams of law. General principles of law recognized by civilized nations would seem to resemble lakes,

183. On the international codification movement as an attempt to modernize international law by making it the product of conscious activity, see Nicholas Greenwood Onuf, "The Conscious Development of International Law," doctoral dissertation, Johns Hopkins University, 1967.

184. Use of the word *community* is deliberate, for the primacy of water is clearest in the small and simple entities that go by that name. All orders require water, but large, complex ones (societies) require so much else for survival that the need to insure water supply may not be related to social organization. Temperate zone societies, for example, take water for granted until they become urbanized. The organization of some tropical societies seems to be closely related to the need to manage the supply of water for intensive agricultural purposes, and these may be grouped with community for our purposes. For a major, controversial treatment of the relation of water management to political economy, see Wittfogel (fn. 171).

into and from which streams and spring water flow. Wells are analogous to treaties or particular law. They take some small part of the rain and ground water generally available and put it in a form suitable for particular needs. Channels are streams purposely formed or re-routed to do even better what streams do. Thus they resemble the results of publicists and scholars to discern and enhance customary law. Reservoirs finally are bodies of water put in that form in anticipation of heavy future use, just as legislation is law stored in quantity and drawn on as needed. It would seem then that legislation is better understood not as making law but as making law available for larger and more complex needs than law occurring in other forms permits.

Stretching the metaphor of law as water to include the several forms that water and law take risks an incredulous reaction. We accept this risk persuaded that the metaphor in extended form is central, though subliminal, for the community of individuals who are responsible for the availability, retrieval, and use of international law. The extended metaphor also bears on the fact that these individuals congregate in clans, which are an entirely characteristic form of organization in small communities. Anthropologists frequently use the term *clan* in connection with tribes of related individuals so that clan membership is determined by kinship criteria. In the instance of the international legal community, all members are related in a professional sense and distinguish among themselves by a reference to professional roles. Thus the community's clans more specifically resemble guilds. We may view guilds as a type of clan, displaying attributes found in communities generally as well as some unique to the apparently sophisticated activities of an occupational community. In other words, the term *clan* is the generic one, referring to a generalized tendency in community life, wherever found, to organize horizontally into small durable clusters of individuals grouped according to the specific nature of their professional activity—legal advisers, judges, publicists, treaty-makers, and arbitrators.[185]

A distinctive feature of clan organization is totemism. Hardly self-evident in the instance of the international legal community, this assertion has an intuitive appeal at the level of metaphor. Totems are natural objects or events, frequently animal or vegetable species, used to name and identify clans. The choice of totems is sometimes explained in myths about clan origins and accompanied by taboos, rituals, and other trappings of religious experience.[186] The purest or most fully developed totemistic communities were found in Australia, although important elements of totemism occurred throughout North America and Africa, that is, wherever primitive culture persisted into the era of systematic gathering of culturally relevant evidence.

We find naturalistic emblems, often accompanied by supporting myths and rituals, setting apart groups in any culture. They are strikingly present in the designations we apply to personal styles, complicated circumstances, or ideological postures far removed from nature: fox and hedgehog, hare and tortoise, bull and bear, sheep and wolf, hawk and dove. When naturalistic emblems are not overtly used, they lurk in the immediate background of our consciousness. If this is the case with international law and its sources, then the several sources may be less analytically discerned categories of law coming into

---

185. Clan membership is generally a lifelong and exclusive affiliation. Professional roles are not mutually exclusive in the same categorical fashion. There is a tendency, however, to treat them as mutually exclusive at any given point in time. Thus World Court Judges and members of the International Law Commission are uninstructed in principle and cannot be understood as functioning as legal advisors or treaty-makers.

186. Emile Durkheim, *The Elementary Forms of Religious Life* (London: George Allen and Unwin, 1915), Book II.

being or use than clan names barely abstracted from the naturalist context of the several sources of water a community can make use of.

To repeat, the several clans of the international legal community would seem to be named for objects, called sources, which are only slightly removed from nature. We may reasonably suppose that each clan is named for the source which its professional activity seems to be most concerned with. By this reckoning, legal advisers would belong to the custom clan, which could just as well be named "stream clan." Treaty-makers obviously belong to the treaty clan, judges to the judicial-decisions clan and scholars to the publicists clan. Less obvious is the membership of the general principles clan. If we recall that general principles were authenticated as a source in 1919, after a half-century burst of international arbitration, then we can easily see that a relatively new clan of arbitrators had emerged, to be rewarded in due course with their own totem, general principles of law recognized by civilized nations.[187]

The alignment of distinct occupational groups with sources of international law does not mean that these groups are meaningfully engaged in separate kinds of law-making or, better, law-finding activity. Their professional activity may relate to the emergence of new law, but the thrust of that activity is, after all, simply daily lawyering. Law-making in the form of framing artifacts and devising standardized procedures has much to do with lawyering but little indeed to do with the five sources of law, so-called. But we should not conclude that the sources typology is merely a fiction or series of historical accidents. It is a categorization of something else entirely, the five major clans of the international legal community. Their survival, achieved through continual adaptation of their craft to social need, accounts for both their individual persistence and the doctrinal fixity of their collective description as sources.

The literature on totemism presents a basic theoretical problem which takes the proverbial chicken-and egg form. Did the emergence of clans precede the attachment of unique labels to each, labels which are therefore uniquely relevant to the experience and activities of each clan? Or do the totems come first, as they might if they are understood as a system of thought, a way of conceptualizing reality which provides the framework for the subsequent social experience of organizing into clans?

The first of these positions is a functionalist view. Its baldest expression is Bronislaw Malinowski's.[188] The second is a structuralist view made famous by Claude Levi-Strauss.[189] The functionalist view, by emphasizing the utility of the totem in the clan's experience, explains the progression from natural object to ritual focus. The structuralist view, by contrast, emphasizes the arrangement of totems rather than their individual content and use. Of interest is the intellectual character of such arrangements, more evident in their pristine form than when they are buried in layers of subsequent social invention. Both views commend themselves to our attention, once we posit the

---

187.   There is no clear a priori basis for assigning World Court judges to either the general principles or the judicial decisions clan. The World Court is a mature phase of the arbitration movement and is organized in the fashion of a high domestic court. The judges themselves show a proclivity to engage in the formulation of general principles borrowed from municipal orders even to the extent of ignoring relevant international custom. Consequently they seem to regard themselves as members of the general principles (arbitrator's) clan. See Richard B. Lillich, "The Rigidity of Barcelona," *American Journal of International Law*, Vol. 65, No. 3 (July 1971), pp. 522-532, for illustration.

188.   Bronislaw Malinowski, *Magic, Science and Religion and Other Essays* (Boston: Beacon Press, 1948), pp. 26-29.

189.   Claude Levi-Strauss, *Totemism* (Boston: Beacon Press, 1963); *The Savage Mind* (Chicago: University of Chicago Press, 1966). Ch. 2-4. Ch. 3 of the former is a critique of functionalist theories of totemism.

international legal community as both a congeries of clans and a group with a specified social function to perform. Since clans in the international legal community are not consciously identified as such by their members, identification and naming of such clans is actually an exercise in functionalist logic rather than the unmediated result of ethnographic fieldwork. To this one observer, at least, the sources of international law appear to be the specific totems they are because of the community's functionally specific character as water tribe in the global community. This argument departs from Levi-Strauss, but in a manner which avoids his devasting critique of Malinowski's generally applied view.

The functionalist position explains the assignment of only a few clan names in functionally undifferentiated communities. Levi-Strauss shows, however, that totems are never arbitrary in arrangement, no matter how obscured the logic. The evident functional relation of clans to sources (totems) in the international legal community, by appearing to explain clan origins, in fact obscures the underlying logic of their arrangement. Just because the functional relations of a complex society are present is no reason to deny the workings of the "savage mind," as Levi-Strauss would have it.

One of the characteristics of the savage mind, according to Levi-Strauss, is an extraordinary concern for orderly arrangements of all kinds.[190] Geometric garden plots, elaborate classifications of natural objects and events, and highly self-conscious kinship systems are manifestations of this urge to order. The legal mind is characteristically savage in its attempt to order its existential situation. The revealing exception is in reference to its own status, which the legal mind sees somewhat indistinctly in functionalist terms.[191] Furthermore, the daily activity of the lawyer, whatever his clan name implies to him, is *bricolage*.[192] Levi-Strauss defines this as the activity of making things from the bits and pieces of things originally made for some other purpose but now lying around at the bricoleur's disposal.

The bricoleur's bits and pieces could just as well be social as physical. In either case they are already available for use. Bricolage yields law only in the sense that the bricoleur produces an indefinite number of unique things which he then proceeds to put in a predefined place and thereby classes as no longer unique. Something is being made, namely law, but at the same time it is being made from something that already exists, including law and anything else that seems relevant. Its making is not really complete until it has been placed for future use. It may not even be law until it is actually used. Law is like cloth in this respect. The tailor uses cloth, along with his tools and skills, to make, repair, or alter clothes (laws) which someone else will use only after they have been put in a desired form.[193] Given the prominence of such expressions as the fabric of

---

190.   Levi-Strauss, *The Savage Mind*, Ch. 1.

191.   Thus Llewellyn's attempt to categorize "law-jobs" is still widely cited. K. N. Llewellyn, "The Normative, the Legal. and the Law-Jobs: The Problem of Juristic Method," *Yale Law Journal*. Vol. 49, No. 8 (June. 1940), pp. 1355-1400.

192.   Levi-Strauss, *The Savage Mind* (fn. 189), pp. 16-36. On bricolage in lawyerly activity, see Gerald Garvey, *Constitutional Bricolage* (Princeton: Princeton University Press. 1971).

193.   Bricolage supposes that things used were originally made for some other use and then discarded. The tailor as bricoleur neither makes the cloth he uses nor even buys whole cloth. Instead he pirates pieces of cloth from old garments. Obviously the tailor can use things made for the purpose at hand, as can the lawyer, but then he is no longer a bricoleur. Almost certainly, the lawyer spends more of his time in bricolage than the tailor does. Garvey seems to suggest that bricolage, as "the art of judges," involves a preference for "received forms" even when new materials are available for use. In this interpretation it is the primacy of form over substance and the celebration of procedure which makes bricoleurs of both lawyers and tailors. Ibid., pp. 5-6, 14-18.

society, the cloth metaphor may be an interesting alternative to the law as water metaphor. Its use here is merely to illustrate the peculiar indeterminancy of the notion of law-making in the bricoleur's world.

Levi-Strauss identifies a third tendency of the savage mind. It is the one most directly relevant to totemism. He calls it the "union of opposites" or making "opposition, instead of being an obstacle to integration, serve rather to produce it."[194] The arrangement of totems reduces to a series of binary oppositions, as do supporting myths. These binary opposites are the heart of systems of classification which order the natural world and human activity (the first such pair of opposites). While it is tendentious to argue that all intellectual activity takes the form of posing oppositions, it is not necessary for our purposes either. We need only note that binary opposites seem to be a principal structural property in the domain of law.

Consider first characteristic pairings provided by legal language: fact and norm, compliance and violation, delict and sanction, right and duty, plaintiff and defendant. Consider the intrinsically adversarial nature of lawyer's activity. At the global level consider the two jobs, pulling in opposition, the New Haven School sees befalling the policy-maker. Again following the New Haven School, consider the fact that legal rules "are commonly formulated in pairs of complementary opposites and are composed of a relatively few basic terms of highly variable reference."[195] Levi-Strauss could just as well have written these words as Myres S. McDougal and Florentino P. Feliciano, who did. They go on to say that:

> the complementarity in form and comprehensiveness of reference of such rules are indispensable to the rational search for and application of policy to a world of acts and events which presents itself to the decision-maker, not in terms of neat symmetrical dichotomies and trichotomies, but in terms of innumerable gradations and alterations from one end of the continuum to the other; the spectrum makes available to the decision-maker not one inevitable doom but multiple alternative choices. The realistic function of those rules, considered as a whole, is, accordingly, not mechanically to dictate specific decision-makers to significant variable factors in typical recurring contexts of decision, to serve as summary indices to relevant crystallized community expectations, and, hence, to permit creative and adaptive, instead of arbitrary and irrational, decisions.

This is precisely a description of bricolage. It identifies a methodology which the social bricoleur can, and perhaps must, employ because he is concerned with the products of the mind, that is, intellectual activity. He fashions new, usable things from bits and pieces of existing intellectually created things specifically by pairing those things into complementary opposites to achieve their orderly representation, which is what makes them useful. The law-maker unites two characteristic forms of intellectual activity — bricolage and the pairing of opposites. A major and frequently intended result is the classification of laws into systems of law, thus reflecting the remaining tendency of the legal mind.

Members of the international legal community commonly exempt themselves from classification. Yet we venture to suggest that, in addition to being functional labels, the

---

194. Levi-Strauss, *The Savage Mind*, (fn. 189), pp. 88-89.
195. Myres S. McDougal and Florentine P. Feliciano, *Law and Minimum World Public Order* (New Haven: Yale University Press, 1961), p. 57, footnote deleted. See further Myres S. McDougal, "The Ethics of Applying Systems of Authority: The Balanced Opposites of a Legal System," in Harold D. Lasswell and Harlan Cleveland, eds., *The Ethic of Power* (New York: Harper and Bros., 1962), pp. 221-240.

sources (totems) of international law are arranged by binary opposition into a classificatory scheme. While the actual sources seem to be the object of classification, the objects standing in for the sources are what we find paired off. We find the following arrangement in *form* once sources are transformed into natural objects. The arrangement thus depends on sources having a form which can be discerned only when they have all been restated in terms consistent with the functional metaphor of law as water.

Three pairs stand out on inspection: streams and channels, springs and wells, and lakes and reservoirs. Each pair embodies an obvious structural correspondence. They can also be arranged as pairs by virtue of an evident principle of opposition, namely, whether these sources are found in natural form or provided through human activity and ingenuity.

FOUND	MADE
Streams	Channels
Springs	Wells
Lakes	Reservoirs

Notice that this arrangement fails to produce obvious functional connections. What legal advisers (stream clan) do is no better related to what judges (spring clan) do than to what writers (channel clan) do. Nor does the activity of legal advisers stand in clearer opposition to that of treaty-makers than that of arbitrators, for example.

Inasmuch as the international legal community is functionally differentiated, is it possible to devise an arrangement that makes functional as well as formal sense? If we use running versus still water as the oppositional principle, we point to an important attribute in form and the arrangement does happen to make functional sense.

RUNNING	STILL
Streams	Lakes
(Legal advisers)	(Arbitrators)
Springs	Wells
(Judges)	(Treaty-makers)
Channels	Reservoirs
(Writers)	(Legislators)

To the legal mind, custom, judicial opinion, and the work of writers go together. Treaties, general principles, and legislation go together only by default. Since general principles are a recent designation and international legislation exists only nominally, the historic opposition of custom and treaty is honored. If functional relations are only partly captured by this arrangement, its real problem lies with the indeterminacy of specific pairings. Why pair streams with lakes instead of wells, or reservoirs, for that matter? The solution to this problem is to use two ordering principles simultaneously. The two already suggested cannot be so used, because they result in irreconcilable oppositions.

We need therefore a third principle, but one which is not of opposition but correlation. This principle is most easily expressed abstractly in terms of generality and particularity. Law finding its source in custom and general principles is general in application. Law from judicial decisions and treaties is particular in nature but, through the agency of writers or legislation, subject to generalizing tendencies. Legislation is after all as general or particular as legislators wish it to be. This principle of correlation in effect categorizes the range of outcomes associated with clan activity.

	RUNNING	STILL
GENERAL	Streams (Custom)	Lakes (General Principles)
GENERALIZING	Channels (Texts and codes)	Reservoirs (Legislation)
PARTICULAR	Springs (Judicial decisions)	Wells (Treaties)

To use the language of anthropology, two moieties, running water and still water, are created through an oppositional principle, naturally expressed, which is insufficient to pair specific clans. An additional principle, which formalizes functional consequences, yields the necessary pairings, but it cannot be transformed into a natural opposition, because it is not, after all, a formal opposition to start with.[196] The arrangement of clans apparently reflects the mixed character of the international legal community as a congeries of clans and a functionally defined group. As such its structure can be understood as an arrangement partly of forms only somewhat abstracted from natural objects and of forms which are abstracted from natural objects and of forms which are abstracted from the consequences of clan functioning and therefore not subject to naturalistic identification.

The discovery of an underlying arrangement to the sources of international law, here meaning the totems of functionally specific clans in the international legal community, suggests that the existence of six sources is mandated by the arrangement itself. Before the definitive articulation of general principles as a source, the imbalance might seem to have been severe. Custom, judicial decisions, and the work of publicists were in opposition to treaties. Yet, as we have already observed, treating judicial decisions and authoritative texts as subsidiary sources has the effect of collapsing three into one, which stands in opposition to treaties on three grounds—running versus still, natural versus man-made, and general versus particular. The reader who thinks the first, naturalistic opposition is a quixotic invention should recall innumerable statements on the subject of international codification referring to the effect of treaties on custom. The recurring phrase was that embodiment in treaty form would have the effect of "freezing" custom.

The difficulty with a simple, unsegmented oppositional structure is its crudity. Arguably the international legal community was enough smaller in past centuries that further functional differentiation was unnecessary. The authentication of international arbitrators as a clan with general principles as their totem, together with the clear designation of five clan names altogether in the Statute of the Permanent Court of International Justice (albeit two explicitly treated as subsidiary) throws the arrangement out of balance. This could help to explain the striking preoccupation of the international legal community with legislation. In the absence of any real possibility of legislative competence attaching to a global institution, the attempt to construe multilateral law-making conventions as international legislation is entirely understandable.[197] So is the more recent effort to construe the General Assembly as quasi-legislative. To the extent there has emerged a functionally distinct group in the international legal

---

196.   Observe that the rejected oppositional principle, made versus found, exists in specific pairs, although it is not to be found in their arrangement.

197.   See the second section of this chapter, under "Traditional Sources." In naturalistic terms the difference between wells and reservoirs is largely a matter of degree.

community whose members see themselves as different by virtue of their law-relevant activities in major plenary forums, the clan exists, although its name is less an accurate functional description than an appealing totem.

As a clan emerges to fill the vacant niche, we perhaps will see a decline in the rhetoric devoted to global legislation. The persistence of such rhetoric, like legislation itself, takes on the proportions of a *fetish*. While anthropologists have largely abandoned this ill-defined and possibly overworked term, it lives on in popular language. A fetish is an object held in awe or reverence, irrationally so to the modern mind, and frequently subject to special rites. More particularly the fetish is not part of a system of identification or classification, as totems are.[198] Legislation at the global level is an objective which, because it is unrealizable, is turned into a revered object instead.

The international legal community's fetishistic inclinations toward legislation have had the interesting effect of supporting its belief that it is better to make law than to find it. In modern orders, apparently dominated by centralized law-making procedures, the law as water metaphor breaks down. Waterworks require administrative rather than legislative competence, as we know from the experience of historic hydraulic societies. In making a fetish of legislation, the international legal community is attempting to foster the impression it is no longer or not simply a savage community. It wishes to be seen instead as an integral, indeed overarching, part of the global liberal order born of Western civilization.

The fetish made of legislation is merely the most extreme example of an important and widespread opposition in the activities of most cultures. As does the savage mind, we oppose the sacred and the profane in our own "advanced" culture.[199] Activities like multilateral convention-making, drafting General Assembly declarations, and divining general principles all display rhetorical tendencies which approach the sacred. Concluding bilateral treaties, availing of administrative procedures, and writing regulations and codes are all the profane, daily professional duties of the lawyers in the community.

If the profane activities of the international legal community are inaccessible, it is not by intent but by virtue of their exceedingly technical nature. Sacred activities by contrast are made inaccessible so that they seem to be the result of some mysterious process akin to legislation, the products of which are held up by the few charged with sacred duties for the admiration of all. Sacred objects are thus made as accessible as possible with their mundane origins shrouded in rituals invoking the idea of legislation. In the language of this essay, artifacts are sacred while standardized procedures are profane; making artifacts is a sacred duty and using law in daily problem-solving is the profane activity which ends up making law of the latter kind.

To go one step further, turning the idea of legislation into a fetish and organizing sacred activity around it suggests an important place in the international legal community for what can only be called a myth of modernity.[200] This myth has other elements.

---

198. Durkheim (fn. 179), pp. 172-180.

199. Ibid., pp. 36-42 and throughout; Robert A. Nisbet, *The Sociological Tradition* (New York: Basic Books, 1966). Ch. 6.

200. Quite commonly those wishing to modernize presume that politicization of the process will speed it up. This is a contradiction to those who are already modern and believe they got there by denying politics in favor ot technics. Here we can see that the myth of modernity is complemented by an equally Faustian myth of modernization. Those wishing to catch up, however, are less likely to believe in technics as a means than as an end justifying political means. The current furor over politicization of previously technically oriented international institutions is more easily understood in this light.

Law is supported by sanctions; a legal order is a potential force monopoly; more generally, international law is law in the usual positivist conception of domestic law. Empirically we can establish the existence of a community, here designated the international legal community, a collection of statements called rules of international law, and a myth or series of myths about the nature, function, and origins of these rules and the way everything fits together as an order. The myth or myths probably have some kind of empirical referent, however distorted, but their structure, if it can be discerned, reveals some basic things about the community, its activities, and the world around it. This is not the place to undertake a structural analysis of the myths of the international legal community. The method for doing so is perhaps the greatest contribution Levi-Strauss has made to understanding the mind's workings. Observe only that Levi-Strauss understands any culture's myths, including their many variations and interpretations, to be analogous to music.[201] Perhaps Manning's metaphor of law as music failed to go far enough. The legal order is the myth surrounding law and the legal community. As such it is akin to music in form and function.

The reconciliation of metaphors of law as water and legal order as music is obviously impossible and may thus betray the absurdity of the whole enterprise. This is not merely a matter of mixed metaphors. The modernity myths of the international legal community, whether understood by reference to music, or the community's clan organization, or whether interpreted through water-related totems, are integral features of what the legal mind insists on regarding as a legal order.

The legal mind speaks for its savage self, once its language is decoded. But it speaks to itself as if modern, changing with the world. That world is unable to sustain indefinitely the material transformation implied by modernization. Stresses caused by differential modernization are sure to be compounded as Western civilization proceeds into post-modern circumstances. How does the ever savage legal mind cope with longstanding myths of modernity juxtaposed against the growing disarray of its civilization? Will it take refuge in the sacred, ritualizing the irrelevant, or persist as bricoleur, patching together bits and pieces of a world that never was what it seemed to the legal mind?

ON THE VOCATION OF OUR AGE FOR LAW AND LAW-MAKING: CURRENT TRENDS, CONCLUDING THOUGHTS

Law-Making as Law-Doing: Legal Vocation

Throughout this essay we have construed laws as opportunity for and consequence of human choices.[202] Even if choices are deliberately random, they produce something called laws, different only in content, not structure, from what other deliberate choices would have produced. Now we must face one of the oddities of the English language. When people accept constraints on their conduct imposed by natural circumstances, we talk about laws of the wild, or life, or nature, or the universe, or whatever else seems to be the constraining element. Such "laws" are not made by anyone; their effects do not include any effect on themselves. Indeed we call them laws only when we believe that

---

201.   Claude Levi-Strauss. *The Raw and the Cooked* (New York: Harper and Row, 1969), pp. 14-26.
202.   Of course all such choices are not necessarily law-relevant. Gottlieb (fn. 26), pp. 372-373.

they describe relations among things or events either fully beyond our control or perfectly regular and predictable. Generally we expect both conditions to be met.[203]

The complex social world of transnational relations is so far removed from the certainties of nature that choice rarely seems to be ruled out entirely. Laws for such a world, it seems, are the ones we choose to make and then make our choices by or find made for us by what others choose. Rules that might be otherwise we ignore or represent in social terms alone. A materialist position such as presented in the preceding section does little to correct this tendency, inasmuch as the domain of the material inextricably includes socioeconomic and other conditions created by people in relation to nature. The physical, as opposed to the social, may in some measure be a matter of choices but not a matter for choice.

The nuclear balance of terror illustrates this point. We think of it as fearsome but discretionary. This our behavior belies. We act as if there were but one course of action; any other would be foolhardy, and this is a physical reality. To be sure, the balance is dependent on the social reality of a system of states in which some states have the physical capacity to inflict unacceptable destruction on any of the others no matter what happens to them first. But constraints imposed by the balance of terror differ radically from those of the balance of power as historically understood. The former incomparably more than the latter result from a nearly inalterable, or at least irreversible, condition which is no less physical for having been created by men in a particular social context. Similarly people often consider frontiers to be social creations but accept them the more because they are also river courses or mountain ridges.

Clearly there is no sharp boundary between physical and social realms as they contribute to our acceptance of certain situations.[204] We may call the behavior determined by the very structure of the international system, as a joint sociophysical (material) reality, rules of the game. We may call the channeling of behavior in response to the sociophysical circumstances of a particular conflict situation rules of the conflict. In both cases we cannot exclude the accepting behavior from the domain of law just because what is accepted is not exclusively social. Insofar as the source of acceptance is tangibly or most saliently a physical thing, we could partition this from other kinds of law. Recalling our discussion of species of law in the third section of this charter, we might identify it as a new species. In fact, we believe there are two such species of international law. The first of these is illustrated by the example of the balance of terror and other basic structural features of the international system, and goes generally by such names as rules of the game or rules of the system.[205] The second is specific with respect to stable or recurring,

---

203. See further Robert Brown, *Laws and Rules in Sociology*: Aldine Pub. Co., 1973), ch. 5-6.

204. This is clearest, but with consequences most insidious, in the instance of physical things made by man. "The reason that the present century is fittingly called the Machine Age is not the abundance of machines, nor is it man's dependency on them. It lies in man's changed attitude. Instead of looking upon machines merely as aids toward the attainment of his ideals, man is now being spiritually overwhelmed. He is beginning to emulate the characteristics of the machine itself. . . . Consequences are taking the place of purposes." R. G. H. Siu, *The Tao of Science* (New York: Technology Press and John Wiley and Sons, 1957), p. 128.

205. The metaphor, *rules of the game,* is widely used, its meaning usually taken as self-evident. In connection with international law, see Richard A. Falk, "The Relevance of Political Context to the Nature and Functioning of International Law: An Intermediate View," in Karl Deutsch and Stanley Hoffmann, eds., *The Relevance of International Law* (Garden City, N.Y.: Anchor Books, 1971), pp. 193-194. Falk's definition and examples refer to informal boundaries on conflict. It differs substantially from the definition provided here, but the two are probably reconcilable. Consider one of Falk's most interesting examples: spheres of influence. Their apparently social origin is in part determined by the physical reality of the uneven

highly patterned situation. Examples drawn from conflict situations are most obvious and would include respect for sanctuaries, discrimination between acceptable and unacceptable instrumentalities of war, and so on. Largely ignored until Thomas C. Schelling pointed out the physical determinants in such apparently social situations, this species of law has yet to receive a conventional name.[206] Elsewhere the present writer has provisionally adopted the expression, *guidance criteria*, which Falk first suggested.[207]

These additional species of international law respectively describe a general imposition of nature, however disguised, and a specific imposition. They are not enforced but rather intrude themselves (the former term connoting social control) and are accepted because they are obvious even when they are not acknowledged.[208] The two species parallel general and specific species of enforced decisions and unenforced but accepted decisions. Thus we can identify six species of law, four of which are clearly applicable to what we see as international law conceived in the broadest sense.[209]

No doubt further inquiry would yield more refined categories, recognition of further speciation, and even more elaborate categories. For example, do the peculiar qualities of random selection from repeating pairs of choices—the coin-tossing model described earlier—constitute law unlike that of any other species, and, if we have a new species, how are we to classify it? To a point such an exercise is justified by the need to disabuse legal thinkers of their cherished notions about law as a homogeneous entity—a single species, whether domestic or international. Nonetheless we think the quest for precision through further taxonomic refinement in this essay would obtain irrelevance as its price.

A better investment is to clarify and order concepts by reference to attributes selected, and defended, as most useful for purposes of empirical anchoring. Inevitably subjective, such an effort is also the inevitable prelude to science, the object of which is to use publicly disclosed and replicable procedures to propose statements (explanations, predictions) which are both derived from theory and existentially meaningful. All branches of social inquiry but law have in the last several decades been launched in earnest pursuit of science as it is normally understood today. They have dismantled their standing doctrines, salvaging such propositions as they can for inventory and evaluation. They hold out theory as their goal. They cast about for research strategies resembling those of natural science, and sometimes they almost seem to be consumed by procedural concerns.

With the study of law the problem is quite different. As we have seen, legal science has not moved in the direction of science as currently understood. It has not been inclined toward the development of testable propositions because it is disinterested in

---

distribution of factors of industrial production, which in turn are more or less consequential depending on previous social arrangements like control over territory. If the territorially defined system of states itself is a social creation, its decentralized nature was forced by vast distances between favored physical locales for social development. Informality prevails simply because the rules work independently of their recognition as such.

206. Schelling (fn. 99), ch. 3.

207. Falk (fn. 205), pp. 199-200; Nicholas Greenwood Onuf, "Law and Lawyers in International Crises," *International Organization*, Vol. 29, No. 4 (Autumn 1975), pp. 1048-1050.

208. But see Haas (fn. 115), pp. 828-838, on the difficulties in establishing just what a natural whole of any complexity might be. In terms of the present discussion, what might appear to one observer as an inalterable physical constraint, e.g., inaccessibility of certain resources or irreversibility of ecological damage, may appear quite differently to another observer. The situations which we have in mind as falling within the legal domain tend to generate a ready consensus, at least among the affected parties, on the constraints imposed by reality. Lack of consensus is a recipe for disaster for at least some parties but not a breaking of the law.

209. The four species of international law are developed in Onuf (fn. 207), pp. 1039-1053, in a separate framework which was erected for a different purpose but is nonetheless compatible with the present one.

theory. Instead it holds onto positivist doctrine. Alternative conceptualizations do not exist. They must be proposed.[210] But once one and then several are proposed, they can be refined only so far. Then they should be used, just as in any branch of inquiry given to the pursuit of theory through science, to find and order testable propositions. There is more to science than legal science knows. To break the latter's thrall, we must learn from accumulating experiences in other social sciences and borrow from them as appears useful.

Among the social sciences, political science is most obviously concerned with the study of law. Historically political scientists have shared their perspective on law with lawyers. We have witnessed in recent decades a revolt against these ties, which were felt to inhibit the investigation of innumerable political phenomena unrelated to legal categories, legal methods, and legally defined institutions. The behavioral movement, as it is called, contrasts such legal or, more pejoratively, legalistic concerns with political behavior, to be understood in terms of social behavior more generally and explored inductively and where possible quantitatively.[211]

Having ended its colonial relationship with legal science, political science has invited neocolonialism from other quarters. Political science tends to be a discipline without a core of its own. Many political scientists see politics as the adjective to some other discipline's noun: economy, community, personality.[212] And they cast their lot with other social sciences for the development of fundamental notions and research strategies. We could hardly do otherwise. The alternative for political science is to hang everything political on the one thin concept of authority, which resembles the Austinian command of the sovereign too closely to advance the study of law.[213] The upshot of recent changes in political science is that its students have little to say about law and law-making, except for what falls within the convenient but limiting categories of legislative and judicial activity. To these we return presently but without promise that they contribute significantly to the furtherance of a comtemporary science of law.

Because political science offers so little, we sought help in this essay from sociology in taking the first step toward science—dismantling doctrine and developing a framework that better organizes the soical complexity of law. Sociology takes us no further. For reasons of its own history, sociology tends to confine itself to change on a societal scale (development) and the absence of such change as stable societies absorb small changes (equilibrium). Moored to the historical and biological metaphors of its Victorian origins,

---

210. We sketched such an alternative in the fourth section of this chapter, under "Law and Community." Although it was specifically directed toward the problem of why sources persist in a world of significant material changes, its explanatory scope need not be restricted to this alone.

211. Charles E. Merriam's *New Aspects of Politics* (Chicago: University of Chicago Press, 1925) was clarion call for the new movement and defined its abiding tenets. Subsequent literature of self-appraisal in political science is voluminous.

212. Correlatively politics may be nothing more than "a cluster term extending range of events loosely linked in a 'family resemblance' way though without the single common property required for class terms." Fred M. Frohock, "The Structure of 'Politics'," *American Political Science Review*, Vol. 72, No. 3 (September 1978), p. 859. Frohock attempts to establish a necessary, but not sufficient, structural core to the concept of politics revolving around the terms *directivenes* and *aggregation*. All political phenomena are thus characterized by at least two collectivities, one providing the other direction—even passively, as through maps (and law). pp. 866-869.

213. As with Frohock's core property of directiveness, the term *authority* invariably connotes asymmetry in collective relations, whether accepted on authority or imposed by authority. The case for authority as the defining concept of political science is made by Harry Eckstein, "Authority Patterns: A Structural Basis for Political Inquiry," *American Political Science Review*, Vol. 67, No. 4 (December 1973), pp. 1142-1163.

For a critical response to this kind of thinking, with particular reference to the consequent exclusion of international relations from the domain of the political, see John Gerard Ruggie, "International Responses to

sociology remains preoccupied with classification and morphological description, which were after all dominant features of later nineteenth century science.

More so than sociology, anthropology addresses all kinds of activities and their effects on things. Although it may have gained us access to the legal mind and the hidden meaning of legal activity, the use of anthropology in this essay took the form of a speculative excursus, if anything moving the inquiry away from the accessible empirics of science. Nevertheless, we have hardly touched on anthropology's concern for law nor exhausted its promise for science.

Anthropological interest in law and other properties of orders without familiar Western institutions inspired an important literature from the discipline's earliest days. Thus, despite its age, Malinowski's *Crime and Custom in Savage Society* continues to receive the attention only accorded seminal works in any field.[214] Malinowski displayed a strong preference for sytematic description based on intensive field investigation. A generally applicable framework about law in many orders failed to develop. Following Malinowski, anthropologists tended to view law in contextually specific terms. To the extent general statements about law were employed, they were casually borrowed from legal thought to describe a given community's ordering nexus in the alien terms of Western legal thought, obviously for the benefit of Westerners. Feuding, for example, is often seen as a system of self-help to enforce the law, since Austinian law is posited as something that must exist if order is being maintained.[215] Reflexive borrowing from Western legal doctrine is less evident in the case of law-making, as opposed to law-using, because only one thing is borrowed. The ill-defined idea of custom is taken to comprehend all varieties of "primitive" law-making.

Well before Malinowski and the emergence of modern anthropology, the study of law in the context of culture held definite promise of developing a sufficiently unified and generalizable perspective that it could have oriented the construction of appropriate frameworks and prompted systematic investigation of the subject. Sir Henry Maine (1822-1888) is, after all, a name equally familiar to anthropologists and legal scholars today. Deserted by field-oriented anthropology, resisted by increasingly formal tendencies in positivist doctrine, and discredited by its own tendency to generalize metaphorically and parochially, the historical school, as it was called, is mostly a matter of history.[216] Had it been otherwise, the Austinian view might be the anachronism, and the gulf between legal thought and social science might not exist at all.

Only with the rise, decades later, of a quite different school called legal realism did the flowering of legal concerns in social anthropology benefit legal thought. Legal realism is but a latter-day branch of sociological jurisprudence, separated from the latter more by

---

Technology: Concepts and Trends," *International Organization*, Vol. 29, No. 3 (Summer 1975), pp. 578-583. Ruggie's position on the relation of authority to things political is quite similar to the position taken in these pages with respect to the nature of things legal. See also Edward H. Buehrig, "The International Pattern of Authority," *World Politics*, Vol. 17, No. 3 (April 1965), pp. 369-376, and Onuf (fn. 1), pp. 259-266, on authority, vestigial and incipient respectively, as may have been or come to be above states.

214.   Cited above (fn. 118).

215.   This point is elaborated in Onuf (fn. 26).

216.   On the historical school and its most famous member, Friedrich Carl van Savigny (1779-1861), see Stone (fn. 18), ch. 2. Parochialism was particularly evident in Savigny's "*Volkgeist* doctrine," articulated in his celebrated tract, *The Vocation of our Age for Legislation and Jurisprudence* (1814; trans. 1831), and subjected to further distortion by his followers. See also fn. 46 and the fourth section of this chapter, under "Law and Order."

style than substance.[217] Indeed legal realism's standing as a distinctive school of thought was thrust upon it. A veritable chorus of critics has insisted that legal realism is rooted in the proposition that law is what judges and other law officials say it is. Perhaps unfairly we are now conditioned by these critics to identify legal realism "as being primarily concerned with judicial processes."[218]

The empirical utility of this orientation has been overlooked in the basically normative controversy over its validity. If it were adopted, the empirical domain of inquiry would be readily defined. The study of judicial behavior in contemporary political science accomplished just this simply by freeing itself from legal thought.[219] Within its tightly defined domain, the study of judicial behavior has made considerable strides (at least when compared to political science as a whole) in the direction of formulating and testing theoretically relevant propositions. Legal realism could have charted the course subsequently taken by judicial behavior but failed to take any real path at all. Instead it manifested itself as a surge of recognition that law, law-making, and law-doing are inseparable concerns. As such, legal realism could hardly present a neatly defined empirical domain to the observer. Either he carves out an empirical domain, like the behavior of appellate judges, because it is accessible and interesting, at least to him, even if it seems arbitrary to others; or the observer ranges over the terrain of legal culture wherever he finds it. By assuming that law not so much *is* as *does,* he makes legal culture the unifying but only loosely organizing element in diverse inquiries.

The notion that law *does* presents a functional view of law. It typifies the work of Karl N. Llewellyn (1893-1962), a central figure in American legal realism. The convergence of legal realism and anthropology is nowhere better seen than in Llewellyn's functional orientation. Llewellyn's basic jurisprudential posture assumes that law is what law officials do, and that what they do is susceptible to inductive treatment, aided by the a priori identification of a few rather broad categories. These he called law-jobs, and they form the organizational basis of legal training.[220] Llewellyn resisted definitions of law. He preferred a deliberately vague and suggestive vocabulary revolving around such terms as law-ways and law-stuff, which emphasize the cultural context of law and permit informal comparisons from widely divergent socio-cultural settings.

The marriage of legal realism and anthropology yielded a general sense of pregnant expectation and one birth (Llewellyn's famous study of Cheyenne law-ways, done collaboratively with anthropologist E. Adamson Hoebel[221]) before the partners drifted

---

217. Roscoe Pound, whom we saw as a towering figure in sociological jurisprudence (the first section of this chapter, under "Positivism"), is also regarded as one of legal realism's forerunners. Wilfrid E. Rumble, Jr., *American Legal Realism* (Ithaca: Cornell University Press, 1968), pp. 9-26. On the famous though misleading controversy between Pound and leading legal realists, see Twining (fn. 39), pp. 70-83.

218. Ibid., p. 409, fn. 22. Twining found this an unfair characterization.

219. Thus the many studies of judicial behavior undertaken by political scientists have an inspirational debt to legal realism but a more direct analytic debt to sociology and social psychology. But see Glendon Schubert, "Behavioral Jurisprudence," *Law and Society Review*, Vol. 2, No. 3 (May 1968). pp. 407-428, for an attempt to reassert the connection between legal thought and the study of judicial behavior by dignifying the latter with the grander term, behavioral jurisprudence. The effort is marred by failure to broaden the empirical domain of his new jurisprudence beyond that of judicial behavior.

220. Llewellyn (fn. 191), pp. 1355-1400. Llewellyn acknowledged a debt to Weber with respect to his idea of law-jobs. Twining (fn. 39), p. 183. A shared concern for legal vocation nevertheless resulted in entirely different analytic orientation.

221. Karl N. Llewellyn and E. Adamson Hoebel, *The Cheyenne Way* (Norman: University of Oklahoma Press, 1941).

away. Llewellyn's legal realism was ultimately a vocational movement, given over to lawyer's daily concerns. Contributing to the demise of the relationship was functionalism's fall from epistemological favor as the social sciences became increasingly preoccupied with the requirements of modern science.

The hostility of vocationally oriented legal realism toward the rigors of science as they might relate to law is well documented.[222] Nonetheless, Llewellyn and others in the movement virtually invited research conducted on scientific premises. Any amount of quantifiable evidence can be found in the detritus of daily law-doing. How are the law-jobs distributed? Who are the doers in each job? Do they have attributes that set them apart from other professional groups, like managers and administrators? Are they constituted in communities, as argued above?[223] Do communities of law-makers overlap at different levels or, for example, is the law-making community at the international level isolated from other such communities? Are law-doers more self-conscious about the social consequences of their activities than are other professional groups? Questions like the last one increase the challenge confronting the researcher guided by the scientific method, but they are familiar enough in present-day sociological and social psychological research.

The political science field of legislative behavior perennially addresses many such questions in the context of just one of Llewellyn's law-jobs.[224] No one asks who the law-makers are, however, on the assumption that legislators are the law-makers of record.[225] Much as can be learned about legislators and legislative behavior, we need to know more, in the sense of science, about all those whose doings are the law. Even if we put science aside, asking who the legislators are contributes little to the speculative dimension of legal thought. Only by asking who all the law-makers are can we develop general ideas about the relation of law, legal culture and its vocational sub-cultures, and public order.[226]

---

222. Twining (fn. 39), pp. 56-69. The emphasis in both modern science and legal realism on prediction creates an illusion of methodological convergence. Modern science is devoted to the isolation and identification of regularities. In this context prediction is an anticipated regularity. Realist prediction comes from assessing multiple factors uniquely generating individual decisions. Each such decision must be predicted in its own exclusive terms. The result is relativism inconsistent with the generalizing and replicating tendencies of positivist, experimental science. See also Hunt (fn. 15), pp. 43-44.

223. See the fourth section of this chapter, under "Law and Community." For stimulating, scientifically oriented discussion of communities in science, see Diana Crane, *Invisible Colleges* (Chicago: University of Chicago Press, 1972); Thomas S. Kuhn, *The Essential Tension* (Chicago: University of Chicago Press, 1977), ch. 12.

224. For a brief overview of legislative behavior as a field, with particular reference to its methodological progress, see Samuel C. Patterson and John C. Wahlke, "Trends and Prospects in Legislative Behavior Research," in ibid., eds., *Comparative Legislative Behavior* (New York: John Wiley and Sons, 1972), pp. 289-303.

225. A blatant example is James David Barber's *The Law-Makers* (New Haven: Yale University Press, 1965). Its subtitle: Recruitment and Adaptation to Legislative Life.

226. Indeed this was Burke's procedure in evaluating the National Assembly of revolutionary France, which he also compared, obviously invidiously, to the House of Commons. While "a very great proportion of the assembly (a majority of the members who attended) were composed of practitioners of the law," the House of Commons is "filled with everything illustrious in rank, in descent, in hereditary and in acquired opulence, in cultivated talents, in military, civil, naval, and politic distinction that the country can afford." Edmund Burke, *Reflections on the Revolution in France* (Indianapolis: The Library of Liberal Arts, 46: 1955). pp. 47, 50. First published 1792; quoted words from ch. III, section 3, entitled "The Men Responsible for this Evil Policy." For contemporary, less judgmental comparative research along these lines, see Mogens S. Pedersen, "Lawyers in Politics: The Danish Folketing and United States Legislatures," in Patterson and Wahlke (fn. 224), pp. 25-63.

Legal realism never asked who the law-makers are. We cannot be sure that knowledge will be furthered by devising research to answer it. But it does seem to offer a promising avenue for inquiry. This avenue has been ignored not so much because it has not been seen as promising but because it has not been seen at all. Without organizing frameworks, legal realists could hardly know what questions might be worth asking.

Legal realism was substantially an American movement, as its vocational concerns might suggest.[227] Though receptive to intellectual influences outside the positivist tradition, the major source of stimulation was Anglo-American social anthropology and not the Continental sociology of Durkheim and Weber. The systematizing tendencies of the latter are notably absent in the former, and the altogether formless character of legal realism remained unaffected. Ideas were absorbed—folkways became law-ways—but the grounding of inquiry in taxonomic ordering design of research, such as anthropology and the other social sciences have come to regard as vital, was not contemplated by legal realism.

The one exception to the tendency of legal realism to borrow from social science but remain formless merely confirms the primacy of the vocational orientation in legal realism. The controversial "parking studies" of Underhill Moore (1879-1949) are this exception.[228] The design of this research was developed from learning theory associated with Watsonian behaviorism. The research itself involved the gathering and analysis of data about law compliance. As one commentator noted at the time, Moore's underlying assumption was that behavior conforms to legal artifacts and not the converse.[229] To assume that legal artifacts conform to behavior might be the first step in developing systematic research on law-making; indeed it was the first step taken in these pages to develop a framework for the study of global law-making freed from positivist assumptions. The point is that Moore was at least concerned to make his assumption, be it the conventional positivist one, into a testable proposition. His effort to make the test meaningful and research manageable was rewarded by the scorn of fellow legal realists.[230]

Fortunately psychologists have not reciprocated the hostility legal realists directed at Moore's work. Quite to the contrary, they have developed a substantial interest in law. In particular their interest, like Moore's, attaches to the effect of law on behavior. The perennial, and eminently researchable, questions are those of compliance and deviance, not of law-making and the uses of law. All legal thought has tended to postulate effects of law, thereby assuming its effectiveness, and then ask questions about its formal qualities and functions. Advances in knowledge of behavior in the face of law put forward by psychologists may challenge assumptions but not help in answering timeless questions of legal thought. Legal thinkers are so absorbed in their questions that such challenges go unnoticed. Thus we account for the distaste legal realists display toward the outbreak of scientific activity within their own rank. In this respect they differ little from legal thinkers of other persuasions.

---

227. A Scandinavian school of legal realism—the free law movement—did appear but failed to gain a major following. In the English-speaking world its best known member is Alf Ross, whose book, *Towards a Realistic Jurisprudence* (Copenhagen: Munksgard, 1946), stays close to standard positivist doctrine on sources.

228. Underhill Moore and Charles C. Callahan, "Law and Learning Theory: A Study in Legal Control," *Yale Law Journal*, Vol. 53, No. 1 (December 1943), pp. 1-136.

229. Hessel E. Yntema, "'Law and Learning Theory' through the Looking Glass of Legal Theory," *Yale Law Journal*, Vol. 53, No. 2 (March 1944), p. 346.

230. Twining (fn. 39), pp. 56-67. For a sympathetic assessment of Moore's effort to further the study of law through modern science, see F. S. C. Northrop, "Underhill Moore's Legal Science: Its Nature and Significance," *Yale Law Journal*, Vol. 59, No. 2 (January 1950), pp. 196-213.

Regimes: A New Vocation for Law-Making

We may fairly credit our age with a vocation for science. And the legal vocation flourishes. Although both vocations are manifestations of the rationalist-instrumentalist spirit in Western culture, they are not for that reason easily connected. Indeed, the evidence suggests that a modern science of law is not forthcoming in this age. The purpose of such a science, beyond understanding for its own sake, is presumably increased control over legal processes and outcomes. Science leads to improved engineering.[231] If control is the ultimate objective, and control through science is thwarted, are we left with no alternative? Can social control be exercised more directly through other means than the acquisition of certain knowledge about how social things work? The answer is simple enough to have preceded modern science. Replace social objects that can be controlled only after they are understood with new ones designed specifically with control in mind.

The legal processes of the global community yield two species of law which resist scientific assessment and mock the ambition to control. The social institution designed to increase control over law-making processes is called legislation. The legislative instrumentality in domestic orders was intended to replace, through the division of labor, existing law-making processes at an early point in the transformation of such orders.[232] As social complexity increases and the division of labor proceeds even further, the use of standard solutions to deal with specialized problems effectively revives non-legislative law-making. Nonetheless, the assumption remains that as an instrumentality lending itself to social control, the legislature is the fount of law. It would be more accurate to say that the legislative instrumentality creates a different species of law—law as a general command, enforceable precisely because it is legislated. Thus the legislature is the fount of Austinian law. To the extent that such law replaces law of the other species, then the legislature has control over important legal processes.[233] New or revitalized legal processes yielding non-Austinian law take place within legislatively established constraints and are thereby subject to control of an indirect sort.

The global situation is marked by different sequences of events. A legislative instrumentality has not been created for the very reason that it implies control unacceptable to many members of the state system. Meanwhile the division of labor has proceeded apace in the many areas of international life tied to circumstances within major members of the system. The result is an extensive body of law not subject to control,

---

231.   Engineering, through trial and error, can proceed with no science and minimal theory. Such craft typically antedates science. We argue only that whatever science is intended for, it can substitute for cumbersome, cut and dried procedures.

232.   Whether legislation actually did replace existing legal processes is another question. More important is the belief that this is what happened. A noted classical liberal thinker, F. A. Hayek, has argued that a related belief—that law relevant to the public welfare can only come from legislation—is the source of what he takes to be excesses in governmental activity. Another consequence of such beliefs is the preoccupation with legal positivism. F. A. Hayek, *Law, Legislation and Liberty, Vol. I., Rules and Order* (Chicago: University of Chicago Press, 1973), pp. 131-134.

233.   Assumed here is a necessary relation between the aggregation of rationally made individual decisions and collectively preferred outcomes in a legislative organ characterized by some kind of majoritarian decision rule. The absence of a necessary relation between individual and collective preferences—"the paradox of voting"—means that control and legislation cannot be taken as synonymous even under the best of circumstances. The paradox of voting has been the subject of extensive and exceedingly formal analysis in recent years. Implications now understood could hardly have been anticipated when the legislative instrumentality was first devised to gain control over legal processes. For a relatively informal statement of the formal reasoning involved, see William H. Riker and Peter C. Ordeshook, *An Introduction to Positive Political Theory* (Englewood Cliffs. N.J.: Prentice-Hall, 1973), ch. 1, 4.

whether direct or indirect, that a legislature is assumed to provide. If it were possible to create a global legislative instrumentality, its law could readily replace only one of the two currently operative species of international law. That of course is artifactual law. At best the law of standard solutions could only gradually be subsumed within the legal structure emanating from the legislature.

Control is hardly automatic simply because a source of general commands is introduced. Somehow the legislature must impose effective control over an existing body of problem-solving practices without having to replace each and every standard solution. As time passes, the difficulty of converting a necessarily limited number of commands into meaningful control increases proportionately. No doubt the point comes when it is simply too late to gain even a semblance of control over the planet's legal product. Active control over complex social situations is increasingly problematic even in those advanced domestic orders with long legislative histories. Complex situations with planetary implications abound. These situations virtually beg for control on the requisite scale. The need for control is as urgent as the hope for it slender.

The need for a controllable world and the promise of control in the form of a global fount of Austinian law are virtual clichés. The utter unlikelihood that such a fount will be created in the near future is a cliché of the same order. In an age of science, law, and legislation, it appears that we have no vocation for the making of a global legislature. Without one, we cannot make Austinian law, or so it would seem, and without Austinian law, we cannot even hope to control the legal processes indispensable to a well-managed world.

$$* \quad * \quad * \quad * \quad * \quad *$$

Legislation, like science, law, and all such features of our experience which arise from and contribute to the peculiar Western belief in the primacy of the individual over society and nature itself, may be nothing more than a massive self-deception on the nature and purpose of man's existence.[234] The other side of this coin, though, is Western man's inventiveness, social as well as mechanical. He invented legislation long after he had public, representative assemblies by drafting the latter in the service of the former.[235] Law had always existed "in the sense of rules defining what kind of conduct is generally right." Legislation is different, consisting largely "of directions concerning what particular officers or agencies of governments are required to do."[236] Legislated law arises in response to the need for ever more complex and organized social orders. Such law is distinctive for this reason, and not because it is Austinian in character (which law not legislated may nonetheless be) or the product of a particular social institution called a legislature. That such law must be consciously devised is another matter.

---

234. Adda B. Bozeman, *The Future of Law in a Multicultural World* (Princeton: Princeton University Press. 1971), pp. 35-49, on the importance the Western mind alone attaches to the ideas of law and legislation.

235. Originally noble assemblies and feudal estates, such public bodies were hardly representative in any literal sense, even if in due course their members came to be elected popularly. Nevertheless they are often called popular assemblies.

236. Hayek (fn. 232), p. 133. Note also: "Modern legislatures clearly derive from bodies which existed before the deliberate making of rules of just conduct was even considered possible, and the latter task was only later entrusted to institutions habitually concerned with very different tasks. The noun 'legislature' does not in fact appear before the middle of the seventeenth century. . . ." p. 129.

If Western man invented legislation in the context of public assemblies, the availability of the latter, or their ready creation to fulfill Enlightenment principles, must have played a part. But the same possibilities do not exist for the globe today. The General Assembly approximates the model of an available assembly, but that body is too busy with its artifactual creations and is too little trusted by influential members of the system to serve the purpose. The creation of a new body specifically to serve as a legislature is inconceivable in a time so different from the Enlightenment. An alternative social institution is demanded.

What is available are those assemblies created specifically to deal with whole bundles of issues and problems apparently related as an objective matter. The labors of such assemblies are intended to take the form of multilateral treaties which, as we saw, may constitute general law directly. As special purpose assemblies, constructed separately for each whole set of concerns, these bodies have a singular advantage over a general assembly. Without sacrificing the representation of numerous constituencies and the balancing of their interests, each one develops a competence in the subject of their concerns which is vastly augmented by soliciting expert advice. The competence of special purpose assemblies and their attention to expert advice mean that they may actually be able to use law to organize institutional activity in a way that substantially controls situations otherwise too large and complex for the controlling effects of the division of labor.[237]

Special purpose assemblies must be viewed collectively as doing the work of a legislature. They would seem to be the only available or readily imagined alternative to the legislative model as a fount of law appropriate to the organizational needs of the planet. The major problem with the argument of functional equivalence is that legislation is normally assumed to take the form of Austinian law. The legal product of special purpose assemblies is clearly not Austinian in the sense of having sanctions attached to it. At the same time, it is not merely accepted law. Most significantly, the legal product of successful special purpose assemblies taken as a whole, has properties simply not to be found in the individual rules produced.

Honoring the difference between a whole and its summed parts, Oran R. Young has defined a coherent, substantively related body of rules a regime.[238] Regimes in this sense may have some other source than a special purpose assembly and need not be the functional equivalent of legislation. By substituting for legislation, the legal product of a special purpose assembly also comports with a more restrictive definition of regime—a body of rules made for specific and identifiable purposes—developed by Ernst B. Haas and his co-workers.[239] There is ample historical justification for Young's definition. The

---

237. One might consider special purpose assemblies legislatures but for the following: they do not exist primarily to make legal rules in the conventional sense, they are not representative by the very fact of being specialized, and they are not usually standing assemblies. None of these considerations are persuasive individually, but taken together differences in degree become a difference in kind. On defining "legislatures as a kind of assembly," see Fred Riggs, "Legislative Structures: Some Thoughts on Elected National Assemblies." in Alan Kornberg, ed., *Legislatures in Comparative Perspective* (New York: David McKay, 1973), pp. 30-93.

238. Oran R. Young, "International Regimes: Problems of Concept Formation," *World Politics*, Vol. 32, No. 3 (April 1980), pp. 332-342. Young has rights and rules at the core of regimes. Rights for one regime participant, however, are merely consequences of rules for others. Young also finds in regimes social choice and implementing mechanisms, which of course are embodied in rules. Nye (fn. 28), p. 222, defines the term similarly but less elaborately.

239. Ernst B. Haas, "On Systems and International Regimes," *World Politics*, Vol. 27, No. 3 (January 1975), p. 175; Ruggie (fn. 213), pp. 570-573; Haas, "Why Collaborate? Issue-Linkage and International

customary law of treaties and the law of the high seas, to use prominent examples, have always been called legal regimes. At the same time Haas has correctly emphasized the importance of regimes constituted of Austinian law, even when clear patterns of authority and enforcement are absent.[240] Regimes of the latter type can only be made, as we have indicated, and their making is a recent phenomenon. We therefore designate the subtype of regime that substitutes for legislation *modern regimes*.

Modern regimes also differ from those that are naturally found because they are characteristically accompanied by organizational instrumentalities to enhance their operation.[241] Of modern, organized regimes we may further distinguish two types: regulatory regimes and management regimes. Regulatory regimes are dense networks of relatively detailed rules which commend themselves to national-level bureaucrats as a help rather than hindrance in conducting their duties, even if the nominal function of such rule-networks is to prevent abuses.[242] Regulatory regimes would thus appear to lend form to the law of standardized solutions.

No government partaking of the advantages of a regulatory regime can do so selectively. The regime is framed and then filled in as a whole, and the integrity of the whole becomes the enforcing agent with respect to individual rules. In effect, rules individually match the specificity of legislation, while collectively, as a regime, they strongly resemble a general command.[243] The same thing does not happen with international law as a whole, simply because it is not a whole. Any member of the international legal order can deny acceptance of any particular rule with tangible effect only on that rule. The legal order is not threatened because the rest of its law is accepted;

Regimes," *World Politics*, Vol. 32, No. 3 (April 1980), pp. 358, 396-400. Haas also recognizes that his definition is more restrictive than Young's but incorrectly states the difference. In so doing he imputes to Young the view that a regime is the product of active agreement. "Why Collaborate? . . .," p. 358 fn. 2.

240.   Ruggie expressed this well in a somewhat different connection: "Not organization *above* states, but an enormously complex and rather fundamental *re-ordering* of political space and *re-structuring* of public authority *across* states appears to be the general pattern of the future." John Gerard Ruggie, "The Structure of International Organization: Contingency, Complexity and Post-Modern Form," *Papers, Peace Research Society (International)*, Vol. 18 (1972), p. 87. Emphasis in original.

241.   We might say that regimes by their nature must be horizontally integrated—a quality that makes regimes distinguishable from the general legal order in which they are lodged. Insofar as they are modern, organized regimes, they are also vertically integrated in some degree. When vertical integration feeds an outward movement of a regime's boundaries, we call it *spill-over*. When horizontal integration promotes organizational growth, we use the phrase *task expansion*. These reciprocal integrative effects are at the heart of the theory of international functionalist growth underlying European integration efforts, at least initially. In effect, functionalist theory assumes a lumpy, or unevenly integrated, regime is unnatural and will therefore integrate sufficiently to smooth out. Even if this dubious assumption were correct, it fails to account for the possibility that disintegration will also yield a smoothed out, more natural regime. The possibility of such an outcome defeats functionalism as a world order strategy backed by theory and suggests that it is doctrine instead.

242.   David M. Leive, *International Regulatory Regimes* (Lexington, Mass.: Lexington Books, 1976) provides useful case studies of representative regulatory regimes. Perhaps the most impressive example, one that is closest to the ideal type, is the Codex Alimentarius jointly developed by the Food and Agricultural Organization and the World Health Organization.

243.   Awareness of this may have been a motive for the rendering of customary international law into code form but not submitting it for adoption as a treaty. Not only would such a treaty weaken the law if it were less than fully ratified and freeze the law if it were, restatement as a whole was the only way to bring the law in question closer to the structure of a general command. This was the tactic favored by British spokesmen during the international codification movement's century-long history. A lucid example of the British view is P. J. Baker, "The Codification of International Law," *British Year Book of International Law*, Vol. 5 (1924), pp. 38-65.

its members go on treating the law selectively, accepting and rejecting as they see fit.[244]

By contrast with regulatory regimes, management regimes are devised more to provide orderly access to such goods as natural resources than to deter delinquent behavior. Despite this apparently restitutive function, to use Durkheim's terms, management regimes revolve around a small number of generally stated principles which approach artifactual status. Unspecified managerial activities take the place of detailed regulation. Management is thus a euphemism for hard bargaining and implicit coercion in the interpretation of high rhetoric for real problem-solving.[245] Underlying open-ended artifacts like the principle of maximum sustainable yield are distributive agreements hammered out in an atmosphere redolent with Durkheim's repressive sanctions exercised on all sides. Not only are management regimes relatively formless, but the principles ostensibly guiding them may be sacrificed to expediency. The troubled history of ocean resource regimes confirms that technical difficulties raised by a principle like maximum sustainable yield pale beside its political vulnerability.[246]

Whatever the internal dynamics of management regimes, they take on the force of a general command precisely because they incorporate an elaborate organizational apparatus to assume managerial responsibilities when and if agreements are struck. While such organizations rarely possess clear enforcement powers, they operate, as do most administrative vehicles, in a way that simultaneously presumes the existence of enforcement power but virtually never calls for its employment. The existence of an administrative vehicle to oversee auto-enforcement of individual rules serves to remind regime participants that in the pursuit of their interests they had agreed to those rules, even if they later regret doing so.

Lest too much be made of the fact that regimes work, often quite well, in the absence of repressive sanctions, we should note that legislative enactments rarely require enforcement in the usual sense of threatening or using force to achieve compliance with law. The law of right conduct, it is true, lends itself naturally to repressive sanctions. But legislatures, or special purpose assemblies, are not principally in the business of making this law. Their chief business is the law of organization—law lending itself to restitutive sanctions, which are not sanctions in the usual sense at all. Networks of reciprocity, typically supported by organizational commitments and benefits, make the law systematically devised by authorized assemblies, general and special, distinctively modern *and* properly Austinian.[247]

---

244. See similarly Oran R. Young, *Compliance and Public Authority* (Baltimore: Johns Hopkins University Press, 1979), pp. 41-44.

245. Even official statements can offer a glimpse into the relation of principle to politics in the instance of a managerial regime. See for example Thomas A. Pickering, "The U.S.-Canada Boundary and Resource Agreements," United States Department of State, Bureau of Public Affairs, *Current Policy*, No. 64 (April 1979). Phrases like "the difference in management approaches and the resultant discord on management and sharing" (p. 2) give the game away. See generally, Oran R. Young, *Resource Management at the International Level* (London: Frances Pinter, 1977), and "International Resource Regimes," in Clifford S. Russell, ed., *Collective Decision-Making* (Baltimore: Johns Hopkins University Press, 1979), pp. 241-282.

246. Consult Lee M. Talbot, "Wildlife Quotas Sometimes Ignore the Real World," *Smithsonian*, Vol. 8, No. 2 (May 1977), pp. 116-124; P. A. Larkin, "Epitaph for the Concept of Maximum Sustainable Yield," *Transactions of the American Fisheries Society*, Vol. 106, No. 1 (January 1977), pp. 1-11. A further complication is the principle's economic irrelevance—yields and revenues are not to be confused.

247. The phrase, "networks of reciprocity," belongs to Wesley L. Gould and Michael Barkun, *International Law and the Social Sciences* (Princeton: Princeton University Press, 1970), p. 182. They use it to explain customary law formation.

Regimes differ not only in type, but in scope, meaning their degree of generality. Naturally formed regimes tend to be spatially general, that is, global in scope, and functionally limited, but broadly so. Modern regimes, made for specified purposes instead of arising from generalizing state practice, are characteristically more limited in functional scope and frequently are spatially limited as well. Some of the more conspicuous modern regimes are regionally and functionally specific in an interlocking fashion. If a region is understood to mean the littoral of an ocean basin, for example, and the function of the regime to manage basin resources, then the criteria for participating in the regime are indistinguishably space and need-defined.[248]

Experience strongly suggests that the more limited in scope a regime, the more readily it can be made or upgraded as needed. The trend therefore is in the direction of the general legal order differentiating into multiple micro-orders, each coherently defined in its own spatial and functional terms. From a global perspective the fission-explosion of new regimes is discernibly lacking in order. And this is not merely an illusion. The proliferation of regimes results in overlapping boundaries, confusion and jurisdictional squabbles. It may even promote conflict between regime operators, and present exploitative opportunities to participants.

It might appear that the advantages of having fewer, larger regimes justify greater investment in their creation. It might also appear that the cost of creating any large-scale regime might be reduced substantially if undertaken within the received framework of a naturally formed historic regime. At the very least, architectural problems, like defining the regime's overarching dimensions and organizing principles would already have provisional answers to them.

The contemporary test case for transforming historic regimes into modern ones is the arduous United Nations law of the sea deliberations. Constructing a renovated oceans regime exposes certain constraining assumptions built into the effort. One assumption is that regimes formed gradually in past times have a natural wholeness which stays with the regime no matter how circumstances change.[249] A second assumption holds that lawyers alone really understand the problems of making regimes, while others are needed only to render technical advice.[250] A third assumption is that the business of making a regime can actually be finished up at some point. Permanence of special purpose assemblies is unthinkable unless they are granted some other responsibilities, that they might look like full-fledged organizations.[251]

Codifying long-standing glacially formed regimes may make sense if codification is merely a matter of tidying up existing law. Codification within a domestic setting tends

---

248. Pertinent here is Lennart J. Lundquist's concept, *community of cobasin states*, as defining criterion and organizing principle for such regimes. "Managing the World's Ocean Resources: Problems in Equity and Efficiency," in Gerald Garvey and Lou Ann Garvey, eds., *International Resource Flow* (Lexington, Mass.: Lexington Books, 1977), pp. 121-122.

249. Haas (fn. 115) has examined this assumption and its implications at great length.

250. This assumption is deeply rooted in the West in general and the United States in particular. See Robert L. Friedheim, "The 'Satisfied' and 'Dissatisfied' States Negotiate International Law: A Case Study," *World Politics*, Vol. 18, No. 1 October 1965), pp. 20-41; N. G. Onuf and Robert O. Slater, "Law-Experts and the Making of Formal Ocean Policies," presented at 1974 Meeting of the American Political Science Association.

251. That states are loathe to take additional steps to make special purpose assemblies permanent parallels their unwillingness to create new specialized agencies for the United Nations Systems, the latter being a model for the former, and their hesitancy to establish an "authority" to supervise exploitation of the seabed and distribution of rewards. It is precisely because authority is at stake.

to be associated with strengthening executive authority, as Weber noted.[252] Consequently, it might seem to be an appropriate vehicle for the transformation of large-scale regimes. Experience with international codification cannot support this conclusion. Using codification to modernize historic regimes is neither associated with increased centralization nor, in the absence of such, is it adequate to the need for directed change on any scale. This is not to say that the transformation of the global oceans regime must fail. Prevailing assumptions deceived participants into thinking that the job would be easier than it has turned out to be. Future efforts at regime transformation on a comparable scale will certainly not be undertaken so readily, or so innocently.

At the moment of this writing efforts to renovate the oceans regime continue. Even if they eventually fail, we should by no means conclude that chaos will ensue. Doubtless the traditional regime will be damaged beyond repair by the stillbirth of its successor. In its place will be a disorderly melange of lesser regimes, some of them modern and well organized, others rapidly emerging in natural form.[253] Some policy-makers in the United States are particularly blithe about the latter prospect because they correctly recognize that the United States is a likely beneficiary of a regime whose ultimate form results from uninhibited competition. Arguably this has happened already in the case of fisheries, whatever the eventual disposition of the oceans question.[254] If regime-making on a small scale lends itself to general disorder, regime-making on a larger scale risks disorder and, in the minds of many in the global community, injustice as well.

*   *   *   *   *   *

That we have made law and law-making a vocation of our age cannot be doubted. We may become as proficient in making laws into regimes, thus fashioning pockets of order for the denser and more complex nodes of contemporary transnational relations, where order is most needed. Yet little of this aids in rationalizing the profusion of existing rules and claims and integrating emergent phenomena into existing arrangements. Even less does it impose order upon the whole. Our instrumental aptitudes, for all the good they do, bring untoward complications: the very intricacy of our plans make them vulnerable; our solutions to problems expose or even introduce additional, more intractable problems; our labors become Sisyphean; everything we do to control our circumstances defiles our dreams of order. Our solutions exceed our problems in complexity, becoming problems in their own right. Our efforts compound, as do solutions, and problems, in ceaseless, accelerating spirals, conjuring images of an inverted cone spinning and wobbling like a top, a cyclone of human activities and consequences, beyond control. The image of social control in Western thought, emphatically present in Western positivism, has the cone set aright: a central point of authority at the top, lines of control neatly extending downward to a broad supporting base. Efficiency and stability thus converge, and simplicity presides in the proverbial equation of law and order.

The law of requisite variety so well known to cybernetics tells us to expect

---

252.   Weber (fn. 25), ch. IX.
253.   But this need not be an entirely haphazard process. States can choose less conflict and more order by their individual actions even after collective endeavors have ceased. Gary Knight, "Treaty and Non-Treaty Approaches to Order in the World Ocean," in *Perspectives on Ocean Policy* (fn. 28), p. 268.
254.   Young (fn. 238), p. 354.

otherwise. It takes variety to master variety.[255] Simplicity is foreclosed but not forgotten. Instrumental man yearns for a simple, direct way to make order for his troubled planet, a modern, popular, duly constituted version of the oracular law-giver, a legislature.[256]

> This is as strange a maze as e'er men trod,
> And there is in this business more than nature
> Was ever conduct of. Some oracle
> Must rectify our knowledge.
> (William Shakespeare. *The Tempest*, Act V)

Without Prospero's magic, there can be no oracle, and no law-giver can extricate us from mazes of our own devising.

---

255. More "picturesquely": "Only variety can destroy variety." W. Ross Ashby, *An Introduction to Cybernetics* (London: Chapman and Hall; 1956), p. 207. See generally ch. 11.

256. In light of Ashby's law of requisite variety, Anthony D'Amato concludes that "the future of the real world has infinite variety, and therefore can never be controlled in the legislative present by means of a finite number of statutory words." "Towards a Reconciliation of Positivism and Naturalism: A Cybernetic Approach," *Western Ontario Law Review*, Vol. 14, (1975), pp. 191-192.

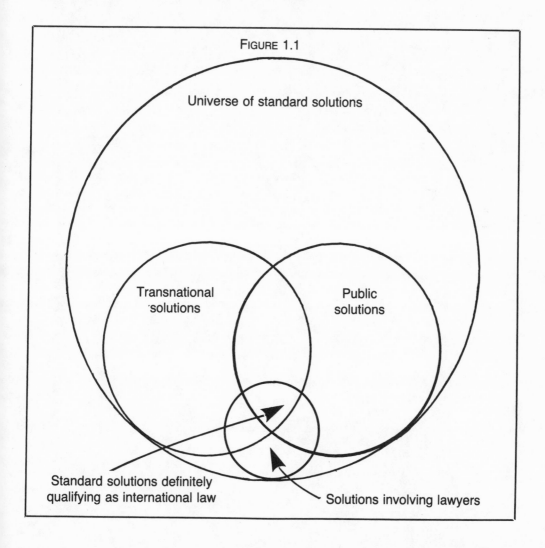

FIGURE 1.1

Universe of standard solutions

Transnational solutions

Public solutions

Standard solutions definitely qualifying as international law

Solutions involving lawyers

What 'Counts' as Law?

Anthony D'Amato

Basic Premises And Building Blocks

The Term Law *in the International Arena*

A reader of jurisprudence might conclude that only philosophers raise the question whether international law may be said to exist or is really law. But in terms of frequency, the question is probably raised more often by governments and states that are not trying to be philosophical. Hitler might have had genuine doubts whether his plans for aggression and territorial aggrandizement were contrary to law, and if told they were contrary to international law he would have felt the same urge to deny the meaning of the term "international law" that other heads of state have felt when purported legal rules stood in the way of their policies. Since Hitler died before the international legal prohibitions against unjustified aggression were actually enforced against individuals at Nuremberg, he may have gone to his death thinking that he had done nothing illegal. But did those legal rules depend upon subsequent "enforcement" before they could claim the title law?[1] In what sense can we divorce law from its subsequent enforcement?

To begin at the most basic level possible, let us consider the categories of possible *words* that can be used to change or modify human behavior. We start with any person who has a choice, who can pick one of two courses of action or who can decide whether to go ahead or not to go ahead with one potential course of action.[2] Certain kinds of words or messages can be communicated to him that might influence his choice. Someone might say, for example, "Plan A would be right but plan B would be immoral." That assertion might be backed up with arguments appealing to all kinds of sources, particularly the would-be actor's, that might give content to the meaning of morality. A second kind of message might be, "If you do A, my friends and I will help you; but if you do B, my friends and I will punish you." This threat of sanction, which may have no moral content, can effectively influence the actor providing that he is persuaded of the likelihood, credibility, and severity of the threat. A third type of message, at first glance quite different from those involving morality or physical sanction, is "If you do A you will be acting legally, but if you do B you will violate the law." Accompanying *this*

---

1. Compare the discussion of the "grudge informer problem" as an example of legal *prediction* of future enforceability in Anthony D'Amato, "The Limits of Legal Realism," *Yale Law Journal*, Vol. 87, No. 2 (January 1978), pp. 506-513.

2. Law is quintessentially a matter of free will. Determinism (as in laws of physics, biology, etc.) is absurd in a legal context (e.g., a person who could not control his actions cannot be judged legally guilty of a crime, in any society). For philosophical expansion of these points, see Anthony Kenny, *Will, Freedom and Power* (Oxford: Blackwell, 1975), and *Freewill and Responsibility* (London: Routledge and Paul, 1978); George H. von Wright, *Norm and Action* (New York: Humanities Press, 1963). But see Onuf's chapter in this volume, the fifth section, under "Law-Making as Law-Doing," for a somewhat different view.

message will be arguments showing that A is indeed legal under the rules of law acknowleged by the actor and B is illegal.[3]

Is the legal message different in kind from the moral message or the sanctions message? Certainly we might postulate a purely imaginary society where the mere invocation of the term *law* is enough to channel all behavior in legal directions. In such a society no one has any intention of violating the law provided information is given as to what courses of action are illegal, and hence there are no violations of law and no enforcement machinery (police, prisons, etc.) Human society probably will never reach such a system, but surely we cannot deny the title "law" to the rules of that system simply because there is no need for enforcement. Nor can we insist that the rules are necessarily rules of morality as we understand the latter term, because my brief description of the imaginary system is complete without reference to the content of their rules. But now, descending to earth and taking human nature as it is, must the legal message have components that are also moral and physically enforceable? Natural-law theorists insist that law is close to morality while positivists insist that it is close to "that which is enforced."[4] How close? How necessarily close? These are questions which would take more space to deal with than is available here. We do not have to ask these particular questions to work out an understanding of the term *international law* for the purposes of this volume. Yet we have some guidelines, at least psychologically if not philosophically, for the interpretation of the legal message in terms of either the moral message or the sanctions message.

If rules of law were consistently at odds with generally understood rules of morality or justice, soon "cognitive dissonance"[5] would intrude to vitiate the influence that the legal message would have upon our conduct. If we live in a system of immoral laws, we will spend our time thinking of ways to act illegally and subvert the system so as to establish a new system where the new laws will be entitled to respect. Surely a system of immoral laws will not last long if there is a psychological dissonance between its rules and those of morality. But now one can argue: what if the immoral laws are strictly and brutally enforced? This brings us to the positivist assertion of the interdependence between law and sanctions. But let us hold for a moment the case of enforcement of *immoral* laws, and consider first the relation between law and sanctions where we do not add the complexity of whether the rules are moral or immoral.

Let us now imagine another strange and purely imaginary society: a dictator has recently taken complete control over the military and police, and he announces that he

---

3.   A fourth type of conduct-influencing message would be an offer of a reward; this is the normal component of economic exchanges. The four types seem to exhaust the range of answers to the question, "Why should I do X?" The answers are: (a) because it's right; (b) because I will punish you if you don't; (c) because it's legal; (d) because I will reward you if you do. The answers can co-exist, but the text departs from writers who insist upon a necessary connection, such as positivists who insist upon a connection between law and punishment (sanctions), or naturalists who insist upon a connection between law and morality.

4.   For a representative naturalist viewpoint, see Lon L. Fuller, *The Morality of Law* (New Haven: Yale University Press, 2nd ed., 1969), pp. 33-94, 152-186; for the positivist view, see H. L. A. Hart, *The Concept of Law* (Oxford: Oxford University Press, 1961); Hans Kelsen, *Pure Theory of Law* (Berkeley: University of California Press, Knight trans., 1967). See also Samuel I. Shuman, *Legal Positivism* (Detroit: Wayne State University Press, 1963). Writers who insist that sanctions constitute the reality of international law include Wolfgang G. Friedmann, *Legal Theory* (New York: Columbia University Press, 5th ed., 1967); Hans Kelsen, *Principles of International Law*, Second Edition prepared by Robert W. Tucker (New York: Holt, Rinehart and Winston, 1966).

5.   See Leon Festinger, *A Theory of Cognitive Dissonance* (Stanford: Stanford University Press, 1957); Anthony A. D'Amato, "Psychological Constructs in Foreign Policy Predictions," *Journal of Conflict Resolution*, Vol. 11, No. 3 (September 1967), pp. 306-309.

will enforce his own wishes whatever they will be and whether or not they are legal. He cares nothing for the legal system as it exists in the country prior to his take-over, and he will neither attempt to change nor enforce it. He then engages in a series of actions, some of which he openly admits are illegal, such as condemning for his own use without paying for it a large house owned by a private citizen and a swimming pool owned by a private corporation. Since he controls the police and the army, private resistance is futile. Perhaps he even enjoys admitting that his actions are illegal, since that gives him a greater sense of power. Now, could we argue that his actions are *not* illegal because he controls the physical power of the state? If so argued, we would be contradicting the express conclusion of both the dictator and all his subjects. We would find ourselves, on the outside of that society, adhering to a definition of legality that is at variance with that of everyone in the society. Quite the contrary, it makes perfect sense to claim that, although the dictator can get away with it because he controls the state's enforcement machinery, his illegal actions are not suddenly made legal because of that control any more than a criminal's theft is made legal because he got away with it. Yet, having said this much, we must also predict that in a short period of time that society will experience a cognitive dissonance between rules of law and morality. Every parent knows that in teaching certain rules to children (such as the rule "Don't play in the street") the rule occasionally must be enforced, so as to make it stick. Otherwise the child will begin to disregard those rules that the parent sees the child violating but does nothing about. Yet it is not necessary that the parents enforce every rule, so long as the rules are clear, obeyable, and subject to enforcement. The authority of the rules will erode if they are not enforced more or less consistently. When the opposite of certain rules are enforced, at first one might conclude that the enforcement is illegal but later one might conclude that it is the opposite of the rules that truly constitute the law. Thus, the dictator's actions at first will be perceived to be illegal; after a period of time people will begin to wonder if they will not be better off it they recognize that the rules that the dictator enforces are those that are truly rules of law and the rules he is apparently violating are only the old rules of the pre-dictator regime.

Applying the preceding example to the case of enforcement of immoral laws, we can now see that if a system of immoral laws is systematically enforced, the people will be caught between two conceptions of law. On the one hand they will be reluctant to recognize the claim that they *ought* to obey the law in a moral sense, but on the other hand they will have to concede that there is no conflict between the asserted rules of law and the enforced rules. Surely this system will persist somewhat longer than one where the laws are simply immoral but there are no sanctions for disobeying them. Yet the seeds of revolution must exist in the system, for the people will resent the enforcement of immoral laws even more than they would resent immoral laws that are not enforced. (Of course, the opposite is possible: the people may begin to *learn* a new standard of morality by virtue of repeated applications of legal rules that are enforced, but we are here dealing only with the assumption that in a given system laws are perceived as immoral and continue to be so perceived.)

Thus, we have some conclusions to draw from the above examples which are not necessarily rigid as a matter of philosophy but rather seem to be dictated by basic psychological observation. A legal system might exist at any moment in time that is totally divorced from moral standards, but it will probably not last long; similarly, it is hard to imagine how it came to exist in the first place since rules of law tend to evolve from moral considerations.[6] Similarly, a legal system might exist at any moment in time

---

6. An immoral regime, however, might be imposed upon a conquered nation.

that is totally divorced from what the state will enforce, but over the longer run an accommodation will set in between what is legal and what is enforced. Yet it is no test of any individual law that it must be enforced to be a law. The international law against unjustified aggression existed in 1939 even though it wasn't going to be enforced until 1946 and even if it hadn't been enforced in 1946. It existed by virtue of the fact that it was contained in the messages Hitler could have received from other subjects of international law at that time. The legal arguments justifying the particular law against international unjustified aggression of course had to be made, and made persuasively, but for present purposes we are assuming that those arguments could have been made. Our preliminary conclusion here is only that if those arguments could have been made, then there was an international legal rule against unjustified aggression in 1939. That rule was not dependent upon its later enforceability. Its status as law was dependent solely upon the assertion and belief by other actors that the rule was in fact a rule of law that was binding upon Hitler and capable of influencing his course of action.[7]

International Law in the Present World Community

The preceding arguments at best have shown only that a communication that a given rule is a rule of international law is prima facie as viable a claim as any other claim that a given rule is a rule of a particular legal system; what remains is the authentication of the given rule and not a dismissal that the claim is erroneous because of considerations having to do with the morality or enforceability of the rule. But even this much may be an important building block toward the construction of international law, since it avoids metaphysical inquiries into the nature of international law or the positivist claims that the content of law depends necessarily upon that which is enforced.

Yet authentication of an alleged rule does depend to some extent upon its congruence with the other two types of messages, those of morality and sanctions, for the simple reason that international law has persisted in roughly its present form through several centuries and hence we are not taking a time-slice of that law at an unrepresentative moment in its history the way we're doing with respect to the imaginary systems considered above. But even with this concession, international law today is undergoing some fundamental changes. Its relation to the normative (moral, *natural law*) realm as well as its relation to the enforcement (sanctions, *positivist*) dimension helps determine its actual content. This is *not* to say that a morally desirable rule is hence a rule of international law, nor to say that what the major powers might enforce (e.g., that only *they* are entitled to have nuclear weapons) is for that reason a rule of international law; such simple correspondences between the desired and the actual are quite alien to my contentions here. Not only are the relationships far more complex, but most importantly we are dealing with an objective realm of law and not with the law as we would like it to be. Any writer of course is tempted to write in his pet contentions to the substance of international law that he purports objectively to describe, and as I have noted elsewhere, the force of one's own contention for what the law ought to be is helped by claiming that such rules of law are objective truths and not mere desiderata.[8] We must try to overcome the temptation to write in our own preferences if we are purporting to describe an

---

7.   The rules of war obviously did act as a deterrent to many German generals and other leaders during the war even if they did not deter Hitler. There were many acquittals and more nonprosecutions at Nuremberg on the ground that the individuals involved did all in their power to comply with the relevant rules of international law. See Burns Weston, Richard A. Falk, and Anthony A. D'Amato, *International Law and World Order* (Minneapolis: West Pub., 1980), pp. 66-68, 76-80.

8.   See Anthony A. D'Amato, *The Concept of Custom in International Law* (Ithaca: Cornell University

objective reality. But nevertheless the previously mentioned relationships of law to the normative and enforcement realms remain and we have to deal with them objectively.

An important beginning has been made in the preceding chapter by Nicholas Onuf. Professor Onuf has set out the basic relationship between international law and the assumed objectivity of the positivist model as appropriately modified by H.L.A. Hart and Gidon Gottlieb. Additionally, he has demonstrated the basic tension in present international law between states as traditional subjects of that law and the rising claims of individuals against foreign states or even their own states. Unquestionably international law is being subjected to a kind of strain that is unprecedented in its history, yet the prognosis is not at all a pessimistic one.

The basic reason for guarded optimism is that respect for international law seems to be going up in a world where the use of military force among states seems to be going down. This simple observation constitutes a deep paradox for positivists, which as we shall see may be a good reason why positivistic theory is quite inadequate in its explanatory power. For if positivism views as necessary a correlation between the efficacy of law and its enforcement, then an increasing diminution in enforcement measures might seem to call for a degradation of the power of law itself. Yet in the nuclear age international law seems to elicit increasing respect. Several explanations ar possible. First, the existence of weapons of mass annihilation may have concomitantly reduced the number of wars but increased the stakes if any war were to break out; thus positivists might claim that international law is more enforceable than ever even if it is less enforced. But this claim would seem to be met by the argument that major powers would hardly resort to the use of nuclear warfare to ensure observance of international law, and hence for this particular purpose ICBM stockpiles are paper tigers. Second, perhaps respect for international law is more importantly connected with the internal stability of most national regimes coupled with increasing literacy on the part of the world population. These factors ensure that people are most sensitive to law in general, and hence their receptivity to international law in particular might be increasing. One might respond, however, to this argument by noting that the factors mentioned here have been around a long time, and thus do not seem to constitute a full explanation for the post-World War II situation. Third, one might contend more frontally that international law in fact is not on the ascendant since the International Court of Justice hardly has any cases they days compared to its predecessor the Permanent Court of International Justice. But this observation would apparently equate the number of international disputes (and hence cases) with the existence of law; surely the fewer the disputes the more we can say that a legal system is truly efficacious. Moreover, the many disputes that exist today are not being resolved, except in rare but highly conspicuous instances, by the force of arms. The disputes *are* being resolved by negotiation and accommodation, with international lawyers playing important roles. Legal arguments are being heard and they are making a difference, even though they are not often heard formally in courts such as the ICJ. Fourth, and lastly, one might account for the increasing role of international law in the world affairs today by claiming that positivists are right after all, except that they have looked for sanctions in the wrong place. Instead of highly visible punitive sanctions, international law today is largely enforced through a spectrum of steps short of acts of warfare. All kinds of harassment might follow upon a nation's violation of an international rule; moreover there will be legal retaliation. (You've broken one rule, we'll break another) or economic retaliation (You've broken a rule, we'll raise tariffs solely against

---

Press, 1971), pp. 218-219, and "International Law—Content and Function: A Review," *Journal of Conflict Resolution*, Vol. 11, No. 4 (December 1967), pp. 505-508.

your country).[9] Let us revert for a moment to the parent establishing a rule for a child; the parent need not spank the child, for many other measures of disapproval are possible. The parent might withdraw some expected reward, or the parent might simply express displeasure, which a well-raised child might find to be as much of a sanction as another child might find physical punishment. But as the notion of sanction becomes attenuated, even conceding that thus it becomes more realistic, it begins to depart from the positivist model. If a parent's mere annoyance that a child has broken a rule constitutes a sufficient sanction in the eyes of the child, we may properly ask whether this is a sanction at all or whether it is merely an inherent attribute of law or authority. Most citizens obeys most laws—even laws that are morally neutral such as obeying a traffic signal—not because they calculate the odds of being caught and penalized but almost reflexively, as if not to do something which the state has rightly said should not be done. Additionally, the notions of legal retaliation and harassment may not themselves be a full explanation for the sanction theory, since many people believe that two wrongs do not make a right. If nation A allegedly violates international law, we do not automatically expect nation B to demonstrate A's violation by in turn doing something illegal. In other words, we do not wait for B's sanction to determine whether A has violated the law. Rather, we simply expect B to respond that A has violated the law—and it doesn't even matter that B in fact does make such a response. The expectation of such a response undoubtedly deters many nations in A's position from violating the law in the first instance.

If we can conclude that an objective reality called international law is increasingly important as a factor in helping to modify conduct in the world community—or, what amounts to the same thing, to structure the range of possible alternatives so that only some courses of action appear reasonable and legal—we must next turn to the substance of the relationship between international law and the naturalist and positivist theories that are so important in determining its content. In the preceding chapter Professor Onuf considered these relations largely from a historical viewpoint. Within that general context, let us look at the relationships analytically.

The Opposing Viewpoints of Positivism and Naturalism

I want to argue in this section that positivism and naturalism represent fundamentally opposing epistemologies; and in the next section I will contend that international law today reflects, and necessarily absorbs, the naturalist position.

Although historically it might appear that positivism was a nineteenth century Benthamite-Austinian movement in jurisprudence, in fact a positivist perspective is implicit in the writings of Plato and St. Augustine and even to some extent in the writings of the "father of natural law" St. Thomas Aquinas.[10] Positivism is more than an insistence upon the importance of sanctions as suggested earlier in this chapter; it is more than the "command" theory of law of John Austin or subsequent refinements as outlined by Professor Onuf in the preceding chapter. Rather, at the essence of positivism is a world outlook that might be described as existential—a denial of imminent purposive-

---

9.   The U. S. freeze on all Iranian assets was a direct punitive step following upon the clearly illegal taking of hostages in the U. S. Embassy in Teheran. It was phrased in terms of securing claims on Iran by the United States and its citizens. See White House Press Release, *Department of State Bulletin,* Vol. 79, No. 2033 (December 1979), p. 50. For an analysis of Iran's primary obligation, see Richard Falk, "The Iran Hostage Crisis: Easy Answers and Hard Questions," *American Journal of International Law,* Vol. 74, No. 2 (April 1980), pp. 411-417.

10.   See Plato, *The Laws;* Augustine, *The City of God;* Aquinas, *Summa Theologica,* Questions 90-92, 95-96 (1a-2ae).

ness, an emphasis on the present fact of existence no matter how absurd those facts might seem to be. A legal positivist believes that a rule is or is not a rule of law, and if it is a rule of law, then what it commands, however absurdly, gives rise to a legal obligation. Lon L. Fuller once suggested an example that indicates this point clearly: a statute is enacted which contains the word *not* preceding its operative paragraph, rendering the entire statute meaningless or exceptionally misleading and frustrating to anyone purporting to divine its command.[11] A court believing in naturalism might take the position that the word *not* was included by error either when the bill was read before the legislature or later when it was printed in the public code, and thus strike out the word. But a positivist court could not do so, no matter how absurd the consequences, because a positivist court would investigate only whether the statute was validly enacted.[12] If valid, it must be enforced as written; only the legislature can later "remedy the mischief" if mischief there be. Positivism does not require a court or an interpretive body to make sense out of law, but merely to apply it as enacted. Nor does positivism place any requirement upon the legislature; the latter may enact anything into law provided it is in fact the legislature validly engaged in enacting rules. A legislature may enact nonsensical, or impossible, or retroactive laws; it may enact some laws but keep their contents secret from the public; it has total license to command, and a court is required to apply its commands as dictated by the *words* of the statute and not any extrinsic test of meaning. Positivism, in short, is a special kind of theory of meaning; it takes the denotations of words and asks for strict application. It treats legal rules as it would treat electronic commands fed into a computer. The computer must obey the commands exactly, with no attempt to omit a word such as *not* or to change the meaning of any words. (Of course, a computer may be programmed to correct for certain errors; but it is nevertheless commanded to obey the program without correcting the program for errors. In other words, the computer is not human.)[13]

An entirely different view of the world is suggested in the teleological philosophy of Aristotle, taken up in the bulk of the writings of St. Thomas and fed decisively into international law by Pufendorf and Grotius. This nonexistential view of law is that the law must make sense as applied to human behavior. A rule of law is something that is enacted by humans in order to fulfill certain human purposes. The purposes, or ends, are really what is important; the law is merely a means to their attainment. Hence a statute that obviously contains a mistake can be corrected by a court. A law that commands people to do the impossible, or that is self-contradictory, or that is deliberately kept secret from those to whom it is purportedly addressed, is not entitled to be interpreted as law by any body, such as a court, that is charged with applying it. A naturalist does not equate courts with computers; he does not strive for realization of the *words* of the law at the expense of its purpose to regulate and order the relationships among people. A naturalist is a peculiarly human interpreter of law; he assumes that the law does not exist

---

11. Lon L. Fuller, "The Case of the Speluncean Explorers," *Harvard Law Review*, Vol. 64, No.2 (February 1949), p. 624.

12. Of course positivist writers will either (a) minimize such examples, or (b) concede that courts "obviously" may correct such errors. But the point is that the positivist writers *lack a theory* to account for the *why* and the *when* of any such corrections. Cf. Anthony D'Amato, "Towards a Reconciliation of Positivism and Naturalism: A Cybernetic Approach to a Problem of Jurisprudence," *Western Ontario Law Review*, Vol. 14 (1975), pp. 186-188.

13. I do not intend to denigrate positivism by this analogy to a computer. In fact, a computer is capable of rendering *exact egalitarian* justice, uninfluenced by the wealth, social prominence, or courtroom demeanor of the litigants. See Anthony D'Amato, "Can/Should Computers Replace Judges?" *Georgia Law Review*, Vol. 11, No. 5 (September 1977), pp. 1277-1301.

for itself but rather is a means toward the attainment of human ends. A naturalist must deny the strictly causal theories of some scientists who assert that only material events can precede other highly correlated material events. As Professor Taylor has shown, a teleologist (or for our purposes, a naturalist) necessarily assumes that a future event (an end) influences in the present a line of conduct.[14] This can only happen for thinking beings who have a vision of an end they want to reach and who use that vision to shape their interpretation of various means that are presented to them. Thus, purposiveness becomes a part of law-interpretation and hence of law-content. The existentialist-positivist, on the other hand, adopts a strictly material causal philosophy, insisting that rules of law be interpreted only according to the present denotative meanings of the words in those rules irrespective of consequences.

Reduced to their essentials, positivism and naturalism thus proceed from two contradictory views of the world: men as machines acting out what could be an absurd drama, and men as teleological beings concerned with future consequences of alternative courses of conduct. While the notion of men as machines may today sound pejorative, in fact for the past three hundred years this picture has been the dominant philosophy in legal circles due to a certain intrinsic attractiveness that it possesses over the naturalist view. One aspect of this attraction is the certainty and efficiency of the positivist view: why allow a court to second guess a legislature when the result may be more "common law confusion" of that type that Bentham excoriated?[15] Another aspect is the apparent scientific quality of positivism: here, at last, is a pure science which, according to Kelsen and other enthusiasts, could finally be made objective.[16] Recent years have seen many positivist theorists trying to account for the loose ends in the framework of scientific positivism; though reality seemed elusive, they hoped that by further refining positivist theory all the disconcerting facts of law as actually applied by human beings might be brought within the positivist framework. A final aspect of the attraction of positivist theory is that it promised to divorce any commentator's own views of what the law should be from his description of the law that is. Here, at least, is an important and significant endeavor, but perhaps one need not embrace positivism to ensure its fulfillment. By exercising great care—more than a positivist writer need exercise—a naturalist-oriented writer can still divorce his own predilections from his description of the law that exists, even though his description of the objective existing law necessarily includes purposive-oriented standards of the law that ought to be.

Historically, positivism certainly corrected the common law excesses of naturalism as ridiculed by Bentham.[17] In this sense it was and has been a healthy corrective. But I want to argue next that present-day international law reflects the naturalist and not the positivist perspective, and that this reflection has great substantive significance.

Natural Law and International Law

The notion of teleology in naturalism is more than an empty formality to the effect that perceived future purposes can guide present actions. The historical development of

---

14.   Charles Taylor, *The Explanation of Behaviour* (New York: Humanities Press, 1964), pp. 5-17.

15.   Jeremy Bentham, *Of Laws in General* (London: Athlone Press, H. L. A. Hart ed., 1970), pp. 184-195.

16.   Kelsen (fn.4), pp. 70-76.

17.   See H. L. A. Hart, "Positivism and the Separation of Law and Morals," *Harvard Law Review*, Vol. 71, No. 4 (February 1958), pp. 595-599.

natural law contributes the essential substantive fact that human purpose is everywhere pretty much the same, that people strive for (roughly) the same basic values, and that the meanings we can attribute to norms of international law make sense in the same sort of way to widely divergent peoples in developed and developing nations alike. Were it not for the essential sameness of human nature, so insisted upon by St. Thomas and assumed in the writings of Myres McDougal and his associates,[18] natural law would be deflated into existentialism, with a person becoming a purposeless being in a world that may be absurd. Natural law is a non-arbitrary set of human standards that retains its meaning for all people at all times in all places. Its claim is, for this reason, arrogant; but the opposite claim sells humanity short.

The increasing assertion of human rights against the depredations of governments is an example of substantive natural law in the international legal arena.[19] Natural law combines two great substantive principles: the goal of survival of the human species, and justice to individuals. Any artificial entity, such as a state, that stands in the way of the attainment of these principles is contrary to natural law (as the greatest philosopher of the state as an entity—Hegel—fully realized in his strictures against natural law). The relation of the state to the naturalist needs of the world community will be more fully considered in the next part of this chapter.

It is instructive to note that anyone's list of basic human rights is invariably universal in its claim. Equality under the law or freedom of speech or the rights of women, for example, are not claimed for a particular region or a collection of states in a certain economic classification; rather, these and other human rights are asserted to apply to all people wherever situated. The push toward universality in such claims is a natural concomitant of the naturalist perspective. If law itself does not mean arbitrarily different things in different places, under naturalist theory, then certainly rights and freedoms should also be grounded in universality.

St. Thomas talked about "right reason" as the meaning to be given to natural law.[20] His scope was global; by "right" he did not mean "right only in the context of Western Europe during the Middle Ages." And "reason" was not the exclusive province of Churchmen (no wonder that true natural law was a subversive doctrine insofar as the Catholic Church was concerned, the Church after St. Thomas emphasizing the primacy of "Divine Law" and canon law over the dictates of right reason). The tendency toward universality is probably inherent in any contemplation of the right as distinct from the expedient course of action for any person to take. If something is right, it is right in all similar contexts whatever the time or place. Surely killing another person for private gain is wrong throughout the world; regardless of the wide variances in cultures, we can still recognize murder when we see it, and we can distinguish it even from tribal sacrificial rites or state executions of criminals or self-defense. But what about abortion? Is that murder? Didn't St. Thomas so hold? Doesn't the abortion example prove the non-universality of so-called natural law? What if the right to abortion were to appear on a United Nations list of basic human rights?

We must relate abortion, as any other substantive claim, to the two fundamental natural law principles: perpetuation of the species and justice to the individual. In St.

---

18.   Aquinas (fn. 10), Questions 94 art 4 (la-2ae) ("truth or rectitude is the same for all, and is equally known by all"); Myres S. McDougal and Associates, *Studies in World Public Order* (New Haven: Yale University Press, 1960), pp. 31-36. For a critique, see D'Amato, *The Concept of Custom in International Law* (fn. 8), pp. 218-219.

19.   See Anthony D'Amato, "Are Human Rights Good for International Business?" *Northwestern Journal of International Law and Business,* Vol. 1, (Spring 1979), p. 22.

20.   Aquinas (fn. 10), Question 94.

Thomas' time, there was a perceived threat of underpopulation to the future of the human race. Indeed, seventy-five years after his death, the plague decimated Europe. In that context, abortion was a crime against the future survival of the human race. Today, perceptions are quite the opposite: the threat to human survival is more a matter of overpopulation than underpopulation. Far from being a threat to human survival, abortion today may be an aid to the future of human life on this planet. But we can well imagine a future where nuclear devastation has left few survivors, and in such a context abortion again might be linked to future survivability and hence be prohibited by "right reason."

But medieval strictures against abortion have had an important psychological effect, which today is manifested in the feeling of the sacredness of human life. This feeling too is very important to the survival of the species. Much of this feeling is manifested by the anti-abortionists, and even those who disagree with their position must concede that the anti-abortionists are not acting out of selfish or hedonistic motives but rather are articulating a basic feeling of the sacredness of life that might tend to be downgraded in an overpopulated world. (Studies of animal overpopulation invariably show behavior that becomes predicated on the pervasive assumption that life is cheap and reproduction is unnecessary.) Thus a U.N. right-to-abortion plank might be counter-productive in downgrading the sacredness of life at the same time that it would be productive in asserting the rights of women and helping to reduce global overpopulation. We can only conclude that the abortion issue is necessarily complex, but certainly does not destroy the universality of the claim that what is paramount is the survival of the species.

Focusing upon species survival also brings out the relevance of environmental protection in the international law context. Persons or governments have no right to destroy the life sustaining environment or permanently deplete it of, for example, an animal or plant species; such actions endanger the future survivability of the human race. Often in the short-term, even if measured by the life span of an individual, environment-depleting actions can be economically profitable (even to the point that it would not pay others to deter such actions.) Only natural law—and the effect it is having upon substantive international law—may stand as a realistic deterrent to such actions.[21]

Professor Falk has well described the fundamental disparities among peoples today and the challenges faced by the world community.[22] There is an extremely unequal distribution of wealth. Nuclear armaments are stockpiled that can destroy all life forms forever. The world is overpopulated and many are starving to death. Our natural environment is being poisoned and resources necessary to organic life are wantonly exploited. And superimposed upon all these problems is the nation-state system, where governments pursue narrowly defined bureaucratic values often at the expense of the people. Such governments can no longer be changed by the threat of war, for nuclear war against any major government will equally destroy victor and vanquished. All that is left is law and, perhaps, right reason. But international law as we know it is largely state dominated. Its subject-creators traditionally have been nations, not persons. And while we are seeing a transition from states as exclusive subjects of international law to people increasingly obtaining international legal rights, described by Professor Onuf in the preceding chapter, we still are faced with the problem that traditional international law might be unable to meet world needs because it assumes subject entities that are nations and not persons.

---

21.   The survival of animal species may have natural-law implications. St. Francis of Assisi attempted to expand the Catholic Church's concept of natural law to include animal rights, but was met with hostility and isolation by the Church establishment which did not want natural law deanthropocentricized.

22.   See Richard A. Ralk, *This Endangered Planet* (New York: Random House, 1971).

Nations as Subject-Creators of International Law: The Basic Context

International law suggests a system of laws between and among nations; in this classic view, states are the creator-subjects of that legal system. But there are other logical possibilities. Mankind might have refused to recognize all artificial entities; international law could have meant, simply, the law governing transactions among individuals across national frontiers (the nations, in this case, not constituting separate legal entities but merely names for aggregations of individuals in geographic areas). Present international law seems to be on the road to recognizing individual actions as part of international adjudication in limited areas such as the European Court of Human Rights. Another possibility would be to recognize artificial international entities other than states—multinational corporations and intergovernmental organizations, for example. A more revolutionary approach would be the extreme form of functionalism described by David Mitrany[23] where all governmental functions are performed by international agencies and bureaucracies, that presumably then would be the sole subjects of international law. The above possibilities are generally conceived at the substate level, but other possible forms of international legal interaction could occur supranationally: regionalism (a region might include states *and* parts of states) and world organizations, both of which could impose law downward upon states and people. As Professor Onuf has remarked in the first chapter, the present system is dominated by the relations of states even though writers disagree about how significant an inroad has been made by other forms.

How do these various forms relate to the overwhelming problems confronting mankind today: environmental degradation and the threat of total nuclear war? How do they relate to other problems that may not involve destruction of the human species but just as seriously affect the meaning of life: human freedoms and rights, relief from overpopulation, freedom from hunger and severe poverty? A natural law perspective would hold that a rational relation between the forms of the legal system and the basic needs of mankind is more than a desideratum; it is a necessity. Yet two enormous tasks impend: First, we must attempt to solve the theoretical problem of determining *what* forms, in detail, are most rationally related to the solution of these problems; second, people and their governments must be persuaded to operationalize these forms. No matter how hopeless or utopian this second task of persuasion might seem, we cannot even undertake it without first solving the theoretical problem.

The remaining chapters in this book are addressed to aspects of the various forms, present and emerging, that constitute the international legal system. My task in the rest of this chapter involves a partial examination of the first and most traditional form of international law, that involving states as subject-creators. I will be concerned primarily with mechanisms of law-creation among states, but some preliminary consideration might usefully be given here to the concept of state in political philosophy and its potential relevance to the basic challenges to human survival on this small planet.

Four possible notions of a state are as follows:

(1) A state is nothing at all; it is a mere word giving a name to all the people within a defined geographic area.
(2) A state is an entity independent of the people within it; it is a force in itself; it is a right in Hegel's sense.

---

23. See David Mitrany, *A Working Peace System* (Chicago: Quadrangle Books, 1966), pp. 157-166.

(3) A state represents more than people in a geographic area, because it represents the human species—dead people (tradition in Burke's sense), living people, and potential people.

(4) A state represents not only past, present, and future persons, but also a symbiotic tie between these people and the land they live on (exemplified in the writings of, among others, Mazzini). Under this view, people living in one state would become different people if they migrated to a different state.

The first possibility might be labelled as liberal in today's terms, the second reactionary. Perhaps without states we would not be in a position today to fear thermonuclear destruction. On the other hand, if nuclear weapons were invented in a nationless world, certain individuals might obtain a monopoly and terrorize everyone else. In short, we must not confuse theories of how mankind got into its present predicament with rational solutions for getting out of it. Now that nuclear weapons *are* stockpiled that can destroy all life and continue to "make the rubble bounce," are they best controlled by a state system or by some other kind of system? Perhaps a state in the third sense given above might have a collective rationality greater than that of individuals. An individual, after all, could believe in taking the world down with him—*après moi, le déluge.* But a number of governmental officials, some of whom have families, might not think the same way. Perhaps there is conservatism in collectivity. Similarly, with respect to environmental degradation, it is not at all clear that governments will act less responsibly than other entities, including persons or multinational corporations or regional associations. There is cause for great despair at the lack of progress among governments in stemming the destruction of species such as whales, in reversing global air pollution or destruction of the stratospheric ozone layer, or in checking the population explosion; yet would other forms of legal organization behave any better; and if there are any, how are they better? These questions are not rhetorical; obviously much thought has to be addressed to them in the years ahead.

My limited task here is to show that some degree of rationality, at least, results from the fact that international law is not created out of the whims of individual states (their policies, their unilateral declarations, their claims) but rather is created out of interstate relations. Since states try to survive, and since their survival is predicated on some minimal degree of order, their interactions—forming universal customary law—will normally be rational in the natural law sense of being purposive.

My discussion will be in terms of a referent—that of a logical validator of what assertions "count" as rules of the system. This attempt to search for a mechanism is prompted by a natural law perspective, for the mechanism presumes that states do not act arbitrarily and that their interactions reflect a consensus about mutually desirable rules. To say this much is not to assert that the present international system is capable of solving the problems of environmental degradation and thermonuclear destruction but rather simply to examine what the capabilities might be in a formal sense. Let us, therefore, turn to an examination of the mechanism for generating interstate rules.

THE RELATION OF RULES TO STATES

International law is more than a communication that affects state behavior. It also defines international reality. The law tells states when they are injured; states feel no pain and hence have to be told when they are hurt. The law also tells states what appropriate responses may be made to such injuries. Law defines the scope of a nation's legitimate interests—its entitlements. A nation may want many things that it is not entitled to have—e.g., to import inexpensive oil, to have exclusive fishing rights to the Atlantic Ocean, to add to its territory at the expense of neighboring nations. But only its entitlements as defined by international law constitute claims which, if not recognized by other states, tend reciprocally to adversely affect the entitlements of those other states. Finally, international law erects a structural perspective for interpreting international claim conflicts.

The competing interests of states inevitably clash in the international arena. International law in the first instance serves as a sort of signal to tell states which of these clashes are acceptable and which are deserving of retaliation. A mental experiment may help illustrate this function of law. State A is wealthier and militarily more powerful than its neighbor state B. If both states need to import oil but state A consistently outbids state B for the oil so that most of the short supply goes to A and not B, state B normally would have no justifiable complaint against A and would not attempt any retaliatory measures outside of possible economic retaliation. If state B were to commit a hostile act against A—e.g., imprisoning 100 of state A's nationals resident in B until state A lowers its bid price for the oil—we can well imagine that A's reaction would *not* be to lower its bid price but rather, perhaps, to imprison 120 of state B's nationals resident in A. In short, B has reacted inappropriately to A's economic aggression by an illegal act; A's economic aggression was not illegal but B's act of imprisonment was illegal and was perceived to be illegal by A which retaliated in kind. If B were then to retaliate again by an even greater illegality, B could only expect another round of retaliation in kind. This no-win strategy is probably why we would not ordinarily expect B to engage in an illegal retaliation for A's legal initial action.

Now let us change the situation by supposing that A, having cornered the supply of oil, decides to drop some bombs on B's few domestic oilfields. The bombing is clearly an illegal act that would engender retaliation by B. Even though A is militarily the more powerful state, it would probably refrain from committing such an overt unprovoked act against B. The sheer illegality of the act would undoubtedly transform B into a tougher opponent than B was on paper, for B would feel justified in fighting back, her citizens aroused, whereas A's citizens might be reluctant to fight very hard in such an unjustified cause. Of course, actual wars are never so simple, and nations can fight for what seem in retrospect to be unjustified causes. But I am trying to show why a great many potential wars never get fought. They do not arise because most nations do not initiate illegal aggressions upon weaker neighbors.

A final point needs to be made about this thought experiment. A's initial cornering of the oil supply might have had extremely deleterious consequences for B; perhaps many more citizens of B starved to death due to the lack of oil to power farm machinery than the 120 citizens that might be hurt if B started a chain of retaliation. Yet the amount of real suffering visited upon a nation is no test of legality. In the present world at the present time, international law tells us that it is legal for one nation to outbid another in the international oil market, but is it is illegal for one nation to imprison the nationals of another nation without legal cause. State B may feel much more pain from a legal economic attack than from an illegal physical attack, yet the law tells B that the legal pain is not a pain at all but the illegal physical injury, however slight, is justification for retaliation or resort to third-party intervention.

What underlies this strange set of legal injuries that states experience? We should examine the fundamental structural assumptions of the international legal system. Perhaps one of the best ways to get a perspective of that system is to take some of the central assumptions of international law and imagine what the world would be like without them. If successful, this exercise in imagination will do more than give us an analytical perspective. It will help narrow the class of purported international norms that cannot become rules of law because they do not share the basic characteristics of international law as we have come to know it.

One of the most basic and deep-rooted postulates of international law is that of the sovereign equality of nations. Suppose, instead, that international law had evolved differently. Suppose the law reflected accurately the differences in the armed might of the various nations. The law would give more rights and privileges to the stronger nation, and fewer to the weaker nation. The United States and the Soviet Union might have, say, an exclusive fisheries coastal zone of 200 miles, Canada 100 miles, Chile and Mexico 50 miles each, and Costa Rica 25 miles. Of course this result seems strange, but its strangeness is because we are all conditioned to accept the notion of legal equality. In particular, the most powerful states naturally assume in negotiations such as the Law of the Sea Conferences that whatever the breadth of contiguous zones may be adopted, the breadth will be the same for all coastal states. In this, among many ways, the notion of equality of states under international law is a powerful force operating to the advantage of weaker states. When newly emerging and third-world states claim that international law was invented by European powers for their own interests and that norms of international law can be freely accepted or rejected by the new nations, they are essentially taking a doctrinal position for bargaining purposes that they might reject if they stood the chance of losing all the benefits of international law.

Another basic characteristic of international law is that any rule in the system must prohibit at least certain kinds of actions. A rule of law means that the actor must refrain from doing something that he otherwise might have been inclined to do. Sometimes writers cast their nets so broadly as to include within international law everything that states do; the result is to find law everywhere, but at the great loss of making it impossible for any state to violate the law. This supererogatory result is sometimes found in the writings of Professor McDougal and his associates when the claim appears to be made that if certain states share the proper values and act with the proper motives, everything they do is legal.[24] On the opposite extreme, some writers claim that the laws of warfare are not true laws of international law because they seem to have little if any power in fact to prohibit the actor from doing what he wants to do in a wartime situation.[25] But this view is probably erroneous both from a factual and a theoretical perspective. Factually, the laws of war like any other laws indicate what initiatives are legal and hence subject to legal retaliation, and what initiatives are illegal and hence open up extreme, impassioned, and sometimes unrestrained retaliation. Even in the bitterest wars there are hundreds if not thousands of understood reciprocal restraints in small and large matters affecting both sides. These restraints are keyed around perceived legalities and illegalities of the conduct of warfare. Of course, the restraints sometimes break down, but even in domestic law not all laws are always enforced by prosecutors, and certainly all laws are not always obeyed (the rising crime rate does not mean that criminal laws are losing their status as legal prohibitions).[26] And from a theoretical standpoint, positivists in the Austinian tradition, particularly Kelsen, have insisted upon finding

---

24. See, e.g., McDougal (fn. 18), pp. 170, 887, 954, 1006-07. For a critique of McDougal's argument on U.S. atomic testing, see D'Amato, *The Concept of Custom in International Law* (fn. 8), pp. 215-219.

25. See P. E. Corbett, *Law and Society in the Relations of States* (New York: Harcourt, Brace, 1951), pp. 32-35, 210-213; cf. Julius Stone, *Legal Controls of International Conflict* (New York: Rinehart, 2nd ed., 1959), pp. 349-351.

26. See Abram Chayes, *The Cuban Missile Crisis* (New York: Oxford University Press, 1974), pp. 25-26.

some sanction behind all laws. These writers find it particularly difficult to deal with the laws of war because in a war there is a breakdown of an authorative sanction-source to enforce laws.[27] What these writers seemed to have failed to appreciate is the consequence of viewing law as a set of words. The words of law that specify primary delicts are not unlike the words of law that command those who would enforce the law. A prosecutor in domestic law can violate the law that commands him to prosecute murderers just as the murderer can violate the primary law against homicide. But if the prosecutor decides not to prosecute—even if he announces that he will no longer prosecute any criminal matters—we do not say that there are no longer any primary laws against crime. A crime is still a crime; someday some official might attach a penalty to it. Similarly, in wartime, the failure, no matter how widespread, to enforce certain laws of warfare does not mean that these laws have vanished. Their violation is always potentially capable of being penalized—after the war, or as retaliation during the war. What is significant is that the law has characterized the event, and in thus characterizing it, has said that a future sanction could legally be applied to it. This is all that law, as a set of words, can ever do. What actually happens as a consequence of the violation of legal norms is by and large a matter of post-legal behavior.[28]

An important consequence of the view that international law minimally prohibits certain classes of actions is that we should view critically any claim that unilateral declarations of law are per se evidence of what the law is.[29] A nation may claim anything; it may make a claim for something that is patently illegal just to see whether other nations will let it get away with the claim. Similarly, an attorney general's opinion is not evidence of the content of international law, nor is a nation's pleadings in an international dispute (obviously there are two sides to a dispute and both cannot be right). The tendency of some writers to amass claims of all sorts—often those made in an international forum such as the United Nations—and use these as evidence of international law can paint a misleading picture of the content of international law. Indeed, it is probably not too great an exaggeration to say that most statements by nations (including their diplomatic speeches and writings, foreign office correspondence, attorney general opinions, writings of their own establishment of international legal scholars, and public mass-media speeches) are carefully contrived for the purpose of eliciting advantage in the vast process of international negotiation, and are not—even though many purport to be—restatements of international law. If anything an interested party says is evidence of law, then international law in total would hardly prohibit any actions at all. There would be no point in calling it law.

Finally, let us consider a third basic postulate of international law: the unidimensionality of rules. It is characteristic of rules that, where they apply, they apply completely and fully to that and to similar factual situations. Rules do not arbitrarily apply sometimes to the same factual situations; nor do they require a mere attempt at compliance or give the affected state discretion whether or not to obey them. Conceivably we could have had

---

27. See Kelsen-Tucker (fn. 4). See also D'Amato, "International Law—Content and Function," (fn. 8), pp. 507-509.

28. Of course, subsequent conduct cannot be irrelevant. If subsequent conduct contradicts the norms of law, then we may have been mistaken in our choice of norms. To see how postvalidation may work in a hypothetical example, see D'Amato (fn. 1), pp. 475-477.

29. Contrast Erik Suy, *Les actes juridiques unilatéraux en droit international public* (Paris: Pichon, 1962), with the more careful study by Alfred P. Rubin, "The International Legal Effects of Unilateral Declarations," *American Journal of International Law*, Vol. 71, No. 1 (January 1977), pp. 1-30.

other dimensions to rules, giving them the character of weights which may or may not be taken into account. To some extent, the notion of "principles of law" as formulated by Ronald Dworkin[30] and as reflected in Article 38 of the Statute of the International Court of Justice[31] applies as a weight to be added into the balance in international decision-making. But rules or norms of law must be sharply distinguished from principles. As to rules or norms, the only important question is whether or not they are rules of the system of international law. Of course, we may have so called emerging rules of the system whose status is uncertain. But as to the latter, the debate is whether the rule has or has not arrived; significantly, the debate never is addressed to a compromise position that would accord to the rule a half-status between law and non-law. We would not know what to do with a rule in this grey area. Nations want to know whether or not they are currently bound by an alleged rule of international law. The line between law and non-law is crucially significant in international law. Our task, then, is to try to specify how the line is to be drawn. Of all the alleged rules and norms that on their face *could* be rules of international law, how do we select the smaller set of rules that actually are rules of that system?

An Objective Validator of International Law

Prior to the nineteenth century it hardly occurred to anyone to desire an objective test for determining what was the law and what was not the law. The law—whether municipal or international—was rooted in immemorial custom, in natural law, in eternal principles, and in reason. If there was a dispute, a judge would decide the question, his decision contributing to the clarity of the law in its restatement of what everyone should have known anyway. But legislative reform gave the impetus to a rethinking of validating procedures for the law. Bentham's desire to change the content of the common law through legislation led him naturally to question the authenticity of the common law.[32] Austin, who did not share Bentham's antipathy to the common law, nevertheless theorized that the common law owed its efficacy only to its being adopted by the sovereign.[33] Breaking from the centuries-old tradition that the law was binding on everyone, Austin, doing for law what Bodin and Hobbes had done for political philosophy, posited a sovereign who was above the law and under whom law existed through his sufferance. The sovereign became the objective validator of all law; what he commanded, or allowed, was law; nothing was law that was contrary to his commands. Finding his view of law inapplicable to the international arena because of the difficulty of locating a sovereign there, Austin redefined international law as not being law but mere "positive morality."[34]

But the simple mechanism of a sovereign being the objective validator of law even in domestic systems increasingly was shown to be deficient. First, laws that defined and accounted for the succession of sovereigns could not themselves be sovereign commands.

---

30.   Ronald Dworkin, *Taking Rights Seriously* (Cambridge, Mass.: Harvard University Press, 1977), pp. 22-31.

31.   Statute of the International Court of Justice, Art. 38 (1) (c).

32.   Bentham (fn. 15), pp. 152-155, 184-195.

33.   John Austin, *The Province of Jurisprudence Determined* and *The Uses of the Study of Jurisprudence*, with an Introduction by H. L. A. Hart (London: Weidenfeld and Nicolson, 1954), pp. 30-33.

34.   Ibid., pp. 140-142. Consistently (and revealingly) Austin thought of constitutional law as also "positive morality" and not truly "law" because, like international law, he felt that constitutional law could not limit the sovereign.

Second, in some systems it became very hard to locate the sovereign at all. Attempting to cope with this latter difficulty, Hart has posited the idea of the sovereignty of a "rule of recognition."[35] But I think that Hart's solution will eventually fail for the same reasons as Austin's. In the first place, Hart cannot account for changes in the rule of recognition or in its replacement by a successor rule. Secondly, in some systems the rule is fairly clear (as in states with a written constitution) but in some it seems so diffuse and so rooted in common law and custom that the rule is too broad to be helpful in its avowed purpose as serving as an objective validator.[36]

If Hart's conceptualization eventually fails for the latter reason, he nevertheless has forcefully reminded us of the necessity for finding secondary rules in a legal system that account for the creation and change of the primary rules. This is no less important internationally than domestically. The set of international secondary rules that one might—if one feels the need—call the international rule of recognition has usually been discussed under the misleading term *sources of law.* The sources of international law do not form a closed set; there is nothing to prevent the community of nations from someday recognizing a new authoritative source. The open-endedness of the possible sources or validators of international law does not make it any the less law than Godel's proof of the open-endedness of any mathematical system of an order of complexity that would include the real numbers has made mathematics any the less mathematical.

Consensus.   One alleged validator of international rules is the consensus of states. We have come to know the term *consensus* as denoting that situation where a rule or policy is proposed and no one actively opposes it. Some may abstain from voting or may not be willing to endorse the group decision, but a consensus may still obtain. But consensus is not the same as a majority vote. There is no international mechanism for creating rules by majority of states through some sort of legislative process. For example, a resolution directed against South Africa in the General Assembly of the United Nations, and actively opposed by South Africa, is not in itself a rule of law by virtue of the consensus of states.[37] Of course, the resolution might reflect already existing law, but then it would be the existing law and not the resolution that counts. As much as nations might want to transform General Assembly resolutions into law, we must acknowledge at this state of world law that one actively opposed dissenter is enough to destroy the consensus. The General Assembly may, in Professor Falk's term, have *quasi-legislative* competence, but this is not the same as legislative competence[38]

Nearly all rules of international law at present enjoy the status of law by virtue of the consensus of states over time. We tend to regard the settled rules of international law as those rules that are not actively opposed by a state or group of states. Sometimes the consensus has not been derived by reference to the specific rule itself but to the other kinds of validators (such as custom) which themselves are a product of the consensus of states. But consensus is not a very useful mechanism for introducing new laws directly because adversely affected states can actively oppose such rules.[39] Proposed rules that

---

35.   Hart (fn. 4), pp. 49-76.

36.   Cf. Fuller (fn. 4), pp. 133-145; Anthony A. D'Amato, "The Neo-Positivist Concept of International Law," *American Journal of International Law,* Vol. 59, No. 2 (April 1965), pp. 321-324.

37.   I have spelled this argument out elsewhere. See D'Amato, "On Consensus," *Canadian Yearbook of International Law,* Vol 8 (1970), pp. 104- 122.

38.   Falk, "On the Quasi-Legislative Competence of the General Assembly," *American Journal of International Law,* Vol. 60, No. 4 (October 1966), pp. 782-791.

39.   I did not mean to suggest, as Onuf infers in his essay in this book, that consensus *replaces* custom, in D'Amato, *The Concept of Custom in International Law* (fn. 8), pp. 41-42. Less felicitous was a sentence I wrote in the *Canadian Yearbook of International Law* that consensus is "merely a definition of what we mean by

adversely affect the important interests of states will not be adopted by the international community through any sort of consensus mechanism. On the other hand, clarificatory rules and those which progressively develop the content of international law are becoming incorporated into the body of international norms through the slow and patient work of groups such as the International Law Commission. By soliciting comments from states, these international groups engaged in progressive development of the law often achieve consensus on a large number of proposed restatements of the law by virtue of the states not objecting to the reformulations.

Clearly the most important function of consensus is in its validation of the other validators. The secondary rules relating to custom, treaty, decisions of courts, and so forth, are the product of the consensus of nations and hence are the most significant means for changing old norms and creating new ones.

Custom. The workability of custom as a validator of international rules stems primarily from a nation's actions being far more conservative than its claims, desires, threats, responses, and wishes. A nation might desire exclusive fishing rights to the Atlantic Ocean; it might make a claim to a large area of that ocean; it might even issue a legal opinion that it owns the fish in the ocean. But these wishes are not translated into reality; the nation does not attempt to bar all other fishing vessels from the Atlantic Ocean. Hence it was early perceived that a nation's actions in the international arena are a far better guide to the underlying rules of law than its claims or its desires. When we sum all nations' actions, we have a fairly good view of the implicit principles that channel such actions in certain directions and not in others. Custom is grounded on this material component of action (or abstention from action).

But not everything a nation does or does not do constitutes custom in the international sense. When a nation taxes its own resident nationals it is not creating an international rule of taxation; although Kelsen theorized that international law *permits* such taxation, his argument was only a theoretical construct to the effect that everything not prohibited by international law is permitted by it.[40] When a nation extends a mere courtesy to another nation (e.g., by displaying the other nation's flag on one of its city streets), such an action does not form part of custom so that a rule is developed *requiring* the nation to display the flag forever.[41] Thus, to formulate a rule of *customary* law, we must have both an act (the material component) and a characterization of that act (the

---

the expression 'international law.'" D'Amato (fn. 37), p. 122. This sentence has been properly criticized by Onuf in the second section of his chapter in this book. What I was trying to say in that article on this point might better be expressed as follows:

International law is what all the nations of the world believe it to be, or in other words, their "consensus." If at any time all the nations suddenly, somehow, were to manifest their belief that a new rule, X, is now a rule of international law; then X has become such a rule, again through "consensus." (To pick a wild example: a nation contacts us from a star system in another part of our galaxy, offers to enter into friendly relations with us, and all the nations of the world—whether through fear, friendship, or both—immediately express the opinion that that other-world nation shall have certain traditional rights and privileges under earth-bound international law; then that new situation would have been accomplished through "consensus" even without any practice or actions on the part of states.) But to say this is not to say that consensus is a *procedure* for deriving new rules; rather, it is a way of saying that a new rule is in fact a rule. There is admittedly a phenomenological aspect to this sort of reasoning, which is why I wrote in an earlier article, "International law, in short, is phenomenological at the national-perception level. Only when we begin to get at the subject from such an approach can the claims of scientific accuracy, which at present are used for propagandistic purposes, become truly persuasive." D'Amato, "International Law—Content and Function," (fn.8), p. 510.

40.   See Kelsen (fn. 4), p. 325.

41.   Nevertheless, Akehurst feels that a similar rather silly example (Japan adopting the Western Calendar in 1872), standing alone, invalidates my entire thesis on articulation as the qualitative element in

qualitative or psychological component) as a norm of international law. I have attempted to spell out these factors elsewhere and would not want to repeat them here.[42] However, I would note a dissent to Professor Onuf's view in the preceding chapter[43] that the only characterization or articulation of an act that international customary rules require is to indicate which acts are *not* law so that all the rest of them can generate rules of law. To my mind this would present an unnecessary burden on states to continually characterize harmless acts as non-law (e.g., if a statesman signs a treaty with a fountain pen, he would need to announce that he is doing so only as a matter of courtesy and not with a view to generating a future law that will require the use of fountain pens if treaties are to be validly signed). Of course, maybe states someday will welcome such a burden, but until they do, all that custom as a validator of rules of law seems to require is a positive articulation and not Professor Onuf's less restrictive negative disclaimer.

The articulation of an act as formative of a customary rule need not come from the acting state; what is minimally required is that states be put on notice of the articulation. Sometimes scholars can play a crucial role in the formation of customary law by writings which amount to an articulation of a rule. A possible example is Professor Falk's characterization of the three types of violent conflict in civil strife.[44] In an area as complex as irregular warfare, such an organizing principle might suddenly clarify what had previously appeared to be divergent practices and suggest an implicit rule of customary law that the actions of states involved in civil strife were in fact substantiating. Inasmuch as Professor Falk's views were published during the Vietnam War, his articulation was contemporaneous with the acts themselves. It is too early to tell whether, in this particular case, new customary rules of universal validity were set in motion that will affect the way nations will react in the future to civil strife.

Treaties. Treaties and other international agreements tend to supply the bulk of articulations of rules.[45] Moreover, entering into a treaty is an act of a state, a legal commitment to act or refrain from acting in a treaty-specified way. As a result, treaty rules tend to become rules of customary international law (unless opposed by contrary rules in other treaties).[46] A treaty that creates a particular law for the parties is thus also an instrument for the universalization of rules, not by virtue of what the parties intend (because all they presumably intend to do is to make an agreement between themselves) but by virtue of international perceptions about the rule-generating ability of treaty provisions.[47]

---

custom. See Michael Akehurst, "Custom as a Source of International Law," *British Year Book of International Law*, Vol. 47 (1974-1975), p. 36.

42. See D'Amato, *The Concept of Custom in International Law* (fn. 8), pp. 47-102.

43. The second section of his chapter, under "Traditional Sources."

44. See Richard A. Falk, "International Law and the United States Role in the Vietnam War," in Falk, ed., *The Vietnam War and International Law*, Vol. 1 (Princeton: Princeton University Press, 1968), pp. 366-368.

45. On a purely impressionistic basis, I would guess that over 90% of the rules of international law owe their origin to treaties. For a historical statement to this effect, see Georg Schwarzenberger, *A Manual of International Law* (London: Stevens, 4th ed., 1960), p. 28, and *The Frontiers of International Law* (London: Stevens, 1962). Armchair perusal of the classics in international law, especially the so-called positivist authors such as Zouche, Bynkershoek, Moser, Vattel, and Wolff, will reveal the tremendous extent to which what they claim were rules of international law were in fact rules found in or derived from provisions in treaties.

46. The argument, with reference to cases and other evidences of state practices, is spelled out in D'Amato, *The Concept of Custom in International Law* (fn. 8), pp. 103-166.

47. This effect given to rules in treaties is *independent* of the actual wishes of the parties thereto. In other words, it is irrelevant whether the parties to a treaty intend nonparties to be bound. For the effect of

Judicial Decisions.   Despite an uneven performance through the years and a noticeably uncrowded docket, the International Court of Justice is perhaps the closest thing we have to a tangible objective validator of rules. Its opinions are greatly respected and frequently cited by states. Its judges today are more representative of the community of all nations than in the past, but whether its caseload will expand is problematical.

Other international courts of all kinds are feeder streams into the river of international law. Can we include domestic courts as well, when they deal with international questions? Professor Falk argues that we should, but in chapter 1 Professor Onuf indicates that such courts are on a par with a unilateral opinion of a nation. Perhaps the truth lies somewhere in between. Professor Onuf is right insofar as he is pointing out that a domestic court does not contribute to the development of international law merely by saying that it is applying international law. But any court does more than issue an opinion; it issues a decision. The decision itself can affect international interests, and if erroneous can lead to retaliation by the foreign state. The decision, moreover, embodies a concession for reciprocal treatment when a similar case comes up in a foreign nation's domestic court system. In these respects, decisions of domestic courts involving international questions directly contribute to the form of international rules by the process of custom. The decisions are acts of states containing, in the accompanying opinions, their own articulation.

Hence, we might conclude that the International Court of Justice, by virtue of its acknowledgement by states, is itself a validator of international norms, whereas domestic courts (which of course have no such international acknowledgement) may make their greatest contribution by the operation of a previously discussed objective validator, namely, custom.

General Principles of Law.   To Professor Onuf's analysis in chapter 1 on "general principles of law recognized by civilized nations" (as found in Article 38 of the Statute of the International Court of Justice), I would like to add an observation based upon Professor Dworkin's work that has not yet been applied to international studies. Professor Dworkin has shown that there is something fundamentally different between a principle and a rule.[48] A principle is entitled to a certain weight in the consideration of a decision, whereas a rule points to an unambiguous result. A rule either applies or it doesn't apply; if it applies, it is decisive. But a principle may apply and yet be overshadowed by other

---

rules in treaties upon nonparties is a function of the way the international community as a whole views rules in treaties as generators of custom, and *not* whether the particular parties to a treaty have "legislative" intent. An entirely different question is whether the rule in a treaty, on its face, objectively manifests universal application. On this particular point, see D'Amato, "Manifest Intent and the Generation by Treaty of Customary Rules of International Law," *American Journal of International Law,* Vol. 64, No. 5 (October 1970), pp. 892-902; N. G. Onuf, "Further Thoughts on a New Source of International Law: Professor D'Amato's Manifest Intent, *American Journal of International Law,* Vol. 65, No. 5 (October 1971), pp. 774-781.

A leading recent article by Akehurst criticizes my theory by the argument that if the parties to a treaty do not intend the rules in the treaty to have customary law-making effect, then the rules do not have that effect. See Akehurst (fn. 41), p. 43. But how would Akehurst *know* whether the parties to a treaty have such a restrictive view of the ambit of the provisions upon which they have agreed? He neither cites evidence of the parties' intent with respect to *any* treaty, nor does he indicate where one would look for such evidence. But even assuming he were to find convincing evidence of what the parties intend, what really "counts" is what the international community of states decides to do with respect to the rules in the treaty. Analogously, would Dr. Akehurst contend that if states A and B interact in the form of a practice that is recognized by the community of states as generating a customary rule of law, what is important is whether states A and B "intend" that such practice be given customary-law effect? But practice is *no different* from signing a treaty. A treaty is in effect a concretization of practice. For an expansion of this point see D'Amato, *The Concept of Custom in International Law* (fn. 8), pp. 149-166. Cf. R. Y. Jennings, "Treaties as Legislation," in Gabriel M. Wilner, ed., *Jus et Societas* (The Hague: Nijhoff, 1979), pp. 166-168.

48. Dworkin (fn. 30), pp. 22-31.

principles. The principle "no man should profit by his own wrong" is one that is found in most domestic legal systems, yet it can be overshadowed in domestic law by, for example, the principle of quieting title to real estate in a case involving adverse possession (where the adverse possessor clearly profits from his own wrong). The principle that tends to invalidate contracts achieved by coercion does not apply to treaties of peace between two states that were previously at war; here another principle, namely the avoidance of further violence, validates unequal peace treaties. In the law of war, competing principles are military necessity and humanitarianism, and, as Quincy Wright pointed out,[49] the principle of ending the war quickly and the principle of securing a just and lasting peace (the latter could be compromised if brutally illegal means are adopted to end the war more quickly). These principles do not decide specific cases but they are factors in the decisions. The numerous post-World War II military trials in Europe and Asia were often decided on the basis of these principles, particularly in the sentences that were meted out, when the defendants pleaded exceptions to the rules of the conduct of war that were applied to them.

General principles of law can thus be very important as weights or factors in international legal decision-making. Their operation in this respect is very much like that described by Professor McDougal and his associates, who however were talking about the rules and norms of international law as well as principles (and thus perhaps cast too wide a net).[50] By virtue of the inclusion of general principles in Article 38, and also through their basic familiarity to lawyers as described by Professor Onuf, "general principles of law recognized by civilized nations" has become prima facie an objective validator of international principles. When a given principle arises in a case or dispute, its proponent should examine the domestic law of all the nations (if he has the time and resources to do so!) and if he can show that most or all nations recognize the principle in their domestic legal systems, he will have made out a prima facie case for the inclusion of that principle in the international legal dispute. However, mere similarity in provisions in the laws of many nations does not itself mean that a similar rule is a rule of international law. To lift the rule from national to international status still requires some showing of customary law—that the rule has been applied in at least one interaction between states.

Unilateral Declarations and International Law Formation. We have seen that a unilateral claim or declaration by a state cannot per se be evidence of customary law inasmuch as the claim may be patently illegal or it may be a trial balloon with the claimant state not intending to follow through upon the claim unless the reaction of other states is favorable. Yet in the past few years we have witnessed a proliferation of unilateral claims on the part of coastal states to various kinds of exclusive jurisdiction or control over contiguous zones of the high seas and submarine areas. Perhaps these claims have been partially inspired by the success of the Truman Proclamation of September 28, 1945,[51] regarding the continental shelf of the United States. This famous proclamation deserves a closer look with respect to the question of its impact upon general norms of international law.

President Truman proclaimed that the policy of the United States was to regard the continental shelf "as appertaining to the United States, subject to its jurisdiction and control."[52] A month later Mexico followed with a similar Presidential Proclamation, and

---

49. In a little-known essay. See Quincy Wright, "The New Law of War and Neutrality," in *Varia Juris Gentium* (Leiden: Sijthoff, 1959,) p. 412.

50. McDougal (fn. 18), p. 778.

51. Proclamation With Respect to the Natural Resources of the Subsoil and Sea Bed of the Continental Shelf, September 28, 1945, *Federal Register,* Vol. 10, p. 12303.

52. Ibid.

before the decade was over another twelve nations had issued similar unilateral decrees.[53] When, if at any time, was any law created by these decrees?

The Truman Proclamation did not descend upon an unsuspecting world. The United States Department of State had shown a draft of the proclamation to representatives of Canada, Cuba, Denmark, France, Great Britain, Iceland, Mexico, The Netherlands, Norway, Portugal, and the Soviet Union, and none of the governments consulted expressed opposition to the American proposal to issue the proclamation.[54] At least with respect to all the governments consulted, we may say that a consensus had been reached prior to the date of Truman's proclamation. In addition to this consensus, we must not overlook the fact that prior to 1945 there was scant attention to the continental shelf, and certainly there was no rule of international law in opposition to coastal state control over its continental shelf. Had there been such a law saying, for example, that the continental shelf belonged to all nations equally, then the Truman Proclamation would have had a harder burden of justification. Moreover, we might even assume that if such a law existed, the nations consulted on the draft proclamation, or some of them, probably would have objected. Therefore, we might conclude tentatively that the Truman Proclamation articulated a rule that the world community was prepared to accept in an area where there was no contrary rule or practice.

Now let us look at the situation a month or two after the issuance of the Truman Proclamation. Other states now had a clear opportunity to protest. In the absence of protest, we have additional evidence of a universal consensus. The evidence is not conclusive, as I have argued elsewhere, because states may reasonably not want to protest even though they disagree with the claim.[55]

Further evidence of consensus occurs when state after state issues decrees similar to the Truman Proclamation. As time has passed and more states have become aware of riches in the continental shelf, more states have issued such decrees. In more recent years when some states have realized that the coastal states' claims deprive others of access to minerals, the have-not states have complained, but then the objections may have come too late. A consensus may already have been formed

But apart from the operations of consensus, customary law was forming when states began to act upon their claims. Truman's proclamation itself did not create customary law; it supplied an articulation of a rule, but not any underlying practice. Nor was there a commitment to act (as would have obtained had there been a treaty relating to the continental shelf). But with the course of time, mining and fishing (sedentary) operations on the continental shelves of various countries that were confined exclusively to nationals or (even stronger evidence) licensed to non-nationals created customary law binding upon all nations. It is by virtue of this practice, rather than the more frail need of consensus, that the rule of coastal state jurisdiction is so strong today.

The continental shelf story contains lessons for claims today for exclusive jurisdiction over wide contiguous zones. Suppose a nation claims that it owns 500 miles of the ocean perpendicular to its coastline. The claim may be expressed in a presidential proclamation, in an amendment to the state's own constitution, or in any similar fashion. Such a claim, unlike Truman's, intrudes upon an area already subject to a clear rule of international law—the freedom of the seas. Now, what are we to make of such a claim?

In the first place, if the nation making the claim has previously shown a draft to a

---

53. See Zdenek J. Slouka, *International Custom and the Continental Shelf* (The Hague: 1968).
54. Ibid., pp. 146-152.
55. See D'Amato, *The Concept of Custom in International Law* (fn. 8), pp. 98-102, 195-197.

large number of states and has received no objections, then the claim might be expressive of a new consensus. (There is nothing logically wrong with a new consensus of all states that wipes out the previous rule of freedom of the seas—states in the aggregate are free to change any rule of international law because they are the creator-subjects of international rules.) If the nation making the claim does not show a draft to other states, we might assume that it chooses not to show the draft because it knows that the other states would object. This assumption, of course, stems from the fact that a contrary rule already obtains in the area of the proposed declaration.

What is the status of the international law of freedom of the seas a month after a state makes a unilateral claim to 500 miles of contiguous zones? Has the claim changed the established rule? Has it even planted a seed of change? Here, I think we have to be careful and analytically precise.

If the claim represents a new consensus, then of course it may be indicative of a change in the underlying rule. But, in all likelihood, the 500-mile claim does not indicate a change of attitude on the part of other states. If it does, then in due course we will see the fruition of that change of attitude as other states make 500-mile claims and respect the claims of states that have already made similar declarations; in that case, the process of consensus would be at work. But let us now look at the single 500-mile claim in isolation. Suppose no other state has (yet) made a similar claim. Does the single 500-mile claim itself change, even slightly, the underlying freedom-of-the-seas rule?

Clearly no change has taken place at this point through the process of consensus, since a single state by definition does not create a consensus. In the absence of other states issuing or respecting similar claims, there is no consensus. A single state's unilateral declaration therefore has absolutely no effect upon the underlying international rule through the operation of consensus. For the consensus operation to work, we need many more than one state. What we need is the participation of other states in the 500-mile rule plus the contemporary absence of protest (or other forms of disagreement) from the rest of the states. Practically speaking, this is unlikely, although, as I have noted, it is not logically impossible.

What then of the operation of custom as a universal validator of the 500-mile claim?[56] Let us look at the single state's unilateral claim. Does the claim constitute a customary practice? Here the answer must be no. At best the claim articulates a rule which could be realized by acts of the claimant state that affect other states. But an articulation of a rule cannot itself be custom, for the basic reason that the claimant state has done nothing internationally except state a claim. The claim itself runs contrary to the rule of freedom of the seas. The state issuing the claim may not even intend to back it up; it may simply be issuing a trial balloon. Moreover, other states would have no reason to protest this claim. They may believe that the issuing state does not intend to follow through on actualizing the claim, or they may believe that there will be enough time to dispute it when the claimant state actually tries to do something in support of its claim (e.g., seize another state's fishing boat 450 miles offshore). Finally, other states may continue to act on the understanding that fisheries 450 miles off any state's coastline are open to all states, and thus state practice is built up daily with respect to the rule of freedom of the seas. This practice, all the other states may believe, is enough to overwhelm any attempt at a contrary practice by the single state making a 500-mile claim.

---

56.   Cf. fn. 29 above.

If the state's 500-mile claim has no impact, standing alone, either upon consensus or custom as validators of the claim, is it a totally futile gesture from a legal standpoint? Of course, it may start the ball rolling so that, if other states emulate and repeat the claim, eventually consensus or custom may create a 500-mile exclusive jurisdiction rule in what was formerly the high seas. But this is saying very little, for the legal impact of the claimant's proclamation depends upon the actions of others. Is there no legal significance to the claimant's proclamation standing alone? The only significance that I can find is that it is an invitation, an offer, for reciprocal treatment that would amount to a treaty. State A makes a 500-mile claim. By such a claim it is inviting state B both to respect the claim of A and to expect A to stay out of B's 500-mile zone. If B acts accordingly, then a tacit treaty has arisen between A and B. (Moreover, B has joined in A's claim, and thus we have the real beginnings of a customary practice and maybe even a start toward a new international consensus.) Thus, A's claim is not without legal significance; rather, it is like an offer to engage in a contract.

International law could not be law if every act or claim made by a nation could be justified. Some acts and some claims must be illegal; they must run afoul of the prevailing law. The possibility for changing international law occurs when more than one state is involved in an act or a claim. When one state acts and another state receives the action (e.g., A fishes off B's coast and B allows the fishing to go on without interference), customary practice is either created or reinforced. When one state makes a claim and another state agrees to the claim, a treaty is established; the treaty itself then has the status of the practice of states and it creates or reinforces universally valid customary rules. In sum, international law cannot be created or changed by one nation acting in splendid isolation. International law is law between (or among) nations; a nation acting alone or making a unilateral declaration with no concurrence from other states is merely operating in the domestic legal realm.

Conclusion: The Importance of Objective Validation

There is something of a feeling among those who are introduced to the study of international law that it is an indeterminate form of law lacking in provable content or authorized validation procedures. According to Hart, international law in the present day lacks this "rule of recognition" which, someday, will make it a "mature" legal system.[57] Advocates in international law cases sometimes throw in the kitchen sink in an effort to prove their contentions; they cite anything that has ever been published if it will help their contention that a given alleged rule is in fact a rule of international law. In so doing, they are imitating the father of international law, Grotius himself, who seemed to draw upon any published source indiscriminately to prove his contentions about the content of international law. And we cannot blame Grotius or his present-day (sometimes unknowing) imitators; they are, after all, advocates. But judges have a different obligation, and so do nations in passing upon the claims of other nations. If Iran believes that diplomatic personnel may be seized from an American embassy in Teheran if they are spies for the American government, no responsible nation in passing upon, or reacting to, that claim should allow the claim to be proved by citation of indiscriminate sources (for example, a Marxist-Leninist tract to the effect that capitalist nations always illegally spy upon other governments). Instead, reference to customary law and to the Vienna

---

57.　Hart (fn. 4), pp. 208-231; cf. fn. 36 above.

Convention on Diplomatic Relations of 1961[58] amply proves that diplomats are expected to gather information about the host country and transmit it confidentially to their own country. Of course, here the rule is clear, but in other cases where the rule is not clear we should not make the mistake of concluding that, therefore, the sources of the rule are indeterminate. Not only is too much at stake (rapid escalation of competing legal claims leading to military confrontation), but also international legal theory has come a long way from the days of Grotius. The increasing attention being paid to the need for, and the procedures for, objective validation of rules of international law in a burgeoning literature of international law evidences the seriousness of the problem, the responsibility of scholars for careful scholarship in this area of legal theory, and ultimately the good possibility of generally accepted standards for that kind of objective validation.

---

58. Vienna Convention on Diplomatic Relations of April 18, 1961, *United Nations Treaty Series*, Vol. 500 (1964), p. 98.

Global Bargaining: The Legal and Diplomatic Framework

Gidon Gottlieb

The emergence of a new world order shaped more by bargains, compromises, and necessity than by grand architectural designs is underway. Deep structural changes are taking place. They follow the decline of the big power blocs and the rise of states organized in global political parties; changes include the emergence of a distinct multilateral mode of diplomacy that involves a shift from parliamentary diplomacy to a novel form of diplomacy based on equality between groups of states which I shall refer to as *parity diplomacy*. Changes are reflected also in the growing importance of non-voting procedures in international negotiating arenas and in the variety of instruments designed to accommodate all types of bargains. These instruments are often characterized by a shift from formal, legally binding accords to other forms of commitment, and in the United States such shifts affect the respective roles of the President and of the Congress in the domestic management of interdependence. Informal agreements are evidently harder for Congress to control or even to monitor. Cumulatively these changes constitute new structures for the contemporary world order. Legal theory, as well as economic and political conventions, must be brought up to date and reflect the rapidly evolving practice of states, as well as the new structural framework in which the great economic issues of interdependence must be resolved. These are the main themes of this essay.

Diplomatic Modes and Procedures of Decision in International Arenas

The headlong flight of developed countries from negotiations in arenas dominated by coalitions of Communist States and Less Developed Countries (LDCs) continues. Since the first meeting of the United Nations Conference on Trade and Development (UNCTAD) in 1964, these coalitions of states have acquired official status. States are formally classified in a number of groups that reflect fairly fixed party alignments in the world economic arenas.[1] These formal groupings function in the economic arena as global bargaining units. They tend to keep their cohesion in political forums as well.

---

1. See U.N. General Assembly resolution 1995 (XIX), December 30, 1964, and Annex. See, for example, the classification adopted in the Reports of UNCTAD IV on International Financial Cooperation for Development, TD/188/Sub.1 (1976) Nairobi. Thus the developed countries are formally identified by reference to their membership in Group D of UNCTAD, in the Development Assistance Committee of the OECD, in the Group of Developing Countries, in the Conference on International Economic Cooperation and in the Group of 10 which meets at various levels both in the International Monetary Fund and in the OECD. Less Developed Countries or LDCs are formally identified by their membership in the Group of 77 and participation in its ministerial meetings. For the purposes of development assistance this group is divided into three segments: OPEC members, Less Developed Countries and Least Developed Countries. They are also identified by their membership in Group A and C of UNCTAD and in the Group of Developing Countries of the Conference on International Economic Cooperation. Socialist countries of the Soviet bloc belong to COMECON and to Group D of UNCTAD.

The emergence of economic interest groupings of states has encouraged the shift toward conciliation and away from the majority voting characteristic of the principal United Nations organs.[2] This trend is noticeable in UNCTAD and in the Economic and Social Council (ECOSOC). It has also had an impact in the Law of the Sea Conference where complicated coalitions of states have sprung up along lines reflecting additional special interests such as those of landlocked states.

Powers that are not ready to forego military parity cannot be expected to accept less than parity in negotiations. Yet positions secured by military might can be eroded at the conference table. The significance of issues on the international negotiating agenda is confirmed by the emergence of a new mode of multilateral diplomacy: I refer to it as the principle of *parity*. It reflects the organization of states into global political parties and alignments which do not follow the big power bloc politics of the first years of the U.N. Parity requires that agreement be reached between the main parties or groups of states on the basis of the equality of the groups of states rather than on the basis of the equality of individual states. It requires the consent of the groups before any decision can be taken or agreement reached. It arises from the organization of states into caucuses or alignments. Parity is a principle applicable in negotiations between groups of states and between powers. It is anchored neither in ideological claims of equality nor in the theory of representation. It emanates from the realities of power relationships and from the need to manage the problems of interdependence and of world order. The principle of parity is well suited to a pluralistic international community with few shared ideological premises. It connotes no particular theory of political obligation or consent but rests entirely on actual patterns of relationships and common concerns.

The principle of parity, which is reflected also in collective bargaining, was applied in the Paris North-South negotiations at the Conference on International Economic Cooperation (CIEC).[3]

---

2. Bloc voting and caucuses in international organizations are not a new feature of the world political order. For example, the West European and Afro-Asian groups at the United Nations have been caucusing regularly during meetings of the General Assembly. But the drafting and development of comprehensive proposals in advance of U.N. meetings were less common. The Group of 77 and the nonaligned now come to the General Assembly with an agreed comprehensive program regarding a large number of agenda items. See, for example, the documents agreed at the Colombo Summit of Non-Aligned Countries in 1976 and circulated to the General Assembly, A/31/197 (1976). See also the Manila Declaration and Program of Action of the Ministerial Meetings of the Group of 77, TD/195 (1976). Generally, on the phenomenon of coalitions in international organizations, see Thomas Hovet, Jr., *Bloc Politics in the United Nations* (Cambridge, Mass.: Harvard University Press, 1960), and his "Political Parties in the United Nations," paper delivered at the 1962 Meeting of the American Political Science Association.

On the principle of majority rule, see Cromwell A. Riches, *Majority Rule in International Organizations* (Baltimore: Johns Hopkins Press, 1940); Wellington Koo, *Voting Procedure in International Political Organizations* (New York: Columbia University Press, 1947); Julius Stone, "The Rule of Unanimity: The Practice of the Council and Assembly of the League of Nations," *British Year Book of International Law*, Vol. 14 (1933), pp. 18-42); F.A. Vallat, "Voting in the General Assembly of the United Nations," *British Year Book of International Law*, Vol. 31 (1956), pp. 273-298; Frederick Sherwood Dunn, *The Practice and Procedure of International Conferences* (Baltimore: Johns Hopkins Press, 1929). John G. Heinberg, "History of the Majority Principle," *American Political Science Review*, Vol. 20, No. 1 (February 1926), pp. 52-68, and "Theories of Majority Rule," *American Political Science Review*, Vol. 26, No. 3 (June 1932), pp. 452-469, provides a useful review of theoretical claims in support of the principle.

3. See the Final Communique of the Conference on International Economic Cooperation, *Department of State Bulletin*, Vol. 74, No. 1907 (12 January 1976), pp. 48-49. See also the Final Declaration of the Second Preparatory Meeting, *Department of State Bulletin*, Vol. 73, 1898 (10 November 1975), pp. 668-669. In some cases, a modification of established instruments of parliamentary organs can be attempted. For example, Rule 59 of the Rule of Procedure of the Economic and Social Council regarding "request for a vote" could be amended to make allowance for the parity mode of negotiation. As it now stands, Rule 59 provides, "[a]

The principle of parity has recently been tied also to the notion of consensus. This notion was the subject of significant analysis in the arbitral award in the dispute between Texaco and Libya. The sole arbitrator, French Professor Dupuy, stated that resolutions of the United Nations which reflect the state of customary law on a given subject and which are supported by a consensus of a majority of states belonging to various representative groups, could—if other conditions were met—acquire a binding force. The arbitrator underscored the importance of representative groups in the process of the development of international law.[4] This is a notion likely to create problems for isolated states not associated with any particular group or alliance. It stands in contrast to earlier official views of the Department of State.

The parity principle avoids the pitfalls of parliamentary diplomacy in a world order dominated less by single states than by organized state groupings. The parity principle can gradually displace the principle of majority rule in international conferences which until recently was itself regarded as a novelty. Earlier this century the progression from unanimity to majority rule had marked the emergence of international assemblies as corporate entities capable of taking action as such. This was in contrast to nineteenth century practice, under which conferences were mere assemblies of states or a medium for negotiating a treaty:

> In the historical development it was necessary that the great political organs of the League should adhere to the traditional system that the corporate personality of the Council and the Assembly soon came to be accepted. It was soon customary to refer to the decisions of the Council or of the Assembly as such and not as the concurrent decisions of the members composing those organs. Yet the complete abandonment of the unanimity rule in the drafting of the United Nations Charter was revolutionary.[5]

Thirty years after the San Francisco Conference on the United Nations, we thus note the further progression from majority to parity.

The range of modes of agreement-making has been broadened. Each mode is endowed with particular attributes that cannot be modified at will. The main diplomatic modes[6] are:

1. The *traditional diplomatic mode* is practiced by states on a bilateral basis and involves consultation, discussion, and negotiation
2. *Conference diplomacy* is adopted in international meetings in which negotiators meet collectively and are bound only by actions to which they consent. Such conferences cannot take action as an entity, but are only an arena for negotiating agreements

---

proposal or motion before the Council for decision shall be voted upon if any member so requests. Where no member requests a vote, the Council may adopt proposals or motions without a vote." (U.N. Doc. E/5715). This rule could be amended to provide for postponement of votes at the request of a group of states.

4.　*Texaco v. Libya, International Legal Materials*, Vol. 17, No. 1 (January 1978), pp. 1-37.

5.　Philip C. Jessup, "Parliamentary Diplomacy," Academie de Droit International, *Recueil des cours*, Vol. 89 (1956/I), p. 248.

6.　The literature on diplomatic modes is considerable. A good beginning is Jessup (fn. 5), pp. 181-320. See also Dunn (fn. 2). For a recent survey see *Journal of International Affairs*, Vol. 29, No. 1 (Spring 1975), full issue. See also Harold G. Nicolson, *Diplomacy* (New York: Oxford University Press, 3rd ed., 1969), and his *Evolution of the Diplomatic Method* (London: Constable and Co., 1954); Charles K. Webster, *The Congress of Vienna* (London: G. Bell and Sons, 1945); Nicholson, *The Congress of Vienna* (New York: Harcourt Brace, 1946); Norman Llewellyn Hill, *The Public International Conference* (Stanford: Stanford University Press, 1929).

3. *Parliamentary diplomacy* is practiced in international organs endowed with a corporate character of their own and authorized to act as such by a majority vote

4. *Parity diplomacy* is a new emerging mode adopted in international arenas in negotiations between groups of states

5. *Third party modes* are characteristic procedures adopted for the settlement of international conflicts, such as good offices, conciliation, mediation, arbitration, and judicial settlement and involve varying degrees of authority exercised by third parties

6. *The managerial mode* is adopted in agencies responsible for performing services requiring managerial decisions

7. *Informal modes* are unstructured, informal processes adopted without the use of formal instruments or arenas

The attributes characteristic of each diplomatic mode permeate and sometimes dominate the process of agreement-making. The choice of mode can on occasion determine the outcome of the negotiating effort itself. Significant attributes of each diplomatic mode include: (1) the procedure of decision-making (i.e., voting, consensus); (2) the character of participation (i.e., universal, regional, bilateral, etc.); (3) the basis of representation (i.e., equality, quotas, special rights); (4) the functions of agreements (i.e., operational, goal-setting, or rule-making); and (5) the range of domestic participants (i.e., the executive or legislative branches, private interest groups, and other constituencies).

Attributes cannot be transplanted at will from one diplomatic mode to another. In parliamentary diplomacy it is thus hard to legitimize unequal voting powers. But these modes can be combined and used simultaneously or in sequence. A conference may thus be called to adopt and sign instruments negotiated in the traditional diplomatic mode. This was done for the Japanese Peace Treaties. President Truman had requested the then New York attorney, John Foster Dulles, to negotiate a peace treaty with Japan. The treaty was eventually submitted to an international conference for acceptance.[7]

The weakness of the majority principle is deepened by the declining authority of two other principles which sustain majority rule: equality and representation.[8] The admission of mini-states to world organizations has accentuated the tensions between the formal equality of states and the extreme inequalities in population, resources, and capacity for independent action. Formally the votes of these states count as heavily as those of the big powers in any tabulation of votes cast, but their political weight is evidently far from equal. Increasingly the equality of states is regarded mainly as a jural principle governing legal rights and duties rather than as a guide for the management of global interdependence and decision-making. The principle of the equality of states is

---

7. See Jessup (fn. 5), and U.S. Department of State Record of the Japanese Peace Conference, Publication 4392 (1951).

8. There is ample literature on these two principles. For example, see the useful work of Hanna Pitkin, *The Concept of Representation* (Berkeley: University of California Press, 1967), and its excellent bibliography. See Edwin DeWitt Dickinson,*The Equality of States in International Law* (Cambridge, Mass.: Harvard University Press, 1920), and bibliography. Adolf Lande, "Revindication of the Principle of Legal Equality, 1871-1914,"*Political Science Quarterly,* Vol. 62, No. 2, 3 (June, September 1947), pp. 258-286, 398-417. See also the Declaration on the Principles of International Law Regarding Friendly Relations and Cooperation Among States, U.N.General Assembly resolution 2625 (XXV), October 24, 1970. For a recent study, see Robert A. Klein, *Sovereign Equality among States* (Toronto: University of Toronto Press, 1974). Different theories were advanced at different times in support of the principle of majority rule. It was only during the lifetime of Locke that the "social compact" theory and principles of "equality" were woven into the majority principle. See Heinberg, "Theories of Majority Rule," (fn. 2).

vulnerable to claims about the need for planetary reapportionment. The vitality of the equality principle as a basis for majority rule in international arenas is fading as reapportionment remains beyond reach.[9]

The moral weight of an international organization varies with the character of its main actors. Police states carry no greater moral authority collectively than they do in isolation. The problem is well-illustrated by the efforts some Communist states made in 1978 in the United Nations Education, Scientific and Cultural Organization (UNESCO) to legitimize press censorship. The increasing number of authoritarian states in the international community has modified the corporate character of international assemblies. Some of these are now analogous to a consortium of tyrannies. The non-aligned group thus had no difficulty in throwing its full support in 1975 behind the Cambodian government of Pol Pot which was then already engaged in the extermination of vast segments of its population. The legitimacy of majority decisions in international organizations is sapped by the repressive and brutal character of many of its constituents.[10] Most cannot in any sense of the word be regarded as representative governments. They meet neither classical nor revolutionary standards of legitimacy.[11] They are not legitimate by reference to their origin, and most are not legitimate under their own principles of constitutionality and law. Many are indeed simply lawless, even in terms of the aspirations which they purport to reflect.[12] Doubts about the domestic legitimacy of

---

9. The formal emergence of negotiating groups is taking place at the expense of the less influential states. On the theory of apportionment, see Alfred DeGrazia, "General Theory of Apportionment," *Law and Contemporary Problems*, Vol. 17, No. 2 (Spring 1952), pp. 256-267.

10. See, for example, Amnesty International, *Report on Torture* (New York: Farrar, Strauss and Giroux, 1975). See further, Freedom House,*Freedom at Issue*, No. 39 (January-February 1977).

11. See Guglielmo Ferrero, *The Principles of Power* (New York: G. P. Putnam's Sons, 1942).

12. On the concept of the lawless state, see Gidon Gottlieb, "Is Law Dead?" in Eugene V. Rostow, ed., *Is Law Dead?* (New York: Simon and Schuster, 1971). See also, the contrasting treatment of the question in Morton Halperin and others,*The Lawless State* (New York: Penguin Books, 1976). The liberal critique of official lawlessness in the United States remains for the time restricted to a discussion of internal domestic politics. It has not led to parallel studies of the lawlessness of foreign regimes other than those which receive U.S. economic and military assistance. See Irving Kristol, "Mortality, Liberalism and Foreign Policy," *The Wall Street Journal*, 19 November 1976. The critique of foreign lawlessness is so far primarily limited to the consideration of human rights violations, such as torture, to treatment of political prisoners, and the right to immigrate.

See Maurice Duverger, *Droit constitutionel et institutions politiques* (Paris: Presses Universtaires, 4th ed., 1955), for a classical treatment of the concept of legitimacy. See also V.I. Lenin,*The State and Revolution* (New York: International Publishers, 1932). Duverger cites Vychinsky's statement that "laws are made to protect the state from the individual and not the individual from the state," p. 49. For a further treatment of Soviet doctrines, see Hans Kelsen,*The Communist Theory of Law* (New York: Praeger, 1955). Charles Maurras, *Enquête sur la monarchi* (Paris: Hachette, 1928), pp. CVII-CVIII, cited in Ferrero (fn. 11), p. 132.

In the past, regimes that sought their legitimacy in the popular character of the revolution that brought them to power often looked for confirmation in a plebiscite establishing the support of the nation. Marxist theory, however, has advanced a new doctrine of legitimacy. It does not claim legitimacy in terms of the ancient order of elective and representative government. Marxist doctrine seeks legitimacy by turning to the future rather than to the past. The dictatorship of the proletariat is the strategy to be followed as long as Marxist legitimacy itself is not solidly implanted. Marxist regimes have been joined by a multitude of other repressive governments in the effort to derive legitimacy from policies for a better furture, in the accomplishment of the "public good." In many new states, the legitimacy derived from the overthrow of alien colonial rule is receding into the mist of history. As the original leaders fade from the scene, new vivifying sources of popular acceptance and support are needed—and hard to find—as economic and social conditions worsen. Nearly half a century ago, the French right wing intellectual, Charles Maurras, wrote:

> Legitimate government, good government, is that which does what it has to do, which does it well, which succeeds in achieving the public good. Its legitimacy is confirmed by its utility. It is considered useful when its means of action, by their vigor and by their structure, appear to be appropriate in

authoritarian rulers do not, however, impeach their international standing to participate in the emerging world order and to bargain and negotiate with states that enjoy governments of unimpeachable legitimacy. These ideological doubts nevertheless undermine the relevance of the principles of majority rule and equality where rulers indifferent to majority rule and equality in their own societies are involved.

Rulers in power, in effective control of territory and people and able to affect global interdependence patterns, cannot be, and on the whole are not, left out of the diplomatic process. But increasingly gross and consistent patterns of violations of human rights are eroding their international legitimacy in the sense that aid to their regimes becomes controversial and assistance to their domestic adversaries elicits support. The developing and as yet unexplored connection between legitimacy and gross violations of human rights is casting a clouded light on the standing of institutions dominated by regimes which flagrantly abuse their populations.

Universality and equality of representation are appropriate principles for deliberative or legislative organs. But their relevance should not everywhere be taken for granted. In institutional architecture, function shapes the design of an institution, its membership, its procedures, and the decision-making process. Difficulties emerge with attempts to rely, for example, on a quasi-legislative organ for collective bargaining purposes. A broad view of institutional design is required to harmonize decision-making processes and outcomes.

The diplomatic record confirms that effective negotiations can be conducted, even in the General Assembly, between influential states that can deliver a decision.[13] It does not follow that the General Assembly and ECOSOC can be converted from majority decisions to consensus procedures. Attempts to deny LDCs and Communist states the benefits of their two-thirds majority may well be futile. Efforts to use the same organs for deliberation, for rule setting, and for collective bargaining were nevertheless attempted.

---

proportion to its aim. Just power is born so that it will provide men with what they need when they are gathered into a community; its existence is determined by the conditions that create it. It exists when this necessary good exists. The absence of this good reveals the absence of the power, that it has been abolished or diverted, or distorted. The harm that the power does is a sign and a confession of its evil nature or of its bad structure, and is proof of its inability to do that for which it was created. . . . But there is a stage at which discussion ceases. This is the criterion before which there can be no doubt. It is called public welfare. A government that does not insure it is a government whose incapacity removes it from power. A government that insures the protection of society and the state acquires an incontestable claim to permanence. It is only a claim, but one that counts. This majesty that surrounds the welfare of the nation and the country is sufficient to create a discipline. This discipline existed at the origin of both transitory government and lasting governments. (Ferrero trans., as cited)

Even the Maurras totalitarian theory of legitimacy sets standards that are too high for many contemporary tyrannical rulers in the international community. Illegitimate governments are not representative—the illegitimacy of regimes vitiates political claims based upon representation. Their illegitimacy weakens their political claims for participation in majority rule.

Freely chosen governments are becoming an anomaly, and a large number of states are afflicted by authoritarian rulers with tenuous domestic legitimacy. According to Freedom House surveys, only 19.6% of the world population is living under free regimes. Only 42 of 159 sovereign countries are classified as free.

Regimes callously indifferent to the majority principle in their own societies have weak claims to participation in majority decision-making internationally. Questions properly raised about the representativeness of the white-racist-minority regimes in Rhodesia and South Africa can be equally raised about scores of military and one-party systems. Ideological doubts about the relevance of majority rule reinforce claims for accommodation of differences between organized groups of states by give-and-take rather than by voting.

13.   See Arthur Lall, "Some Thoughts on the UN General Assembly as a Forum for Mediation and Negotiation,"*Journal of International Affairs*, Vol. 29, No. 1 (Spring 1975), pp. 63-67. See more generally his *Modern International Negotiations* (New York: Columbia University Press, 1966): K. Venkata Raman,*Dispute Settlement Through the United Nations* (Dobbs Ferry, N.Y.: Oceana, 1977).

An interesting effort to mix the deliberative and bargaining functions of ECOSOC and the General Assembly with built-in mediation and consensus procedures was made in the 1975 Report of a Group of Experts on "A New United Nations Structure for Global Economic Cooperation."[14]

The collective bargaining process, or "consultative procedure" as it was referred to in the report, was designed to promote agreement on major policy issues "where agreement might otherwise be unobtainable." The report suggested:

> With this end in view, the procedures would normally be initiated at an early stage in the discussions of a given subject and before the stage of the passing of resolutions, but the procedures could also be initiated at the end of a process of debate or even after a decision where this seemed to be appropriate. It would be for the Economic and Social Council, if the recommendations in this section were accepted, to work out these consultative arrangements in appropriate rules of procedure which would specify, among other things, the kind of subject on which consultative procedures could take place.[15]

The report drew inspiration from the experience of the UNCTAD in employing the conciliation procedures contemplated in Resolution 1995 (XIX) December 30, 1964 of the General Assembly and from the work of Mr. Jeremy Morse, Chairman of the Committee of Twenty on the Reform of the International Monetary System.[16]

The Report of the Group of Experts did not, however, adopt the UNCTAD conciliation procedure which postpones for a fixed period voting on resolutions on which no agreement has been reached. Such a procedure would presumably be too considerable a limitation on the majority's voting rights to be contemplated at this stage of United Nations development. The majority's rights are confirmed in Article 9 of the 1969 Vienna Convention on the Law of Treaties, which provides, with regard to voting at international conferences, that "The adoption of the text of a treaty at an international conference takes place by the vote of two-thirds of the States present and voting, unless by the same majority they shall decide to apply a different rule."[17] Although the Report of the Group of Experts on "A New United Nations Structure for Global Economic Cooperation" did not refer to voting procedures at United Nations conferences, it was an attempt to limit the effects of bloc voting in the United Nations.

Neither the recommendations of the Group of Experts nor the procedures adopted at the Conference on the Law of the Sea can modify the basic political attitude of states and little can be done by way of rules when a majority wishes to avail itself of its voting power or when a significant minority refuses to accept the will of the majority.[18]

---

14. U.N.Doc. E/AC.62/9.

15. Ibid., p. 30.

16. Resolution No. 27-10, in International Monetary Fund, *Annual Report of Executive Directors* (Washington, 1972), pp. 92-93; see also Joseph Gold, "Weighted Voting Power: Some Limits and Some Problems,"*American Journal of International Law*, Vol. 68, No. 4 (October 1974), pp. 687, 702.

17. On the history of this provision, see Shabtai Rosenne, *The Law of Treaties* (Dobbs Ferry, N. Y.: Oceana, 1970).

18. Rule 37 of the Rules of Procedure of the Third Conference on the Law of the Sea provides an elaborate procedure for determining whether all efforts at reaching general agreement have been exhausted. It is worth describing in detail:

> (i) Automatic deferment of a vote: When a matter of substance comes up for voting, the President shall defer the question of taking a vote on such matter for a period not exceeding ten calendar days, "if requested by at least 15 representatives." This can be done only once, and the period of deferment could be less than ten days, depending on the circumstances.
> (ii) President's right to defer: Even when not requested by a group of representatives, the

Consensus procedures designed to get important states to agree on substantive proposals are vulnerable to criticism of the kind made by the Representative of China at that Conference:

> A super-Power, under the smokescreen of practicing "consensus," asserted that the rules of a new Law of the Sea would have international observance only if they were supported by all countries and that the holding of the Conference on the Law of the Sea should also depend on the aforementioned conditions. The intent of these remarks was all too obvious: that is, as long as the super-Power alone does not agree, the Conference cannot be held and the new Law of the Sea cannot be established. Is this not typical hegemonism? As is well known to all, it is necessary now to formulate a new Law of the Sea, precisely because the old Law of the Sea protects the interests of the imperialist Powers, while subjecting the numerous small and medium-sized countries to plunder and humiliation. If the new Law of the Sea would be the same as the old, what is the need for the drafting of a new Law of the Sea? Would not the six year work of the Sea-Bed Committee be in vain? The representative of a developing country had put it rightly: that is, an attempt at the "establishment of the veto" at the Conference by big Powers, which consider

---

President "may" make a similar deferment for up to ten days, but again only once with respect to a particular matter.

(iii) Deferment by the Conference itself. The Conference may, at any time, decide to defer the question of taking a vote on any matter of substance, "for a specified period of time." Such decision shall be made by a majority of representatives present and voting. It can be done either upon proposal by the President "or upon motion by any representative." Such a motion can be made "any number of times" and the final decision will be up to the Conference.

(iv) Special negotiating effort during the period of deferment: In order to ensure that the period of deferment is used for intensive negotiations, the President "shall make every effort" to facilitate the achievement of a general agreement, "having regard to the overall progress made on all matters of substance which are closely related." Negotiations should thus be directed not merely to the solution of a particular problem but should, whenever possible, contemplate the conclusion of a package deal, solving simultaneously a number of problems. The conduct of such negotiations is to be primarily in the hands of the President, the role of the General Committee, stressed in some earlier proposals, having been relegated to assisting the President "as appropriate."

(v) Determination that no agreement can be reached: On the basis of a report by the President, to be made before the end of the period of deferment, the Conference may decide, by the double majority specified in Rule 39(1) for matters of substance, that all efforts at reaching a general agreement have been exhausted and that the matter of substance be put to the vote. Should, however, the Conference prove unable to make such a determination because of a lack of sufficient majority under Rule 39(1), the matter can be resubmitted to the Conference after five calendar days for another vote, on the motion of the President or of any representative. This requirement of five days' delay does not apply during the last two weeks of the session.

(vi) Proper notice for each vote on any matter of substance: To avoid surprise votes and to provide a last chance for compromise, the rules require that no vote shall be taken on any matter of substance less than two working days after an announcement that the Conference is to proceed to vote on the matter has been made, and only after this announcement has been published in the Journal of the Conference. In addition, the Convention as a whole shall not be put to the vote less than four working days after the adoption of its last article.

Louis B. Sohn, "Voting Procedures in United Nations Conferences for the Codification of International Law," *American Journal of International Law*, Vol. 69, No. 2 (April 1975), pp. 310,349; U.N. Doc. A/Conf.62/30/Rev.; Daniel Vignes, "Will The Third Conference on the Law of the Sea Work According to the Consensus Rule?" 69 *American Journal of International Law*, Vol. 69, No. 1 (January 1975), pp. 119-129; John R. Stevenson and Bernard H. Oxman, "The Third United Nations Conference on the Law of the Sea: The 1974 Caracas Session," *American Journal of International Law*, Vol. 69, No. 1 (January 1975), pp. 1-30.

that their economic interests and political ambitions must prevail over the fate of the rest of the nations of the world. Obviously, if those views of that super-Power were accepted, it would be impossible to work out a fair and reasonable new Law of the Sea. In our opinion, consultations are desirable; but there certainly should be some method of voting in formulating a new Law of the Sea. The Chinese delegation firmly opposes the attempt by a certain super-Power to impose on the Conference th so-called principle of "consensus" which is tantamount to a veto.[19]

In conferences in which all United Nations member states participate, some states will seek an operational outcome that is effective, binding rules of conduct actually followed by states, for which consensus is the best guarantee. Other states will be satisfied instead to modify standards of legitimacy by a full utilization of voting majorities over the objection of dissident states, however important and influential, without being unduly preoccupied with the implementation of texts adopted.

United Nations parliamentary diplomacy cannot escape these tensions. Consensus rules operate only when major states or groups of states are politically disposed to let them work. They fail when a majority is determined to use its voting power to adopt an instrument, or when a minority will be reluctant to continue a process of negotiations under the threat of a reversion to naked voting power. Thus, in economic matters, the Group of Seventy-Seven may find it difficult not to press for the political advantage that voting power assures in the United Nations system, while the less numerous developed states may yet prefer a process of bargaining in a forum far removed from the unsettling influence of a well-organized and hostile voting majority, timidly avoiding confrontation in the U.N. itself.

The introduction of collective bargaining procedures in United Nations parliamentary diplomacy by using the device of representative committees, consultative groups, or small negotiating groups, operating on the basis of unanimity, is an attempt to strike a balance between the principle of unanimity on the one hand and the participation of only those states that are principally interested in the subject matter on the other. This balance is open to the same tensions that affect consensus rules and can work only when major states or controlling groups of states are politically disposed to accept it.

The recommendations of the Group of Experts attempted to strike this delicate balance. Under the proposals of the Group of Experts during the two–year period in which the negotiating groups would operate "the General Assembly and ECOSOC would be free to consider subjects under discussion in the group and to vote resolutions thereon, but in deciding whether to vote a particular resolution, the General Assembly and ECOSOC would take into account the progress of the negotiations."[20] At its 31st Session, the General Assembly had received proposals to utilize its functions and powers both as the highest policy-making body in the United Nations system and as a negotiating forum. These proposals were intended to strengthen the role of the Assembly in monetary, trade, and financial fields. As part of the restructuring effort, the Assembly also had proposals to transform UNCTAD into an effective institution for deliberation, negotiation, and review in the field of trade and international economic cooperation, "maintaining its close relationship with the General Assembly." UNCTAD was to be a "generator of new ideas and policy approaches," while its "negotiating function" would also be strengthened. UNCTAD, it has been proposed, would exercise an overview of "negotiations being conducted elsewhere," thus subjecting them to the domination of the Group of 77. The terms of reference of the Committee which considered proposals for

---

19.   Cited in Sohn (fn. 18), p. 336; U.N. Doc. A/C.1/PV.1932, pp. 22-23.
20.   U.N. Doc. E/AC.62/9, p. 1; U.N. Doc. A/AC.179/L.10/Rev. 1, p. 7.

restructuring the United Nations system in the economic and social sections were set out in Resolution 3362 (S-VII), September 16, 1975. The Seventh Special Session of the Assembly instructed the Committee to take into account also the report of the Group of Experts on the Structure of the United Nations system. But it appears that the Committee favors leaving the existing Assembly majority with the power to initiate its new ideas and policy approaches as well as subject all negotiations of an economic character to the overview of the self-same dominant majority. Predictably, the Assembly followed a different course and adopted resolution 32/197, December 20, 1977, "Restructuring of the Economic and Social Sector of the United Nations System." The proposals of the Group of Experts were not followed.[21]

Collective bargaining arenas and technical two-group or three-group negotiating forums removed from parliamentary diplomacy are multiplying. An incentive is needed if the U.N. is to adopt new consensus procedures. If need be, interdependence and crisis management can be conducted in arenas outside the United Nations: The Paris Conference on Vietnam, the Geneva Conference on the Middle East, and the CIEC are major negotiating efforts insulated to a large extent from majority decisions.

The choice between arenas involves a choice among modes of decision. Voting, the method of collective bargaining, or the hybrid method of consensus procedures, representative committees, and negotiating groups must be seen as alternatives. But other important models also exist. The method of informal meeting and gentlemen's agreements adopted by the Heads of the Central Banks of the industrialized nations in their frequent meetings in Basel, Switzerland under the auspices of the Bank for International Settlements has shown its value in a period of great monetary and financial turmoil. A French observer wrote that

> [d]iversification (or informality) is the second characteristic trait of the international monetary system. International monetary cooperation which has developed so fast in recent years between Central banks and the concentration of national economic policies rests only on informal bases known as arrangements or gentlemen's agreements. Those in charge of national monetary policy have taken care to establish a vast network of consultation and cooperation removed from any juridical link and from any formal basis. For bankers in particular, the very idea of formality is synonymous with ineffectiveness. Moreover, national governments, while concerting their domestic policies or while taking specific unilateral measures which went beyond what they were required to do by the positive juridical norms of the international monetary system, have not wished to crystalize those practices into international obligations. This is how, for example, states have followed the practice of keeping part of their official reserves in the national currencies of third countries, in large measure United States dollars, pound sterlings and to a smaller extent, French francs. Similarly, it had been the traditional policy of the United States until 15 August 1971 to convert on demand gold for dollars held by foreign monetary authorities. In these two cases, and they are not the only ones, these were simple practices which have greatly facilitated the work of the international monetary system; the states concerned did not have the feeling that their action, that their policies in these fields, flow from international obligations assumed by treaties or from international custom. This coexistence of legal factors and factual factors in the midst of the international monetary system makes delicate the determination of its true nature and its classification under the traditional typology.[22]

---

21.   U.N. General Assembly resolution 32/197, adopted without vote on December 20, 1977.

22.   Dominique Carreau, *Le système monétaire international* (Paris: A. Colin, 1972) pp. 31-32.

In the economic field, weighted voting plays an important role. The International Monetary Fund is a model for management by such voting procedures. It is significant, as another observer comments, that

> [t]he experience of the Fund demonstrates that even in an international organiza-
> tion in which the principle of the weighted voting power of members prevails, it
> may be necessary to provide that certain decisions are to be taken on the basis of
> equal voting power or by unanimity, the practical effect of which is equal voting
> power. The number of decisions, including action by members to amend the
> articles, for which weighted voting power has been eliminated in the Fund is
> modest. Originally, the decisions were limited to those for which the need for
> special safeguards was almost beyond controversy. . . . Obviously, members with
> sizable proportions of the total voting power are likely to resist any suggestions for
> extending the scope of equal voting power or the requirement of unanimity.[23]

The World Bank is also a significant model for management by weighted voting. Just how far this weighted voting can go is illustrated by the method used for drafting international treaties. The Executive Directors of the World Bank formulated treaties which they submitted to member states under which three international organizations in the Bank's structure were created. Again, it is worth noticing that

> [t]here was no express provision in the Charter of the Bank empowering the
> Directors to engage in this activity and there was no opportunity for individual
> governments (with the exception of those—five in number—who appoint their
> own Directors) to participate directly in the task of formulating these agreements.
> Moreover, the Executive Directors vote in accordance with the weighted-voting
> formula laid down in the Bank Charter. Under this formula voting strength is
> closely related to participation in the Bank's capital and the Executive Directors
> cast a number of votes to which the governments electing or appointing them are
> entitled. This means that one–third of the Directors can control decisions of the
> Board by their vote.[23a]

An increasingly important model of decision-making is decision by consensus in organs in which decisions can be taken by a vote. Many General Assembly decisions are now adopted by consensus. This mode of decision also has currency in the Security Council where the adoption of "a consensus" of the members of the Council is expressed in a statement made by the President of the Council. During the discussion of the invitation extended to the Palestine Liberation Organization (PLO) to participate in the Council's proceedings, an interesting development took place. The President of the Council reported the "understanding of the majority of the Security Council," not of the Council as a whole, that during discussions on the question of Palestine, the PLO would be invited to participate in the proceedings of the Council.[24] A procedural precedent had earlier been set by Western states during a debate on the Laotian question. It paved the way for agreed statements by a majority of the Council in caucus using the Presidency of the Council to overwhelm the veto. The dangers of such a procedure are apparent:

> What we may very well have to come to judge and are seeing here today is the
> commencement of an effort to subvert the open and public proceedings of the

23.   See Gold, (fn. 16), p. 707; see also Joseph Gold, *Voting and Decisions in the International, Monetary Fund* (Washington: International, Monetary Fund, 1972).

23a.   A. Broches, "Development of International Law by the International Bank for Reconstruction and Development," *Proceedings of the American Society of International Law at its Fifty-Ninth Annual Meeting* (1965), p. 34, quoted in Gold (fn 16), p. 706.

24.   U.N. Doc. S/PV.1870, pp. 51-52.

Security Council and replace them by the rule of an extra-legal, semi-secret apparat, which is inaccessible to the membership of the United Nations and inaccessible to the process of inquiry. There is a term for this: the term is totalitarianism.[25]

The form of decision is intimately tied to the type of arena used. The four principles of the sovereign equality of states, of universality, of representative rule, and of majority rule transposed to international organizations have spawned the pattern of majority voting now in common use. The bloc party coalitions of the General Assembly are replicated in many other organizations and agencies.[26] Having captured control of the legitimacy machine, the coalition of Arab, Socialist states and LDCs continues to press the ideological and diplomatic advantages which the United States and its Western allies had enjoyed in the early days of the organization.

As a result, Assembly resolutions such as the Charter of the Economic Rights and Duties of States have been resisted as mere "ideology" by the West. These instruments nevertheless have a tendency to legitimate claims of the 119 members of the non-aligned groups once negotiations begin, although resolutions adopted by consensus cannot acquire legal force in the face of opposition by a major group.[27] The intimate connection between majority votes and the principles of equality, universality, and representation informs the design of other arenas and forums such as the CIEC, in which accommodation and give-and-take are encouraged. In summary, decisions in international organizations are generally taken under one of the following procedures:

1. Unanimity, requiring the concurring votes of member states
2. Consensus, when proposals are adopted without a vote
3. Vote by a majority (simple of two-thirds)
6. Vote by a majority subject to the veto or other special rights of particular states or groups of states
7. Decision by consensus of a majority (the majority must be large enough to be able to obstruct procedural challenges to rulings by the Chair)

The Many Forms of Agreement

The complexity of global bargaining and its diplomatic modes is compounded by the importance of informal instruments of legal interest that are negotiated in multilateral forums and in traditional channels. The new diplomacy, multilateral as well as bilateral, is characterized by the design of many agreements in forms other than those which constitutional experts in the United States have been accustomed to. These formal changes affect the division of responsibility between the President and Congress. They impact on domestic constitutional arrangements for the management of interdependence. Global and regional bargains are struck in instruments of all shapes and forms. The elusive character of many of these instruments reflects the wish of states to structure not only the substance of obligations, but also their weight, legal effect, and domestic processes. States are intent to structure their freedom to retain, modify or terminate agreements. In a regime of global interdependence, some states find it difficult to end

25. Leo Gross, "Voting in the Security Council and the PLO," *American Journal of International Law*, Vol. 70, No. 3 (July 1976), pp. 470-491.
26. See in general Hovet (fn.2); see also Gold (fn. 23), pp. 93ff.
27. On decision by consensus see Giuseppe Sperduti, "Consensus in International Law," *Italian Yearbook of International Law*, Vol. 2 (1976), pp. 33-38.

and reduce commitments. The demands of mutually deeply impacting and sustained relationships between the powers give rise to inertial forces that stabilize the agreements which consecrate and define these relationships. This inertial force can make it truly difficult to modify or end them. Less formal instruments give states greater leeway. Informal agreements can be terminated or revised or suspended with greater ease—and this can then be done, in the United States at least, without requiring formal Congressional support.

The international law concept of international agreement must not be confused with domestic constitutional classifications. Internationally binding commitments can be made in writing or orally, with a minimum of formality. Constitutional and statutory requirements regarding treaties and executive agreements contribute to confusion about the international and domestic effects of instruments under domestic law on the one hand and international law on the other.

It is not surprising that the formality or legal character of international agreements and arrangements can itself become the object of negotiations. This should be illustrated.

Some instruments are intended to have an ambiguous juridical status. Thus, the Final Act of the Conference on Security and Cooperation in Europe signed in Helsinki on August 1, 1975 is neither a treaty nor an executive agreement. A U.S. negotiator commented that

> [f]rom the very earliest discussions in Geneva, it became clear that virtually all delegations desired documents that were morally compelling but not legally binding. As the negotiations progressed, however, and as various delegations gained enthusiasm for texts which were to their liking, certain texts took on some of the tone of legally binding instruments. This trend was a cause of concern to the U.S. delegation, which considered that the intent of the participants should be clearly reflected in the language of the documents. Given the predisposition of Congress to question the right of the President to conclude important international agreements without Congressional consent, any ambiguity as to the legal nature of the texts could become the source of unnecessary dispute with the Congress.[28]

Even though the Declaration as such was clearly not intended to be legally binding, it remained possible, on account of the language used, for the "Document on Confidence-Building Measures and Certain Aspects of Security and Disarmament" which is part of the Final Act, to be regarded as binding. Some doubts were dispelled by tabling interpretative statements in the course of the negotiations. Despite the lack of intent to create legal obligations, the United States, the Soviet Union, France, and the United Kingdom faced the problem of how best to protect their existing special rights in Germany under the German Instrument of Surrender at the end of World War II. An express disclaimer of modification of Four Power Rights in Germany was thus included by the three Western powers in the text of their acceptance of the invitation to the second stage of the Conference and in a statement in the opening week in Geneva. The Powers eventually felt, despite the non-binding character of the Final Act, that some form of disclaimer should be included in the Final Act itself.[29]

---

28.   Harold S. Russell, "The Helsinki Declaration: Brobdignag or Lilliput?" *American Journal of International Law*, Vol. 70, No. 2 (April 1976), pp. 242-272. For the text of the Final Act, see *International Legal Materials*, Vol. 14,No. 5 (September 1975), pp. 1292-1325.

29.   The language adopted is as follows, "The participating states, paying due regard to the principles above and, in particular, to the first sentence of the tenth principle, 'fulfillment in good faith of obligations under international law', note that the present Declaration does not affect their rights and obligations, nor the corresponding treaties and other agreements and arrangements."

To have regarded the Final Act as legally binding would have had a number of significant consequences. The Department of State was concerned that "euphoria over this event might lead to increased pressure for withdrawal of U.S. forces from Europe and for other forms of unilateral disarmament." It played down the Conference as an exercise which "was primarily of interest to the allies of the United States and which, in any case, had not produced documents of a legally binding character." The United States was also reluctant to concede that the Conference had finalized the status quo in Europe and recognized the frontiers in Europe, confirming Soviet hegemony in Eastern Europe and in the Baltic States. According to the same participants, it was the view of "all" the Western negotiators that the Declaration does not depart materially from previous international arrangements on frontiers and "does nothing to recognize existing frontiers in Europe."[30] To this end, Western representatives sought to avoid legal obligations of any kind and treated the question of frontiers merely as a facet of the principle of the non-use of force which had been developed in the United Nations Declaration on Principles of Friendly Relations and Cooperation among States.[31] Recognition of the existing frontiers was also resisted because of the interest of the Federal Republic of Germany in a possible reunification with the German Democratic Republic and because of concern by States in the European Economic Community that no language be used in the Final Act that might inhibit an eventual political union of the Community.

The formal character of diplomatic auspices is also often the object of negotiations. For example, the decision to hold the Middle East Geneva Peace Conference under the "auspices" of the United Nations but not under its authority reflected the participants' agreement on the avoidance of Security Council voting majorities and procedures and on limiting the terms of reference of the Conference to resolutions 242 and 338 of the Security Council. It made the conference independent of the major United Nations organs, structured the agenda and, most importantly, postponed the question of the participation of the PLO to a later stage. On the other hand, the Security Council decision to invite the PLO to participate in the debate of the question of Palestine expressed the agreement of the Council's majority, with the ambiguous acquiescence of the United States, to recognize the authority of the PLO to speak on behalf of the Arab people of Palestine.[32]

At times when agreement on a difficult point is beyond reach, efforts may be made to substitute informal unilateral undertakings for agreed provisions in the hope that the desire for progress in negotiations will lead the other side to respect expectations expressed in a unilateral understanding. For instance, at the 1973 Moscow Summit meeting between President Nixon and Secretary Brezhnev an effort was made to reach agreement on the important definition of "heavy missile" in the SALT negotiations. No one on the U.S. side, which pressed for an agreed definition of heavy missiles (in which the Soviet Union has the advantage), suggested that the negotiations with the Soviets be broken off if the definition was not agreed upon. Instead, in instructions from the White House, the United States delegation was directed to put into the record the following statement:

> The U.S. delegation regrets that the Soviet delegation has not been willing to
> agree on a common definition of a heavy missile. Under these circumstances, the
> U.S. delegation believes it necessary to state the following. The U.S. would

---

30.   See Russell, (fn. 28).
31.   U.N. General Assembly resolution 2625 (XXV), October 24, 1970.
32.   See Gross (fn. 25).

consider any ICBM having a volume significantly greater than that of the largest light ICBM now operational on either side to be a heavy ICBM. The U.S. proceeds on the premise that the Soviet side will give due account to this consideration[32a].

The head of the Soviet delegation made it clear that no understanding had been reached on this point.[33] The Secretary of Defense later stated that the Soviet Union could not be bound by a unilateral understanding on the part of the United States. The device did not work. But it did inject confusion about the question whether the Russians had violated the letter or the spirit of the 1972 SALT agreement to limit strategic arms.

The adoption of conference texts or resolutions in parliamentary arenas is pregnant with legitimizing powers even when these texts lack binding power. They are invoked in disputes and in situations in which the legitimacy of a policy is in issue. Quite apart from the question of their binding effect, assembly resolutions tend to have a self-enabling, self-licensing, or self–authorizing power for states supporting them. Formal limitations on the competence of representative parliamentary organs are *not* an effective restraint in the face of a willful majority.

Emphasis on binding texts has been a costly bias of legal investigation. Preoccupation with binding texts, obligatory resolutions, and enforceable decisions, which are at the core of conventional legal inquiry, has led to the neglect of the authorizing, licensing, recognizing and constitutive properties of resolutions that do not aspire to obligatory status. Concern with binding force and enforcement in the decentralized international system is a relic of legal habits developed in the hierarchical milieu of the state system. The conventional legalistic approach to pay little heed to non-binding texts has encouraged those who would vote for, or permit a consensus on, resolutions inimical to the West on the ground that these texts are only recommendations devoid of obligatory force. It is the licensing, authorizing, recognizing, and constitutive powers of the recommendations of the General Assembly of the United Nations which largely account for its political potency.[34]

Coherent majorities expressed in voting blocs seek to enhance the authority of the arena in which they prevail. The policy of the United States in the General Assembly of the United Nations at the time of the Korean War is a good illustration. In pressing for the "Uniting of Peace" resolution, the United States asserted for the General Assembly powers for the maintenance of international peace and security which at the San Francisco Conference had been reserved to the Security Council. The theory was that when the Security Council fails to exercise its primary responsibility for the maintenance of international peace and security owing to the use of the veto power by one of the Permanent Members, then the Assembly may act to discharge the responsibilities of the organization.[35]

A point may be reached at which multilateral negotiations become simply too involved. The mammouth United Nations Conference on the Law of the Sea has

---

32a. United States Arms Control and Disarmament Agency, *Arms Control and Disarmament Agreements* (Washington, 1980 ed.), p. 157.

33. See the account of Gerard C. Smith, Chief of the U.S. Delegation at the SALT Talks from 1962-1972, in the New York Times, January 16, 1976; see also his account, "SALT after Vladivostock," *Journal of International Affairs*, Vol. 29, No. 1 (Spring 1975), pp. 7-18.

34. See Gidon Gottlieb, "The Nature of International Law: Toward A Second Concept of Law," in Cyril E. Black and Richard A. Falk, eds., *The Future of the International Legal Order, Vol. IV, Trends and Patterns* (Princeton: Princeton University Press, 1972), pp. 331-383.

35. General Assembly resolution 377 (V), November 3, 1950. This episode is discussed in Julius Stone, *Legal Controls of International Conflicts* (New York: Holt Rinehart, 1954), pp. 266-284.

generated intense analysis of the characteristics of the parliamentary mode of negotiations. Policy-makers and analysts have been overwhelmed by the complexities of the negotiating process. Here the magnitude of the task can be numerically expressed. At the 1973 Caracas meeting of the Conference, approximately 1450 persons were officially accredited by states. Other accredited persons, journalists, and observers numbered about 5,000. In negotiations involving 140 states, with an agenda of 100 issues, or articles, a participant was required to know something about 14,000 "decision cells." But even this was an oversimplification, for "14,000 decision cells presumes unified states without internal dissonance in decision."[36]

Particular useful materials on the fomality and legal effect of international engagements can be found in the Senate Hearings on an Early Warning System in Sinai.[37] In seeking the Senate's approval for the American proposal to send technicians to Sinai, the Secretary of State distinguished between several types of documents submitted to Congress. He referred to documents which include assurances, undertakings, and commitments which are considered to be legally binding upon the United States and which were initialed or signed by the United States and one of the parties. He warned that not all the provisions of documents which also contain legally binding commitments are considered to be legally binding. Some are and some are not so binding; some provisions reflect assurances by the United States of political intentions:

> These are often statements typical of diplomatic exchange; in some instances they are merely formal reaffirmations of existing American policy. Other provisions refer to contingencies which may never arise and are related — sometimes explicitly — to present circumstances subject to rapid change. The documents submitted to Congress contain all assurances and undertakings which are binding on the United States. That means the Administration will make no contrary claim in the future, nor will it accept any contrary claim by any other government.

The Secretary of State pointed out that

> [t]he fact that many provisions are not by any standard international commitments does not mean of course that the United States is morally or politically free to act as if they did not exist. On the contrary, they are important statements of diplomatic policy and engage the good faith of the United States so long as the circumstances that give rise to them continue. But they are not binding commitments of the United States.[38]

He submitted to the Committee extracts from documents in the negotiating record which the Administration believes are legally binding assurances, undertakings, or commitments. These include certain provisions which, although not regarded by the Administration as binding, might be so regarded by others. The Committee was also supplied with documents which are explicitly described *as a part* of the Agreement between Egypt and Israel, without the United States being a party to that instrument.

---

36. The Law of the Sea Conference has generated considerable academic and professional interest. In the vast literature, a good starting point is Robert L. Friedheim, *Parliamentary Diplomacy—A Survey*, Institute of Naval Studies, Center for Naval Analyses, 76-0046 (1976); see also his "The 'Satisfied' and 'Dissatisfied' States Negotiate International Law: A Case Study," *World Politics*, Vol. 18, No. 1 (October 1965), pp. 20-41.

37. U.S. Senate, Committee on Foreign Relations, 94th Congress. 1st Session, Hearings on Early Warning System in Sinai.

38. The testimony of Dr. Kissinger is also printed in *Department of State Bulletin*, Vol. 73, No. 1896 (27 October 1975), pp. 609-613.

By inference, other kinds of documents might also be in existence: minutes, notes and other documents in the negotiating record which contain assurances, undertakings, and commitments of a non-binding character only.

The statement of the Secretary of State highlights the delicate distinction between types of assurances, undertakings, commitments, and political intentions of the United States. They suggest several categories of material:

1. Legally binding provisions in an agreement which are recognized to be binding in the sense that the United States recognizes it is not free to disregard them and which are governed by the rules of international law regarding legal agreements

2. Provisions which one party to an agreement may regard to be legally binding but which another party may not

3. Assurances, undertakings, commitments, and statements of political intentions which declare or reaffirm existing American policy and which are not intended to be legally binding

4. Assurances, undertakings, commitments, and statements of political intentions which refer to contingencies which may never arise and which are related to present circumstances subject to rapid change

5. Undertakings or assurances which are conditional on existing or prior legislative authority and approval

Statements and provisions of documents which are not legally binding engage states politically and morally, in the sense that they are not free to act as if they did not exist. They engage their good faith so long as the circumstances that gave rise to them continue.

The distinction between legally binding provisions and those not intended to bind requires clarification. When a provision is regarded as legally binding, the parties agree that they:

1. Will make no contrary claims in the future

2. Will accept no contrary claim in the future

3. Cannot fail to honor the binding provisions without being in breach of a legal obligation which entails international responsibility

4. Recognize that the provisions agreed upon are subject to the rules of international law governing international agreements

5. Consider that all appropriate constitutional requirements regarding existing or prior authorization have been met

6. Affirm that claims, rights, and obligations under relevant treaties and other agreements and arrangements under international law are affected and modified by the new agreement to the extent required

Provisions and instruments are not binding without the intent to give them a legal character. Treaties and executive agreements are legally binding instruments by virtue of their formal character. However, other memoranda of agreement which may not be binding instruments can contain legally binding provisions. The requirement of publicity attached to the Senate consent power involves the Congress in the process of agreement, reducing the possibility that it may not wish to honor the commitments of the Administration. In the case of the Sinai Agreements, the Administration made it clear that the Congress was only invited to approve the American proposal regarding the limited U.S. role in the Early Warning System in Sinai. Dr. Kissinger emphasized that a vote in favor of that proposal would not commit the Congress to a position on any one of the elaborate U.S. commitments to Israel made as part of the package deal. Congress was not asked to approve the undertakings and assurances to the parties, the relationships with the countries in the area, any given level of budget support, or policies and programs in the Middle East. The Secretary of State stressed the distinction between legal obligations of the United States and the commitments of Congress. What then does a provision which is not a legal commitment involve? Such provisions indicate the agreement of the parties that they:

1. Cannot fail to honor a provision that is not legally binding without being in breach of their moral or political obligations which engage their good faith, provided the circumstances which gave rise to them have not changed

2. Recognize that their rights and obligations under relevant treaties and other agreements and arrangements are not affected, modified, or waived

3. Agree that no new jural acts (such as recognition) can be inferred in the absence of an intent to the contrary

As a result, the legal binding force of particular documents or provisions may become a matter of great delicacy. For example, the Legal Adviser of the Department of State submitted to Congress on a classified basis a memorandum with his assessment of the legal character of all the documents given to the Congress in connection with the Sinai agreements. His judgment about which commitment is legally binding was itself classified, although the documents analyzed were made public.

The Legal Adviser to the Department of State, Monroe Leigh, gave an opinion that the two memoranda of agreement between the United States and Israel, reached in connection with the disengagement agreement, are properly described under U.S. Constitutional practice as "executive agreements." These are the agreements which in the opinion of the Secretary of State also contain provisions which are not considered legally binding. Nevertheless, in the Legal Adviser's opinion, the memoranda of agreement when executed become international agreements. The identification of the provisions not intended to be binding remains classified.[39]

The Legal Adviser did not discuss in his opinion the character of the other legal commitments that were included in the negotiating record.[40] The question arises whether binding commitments found in extracts from negotiating records and other informal materials are included in the constitutional category of internationally legally binding commitments.

When provisions of agreements are publicly declared and when Congress expresses its support for them, for example, in a Joint Resolution, then many of the political distinctions between legal and non-legal undertakings are removed. But a difference that remains regards the duration and termination of undertakings. The case of the Mutual Defense Treaty with the Republic of China is in point. Let us assume that in lieu of the Treaty, the United States had adopted another procedure to express the American

39. See U.S. Senate, Committee on the Judiciary, Subcommittee on the Separation of Powers, 94th Congress, 1st Session, Hearings on Congressional Oversight of Executive Agreements—1975. For Mr. Leigh's opinions and letters and the conflicting opinions of the Senate Office of Legal Counsel, see ibid., pp. 365-415. Problems of interpretation may also arise under the Vienna Convention on the Law of Treaties when provisions not included in instruments known domestically as either executive agreements or as treaties, may constitute nevertheless international agreements under the Convention.

40. See, for example, interpretations of the concept of international agreement by the Department of State in *Foreign Affairs Manual*, Vol. 11, reprinted in U.S. Senate Hearings, ibid., pp. 279-301. Compare with the text of the Case Act, Public Law 882, September 23, 1950, *Statutes at Large*, Vol. 64, Part I, p. 980. See also Department of Defense Instruction No. 5530.2 in the selfsame Senate Hearings, pp. 97-98. See further, Mr. Leigh's letter discussing the definition of an international agreement, ibid., pp. 237-239, citing the Restatement on Foreign Law. See also the text of a letter by Kenneth Rush, Acting Secretary of State, ibid., pp. 187-188.

commitment to the defense of the Republic of China and that the President had instead proclaimed a "Defense of China Doctrine" which would have been approved in a Joint Resolution of Congress. Such an American commitment, not in legal form, would in effect have been modified by the Shanghai Communique issued at the end of President Nixon's visit to the People's Republic of China. There would have been no requirement to bring such a commitment formally to an end, assuming the Administration had so wished. On the other hand, abrogation of the Mutual Defense Treaty required formal denunciation, a difficult matter for an Administration facing political constituencies with an interest in the status quo. The role of Congress in terminating treaties is itself unclear. The Shanghai Communique is one of the key diplomatic instruments negotiated in recent years, outlining as it does the character of relations between the People's Republic of China and the United States pending full recognition, and the political commitment of the United States to the People's Republic of China in the event of an armed attack. But this instrument was not endowed with legally binding force, and merely outlined the positions, intentions, and policies of the parties. It did not suggest that the parties intended to enter into a legal relationship capable of modifying existing legal commitments. Only formal recognition could accomplish this.

The subtleties of international negotiations have engendered forms of agreement which Congress finds difficult to control. The Case Act which requires communication to the Congress and publication of international executive agreements has in a sense strengthened the hand of the President in his relations with the Congress, a result not intended by the authors of that enactment. The Act has in effect created a new category of agreements, those that are transmitted to the Congress and on which the Congress takes no position. Where the President would not previously have communicated an executive agreement on a delicate matter to the Congress, he is now bound by law to do so. But as a result, the Congress can no longer claim it was not informed of the President's commitments, and this knowledge implicates it to a greater extent than ignorance would have done. It can no longer pretend ignorance. For example, President Nixon's unpublished assurances to President Thieu with regard to U.S. military assistance in case of Communist violations of the Vietnam-Paris Peace Agreements engaged the good faith of the United States less than if it had been communicated to the Congress at the time. It would then have been necessary for the Congress to take a position on the whole Vietnam agreements package, including the President's assurances.[41] Failure to disavow such assurances would have come closer to acquiescence.

The function and character of an agreement between parties not involved with each other beyond that particular transaction are fundamentally different from those of an agreement which forms part of a complex pattern of interdependence and mutual dealings. In a casual relationship it is natural for the parties to look first and foremost to the performance and enforcement of their accord, which is the raison d'être for their having a relationship. In a complex relationship the parties look to the maintenance of their relationship by honoring their commitments or by further negotiations about the performance and modification of their accords. In such relationships agreements are rarely enforced. They are primarily the basis for future negotiations to modify them. Enforcement is an effective guarantee in a casual relationship. In a fixed relationship the effectiveness of accords rests in the character of the relationship itself.

International negotiations proceed on the basis of agreed rules, principles, and policies that outline the perimeter of what can be claimed. It is difficult for states locked in negotiations—just when good faith is so important—to repudiate principles and rules

---

41.   Ibid., pp. 322-326, for the text of the Nixon letters to Thieu.

to which they have subscribed or to which the community of nations defers. International law furnishes an ample store of agreed principles to structure negotiations and their product. The skillful management of principles already agreed upon gives no mean advantage to the negotiator.

Wherever we turn in the design of agreements and of modes of agreements, a recurring feature stands out: the options and the modes are few and the choice between them inescapable. Failure to choose is nothing more than passive acquiescence in the status quo or in a dominant trend. In the international arena, as in social choices generally, the range of possibilities is restricted. Invention consists in the departure from pure formal models and the generation of mixed modes which strive for delicate balances. The narrow range of options is a significant characteristic of social arrangements limited by natural necessity to a range of choices which cannot be meaningfully widened. The practice of agreement-making remains distinct from that of a rule-guided decision. It belongs to a separate logical field. Other objectives are sought, other mental operations are involved. The area of negotiations is a basic skill of lawyering.

In a global society, increasingly vulnerable to domestic and foreign enemies because of the fragility of its technology and its exposed lifelines, a movement toward negotiations and away from the enforcement of accords was to be expected. The confrontations and violence that enforcement imports have become too costly.

The demands of world order politics are in fact no longer ignored.[42] Without prejudice to the question whether world order can be deliberately created, another preliminary question has been considered: what are the diplomatic modes and structures for a world order built on bargaining and accords. The U.S. is now confronted with the necessity of bargaining with others rather than laying the groundwork for the new order by itself. Esoteric new structures for bargaining, the emergence of parity diplomacy, the creation of new arenas for negotiations, and the wise use of a rich variety of forms of agreement, binding and non-binding, are all elements of the world order now taking shape. Flexibility in voting procedures and a greater variety of forms of instruments is required for managing interdependence and moving to the next world order. They are all part of the transition to the world of the 80's.

We have every reason to think that this world order can be neither easily comprehended nor easily made manageable. It does not fit into any of the blueprints for a new order. The ever-widening circle of arenas, both domestic and international, and the variety of procedures for addressing a complex agenda of interconnected issues that deeply influence national economic policies defies anything but expert analysis. It threatens to exclude significant segments of the law and economics community from involvement in the domestic and international dimensions of global interdependence—a development much to be feared in the absence of a commitment by this community to make this field its own.

---

42. See, for example, the "third century" series of articles by distinguished writers in the review *Foreign Policy*. As Stanley Hoffman observes in "No Choice, No Illusions," *Foreign Policy*, No. 25 (Winter 1976-1977), p. 97, "world order politics is obviously in." For a review of some of the literature on the new order, see Geoffrey Barraclough's articulate if opinionated "Waiting for the New Order," *New York Review of Books*, Vol. 25, No. 16 (26 October 1978), pp. 45-53.

CHART 3.1

Some Principal Diplomatic Modes

The Parliamentary mode: characteristic of representative conferences and assemblies: the U.N. General Assembly.

The Traditional mode: characteristic of bilateral negotiations: U.S. -Japanese trade negotiations.

The Parity mode: characteristic of conflicting interest groups: North-South conference.

The Managerial mode: characteristic of functional agencies or corporations with agreed objectives: World Bank.

The Conference mode: characteristic of situations in which the parties must act in concert to reach agreement: Vietnam Peace conference.

Third party modes: mediation, conciliation, good offices: U.S. role in Egyptian-Israeli disengagement agreement.

CHART 3:2

Sets of Necessary Choices Regarding the Character of International Agreements

---

Process	Legal. . . . Mixed (i.e., UNGA Declaratory Resolutions). . . . Political
Participation	Universal. . . . Plurilateral, Bilateral. . . . Unilateral
Formality	Treaties. . . . Executive Agreements, letters, speeches, toasts. . . . Understandings
Actors	States. . . . Non-recognized States, Non-recognized movements. . . . Corporations, Individuals
Institutions	Inter-governmental. . . . Mixed IGO/NGO. . . . Non-governmental
Stability	Ratification by referendum. . . . Commitment of all branches of the government (majority and opposition). . . . Commitment of Executive Branch only. . . . Personal commitment of officials
Decision Technique	Unanimity. . . . Agreement of Parties, Consensus. . . . Majority voting, coalitions, veto
Inputs	State Civil Service. . . . Advisory boards, private participation in delegations. . . . Private interests
Time Frame	Permanent. . . . Temporary
Negotiating Forum	Universal Organization. . . . Plurilateral Conference. . . . Bilateral Conference, Collective Bargaining Setting. . . . Unilateral Proclamation
Representation	Formal equality. . . . Weighted participation. . . . Special rights. . . . Parity of groups

CHART 3.2 (continued)

Modification New agreement or amendment . . . agreed interpretation and development . . . unilateral interpretation and development . . . new practice without reference to old agreement

Termination Agreed termination . . . claim that arrangement is no longer in force . . . unilateral denunciation

Dispute Settlement Judicial, compulsory or ad hoc. . . . Third party binding arbitration. . . . Third party recommendation. . . . Third party good offices. . . . Bilateral negotiations

Publicity Public negotiations and arrangements . . . secret negotiations and published agreements . . . secret negotiations and secret agreements

Linkage Linkage to character of relations. . . . Linkage to other non-related issues. . . . Linkage to related issues . . . no linkage

Bases of Effectiveness Agreement. . . . Relationship between the parties. . . . Expectations of allies or of adversaries . . . common ends . . . reciprocity . . . legitimacy . . . consensus of big powers . . . sanctions

Dissenting and Third Parties Imposed acceptance . . . negotiated acceptance . . . license action against . . . exclude . . . ignore

Procedure Formal rules with public debate. . . . Formal meetings behind closed doors . . . informal negotiations behind closed doors . . . private talks

Consent Submission to imposed arrangement . . . deference to recommended arrangement . . . acquiescence to arrangement. . . . Tacit agreement. . . . Express agreement

International Law-Making:
A View From Technology

ZDENEK J. SLOUKA

PREVIEW

New actors, new issues, new demands, and new hopes enter the processes of international law-making at an ever-increasing rate. This is not just a quantitative growth of interacting elements and forces. It has a qualitative core: we are witnessing not a mere proliferation of law-making factors but a metamorphosis in the total process of world order, a metamorphosis both subtle and profound. The subtlety is in the real-world manifestations of the change; they come from all directions and yet are difficult to detect, to describe, and to measure. The profound dimension of the change lies in the world of concepts, values, and dreams; the pressure for their rethinking, reappraisal, and redreaming is relentless. The two worlds, of course, completely pervade one another, and a change in one deeply affects the other.

The over-all direction of the change in international law-making is towards specificity, softness, and refinement of new rules and regimes. Within that change two trends are visible; both arise from the observable reality of international relations, and both demand major conceptual adjustments.

One trend is the relative weakening in the power of the treaties and of codifiable customary rules as the chief pillars supporting the global system of order. Ever harder to make, and with ever shorter life-spans, traditional treaties and general customary rules function less than effectively in the regulation of newly erupting international activities. Since international life cannot go on without rules, the traditional processes of international law-making are being supplemented and sometimes replaced by a swiftly pulsating interplay of rising and falling norms of international behavior, filling in the normative vacua as they emerge. The definiteness of these flickering norms, and so their legal quality, may be sometimes doubtful; but they are often all we have.

The second trend stems from the first. Since the normative responses to new demands for guideposts must be quick, there emerge and spread throughout the global system of order visible streams of particularistic, diversified living norms, each individually made-to-measure, and all of them densely intertwined. They do not replace the universal and general rules of behavior of more traditional ancestry. They just join them, but in multitudes. As a result, the traditional general and universal rules no longer are the hierarchical pinnacles towering over the lesser legal forms. They have simply become particles in an increasingly amorphous mass of normative phenomena.

These two trends are separable from each other only as analytical categories. In reality they constitute one indivisible flow. New, abruptly arising issues and conflicts among nations and other global actors stimulate the search for swift, issue-specific responses; once these are found and shown to produce results, they become parts of the total repertoire of problem-solving procedures, and a resort to them in other instances is likely.

This condensation summarizes one of the basic conceptual prisms of this study: through it, the international normative process is viewed as an increasingly diversified, dynamic, highly politicized and particularistic system of interactions and relationships. This is a major trend leading far out into the foreseeable future; technological forces and their social reflections and impacts contribute to the continuity, direction, and scope of this trend.[1]

* * * * * *

Technological change is singled out for analysis although it need not be the sole determining force in the evolution of a diversified process of world order. Indeed, other massive influences, whose specific impact on the processes of world order is beyond the analytic limits of this study, are at work: nationalism; the proliferation of international actors; the post-colonial resurfacing and magnification of cultural diversity; rapid shifts in the distribution of economic power; the "democratization" of the diplomatic and negotiating processes; and many others. In this orchestration of awesome forces, the technological phenomenon plays only one part. Yet the salience of the technological trait in the contemporary and, even more so, in the emerging international society of the future is clearly visible. The technological phenomenon pervades so many if not all social structures and functions; it comprises so durable and probably permanent an element of society; and it so easily penetrates through social boundaries of all types that, at the very least, it provides a useful focus for an inquiry into the ways through which the global community is likely to be ordering its affairs in the future.[2]

* * * * * *

This, then, represents the gist of the forthcoming argument: Technological change, being largely coterminous with the change in the nature of the contemporary civilization and its life-style, helps in a significant way to steer the international normative process—not necessarily the final shape of the system of order—towards the production of an endless multiplicity and diversity of norms distinguished more by their temporariness and flexibility than durability and firmness.

In terms of such values as reliable peace, just order, and human dignity and solidarity, is this trend toward dynamic diversity good or bad? As the technological phenomenon drives the processes of world order off their traditional, slow channels and into swift and unregulated currents, what is gained, and what is lost, from the quality of such processes?

On the positive side we shall see a global normative process much more pliable, and

---

1. A valuable examination of the increasing diversity of normative processes in international society is Oscar Schachter's "Toward a Theory of International Obligation," Stephen M. Schwebel, ed., *The Effectiveness of International Decisions* (Dobbs Ferry, N.Y.: Oceana Publications, 1971), pp. 9-31. Among the factors contributing to the increase of normative activity outside the formal procedures of international law-making Schachter refers to technology: "The expansion of science and technology with international impact both beneficial and harmful has given rise to informal means of setting standards and exercising supervision without entering into tight and tidy legal instruments" (p. 12).

2. Sprouts go farther out when they see focus on technological advances and innovation directing attention to changes in every other sector of our milieu and providing "possibly the most productive point of entry from which to explore the whole range of conditions and trends that are shaping our world." Harold Sprout and Margaret Sprout, *Towards a Politics of the Planet Earth* (New York: Van Nostrand and Reinhold, 1971), p. 205.

much more responsive to social change. Its greater pliability and responsiveness may increase its potential contribution to a more equitable international allocation of all values, political, economic, social, and psychological. These are not small benefits given the present state of world affairs.

The costs are not insignificant either. The legal quality of international order will be further dissipated with the consequent weakening of its legal stability. Expectations and understandings about the substance of norms and about the ways and means of changing them will grow increasingly soft and uncertain as we continue to move from consent to consensus as the order-creating energy in the international politics of the technological age.[3] The classic image of a universal system of international law as the foundation of global order will keep on losing its sharpness and its ability to serve as a vivid guide to thought and action.

This balance sheet has one peculiarity. The positive changes take place in the fields of global interaction, in the real world of nations. The losses are chiefly in the minds of men. It is, of course, possible that the Westphalian syndrome has been so deeply burned into our thinking processes and organizational tendencies that we can no longer effectively design, accept, and operate a mechanism of global order sharply different from the nation-state model—a mechanism, that is, based on diffusion rather than centrality of power; working more through the relative dimness of consensus than the authoritative sharpness of consent; capable of discriminating between subjects, issues, and principles; a mechanism which is infinitely malleable, pluralistic, and kaleidoscopic, an almost precise opposite of the ultimate apotheosis of the Leviathan cast in the form of a world government. This ability to readjust our thinking and actions to new models of the international normative process may eventually determine the productivity of the process and the quality of its outcomes.

TECHNOLOGY AND MODELS OF WORLD ORDER

Considerable thought and much imagination have gone into inquiries and speculations about the possible *outcomes* of the international normative process stimulated or otherwise affected by the technological phenomenon. Painting distant images which leap over generations and over much of the detail of life has always held certain fascination and, to some, offered certain comfort: shooting at a target beyond one's lifetime is a low risk activity. Focused on the product of the normative process, numerous studies examined the possible impact on the quality of life of various mostly material technologies, and from this they postulated the new forms of world order as the necessary and rational reactions to the technological challenge. Skills such as the green revolution, nuclear weaponry, supersonic transport, remote sensing of earth resources, direct satellite broadcasting, weather modification, or deep ocean technologies have all been looked upon not only as technological feats, as more efficient ways of doing things that needed to be done, they have also been recognized for their potential effect on the international calculus of power, and more: they have been seen as possessing the greatest power of all, the power of evoking in men a higher, transnational level of rationality needed for reconstructing the system of world order along more effective, almost technologically reliable lines.

Most predictions about nations going to be forced into working together once they have squarely faced the technologies of global dimensions and extreme complexity have

---

3. Cf. formulation in Richard A. Falk, *The Status of Law in International Society* (Princeton: Princeton University Press, 1970), p. 401.

been actually based on two assumptions so manifestly false that their fallacy requires no documentation: (1) that national policies result from rational decision-making processes and, a corollary of the first, (2) that a rational collective behavior is the product of adding up appropriately related rational policies of individual nations. Yet the scanning of some of the attempts at modelling the system of world order directly from the models of technological change is important here because that type of literature is both fairly prevalent and, more importantly, it reveals by implication some of the assumptions about the process leading from technology to other social institutions.

The two major tendencies—the preoccupation with specific material technologies, and the inclination to vault from the nature of a technology to the nature of the political system supposedly necessitated by it—have been fairly dominant in the last three decades of efforts by students, observers, and practitioners of international affairs concerned with the relation of technology and society.

The ultimate form of ascribing to technology politically imperative power was the "one world or none" projection of the direct political outcomes, one of them a world government, of the existence of the atomic bomb, as seen and wished in the late forties by scientists reacting to the Hiroshima and Nagasaki bombing.[4] Some of these technologically inspired visions have continued to come up through the subsequent years; while the predictions of the inevitable future have lost some of their immediacy, they have come to be only slightly less categorical. More than a quarter of a century after the bomb, the "ultimate" weapon is no longer seen shaping the international political system. It has been replaced by technology at large as the driving force pushing the world inexorably and "swiftly into a universal internationalism."[5]

Although most social scientists were considerably more cautious in predicting the political outcomes of the tensions generated in the international system by technological change,[6] they too have had their share of overdrive. Writing from different theoretical premises, in different times, and with different tools, John Herz[7] and Silviu Brucan,[8]

---

4. For instance, see the demand for "world government right now" in a statement issued by the Association of Los Alamos Scientists on 13 October 1945 in *The New York Times*, 14 October 1945, quoted in William T.R. Fox, "International Control of Atomic Weapons," in Bernard Brodie, ed., *The Absolute Weapon: Atomic Power and World Order* (New York: Harcourt, Brace, 1946), p. 170.

5. Arthur B. Bronwell, "Peace, War, and Technology," Bronwell, ed., *Science and Technology in the World of the Future* (New York: Wiley-Interscience, 1970), p. 387. Of course, none of the sociotechnological imagery of the modern day has ever come anywhere close to the elegance and sophistication of the Teilhardian vision of a noösphere, a zone of spirit-liberating knowledge enveloping the planet in the ultimate phase of peaceful unity. One of the more powerful prophets of a scientific millenium and an ardent believer "that the earth is more likely to stop turning than is mankind, as a whole, likely to stop organising and unifying itself" [Pierre Teilhard de Chardin, *The Future of Man* (New York: Harper and Row, 1964), p. 152] Teilhard saw the certain coming of peace ("peace . . . is certain; it is only a matter of time," p. 153) heralded not by official utterances, pacifist manifestations, or conscientious objectors, but by "the ever more numerous institutions and associations of men where in the search for knowledge a new spirit is silently taking shape around us" (154).

6. Similarly, with reference to the atomic bomb, William T.R. Fox, "Science, Technology and International Politics," *International Studies Quarterly*, Vol. 12, No. 1 (March 1968) p. 10: "Some social scientists were more nearly correct than some natural scientists in projecting the political consequences of the great events at Hiroshima and Nagasaki. They appear to have understood better than the scientists who advocated "one world or none" that even nuclear weapons cannot persuade a representative of a great power to yield his country's veto in an international organization." (Footnotes in original text omitted.)

7. John Herz, *International Politics in the Atomic Age* (New York: Columbia University Press, 1959). This volume, especially because of its chapter on the demise of the territorial state [its original statement was "Rise and Demise of the Territorial State," *World Politics*, Vol. 9,No. 4 (July 1957), pp. 473 ff.], has been much belabored in the literature of world politics as an example of an insufficient or premature analysis breeding incorrect conclusions, and the author himself has returned to review and back away from his original

typifying many others, have covered considerable distances to converge, eventually, on one point: the withering away of the state. Herz, a Western international relations theorist writing in 1957, saw the demise of the territorial state brought about primarily by the technologies of the atomic age. Brucan, a Marxist scholar-diplomat writing in 1971, has been carried by his dialectic to the conclusion that "power and its modern embodiment, the state, will perish as a result of their own development," to be replaced by a "self-regulating international system, whose inner motions will no longer be interrupted by states' decisions."[9]

Images of a very different kind, or at least doubts about the type of order that technology may generate, result from some of the more systematic, more clearly focused studies.

While noting "the erosion of traditional spheres of exclusive national authority as a consequence of technological developments and functional imperatives,"[10] Richard Falk also recognizes that technological change is only one of the forces affecting the system of world order, not necessarily its prime determinant:[11] to Falk, the structural framework of the international legal order has many other features, and is subject to too many dynamic forces for any one of them to become dominant.[12]

A highly differentiated and exceedingly complex international order, rather than the emergence of higher forms of sociopolitical organization above states, is among the conclusions of John Ruggie's study of the relationship of technological developments to international organization.[13] Also using international organization as his focus, Eugene

---

study in "The Territorial State Revisited: Reflections on the Future of the Nation-State," *Polity*, Vol. 1, No. 1 (Fall 1968), pp. 12-34. Reprinted in John H. Herz, *The Nation-State and the Crisis of World Politics* (New York: David McKay, 1976), ch. 8. Yet in many respects the original essay and its premises still warrant attention, particularly when seen as the first broad-brush strokes on a large canvas which now requires more detailed, painstaking work by those capable of applying the methodical tools of sociology, social psychology, political science, economics, legal science, and possibly other disciplines so as to map with some precision the trails connecting technology with the political system.

8. Silviu Brucan, *The Dissolution of Power: A Sociology of International Relations and Politics* (New York: Knopf, 1971). The reference to this volume is made not so much because of the analytical strength or persuasive power of the book as to emphasize that the tendency toward technological determinism is not an affliction of western observers alone. Brucan is striving to analyze what he calls the major forces at work in world politics: the pressures of modern technology and interdependence; big power politics; the thrust of nations toward self-assertion and social change. Of the four, technology and interdependence are seen as "working for larger units than the nation-state" (30) and eventually resulting in a world community which will have absorbed "the diversity of cultures, systems, values, and ways of life" (318).

9. Ibid. 32, 318.

10. Richard A. Falk, "The Interplay of Westphalia and Charter Conceptions of International Legal Order," Richard A. Falk and Cyril E. Black, eds., *The Future of the International Legal Order: Trends and Patterns*, I (Princeton: Princeton University Press, 1969), p. 61.

11. However, Falk also tends toward shortcuts: "Form follows function in organizing human affairs (as well as in organizing architectural space), and function appears increasingly to be eroding national forms and evolving supranational and multinational forms. In this respect, the functional foundations of the Westphalia conception are weakening" (p .61). The problem here is with the definition of function; a technological development may obviously serve many functions of different users and, consequently, the organizational response may have many forms, or remain formless.

12. Ibid., p. 35. In a broader context, examine the cluster of organizational options for an ethically and ecologically directed global reform offered in Richard A. Falk, *A Study of Future Worlds* (New York: Free Press, 1975). Also note his view that "the drift is toward some new kind of geopolitical and geoeconomic hegemony sustained by a neo-Darwinian ethos and implemented by persuasion where possible, coercion where necessary, and violence wherever lesser forms of coercion seem insufficient." "A New Paradigm for International Legal Studies: Prospects and Proposals," *Yale Law Journal*, Vol. 84, No. 5 (April 1975), p. 1021.

13. John Gerard Ruggie, "Collective Goods and Future International Collaboration," *American Political Science Review*, Vol. 66, No. 4 (September 1972), pp. 892-893.

Skolnikoff warned against "any temptation to argue that technological developments lead inevitably to diminution of tension between states or to the modification of competing national policies. . . . Technology alters the physical reality, but is not the key determinant of the political changes that ensue."[14]

In an inquiry emphasizing the impact of national structures of interest on international technological and economic activities, Henry Nau finds that

> it seems too early to conclude that the kind [of global community] emerging under the pressures of modern technology is one in which the locus of decision-making inexorably shifts from the national to the international level. It is just as possible that global community will emerge with national units very much intact, perhaps even stronger than ever.[15]

In all of these probes into the effects of technology on the alternative futures of the international system, little systematic attention is given to the actual process, the international normative activity, which will have to get us from here to there. Skolnikoff touches on some elements of that process during a discussion of large-scale climate modification when, for instance, he notices that "the development of the knowledge in an international environment creates the opportunity to prepare international means to monitor its use."[16]

Similar attention to some elements of the normative process is shown, for instance, in Falk's references to supranational professionalism "arising from the proliferation of contact between various kinds of professional groups located in different national societies" and represented for example by science as "an increasingly supranational enterprise."[17]

Among students dealing explicitly with the relationship of technology and international law, the normative process and its possible development and change remain again largely unexamined.[18] Two significant exceptions are studies by Oscar Schachter[19] and Dennis Livingston.[20] Schachter's brief paper, best read in conjunction with his "Towards

---

14. Eugene B. Skolnikoff, *The International Imperatives of Technology: Technological Developments and the International Political System* (Berkeley: University of California Press, 1972), p. 2. The title of this volume and a few isolated statements by Skolnikoff have misled some commentators into believing that Skolnikoff's technological determinism points to only one type of a resultant political system with distinctly supranational characteristics. However, careful reading shows the study to be analytical and nondeterministic and the brief quotation used here is not taken out of the context of the study.

15. Henry R. Nau, *National Politics and International Technology: Nuclear Reactor Development in Western Europe* (Baltimore: Johns Hopkins University Press, 1974), p. 32.

16. Skolnikoff (fn. 14), p. 27. Even more significant implications for process are contained in the following statement whether or not one accepts its underlying assumptions as correct: "When an organization has responsibility in an area involving sophisticated technology, there automatically exists a built-in set of reasonably 'objective' criteria to form the basis of decisions. This creates a common denominator throughout the secretariat and among governments that can be a powerful aid to the smooth functioning of the organization. Disagreements that arise can often be resolved into questions of fact, for which it may be possible to obtain reasonably concrete answers" (p. 132).

17. Falk (fn. 10), p. 62.

18. C. Wilfred Jenks lists in a single brief article several technology-related treaties which may be needed very soon—World Weather Treaty, Ocean Depths Treaty, Sonic Boom Treaty, Center of the Earth Treaty, Cybernetics Treaty, and a Molecular Biology Treaty—but has little to say on how they can be arrived at. Jenks, "The New Science and the Law of Nations," *International and Comparative Law Quarterly*, Vol. 17, No. 2 (April 1968), pp. 327-45.

19. Oscar Schachter, "Scientific Advances and International Law Making," *California Law Review*, Vol. 55, No. 3 (May 1967), pp. 423-434.

20. Dennis Livingston, "Science, Technology, and International Law: Present Trends and Future

a Theory of International Obligation,"[21] examines in a straightforward manner the role played by international normative institutions in coping with the problems of scientific and technological change. The study points toward the growing importance of non-traditional means of setting international standards and establishing controls required as responses to technological change.[22]

Livingston's contribution is particularly valuable as a systematic examination of the interplay of international law and technology in several areas of international activity. One would expect a fuller analysis of trends before concluding that the impact of technology on the operational structure of international law will lead "toward the rationalization of international law."[23] Nor is it at all obvious that "in responding to the challenges of science and technology, international law is . . . caught in the paradox of centralizing its norms and organization, while decentralizing its process."[24] However, both Livingston and Schachter are cautious about building deterministic models of world order in the technological age and, by their concern for the international normative activity, make an important initial contribution to inquiries into that process.

CONCEPT I: THE NORMATIVE PROCESS

The international normative process, that cluster of activities which fill the time needed to subject a social phenomenon of international significance to international social control, consists of a number of phases separable from each other for analytical purposes. Many breakdowns are possible, and any breakdown into individual functions of the normative process can be subdivided in a variety of ways. For the purposes of this study the following analytical categories will be used.

1. *Identification of issues for normative action.* Who identifies the issue, where, when, and how—these are the elements determining the nature, quality, and direction of the ensuing normative process. Most emphatically, the normative process does not begin with the coming into objective existence of a new technological phenomenon. The discovery of polychlorinated biphenyls in the food chain or the development of a sonar system capable of monitoring undersea movements at great distances are events which in themselves play no role in international law-making. Until they have been recognized by policymakers as subjects of political control, they are as much outside the normative process as star dust.

2. *Mobilization of interests.* Who gets into the normative action, when, how, and why? This category refers to all effective actors, that is, all those who may directly influence the normative process although they may not be the primary or the formal decision-makers. Transnational forces, subnational groups, or individuals fulfilling specific functions may all populate the normative scene. Communication links between the various interests, the levels of actors' responsiveness to the issue, and the relation of the issue to the actors' accumulated experience are some of the salient subcategories.

3. *Selection of arenas and mechanisms for normative action.* Theoretically the range of choice is wide. It lies between the inarticulate unilateral action taken by one actor and an international legislative conference of all the actors. However, the selection of normative

---

Developments," Richard A. Falk and Cyril E. Black, eds., *The Future of the International Legal Order: The Structure of the International Environment*, IV (Princeton: Princeton University Press, 1972), pp. 68-123.

21. Schachter (fn. 1).
22. Ibid., p. 12.
23. Livingston (fn. 20), p. 74.
24. Ibid., p. 119.

arena is much more limited when it comes to particular issues surrounded by a given set of mobilized interests. If and when the legal status of the Senkaku or Tiao–yu–t'ai islands in the East China Sea, claimed by both China and Japan, is identified as an open issue for normative action,[25] the U.N. General Assembly is not very likely to be the prime normative arena or, if it is, the real issue would be probably something else than the need to determine the true sovereign of the island group. Among the significant subcategories are the following: the available arsenal of normative instruments in different arenas (e.g., resolutions and consensual flows in the United Nations, understandings through high-level diplomacy etc.): the availability of mechanisms supporting, directing, accelerating, or slowing down the normative action (e.g., access by primary actors to expertise, access by experts to the normative process, access by non-actors to the normative arena, etc); and the continuing availability of the normative arena for action (e.g., the shifting of an issue from one arena to another may critically change the set of participating interests and even the definition of the issue).

4. *Normative dynamics.* The determination of the urgency of the issue to be internationally regulated, the impulses which keep it alive and moving or slow it down, are closely related to the effectiveness of the normative process. The normative dynamics are obviously influenced by all the other aspects—the identification of the issue, interests involved, and arenas of action. However, it is here treated as a separate category because of its critical importance to the normative process: productivity depends on timeliness. A protracted normative process may produce a rule, or a system of order, for an issue which may have in the meantime lost its objective foundation—a stillborn norm.[26]

5. *Normative search and identification of normative options.* Exchanges of views, the testing of the carrying capacity of specific policy preferences, attempts to identify the outer limits of the political feasibility of a given mode of issue resolution—all these are subcategories of the negotiating process itself, the process of claim and counterclaim, the interplay of authoritative decisions, and the inputs into such decisions.

6. *Emergence and articulation of mutual expectations and reliances with an obligatory component.* This category designates the culmination and formalization of the normative process. The specificity, the clarity, and the lifespan—i.e., the effectiveness—of the rising norm are likely to be profoundly influenced by the way the norm is articulated, by whom, where, and when.

Because these categories do appear to represent a sequence, their analytical character needs to be reemphasized. In reality, for instance, the phase of the identification of an issue may contain norm-producing acts: an authoritative act defining an issue as one in need of regulation may simultaneously contain normative elements by creating specific expectations with an obligatory core.[27]

This, of course, makes only more explicit what has already been implied: in this

---

25. It is, of course, very likely that it has already been so identified and the normative process, with Tokyo and Peking as the only actors in a closed negotiating arena of bilateral diplomacy, is well under way. The Senkaku group, considered by the Japanese as administratively and historically belonging to the Ryukyus and thus to Japan, has also been claimed by China (Peking and Taiwan) but, after a flurry of public exchanges of view, the issue has now receded from public view. See also below.

26. At the time the Convention on the Continental Shelf entered into force the original issue was no longer there; in this case, the normative process shifted to an arena different from the formal treaty-making process which had ceased to be normatively significant.

27. For an earlier analysis of the obligatory essence of some unilateral acts undertaken with normative intentions see examination of the origins of the doctrine and the rule of the continental shelf in Zdenek J. Slouka, *International Custom and the Continental Shelf* (The Hague: Nijhoff, 1968).

study, *system of order* and *normative process* are nonformalistic and nonlegalistic concepts. A minimal system of order is understood to be the existence, between two or more international actors, of a consensuality based on expectations which have been articulated with a clarity and authority sufficient to produce a normative effect. This system of order can be arrived at through a variety of techniques and practices which may be structured or unstructured and which include informal and often indeterminate sources of international obligation.[28] Hence the political and legal spheres are seen as tightly meshed, but meshed in a disciplined way which preserves the identity of the individual strands of law and power. [29]

CONCEPT II: THE TECHNOLOGICAL PHENOMENON

Technology is more than a set of machines and skills. More properly one should speak of the technological phenomenon, a complex cluster of social and human abilities, processes, attitudes, and perspectives. For analytical purposes only, this complex can be subdivided into conceptual segments.

Starting at the lowest and possibly the least significant level, there are machines and skills. This already includes a formidable array of technologies. On the one hand there are material technologies—that is, sets of machines and skills combined to do specific technical jobs such as reaching the moon or the ocean depths, creating synthetics, travelling faster than sound, or fitting a man with a double heart. On the other hand, there is an equally impressive collection of so-called soft technologies such as computer programs or methods of work by which we extend the otherwise extremely limited human capabilities.[30]

Slicing the technological cluster somewhat differently brings its comprehensive nature into a clearer focus. Following Daniel Bell and Harvey Brooks, and starting with the definition of technology as "the use of scientific knowledge to specify ways of doing

---

28. This view generally parallels Schachter's (fn. 1) theoretical acceptance of a large body of normative phenomena occuring outside the formal and traditional procedures for international law-making. The normative authenticity of the nontraditional phenomena depends on five necessary and sufficient conditions stated by Schachter in the form of processes: "(i) the formulation and designation of a requirement as to behavior in contingent circumstances; (ii) an indication that the designation has been made by persons recognized as having the competence (authority or legitimate role) to perform that function and in accordance with procedures accepted as proper for that purpose; (iii) an indication of the capacity and willingness of those concerned to make the designated requirement effective in fact; (iv) the transmittal of the requirement to those to whom it is addressed (the target audience); (v) the creation in the target audience of responses—both psychological and operational—which indicate that the designated requirement is regarded as authoritative (in the sense specified in (iii) above) and as likely to be compiled with in the future in some substantial degree" (17). Another cognate set of concepts is Gottlieb's much broader theoretical canvass with the same basic perspective of international normative activity as an increasingly nonhierarchical, horizontal movement, a flow of practices and techniques resulting in international obligations and having some common features: "– They are based on consensus rather than on consent; – they erode the status of formal sources of law such as treaties and enhance the importance of informal sources like declarations; – they favor informal and rapid normative change; – they involve fairly general principles and standards rather than precise contractual obligations, and therefore leave states with considerable discretion in the interpretation of obligations." Gidon Gottlieb, "The Nature of International Law: Toward a Second Concept of Law," Falk and Black, eds. (fn. 20), pp. 332-83 esp. p. 343.

29. Cf., Richard A. Falk, "The Interplay of Westphalia and Charter conceptions of International Legal Order," Cf. Falk (fn. 10), p. 35.

30. This hard-soft division is used, for instance, by Donald A. Schon, "Forecasting and Technological Forecasting," Daniel Bell, ed., *Toward the Year 2000: Work in Progress* (Boston: Houghton Mifflin, 1968), p. 127.

things in a reproducible manner,"[31] one identifies three fundamental types of technologies: machine technology, social technology, and intellectual technology. While machine technology is a largely self-explanatory term, and social technology is best characterized by illustration (organization of a hospital; international trade system;[32] the "pay-as-you-go" or withholding income tax; application of farm subsidies; U.S. social security system[33]), intellectual technology requires greater attention.

Bell depicts intellectual technology as "the substitution of algorithms (problem solving rules) for intuitive judgments."[34] Intellectual technology, as an application through the computer of new fields (e.g., cybernetics, decision theory, stochastic processes) and their techniques (e.g., linear programming, minimax solutions) to real-life social and human problems,[35] is not only a distinct component of the technological phenomenon but also an element supporting at many points the full utilization of machine and social technologies.

Intellectual technology deserves this emphasis not only because of its dominant role among the technological categories but also because it leads almost directly to the second and higher level of technological traits: the spread of secular and manipulative rationality applied not only to material problems but, increasingly, to social problems as well.[36] And this, of course, signals a wholly new style of thinking about problems and of doing things, a style beginning with and characterized by an effort of defining rational action and identifying its components. In short, this is the element of conscious policy-making on the basis of planning and forecasting—to Bell "the heart of the postindustrial society"[37] and as such one of the central features of the technological phenomenon.

With the new, more deliberate, rational way of doing things goes its social corollary: the emergence of a new class of doers, the professional and technical class. The technological phenomenon comprises not only the rapid quantitative growth of this class but its qualitative position in society as well. "In the post-industrial society, technical skill becomes the base and education the mode of access to power; those who come to the fore in this fashion are the scientists. . . . As a stratum, scientists, or more widely the technical intelligentsia, now have to be taken into account in the political process."[38]

The entry of the new technological class into the political process need not mean

---

31.   Harvey Brooks, "Technology and the Ecological Crisis," lecture given at Amherst, 9 May 1971, p. 13 in an unpublished text quoted by Daniel Bell, *The Coming of Post-Industrial Society: A Venture in Social Forecasting* (New York: Basic Books, 1973), p. 29.

32.   Bell, ibid.

33.   Following examples of Joseph Coates, "Technology Assessment," *The Futurist*, Vol. 5, No. 6 (December 1971), p. 225.

34.   Bell (fn. 31), p. 29.

35.   Ibid., p. 30.

36.   Herman Kahn and B. Bruce-Briggs, *Things to Come* (New York: Macmillan, 1972), pp. 7-30.

37.   Daniel Bell, "The Measurement of Knowledge and Technology," Eleanor B. Sheldon and Wilbert E. Moore, eds., *Indicators of Social Change: Concepts and Measurements* (New York: Russell Sage Foundation, 1968), p. 157. Bell derives this view from what he sees as the primacy of theoretical knowledge in his postindustrial society: in technology, economics, and in other fields, advances become increasingly dependent on the centrality of theoretical work; hence "theoretical knowledge increasingly becomes the strategic resource, the axial principle, of a society." Bell (fn. 31), pp. 18-26, esp. p. 26. Also consider his observation that "technology is not simply a 'machine,' but a systematic, disciplined approach to objectives, using a calculus of precision and measurement and a concept of system that are quite at variance with traditional and customary religious, aesthetic, and intuitive modes. Instead of a machine technology, we will have, increasingly, an 'intellectual technology' in which such techniques as simulation, model construction, linear programming, and operations research will be hitched to the computers and will become the new tools of decision-making." Daniel Bell, "The Year 2000—The Trajectory of an Idea," Bell, ed. (fn. 30), p. 5.

38.   Bell (fn. 31), pp. 35-39.

substantive changes in political strategies; the technologists may have common ways of doing things and a common emerging ethos, but they are not a political class held together and activated by common interest. Their presence, and their role, within or close to the political process derives from the fact that they have the tools so essential to planning and decision-making.[39]

The purposes of this study do not require the acceptance or rejection of any one general characterization of society in the technological age, be it Bell's conceptual scheme of postindustrial society or some other image.[40] Only some specific aspects of these concepts, rooted in empirical data and acceptable as trends likely to continue into the future, need to be isolated here as elements comprising the major dimensions of the technological phenomenon:

1. *Decision-making style.* This involves application of rational methods, initially developed for the handling of technical problems, in the manipulation of social issues, including planning and forecasting as modes in social decision-making. The role of science and of cognitive values is intensified.

2. *Participants.* Technological intelligentsia and, more generally, the professional and technical classes become more intimately related to the political process, often as its essential participants.

3. *Technologies.* Machine, social, and intellectual technologies as extensions of human and social capabilities proliferate and, while requiring social controls, are themselves seen as the best instruments for such controls.

Most of this, of course, characterizes the degree of socio-technical evolution in the United States and a few advanced countries. Where are the contact points between the technological phenomena and the international normative process?

On the most generalized level, the technological phenomenon, while generated by relatively very few people in only very few countries, saturates the international normative process by the issues it creates, by the conditions it sets for their effective handling, and by the solutions it offers. The international normative process is in fact the ground where those belonging to technologically highly developed countries meet and communicate with others from lands on much lower levels of technological development. Yet the distance between these two categories of men is not very great. They are the elites, and whatever may have been their earlier formal education, their learning capacities are usually very high, if not in technical matters, then in decision-making styles. While absorbed in issues growing out of the technological phenomenon, they are absorbing the technological styles of decision and action. As we shall see more clearly in the specific instances examined further below, all the participants in the international normative process carry in them the seeds of the postindustrial society on the international level: they are acting out roles into which they have been cast by the technological age, whether they come from and speak for America or Zambia.

In sum, the technological phenomenon we are facing is not a social anomaly, a

---

39. Political and sociological literature dealing with the growth and positioning of the technological intelligentsia in society is too voluminous to list here; Bell (fn. 31 and fn. 37) provides a good entry point for those with a general interest.

40. Lane's knowledgeable society, Etzioni's active society, Brzezinski's technetronic society, and Ellul's technological society, to name a few, have been described in the following: Robert Lane, "The Decline of Politics and Ideology in a Knowledgeable Society," *American Sociological Review*, Vol. 31, No. 5 (October 1966), pp. 649-662. Amitai Etzioni, *The Active Society* (New York: Free Press, 1968). Zbigniew Brzezinski, *Between Two Ages: America's Role in the Technetronic Era* (New York: Viking, 1970). Jacques Ellul, *The Technological Society*, trans. Konrad Kellen (New York: Knopf, 1964).

pathological aberration on the social body that could be—if only we had the technology and the nerve to do it—surgically removed and placed in vitro for observation. Criticizing it is pointless. One can only criticize men and groups for their inadequate, or excessive, or misdirected use of technology because technology is simply a lifestyle, a way of doing things faster, sometimes better, and quite often doing things which otherwise could not be done at all.[41]

But being largely a lifestyle, technology affects the processes of international law-making and, more broadly, the processes of world order at all levels and stages. It generates, or stimulates the generation of, instances occasioning international regulation. It influences the definition of contentious or disruptive issues in need of regulation; it enters the assessment of preferred outcomes of policy; it seeps into the processes of negotiating new rules; and it plays a role in the implementation, maintenance, monitoring, and modification of rules.

POLITICAL IDENTIFICATION OF ISSUES FOR NORMATIVE ACTION

Since issues open to international regulation arise from social interaction of transnational dimensions, and since the technological phenomenon is a major characteristic of the lifestyle of the transnationally active societies, issues with technological substance or implications are likely to dominate the normative horizons of the global community through the foreseeable future.

An initial two-step sequence changes a potential issue into an active concern of the international normative process. There must be, first, the recognition that an issue should be subjected to international regulation in order to avoid or resolve a conflict or to facilitate some other social goals. Second, the recognition must be acted upon in the international arena by someone with sufficient authority to act internationally or with an influential access to the process of authoritative decision-making.

Starting from this base, one can examine the following points regarding the effects the technological phenomenon may have on the political identification of international normative issues.

1. There will be an increasing proliferation of a new type of issues brought into the international normative arenas in the forthcoming decades. It will be of the technology-bred category—mostly issues of the cognitive rather than reactive type, i.e., issues recognized more for their potential future impact on the participants' goals and values than for an immediate significance.

2. This cognitive and predictive nature of normative issues will intensify the activism of indirect or distant (notional) participants and hence it will increase the numbers of those capable of raising such issues in the normative arenas.

3. The proliferation of the cognitive issues in the global normative arenas, and of actors capable of raising such issues, will get an additional impetus from two factors: (a) the manipulative, conscious rationality, rubbed off from analytical and essentially technological pursuits onto social decision-making, will stimulate the identification of future-impact issues for advance, preventive regulation; (b) experts, expert groups, and those able to manipulate knowledge and expertise from various bureaucratic and other positions will play an increasing role in the processes leading to the identification of issues for normative action.

---

41.   A useful collection of materials dealing with the diverse roles of technology in society in terms of their general relationship is Albert H. Teich, ed., *Technology and Man's Future* (New York: St. Martin's Press, 1972).

4. Summed up, all this opens widely the possibility that technical knowledge, socially interpreted and internationally diffused, may in the future further reduce the once traditional role of actual state involvement and of interstate conflict as the sole catalysts of the normative quest for order.

International Concerns with Technology

All these propositions simply extrapolate today's trends and relations into the next one or two decades. The number of new transnationally significant technologies, by their nature potentially open to international regulation, is growing rapidly and possibly exponentially. Each new technological cluster of machines and skills may give rise to one or more normative issues if properly introduced and activated in the international arena. Technology-bred issues such as allocation of deep ocean resources, responsibility for weather modification, controls on direct broadcasting via satellites, or legitimate uses of space technology for remote sensing of earth resources are only a few of the more visible and dramatic sociotechnological complexes already in the process of normative negotiation.

There is no global institutionalized procedure for determining the regulatory requirements for new technologies of international scope. Over the years such procedures were proposed, and sometimes they were even predicted as the next coming thing made inevitable by the technological age. Ernst Haas spoke more than ten years ago about the possibility that from ad hoc consultations "there may emerge a modest international brain trust for the general planning of innovation" composed of eminent scientists and philosophers and charged with reviewing "all technical and scientific inventions in order to assess their probable impact on society."[42] In a different context and while examining various models of the international system, Haas posited a hypothesis that "the unchecked movement toward scientific and technological innovation in all UN member states will cause concern over the increasing pace of social change unmatched by a clear picture as to where the social change will lead; hence the UN will be given the task of assessing the social change implications of scientific innovations."[43]

In a more activist mood, Livingston proposed the creation of an international technology assessment body authorized to guide states in the control of harmful technologies and in the employment of useful ones.[44] And an altogether sweeping and highly rational system, created to regulate technological innovation through "Councils of Urgent Studies," has been proposed by Richard A. Cellarius and John Platt.[45] The Cellarius-Platt system would set up coordinating assessment councils at all levels from the university up through local and national bodies to an "International Council of Urgent Studies"; the system would be focused on the legitimization of research aimed toward solutions of problems of critical proportions.

Institutions have been set up to serve the general functions of assessing technological change and alerting the members of the global community to the resulting opportunities

---

42. Ernst B. Haas, "Toward Controlling International Change," *World Politics*, Vol. 17, No. 1 (October 1964), p. 9.

43. Ernst B. Haas, "Collective Security and the Future International System," Falk and Black, eds. (fn. 10), p. 231.

44. Dennis Livingston, "International Technology Assessment and the United Nations System, Proceedings of the American Society Law, *American Journal of International Law*, Vol. 64, No. 4 (September 1970), pp. 120-122.

45. Richard A. Cellarius and John Platt, "Councils of Urgent Studies," *Science*, Vol. 177, no. 4050 (25 August 1972), pp. 670-676.

and challenges. On the global, institutionalized level, the United Nations spawned several committees and offices devoted to technology-watching and sponsored a full-scale Conference on Science and Technology for Development in 1979. Acting on Conference recommendation, the General Assembly reorganized existing institutional arrangements in both administrative and coordinative political areas and instituted an ambitious "Financing System for Science and Technology for Development."[46] These latest arrangements make science and technology an integral part of the United Nations' dominant concerns. They also represent a step toward the long and seriously considered goal of a central planning and programming mechanism, within the United Nations System, "whereby the United Nations, together with the specialized agencies, would plan and outline research and development programmes for the system"[47]—an extremely difficult task considering that most technologies are products of nationally controlled and nationally motivated efforts and that the nation-state is not as yet ready to let go, or at least not in this formalistic and institutionalized fashion.

All the technology-watching institutions at the international level have little real or potential direct impact on the political identification of international normative issues. They are oriented toward problems, not order. Although they may deal with technologies whose international regulation could be desirable, their main goal is the modernization and development of the preindustrial societies. This type of international valuation of technology is, of course, also going on almost routinely in the various functional agencies and programs within the United Nations system and outside it.[48] These too, and even more, are oriented toward problems and specific tasks, and not necessarily, or not at all, toward rule-making. In addition, the direct coupling of all of these institutions to the global normative process is weak and ineffective.

Their indirect role is much larger and more significant. While technology-watching institutions may serve their primary function only very inadequately, and while the major tasks of many specialized agencies in technology transfer and technology management may remain largely unfulfilled, all these activities provide a broad and intensive learning experience for their participants. Their contribution toward new styles of decision-making stems from their ability to intensify communication between preindustrial, industrial, and postindustrial societies; to diffuse not only technical information, but the ways of using technical information for ends of policy; and in general to assist the less experienced nations in developing decision-making procedures that would help them to a greater share of the values to be had through international activity.

New Players in the Normative Field

The political identification of issues for international normative action is still the almost exclusive sphere of forceful state action, not the product of a cool international

---

46.   UNGA resolution 34/218 (19 December 1979). There is now a Centre for Science and Technology for Development, replacing the Office of Science and Technology in the Secretariat, and an Intergovernmental Committee for Science and Technology for Development, reporting through ECOSOC to the General Assembly.

47.   Alexander King, "The Proposed United Nations Conference on Science and Technology," a report for the U.N. Panel of Experts on the Proposed United Nations Conference on Science and Technology, issued as Doc. ESA/S&T/AC.4/2 (30 September 1974), 53 (Par. 113).

48.   Livingston (fn.20), p. 121, samples international fora in which international evaluation of technology takes place, among them the World Health Organization, International Whaling Commission, and Rhine Pollution Commission. There are, of course, dozens of agencies and programs in which similar sociotechnological tasks are being performed, for instance, some of the fisheries commissions or, in the U.N. system, the regional Economic Commissions.

analysis of alternative choices, costs, and benefits. It simply takes too much political energy to warm up the normative process, and it takes a type of energy only the nation-state can effectively generate: energy capable of building up an atmosphere of conflict which ought to be resolved with relative urgency. No less than that seems to be needed to bring about political action of sufficient velocity to launch an international norm.

Many technology-generated issues lend themselves well to this type of political treatment. Unlike several other social phenomena, technologies have one dominant characteristic in what may be called the cognitive phase of law making: some of their impacts are predictable or at least imaginable. This perception of what may come if we employ our engineering capabilities in a particular way generates a social response—the demand that the technology be controlled or managed so as to maximize its social benefits and reduce its social costs.

The truly significant point is, however, that technology-related issues can be seized upon and politicized for normative action by anyone with sufficient energy and authority to do it.

The beginnings in 1966-67 of the policy process focused on the seabed issue are a classic illustration of the new trend represented by the multiplication of the potential and effective initiators of international normative action. When in 1967 Ambassador Pardo of Malta, alerted to the rule-making opportunity and mobilized into diplomatic action by the earlier preoccupation of the United Nations with potential seabed resources, introduced the seabed issue in the General Assembly, he was joined in his effort to get the issue up and to keep it alive as a normative issue by a number of mostly less developed countries. They, rather than those who controlled the deep ocean mining technology and who had a traditionally large involvement in the sea, became the initiators and supporters of the normative process.[49]

The annals of the United Nations are replete with examples of normative initiatives taken up by those without any direct and immediate link to the activity to be controlled; the general responsiveness of nations to issues of a future, as yet unrealized, global significance appears to be increasing. One can detect here a major substantive shift toward a democratization—for better or worse—of the international normative process. So far it has been tacitly accepted that new norms are, and perhaps ought to be, created by those whose activity has occasioned the need or the opportunity for them. This tendency to look for law-creation only to those who have had the ability to act in the area to be regulated appears very reasonable in cases such as *The Scotia* where a British system of colored navigation lights became recognized as mandatory for all users of the sea. Traditionally, international law has been the product of the doers: customary law is the doers' law by definition, and the same is true of most treaties except for a few global conventions of the modern era. And these conventions are themselves but symptoms of the emerging trend in which the ability to act materially in a given area no longer represents a special law-making license for that area. If Malta could initiate a major normative activity involving deep ocean mining, Maldive Islands can do the same for remote sensing satellites; what is needed is political erudition in choosing the issue, time, form, and forum, not political muscle, economic vigor, and technological prowess.

---

49. Detailed account of the complex process through which the seabed issue evolved from its 1966 beginnings into a new global normative effort is Zdenek J. Slouka, "United Nations and the Deep Ocean: From Data to Norms," *Syracuse Journal of International Law*, Vol. 1, No. 1 (October 1972), pp. 61-90.

Learning, Knowledge, Forecasting, Planning

The trend towards an increasing number of international actors raising more and more normative issues has its roots in the changing style and pattern of decision making within and between nations.

That many nations are no longer content to watch the world go by and quietly accept the law of the doers is itself an outcome of the accumulating experience of so many new members of the international community through their participation in the world political process. Planning rather than reactive, intuitive diplomacy; more systematic concern with the future as it may be conjectured on the basis of present data and experience; efforts to follow rational, calculated paths in foreign policy: these are the elements of the emerging workstyle of many national policy-makers active in the international normative arenas even though their countries may be still at very low levels of development. Haas' hypothetical prediction that the growing dependence of modern society on the increasingly specialized artifacts will necessitate a greater reliance on technological-scientific elites, and that those who will be making crucial decisions on behalf of the various nations "will be increasingly part of an international meritocracy,"[50] is now a visible trend pointing well into the future.

The international community may be still lacking even rudimentary political competence and operational mechanisms for acting today on the problems of tomorrow. Yet, future-oriented efforts aimed at creating new norms or at erecting political stop signs multiply—the deep ocean mining issue, direct satellite broadcasting, remote sensing of earth resources, environmental problems in general and pollution issues in particular, brain drain, resource conservation are only a few examples from a wide and expanding field. The normative initiatives or at least active participation by less developed countries in international undertakings aimed at these technological issues suggest that, as a result of the on-going learning process, those who speak for their countries in the global arena have become conscious of these problems as problems and have set out to handle them accordingly. The newness of this trend has been evidenced by public statements of national representatives of advanced as well as less developed countries registering their surprise and satisfaction that normative activity aimed at a relatively distant future is becoming possible.[51]

The real scope and the carrying capacity of this new tendency of many countries toward acting today for the regulation of future issues is difficult to gauge. At this point, international systems of order are still more effectively produced through actual disorder

---

50. Haas (fn. 43), p. 232.

51. E.g., compare the two following statements coming from countries at very different levels of development and involvement in the issue concerned, the Maltese proposal for international seabed regulation. In the General Assembly debate, Sir Leslie Glass, United Kingdom, stated: "Here in the United Nations we spend so much time trying to solve old problems—problems born of the past errors and wickedness of mankind—that it is immensely stimulating and encouraging to be asked to look forward—forward to the new world made possible for mankind by technological advance. I think we should all be deeply indebted to the representative of Malta for jolting us out of our preoccupation with the present and the past and forcing us to raise our eyes and look at the wider horizons of the future." Doc. A/C.1/PV.1524 (8 November 1967), p. 8. And a statement by Mr. Akwei of Ghana: "In the past, the United Nations has been what I may call conservative in the sense that it has mainly concerned itself with the past and the present: where we could have looked ahead and taken firm steps to deal with matters still in their embryonic stages, we have been wont to shirk such action. . . . We all know too well how dearly that attitude has cost us. Having delayed too long, we have often been confronted with far more complicated situations which we have then frantically tried to solve but, alas, too late. Thanks to the Maltese initiative, we have a unique opportunity to get out of the rut, to look ahead and to take decisive action now to prevent future difficulties." Doc. A/C.1/PV.1526 (13 November 1967), p. 36.

than by preventive, anticipatory regulation.[52] However, the new planning and forecasting impulse on the part of many previously inactive participants in the normative process is, as a minimum, likely to increase the number of issues in normative arenas, whatever may be their eventual outcome.

The long-range nature of this growing orientation of the normative initiatives toward issues of the future has been viewed prescriptively as an imperative of foreign policy which, without planning, cannot be successful:

> Whatever hope we have of controlling and influencing these developments depends on a serious commitment to long-range planning. The policymaking system will come under increasing pressure to make decisions on both traditional and nontraditional issues for which there are no familiar or simple choices. It is futile and irresponsible to wait until these issues have become so salient that everyone recognizes that something must be done, because by this time everything that can be done is inadequate.[53]

One can also adopt a deterministic pose and state categorically with Galbraith that "technology, under all circumstances, leads to planning."[54] Or, on a still broader and more fundamental base, it can be shown that "this turn to the future is deeply rooted in the nature of contemporary civilization processes."[55]

However, more persuasive indicators of the expanding concerns with the future are to be found in the empirical world. The development of long-term strategies is among the goals of many international programs with global participation so that the experience with planning methods and problems is practically universal and continuous. The preparatory work for the U.N. Conference on Science and Technology for Development amply reflects the focus on the planning for distant future.[56] The United Nations Institute for Training and Research (UNITAR) has proposed a "Project on the Future" to alert the international system about evolving problems and to stimulate systematic inquiry into and public discussion of the emerging issues.[57]

This future-oriented trend in international activity is itself driven by the multiple entry into the decision-making processes by technical experts and international bureaucracies with their well-tested tools, analytical methods, and planning. In recent years, their role in the political identification of issues for normative action has become quite conspicuous. Resorting again to ocean politics, the classic laboratory of the international quest for order, one finds at the very beginnings of the normative process aimed at the deep ocean floor a significant input from technical experts and international bureaucrats: an imaginative use of technical reports[58] supplemented by a political analysis injected by

---

52. For earlier discussion of this aspect in a different, functional context, see Slouka (fn. 49), pp. 80-83; also Slouka, "International Environmental Controls in the Scientific Age," John L. Hargrove, ed., *Law, Institutions, and the Global Environment* (Dobbs Ferry, N.Y.: Oceana Publications, 1972), pp. 219-221.

53. Robert L. Rothstein, *Planning, Prediction, and Policy Making in Foreign Affairs* (Boston: Little Brown, 1972), p. 10.

54. John K. Galbraith, *The New Industrial State* (Boston: Houghton Mifflin, 1967), p. 20.

55. Radovan Richta et al., *Civilization at the Crossroads: Social and Human Implications of the Scientific and Technological Revolution* (White Plains, N.Y.: International Arts and Sciences Press, 3rd expanded ed., 1969), p. 268. This exceptionally interesting study by an interdisciplinary team under Radovan Richta of the Czechoslovak Academy of Sciences in practically unknown in the United States; the only major reference to it is to be found in Bell (fn. 31), pp. 106-112.

56. King (fn. 47), pp. 39-40.

57. Alexander Mironov, "Forecasting the Technological Future," *Technology and Development, UNITAR News,* Vol. 6, No. 4 (1974), p. 31.

58. In 1966, before the Maltese initiative and in the context of the development of global resources, the U.N. Secretariat moved systematically to intensify the awareness of governments and other organizations

international bureaucrats[59] helped to get the seabed issue directly into the Political Committee of the General Assembly.

Still more direct although less visible forms of normative initiatives on the part of technical experts and international bureaucrats are made possible by the personal contact with national representatives; advice, inspiration, and sometimes outright guidance regarding specific policies are communicated along these channels, together with model draft resolutions prepared for national delegations by the anonymous international officials. There is probably no accessible and safe research route to this type of information on a larger scale. However, private discussions with U.N. officials and national diplomats suggest that these types of activities are both widespread and growing.[60] Again, the climate allowing and encouraging the use of analysis and planning as tools in the business of normative politics is certainly conducive to the development of symbiotic relations between experts, bureaucrats, and diplomats; and this results in an increased likelihood that the interaction will breed new normative initiatives spurred by the process of mutual learning. [61]

---

in the potential of the seabed issue. The Secretary-General, empowered by the General Assembly to prepare a special survey of marine science and technology, created a prestigious group of thirty-two participating experts and six observers. The size of the group, the scientific prominence of many of its members, and the number of organizations represented were elements likely to mobilize considerable interest in the international scientific community as well as in the national systems. Doc. E/4487 (24 April 1968), Annexes.

59. An illustrative case of mixing technical expertise with value judgments made by the officers of the Secretariat was the implementation of ECOSOC resolution 1112 (XL) which helped stimulate among the developing states an active interest in the deep ocean floor issue. That resolution called for a survey of "the present state of knowledge" of the sea resources and their exploitability and also asked that "any gaps in available knowledge which merit early attention by virtue of their importance to the development of ocean resources, and of the practicality of their early exploitation" be also identified. In the context of the resolution, and as was later stressed by the sponsors (especially the United States), the reference to "gaps in available knowledge" meant "scientific and technical knowledge." However, the Secretariat chose to identify as gaps "the legal status" of the seabed resources and the "ways and means" of ensuring that the resources benefit the developing countries—gaps not so much in knowledge as in social organization. See U.N. Doc. A/C.1/952 (October 5, 1967). To implement this interpretation of its mandate, the Secretariat added a number of paragraphs amounting to a clear advocacy of a seabed regime placed under a public international body and based on the principle of universal sharing in the benefits. While the technical substance of the survey was prepared by Dr. Frank Wang, Marine Geologist of the U.S. Geological Survey serving as a special consultant to the Secretary-General, the closing paragraphs regarding the preferred political solution were the work of the Ad Hoc Unit on Marine Science and Technology. The entire document, U.N. Doc. E/4449/Add.1 (19 February 1968), was issued as a report by the Secretary-General.

60. Over a period of some five years (1969-74) of intermittent discussions and interviews with U.N. officials and delegates I have found seventeen direct and over thirty strongly implied instances when international officials, often relying on expert knowledge and on the use of analytical methods, were the direct initiators of diplomatic moves aimed at normative goals. All the cases except for three in the "implied" category involved less developed countries. The exceptions seem to have been instances of young diplomats who, either genuinely interested in the subject matter or in order to enhance their careers, accepted draft resolutions prepared by an international official, cleared them with their missions and foreign offices, and were eventually authorized to propose them formally in the name of their country. There is, of course, no way to judge the statistical or even the individual substantive significance of these cases except to note that they occur probably more frequently since the mass entry of less developed countries into the United Nations in the late fifties and early sixties. For nondocumented statements about international officials sometimes preparing draft resolutions that are then submitted by members of national delegations and about the influence of international bureaucracies over decisions depending on the use of analytical methods, see Robert W. Cox and Harold K. Jacobson, *The Anatomy of Influence: Decision Making in International Organization* (New Haven: Yale University Press, 1974), pp. 12, 390.

61. A brief examination of the role of technical expertise in multilateral diplomacy and of the potential forms of the expertise-diplomacy interaction, is Zdenek J. Slouka, "The Diplomat in a Technological World," UNITAR, *Technology and Development UNITAR News,* Vol. 6, No. 4 (1974), pp. 32-34.

At the functional levels of international activity the norm-creating roles of experts and bureaucrats are more fully developed and often well established. For instance, an expanded program in environmental health under the World Health Organization (WHO) was developed on the basis of the conclusions and recommendations of an expert committee. At WHO, the expert committees and scientific groups have a considerable rule-creating force since their reports, widely disseminated, are adopted on the sole authority of the experts, and the WHO Director General and Executive Board cannot interfere with their substance.[62] Similarly, Technical Annexes adopted by the narrowly based Council of the International Civil Aviation Organization automatically bind all members who do not expressly reject them, and the authoritative Codex Alimentarius is the product of a joint group of WHO and the Food and Agricultural Organization (FAO).[63]

Finally, there is a special class of instances when research activities of international and transnational organizations generate new knowledge with a high potential of setting into motion a normative process. The Senkaku Islands are a case in point.[64] The Senkakus or, in Chinese, the Tiao-yu-t'ai Islands in the East China Sea have become a center of controversy between Japan, China, and Taiwan after the Committee for Coordination of Joint Prospecting for Mineral Resources in Asian Offshore Areas, established under the auspices of the U.N. Economic Commission for Asia and the Far East (ECAFE), since renamed the Economic and Social Commission for Asia and the Pacific (ESCAP), reported that "a high probability exists that the continental shelf between Taiwan and Japan may be one of the most prolific oil reservoirs in the world."[65] The area of the Senkaku Islands had seen oceanographic and geological exploration before.[66] Whether or not these explorations had pointed toward the possibility of oil-bearing strata, it would have been normal for the three countries involved to stake out their claims, oil or no oil. However, purposive political action aiming at the allocation of the presumed resources was precipitated only by the ECAFE report.[67]

Perspectives on the Proliferation of Normative Issues

Only the quantitative impact by the technological phenomenon on the initiation of future normative activity in the global community can be assessed with any degree of confidence. It seems safe to say that, because of the rapid rate of technological innovation

---

62. Cf. Harold K. Jacobson, "WHO: Medicine, Regionalism, and Managed Politics," Cox and Jacobson (fn. 60), pp. 192, 202.

63. A useful survey of these and other techniques for creating international legal rules through U.N. specialized agencies is in Charles H. Alexandrowicz, *The Law-Making Functions of the Specialised Agencies of the United Nation* (South Hackensack, N.J.: Fred B. Rothman, 1974).

64. See also fn. 25 and accompanying text above.

65. CCOP-ECAFE, "Geological Structure and Some Water Characteristics of the East China Sea and the Yellow Sea," Technical Advisory Group Report, *Technical Bulletin*, II (1969), 3.43.

66. See research reports containing accounts of earlier exploratory work focused on the topography and sediments in this area: Hiroshi Niino and K.O. Emery, "Sediments of Shallow Portions of East China Sea and South China Sea," *Geological Society of America Bulletin*, Vol. 72, No. 5 (May 1961), pp. 731-762; John M. Wageman, T.W.C. Hilde, and K.O. Emery, "Structural Framework of East China Sea and Yellow Sea," *The American Association of Petroleum Geologists Bulletin*, Vol. 54, No. 9 (September 1970), pp. 1611-1643, esp. pp. 1612-1616.

67. For an account of the controversy and its legal and political implications see Choon-ho Park, "Oil under Troubled Waters: The Northeast Asia Sea-Bed Controversy," *Harvard International Law Journal*, Vol. 14, No. 2 (Spring 1973), pp. 212-59; Park, "Continental Shelf Issues in the Yellow Sea and the East China Sea," Occasional Paper No. 15, Law of the Sea Institute, University of Rhode Island (1972).

coupled with the increasing number of international actors capable and motivated to make claims in international normative arenas, normative issues in need of resolution will proliferate.

This, of course, does have some qualitative connotations. It immediately raises the question whether the international normative system will be able to handle the traffic and, if not, what will give—the desire for norms, the normative productivity, or the system itself. But since these questions go beyond our first concern with the political identification of normative issues, they may be left for examination under other categories.

At this juncture another point needs to be lifted from our earlier discussion for a closer look. Observers of world politics often imply, and sometimes explicitly show, their satisfaction with the growing tendency of various actors on the international scene to employ rational, evaluative, "cool" methods in their international decision making, and see it as a signal of a more orderly world political process. The technological phenomenon certainly makes that tendency in decision-making a trend of the future. As long as rationalism, forecasting, and planning do not become strait jackets on necessary social action, this trend may indeed point to a healthier international life in the future.

Unfortunately we are not there yet. The growing rationalism, which is manifesting itself also in the normative initiatives, is a primarily national phenomenon although it may be driven by international stimuli. Since there is no unified system of accepted social values at the international level, there cannot, to that extent, be any international rationality guiding the normative process at all its stages. In fact, the more the international community seeks to organize itself to regulate technology and to undertake systematic social planning by preventive, anticipatory rule making, the more will the divergence of national and even subnational values become visible, explicit, and intransigent. Future-oriented normative action in which planning is an essential ingredient requires that goals be first clearly stated on the basis of value priorities—and this unavoidable specification of values brings to the surface value conflicts which would otherwise remain invisible and inert.[68] If each interest group in a normative process is led to calculate as precisely as possible what it has, what it wants, and where to get it, international normative arteries may harden with the sharpening of the conflicts. Such conflicts, in the long run, may indeed have an all-important social function of bringing better balance into the global system so far dominated by the more assertive social groups and their normative goals. But this can only be a second-order consequence of the policy clashes stemming from the proliferation of international normative issues.

A point closely related to the same problem rises from the notion that it is intrinsically good to get issues into the international normative arenas long before they become hot political isssues. The first difficulty is with timing. Until an issue is ripe for international action, it is a nonissue: an effort in the twenties or thirties to determine a jurisdictional regime for outer space, or to allocate rights to deep ocean manganese nodules, would have been utterly futile although space as well as the nodules were known to exist and the technological prediction that sooner or later we can get at them would have been reasonable. The second difficulty is with the actual conversion of a nonissue

---

68.   Cf. Mesthene's discussion of the relation of technology to values in a general context and without any reference to the international system: "Questions of values can become more pointed and insistent in a society that organizes itself to control technology and that engages in deliberate social planning. Planning demands explicit recognition of value commitments and value priorities and often brings into the open value conflicts that remain hidden in the more impersonal and less conscious workings of the market system." Emmanuel G. Mesthene, *Technological Change: Its Impact on Man and Society* (Cambridge, Mass.: Harvard University Press, 1970), p. 45.

into an issue before it ignites a political contest. Issues with technological content lend themselves well to such a conversion, or politicization, through the assessment and articulation of the range of possible future consequences of the given technology. But this means that, in fact, a new, notional conflict is being stimulated; a preventive, controlled fire is being started to burn off flammable material before it would ignite spontaneously, and as with every preventive fire it is being started in the hope that it will remain under control until it has done its work. One of the questions still to be faced is whether in the international normative process, with relatively very few participants mutually connected in numerous ways, all the new normative issues do not become tangled up beyond the capacity of the decision-makers to keep them reasonably separate for effective control, management, and resolution.

ACTORS AND ARENAS

The technological phenomenon affects in several diverse ways both the mobilization of participants into an international normative process and the selection of the arena in which the process takes place. Analytically, these two categories are separate. However, the density and nature of their couplings, technological couplings in particular, necessitates their joint treatment before they can be separated again for evaluation.

It is not enough to conclude, as we will, that under the thrust of technological forces the players in the international normative process will proliferate, and that arenas of action will multiply. While these quantitative changes are important, in themselves they suggest little about the quality—the effectiveness, sufficiency, and direction—of the normative process in the future. A qualitative valuation leads to the following hypothetical propositions regarding the future forms and dynamics of the international normative process.

1. The technological phenomenon will enable many more national actors to enter an international normative process, even if their immediate interest in a given issue is low and their technological competence relative to that issue nil. But whether such quantitative change will significantly raise the influence in the normative process of these countries is indeterminate. While their opportunities to act decisively will increase, their relative capabilities may be largely undercut by the growing influence of other actors.

2. Nonstate actors will go up in numbers, in prominence, and in influence. They will be entering the process at many points and in many guises; as transnational organizations and groups; as subnational interest groups, often of the subgovernmental variety; as international bureaucracies; as expert groups; or as individual experts. They will restrict the freedom of action of the nation-states when, by injecting rational methods into the resolution of issues, they will delineate the technological perimeters of issues. Gradually, they will significantly affect, or at least will have the potential to affect, the distribution of normative influence between developing and advanced states.

3. The technological phenomenon will operate toward increasing the number and variety of normative arenas within which an international issue can be settled. In particular, this may come about when a normative process becomes, for some of the participants, too difficult and too lengthy because of too many interests involved. Some will then seek their normative goal through other channels. States may also resort to varying normative arenas whenever an analysis of an issue discloses that it has local, regional, or other particular traits inviting particularistic action. Finally, states may seek to shift an issue from one arena to another whenever they feel that their interests would be better served by a more technical or a more political work-style within a given normative arena. A diversity of rules with varying and sometimes overlapping spheres of authority is likely to result.

Nation-States as Participants

While the technological phenomenon greatly enhances the opportunities and capabilities for political identification of issues to be set up for international normative action, it also affects the number of potential participants joining in the action.

The three closely related factors leading towards the increased participation of states in the normative process are: (1) the technological nature of many issues coming up for regulatory action, (2) the more rational and future-oriented work-style of many national decision-makers, and (3) the increasing experience and expertise of many state representatives with such forms of international bargaining as caucusing, bloc action, and division of diplomatic labor. The first two factors are components of the technological phenomenon. The third is independent of it but related: technological issues often function as exemplary lessons in the diplomatic learning process.

The mobilizing potential of technological projections is high. Technology is still viewed as the cutting edge of civilization and a multiplier of man's capabilities, and hence it holds certain fascination for many people, those without technology in particular. And, of course, at least the first-order consequences of a new technology are seemingly easy to imagine and, if they agree with one's values, easy to believe. A statement by the representative of Trinidad and Tobago in the initial phase of the seabed debate at the United Nations reflects the mobilizing potential of the projections of technological capabilities and their consequences:

> Ambassador Pardo, in his very excellent presentation, gave us some detailed facts and figures which to many of us were extremely fascinating, but which others have described as over-optimistic. My government has neither the technical nor financial competence to determine the accuracy or otherwise of the Maltese figures, but it would be strange indeed if, on the basis of the information available to him and to the world, his figures should prove to be widely over-optimistic. There is at least a sound basis for believing that both wealth and opportunity are to be found on the sea-bed and ocean floor for those who are able and willing to seek them.[69]

States without their own scientific knowledge about the seabed resources and without any data regarding the technological and economic feasibility of deep ocean mining were instrumental in keeping the seabed issue, after it had been raised by Malta, not only alive but moving toward some recognition of communal claims to the resource.[70] Certainly a less intensive but essentially similar surge of political interest

---

69.   Mr. Solomon, Doc. A/C.1/PV.1530 (16 November 1967), p. 7.

70.   The mobilizing efforts, significantly aided by the availability and manipulation of technical data and by the need for technical information, resulted in an expanded and diversified field of participants in the policy-making process. The effects were very obvious on the governmental level. During the initial phases of the seabed debate in the General Assembly and in the Ad Hoc Seabed Committee, sixty-four countries contributed to the recorded exchange of views between November 1967–July 1968. Of these sixty-four, spokesmen for thirty states advocated the establishment of an international regime for the deep ocean floor. Most of these (twenty-five) were countries relatively uninvolved in marine affairs and without appreciable levels of national expertise in marine science and engineering. On the other hand, most of the nations with such expertise and with well-developed and active interests in the uses of the ocean showed almost no inclination to move toward an international regime. Thus, the political burden of maintaining the seabed question as a live issue in the U.N. policy process rested primarily on states which until then relative strangers to marine affairs, were mobilized into action by the dissemination of the technical data and by the resulting images of more or less readily accessible submarine riches threatened by imminent but unequal exploitation by the advanced countries. To some extent the intensity of the newly formed national interest in the economic resources of the seabed and in the political potential of the seabed issue also manifested itself in the swelling of the membership of the Seabed Committee: starting with thirty-five in 1967, it went to forty-two in 1968 and to eighty-six in 1970.

accompanies the search for international regulatory mechanisms for such technologies as space satellites for direct broadcasting or remote sensing of earth's resources.

It is, of course, difficult to judge to what extent the expanding adoption of more rational styles of policy planning has been generating the relatively new tendency of states to participate in normative issues fairly remote from their immediate and pressing concerns. However, two factors appear to be at work here: the incessant learning process regarding effective policy-making and bargaining methods as it is experienced by national representatives involved in international organizations and conferences; and the domestic pressures arising from the goals of modernization and pushing towards a priori as against a posteriori design in all policy making. This pervasive element—the intrusion of postindustrial attitudes and styles into global processes—cannot be overemphasized. It seems to have the potential needed to force the international normative process into a pattern led more by foresight than hindsight, and to make the normative outcome more the result of authorship than of editing.[71]

Various forms of bargaining trade-offs are being rapidly mastered by most countries: issue-for-issue exchanges of support, bloc decision-making, collective policy statements, caucusing as a form of information exchange, these and their many variations are a part of an almost routine arsenal of negotiating instruments used by diplomats in all areas. They are too prevalent to require detailed examination, especially since their relationship to the technological phenomenon is only secondary. It is true, of course, that trade-offs in international negotiation also reflect the increasing ability and inclination of countries to plan and orchestrate, i.e., rationalize, their policies more systematically and consciously. In any case, in the present context it only needs to be noted that trade-offs tend to bring into the normative arena actors which would have no special interest in an issue-area except as general members in the global community whose influence can be traded for other values on the international market.

Finally, the choice of the normative arena also influences the number of participants in the normative process as well as the intensity and political force of their participation. The ways in which the locus of normative activity is influenced or even determined by technological forces will be examined later in this section. The present purpose is served by noting that the strategy of many less developed countries to have large-scale, technology-rich issues brought up for regulatory action into highly political arenas— i.e., U.N. General Assembly rather than the International Telecommunications Union, General Assembly's First (Political) Committee rather than the Sixth (Legal), etc.— increases the mobilizing opportunities with the result that still more countries are likely to enter the normative process as its active participants. The mobilization of new participants seems to follow three major routes: (a) national diplomatic interests are simply alerted to an issue given political visibility in the global arena; (b) the introduction of an issue in the form of an agenda item normally activates the secretariats or other conference organizers into the preparation of background materials which, when disseminated to potential participants, require some response and therefore attention;[72]

71. Cf., Terence K. Hopkins, "Third World Modernization in Transnational Perspective," Wayne Wilcox, ed., *Protagonists, Power, and the Third World: Essays on the Changing International System, Annals of the American Academy of Political and Social Science*, Vol.386 (November 1969), pp. 130-131. Hopkins, dealing with social change, borrows from the biologist George Wald the concepts of *organic* as opposed to *technological* evolution, the contrast being between modes of social design in which intentional, collective actions on a large scale play no regularly important causal role, and in which they do.

72. While it may be true that the production of documents and background materials in organizations such as the U.N. may have reached the level of a complete overload, especially for smaller missions, there are still instances in which the Secretariat effectively serves the mobilizing function. For instance, the Secretary-General used his mandate to prepare a study of seabed resources by sending to all U.N. members a

(c) in general political organizations such as the General Assembly where trade-offs are routine, the pressures on national delegations to act collectively with their regional, political, or other group are considerable—weak states in particular must be mindful of relations with their neighbors.[73]

The technological phenomenon thus leads to an increased state activity in the international normative process. This does not automatically imply that the role of nation-states, relative to other actors, is also on the increase, or that the newcomers to the process necessarily gain more influence at the cost of the well-established players. Before evaluating these relationships two other categories need to be examined—those of non-state actors and of normative arenas.

Nonstate Actors

Normative issues with high technological content and decision-making styles characterized by long-range planning and technology assessment require the involvement of persons with technical expertise, or of those with access to it, or of others with some alternate way of manipulating specific types of information or knowledge. Who are they and how are their roles cast? Where and how do they enter the normative process? Do they influence the substance of issues? If they do have influence, and if they use it rationally, what are their goals?

Inventorying such questions and assessing their relevance for the future can only be undertaken with a sense of inadequacy of both concepts and data.

Organizing concepts which would help in sorting out the roles and functions in international normative activity of various types of expertise are generally unavailable. One of the main reasons for this is that these roles and functions crisscross the boundary between the international and the domestic processes and systems; the political relevance of expert roles and the impact of expert functions inevitably change as they move from one political framework into another. And this, of course, is further complicated by the diversity of national systems and their own relative ability to manage expertise and control its influence.

Reliable data on the relations between knowledge and power at the international level is difficult to get since at least some of the intercourse takes place in the intimacy of closed policy meetings, briefings, background documentation, social contacts, and hundreds of other recesses of the policy-making, diplomatic, and normative processes.

One generalization is possible. The role of experts cast as *actor* in the international normative process will be increasing at a fairly modest pace if at all, while they will be more and more conspicuous, and rather rapidly, as *instrument*. The line between these two functions of expertise is blurred, the media often blend into the message. To what extent expertise consciously guides and manipulates the normative phase of the political process, and to what extent it is used to serve a normative goal may be beyond measurement. In some instances the two may represent a completely fused unit highly resistant to detailed analysis.

---

note verbale and a questionnaire requesting, in addition to data describing each country's activities in marine science and engineering, the views of each government regarding the need for international activities in the marine field. It is of some interest to note that the Secretariat's request for data and policy review was sent on 6 July 1967, while the Maltese submission of the seabed item for inclusion in the agenda of the General Assembly followed on 18 August 1967. For the respective documents see Doc. E 4487/Annex II (24 April 1968); and UNGA, 22nd Session, *Official Records* (Annexes: Agenda Item 92), Doc. A/6695 (1967).

73.   For further comments on this point see A.A. Fatouros, "Participation of the 'New' States in the International Legal Order of the Future," Falk and Black, eds. (fn. 10), p. 356.

There are many signs of expertise entering the international normative process at various stages and with different impacts. Relatively little has so far moved on the most fundamental level, namely, the management of the international normative process. The technocratic elites with the aid of modern techniques of decision-making such as systems analysis, linear programming, and others, have risen to prominence on the national level in the highly advanced societies and such limited overflow as there has been into the international system can be detected only in functional or highly selective organizations—in some of the U.N. specialized agencies, the European Economic Communities, or the Organization for Economic Cooperation and Development. However, since the making of international decisions—and the normative process is only one form of decision-making—in all arenas will have an increasingly technical character due primarily to the densely intermeshed consequences of such decisions, the skill-elites are likely to populate the normative process of the future more visibly and possibly with greater direct influence.

The situation is somewhat different where the expertise is needed to handle the substance of normative activity rather than its procedures. Whether the expert plays the role of an actor or an instrument is largely determined by the nature of the issue and of the arena within which it is being handled, the general rule being approximately as follows:

The more technical the issue and the more select and homogeneous the group of participants, the tighter is the coupling of the expert to the policy process and the more immediate the influence of the expertise on policy. However, the equation changes in a subtle and diffuse way if one posits a less technical—but still technology-related—issue handled in a global, highly politicized arena. Then the important conclusion is not so much that the influence of the expert diminishes but, more importantly, that there will be an increase in the number and influence of the brokers of knowledge, the intermediaries between the experts and the primary actors.

The direct, rule-creating role of expert committees and scientific groups in WHO has already been noted in another context.[74] Somewhat similar, but with a heavier involvement of national policies, is the role of expertise in the normative activities in the International Telecommunications Union (ITU).[75] As one moves into the more politicized environment of the International Atomic Energy Agency (IAEA), the knowledge-decision linkage begins to change. There is more of a symbiotic relationship, with the brokers in a stronger position. The panels of IAEA experts are appointed by the director-general on the basis, to at least some extent, of their technical capability. And it then "depends on the skills of the participants from the secretariat" how effectively the secretariat uses the panels to influence agency decisions.[76]

---

74. See above in this essay.

75. Harold K. Jacobson, "ITU: A Potpourri of Bureaucrats and Industrialists," Cox and Jacobson (fn. 60), pp. 72-74.

76. Lawrence Scheinman, "IAEA: Atomic Condominium?" Cox and Jacobson (fn.60), p. 242. Scheinman's study also includes the following observation: "Some outside experts who have served on these panels have remarked on the adeptness of the secretariat in fashioning the limited technical advice of experts into endorsed recommendations for wider action. The agency also has a Scientific Advisory Council (SAC), composed in the past of such prestigious scientists as Isidore Rabi, Sir John Cockcroft, and Homi Bhabha, among others. SAC reviews the overall scientific program of the agency and passes scientific judgment on panels, conferences, and symposia. Despite its prestigious composition, however, SAC is less influential in agency decisions that the panels of experts convened for particular purposes. It rarely takes a strong position, and on one of the few occasions that it did—when it unanimously rejected the idea of a center for the study of theoretical physics—it was overridden. In general it can be said that SAC is influential if and when the director-general and the board choose to make it so; and this has not been their common practice, especially in recent years."

Still broader and more infused with political considerations are some of the global normative processes taking place at the United Nations. The relative transparency of the United Nations decision-making system enables one to see more clearly than elsewhere how the individual scientist or technical expert, acting as such, comes into close contact with trained international officials administering the flows of scientific and technical knowledge in the normative process.

Two fundamental prerequisites determine the capability of international staffs to perform a given normative function by controlling or influencing certain flows of knowledge. First, their role depends on their responsiveness to the interests of those nations to whom they would communicate scientific and technical data so interpreted as to lead to normative demands. Second, they must be so situated in relation to the normative process as to have a continuous opportunity to employ scientific and technical knowledge as instruments of policy.

As used here, the criterion of responsiveness is primarily phenomenological in nature: to communicate effectively, i.e., to transmit and interpret scientific and technical data, the international staff member must be perceived by those nations to whom the interpreted data is being transmitted as responsive to their general interests. This element of responsiveness plays an important role in many diverse areas where scientific and technical knowledge and international politics meet. Its formal aspects are often reflected in the demands that members of international staffs be as independent of their national states as possible, that scientific and technical consultants be recruited by international staffs rather than selected by their governments, and that they come, as far as possible, from countries not involved in the issue-area concerned. In their interactions, states often rely on these formal aspects of an individual's impartiality to a remarkable degree, and because they do so, the neutral status of international staffs and consultants can become an effective instrument in the international normative process.

Examples of these various phenomena abound. For instance, the availability of independent research effort was stressed as an important element determining the success or failure of international organizations engaged in norm-setting, regulatory tasks in fishery management.[77] In 1960, when the International Whaling Commission (IWC) decided to make a new effort toward the scientific assessment of the whale stocks in the

---

77. Among the important reasons for the success of the U.S.-Canadian salmon and halibut commissions was, according to Kask, "that each of the conventions specifically provided for an international research staff for the commission itself . . . . As the scientific staff members were not the direct employees of the member governments, doubts as to the authenticity of the scientific results presented to the commissioners were minimal, and . . . results of researches have never been seriously questioned." As a contrast, Kask refers to the experience of the International North Pacific Fisheries Convention, under which all researches "are carried out by agencies of members countries, with programs coordinated by the Commission at its annual meetings. Some researches that touch the interests and the sensitivities of members are vigorously contested. They are only passed and reported upon after long joint working party sessions between scientists of all countries and then only if their usually toned-down results are found acceptable to the Government heads of the Commission." John Kask, "Present Arrangements for Fishery Exploitation," Lewis M. Alexander, ed., *The Law of the Sea: International Rules and Organization for the Sea,* Proceedings of the 3rd Annual Conference of the Law of the Sea Institute, June 1968 (Kingston, R.I., 1969), pp. 59-60. Of course, this instance as well as others of similar nature also reflect the more fundamental question whether it was the presence of an international research staff that contributed to the success of some fishery commissions, or whether it was the prior underlying consensus among the member states that provided the climate permitting the international research effort and allowing it to grow. But, as in so many other cases, there is unlikely to be a simple, one-way causal relationship: even if international research arrangements simply mirror an underlying consensus, the high acceptability of data produced through such arrangements can easily be seen as an effective factor fortifying and enlarging the original consensus.

Antarctic and the regulation of whaling, the members of the newly created Committee of Three Scientists had to come from "countries not engaged in pelagic whaling."[78] Later, the neutral standing of the sources of scientific advice for IWC was enhanced when IWC arranged with FAO to receive regular reports on the status of the Antarctic whale stocks from an FAO Assessment Group.[79] Even then, however, care seems to have been taken not to have any nationals from the countries engaged in Antarctic pelagic whaling directly associated with the FAO Assessment Group reports; while, at the same time, the fact that some members of the Assessment Group attended IWC meetings in the added capacity of advisers to their national governments appears to have been entirely acceptable.[80]

There are then certain formal prequisites affecting the ability of individuals involved in an international normative process to function as transmitters and interpreters of scientific and technical data, especially where such functions are to support the needs of developing countries. In the case of staff members of an international secretariat, the minimal prerequisite is automatically fulfilled by their status of international civil servants; beyond this, it depends on other critieria whether or not, and how, they use that potential to traverse the twilight zone separating administration and policy-making. The situation of scientists and technical experts called upon by an international organization to serve in an ad hoc capacity is somewhat different. The act alone of accepting an assignment from an international organization to serve as a scientific and technical adviser potentially elevates an individual into an international or, more precisely, extranational category. It is not that the scientist's politics is presumed to have changed because of his new relationship with an international organization; rather the case is one of assuming that only scientists with transnational perspectives or even loyalties would accept assignments from international organizations. Where such an assumption would be difficult to sustain, the scientist's contribution must be formally "internationalized" in some other way, if necessary by obscuring his authorship.[81]

Two other categories of actors are ushered into the international normative process by the technological phenomenon or, if they are already present, their roles in that process are strengthened. International scientific and other nongovernmental organizations representing specific communities of knowledge or skill are one such category, while subnational groups and subgovernmental groups, while politically distinct, can be collapsed into another category.

Both the increasing technology-inspired reliance on professional input into decision-

---

78.   International Whaling Commission, *Twelfth Report of the Commission* (London 1961), p. 8.

79.   International Whaling Commission, *Fifteenth Report* p. 18; *Sixteenth Report* p. 8; *Seventeenth Report* p. 28.

80.   For instance, J.A. Gulland of the Lowestoft Fisheries Laboratory in the United Kingdom, a prominent member of the FAO Assessment Group, also served as an adviser to the U.K. representatives on IWC. See lists of Commissioners and Advisers attending the 15th, 17th, and 18th meetings in the respective IWC reports.

81.   A rather clear instance of obscuring the authorship of a technical report commissioned by an international organization is to be found by comparing two closely related documents issued by the United Nations in the early phase of the seabed debate. Both were prepared by U.S. scientists. One (U.N. Doc. E/4449/Add.2 of 7 February 1968), dealing with food resources of the sea, was prepared by an academic scientist, Professor C.P. Idyll of the University of Miami. This is clearly stated on the cover page. The other (E/4449/Add. 1 of 19 February 1968), on mineral resources, was done by a scientist in a high governmental position, Dr. Frank Wang, Marine Geologist of the U.S. Geological Survey, with the last policy-oriented chapter added by the U.N. Secretariat. These facts are not given anywhere in the document itself—the whole thing gives the impression of an anonymous technical report. The authorship can be found only in the text of a separately issued cover document, appearing later (E/4449 of 21 February 1968).

making, and the objective need for such an input enable international nongovernmental (transnational) entities to participate in the global normative process. Their specific technical competence allows organizations as different as the International Committee for the Red Cross, the International Confederation of Free Trade Unions, and the International Chamber of Commerce to play major roles in preparing initial studies, recommendations, and drafts of proposed conventions.[82] The granting of a formal consultative status to transnational scientific associations by intergovernmental organizations with normative competencies, and the arrangements for informal consultation between them are becoming routine matters in the life of the global community.[83]

The experience of the constituent groups of the International Council of Scientific Unions (ICSU) and of ICSU itself in providing guidance and advice to decision-making bodies signals a trend likely to grow with the increasing involvement of the global community in technology-related issues.[84] This linkage will not necessarily grow at the U.N.-system level. The inability of the U.N. system to respond adequately to problems which are of primary concern to advanced countries—and many technology-related issues fit this category—leads to the shifting of such problems from the U.N. to regional and narrowly functional organizations. Within them, however, transnational expertise is likely to become even more effective and wanted.

The direct impact by subnational groups—with technical expertise as their admission ticket to the international normative process—is somewhat less visible but not necessarily less penetrative. First of all, transnational scientific organizations may, in fact, represent subnational interests in those instances where a strong national group dominates the scientific organization either through funds or by the sheer weight of its expertise.[85] Private groups sometimes directly contribute to the formation of international norms when, usually through their technological competence, they have been granted operating rights and responsibilities of transnational dimensions. Airline companies and oil companies have already started to accumulate such normative credits for their practice undertaken in pursuance of international agreements.[86] Following Oscar Schachter's observation that "an organ which dispenses funds, supplies and services may lack formal authority to lay down binding rules but its resolutions and practice on the disposition of its resources will clearly be a factor in enhancing its authority in respect of rules governing the use and distribution of those resources,"[87] one can generalize and extrapolate by saying that the growing number of nonstate actors dispensing essential services in the production, management, or operation of technologies of transnational dimensions will have an increasing influence on the formation of rules guiding the use of such technologies. Whether or not the technology-based groups are private companies or

---

82.   Gerald A. Sumida, "Transnational Movements and Economic Structures," Falk and Black, eds. (fn. 20), p. 558.

83.   For numerous references to this practice see Robert O. Keohane and Joseph S. Nye, Jr., eds., *Transnational Relations and World Politics, International Organization* Vol. 25, No. 3 (Summer, 1971), *passim*, and within it in particular the essay by Edward Miles, "Transnationalism in Space Inner and Outer," pp. 602-625.

84.   International Council of Scientific Unions, *The Yearbook* (1974), p. 60.

85.   Amounts contributed by a national unit to a transnational scientific organization, or the number of nationals of one country active in the organization, are not necessarily the best indices of its character: in each case a detailed inquiry into the organization's system of governance, formal and informal, would be necessary for reliable evaluation.

86.   Air Traffic Rights Dispute (United States v. France) (1963), *International Legal Materials*, Vol. 3, No. 4 (July 1964), pp. 668-720; Air Traffic Rights Dispute (United States v. Italy) (1965), *International Legal Materials*, Vol. 4, No. 5 (September 1965), pp. 974-987; Saudi Arabia v. Aramco (1958), *International Law Reports*, Vol. 27 (1963), pp. 117-233. As cited in Schachter (fn. 1), p. 18.

87.   *Ibid.*, p. 19.

subunits of a state is not of crucial importance: even the subgovernmental unit derives its normative influence from its technological rather than political position and to that extent it is a nonstate actor.

It is in fact quite likely that the role and frequency of subgovernmental units with technical experience entering the international normative arena will grow in the future. The trend has its logic: the more a state strives to control technological developments and those behind them, the more it will need specialized units to do the controlling. But the trend also has its empirical manifestations in the way some countries, especially those with a highly developed social, political, economic, and technological infrastructure are represented in international organizations. In some of them, for instance, the chief decision-maker for the United States need not be a State Department official but a representative of other agencies and interests. The State Department is conspicuous through its Office of the Coordinator of Ocean Affairs in the work of the Intergovernmental Oceanographic Commission (ICC) but it shares its responsibility with an Interagency Panel consisting of the representatives of the National Science Foundation (NSF), U.S. Navy, National Oceanic and Atmospheric Administration (NOAA), Environmental Protection Agency (EPA), U.S. Geological Survey (USGS), and U.S. Coast Guard (USCG). In the intergovernmental International Hydrological Decade (IHD) and in its successor, the International Hydrological Program (IHP), the United States representation is different—Atomic Energy Commission (AEC), Agricultural Research Service (ARS), U.S. Army Corps of Engineers, EPA, NOAA, NSF and USGS are the main influences. A still differently constituted "United States" acts out its membership role in the International Monetary Fund (IMF); the decisions are influenced by—in addition to the U.S. Treasury and the Federal Reserve—other financial agencies and, according to Cox and Jacobson, probably by Wall Street bankers and by individuals with particularly strong financial roles.[88] The structurally subnational and functionally nonstate participation in international regulatory agencies is clearly visible in organizations such as WHO where the governmental representatives are predominantly technical specialists, most of them medical doctors.[89]

As we have noted earlier, it is extremely difficult to determine the extent to which the experts in the various institutions participating in the national decision-making and in the international normative processes are simply instruments and to what extent they are actually actors. Yet a preliminary conclusion seems inevitable: in the international normative process the nation-state has company where it used to have none. Both the invited expert guests and expert gate-crashers enter in numbers, and their volume as well as their influence is likely to grow as the world goes more and more technological, and as global concerns become more and more intertwined in ways demanding expert definition and skilled management of the innumerable linkages and dependencies. Whether this is desirable or not for a global community seeking to achieve an orderly and just system is still somewhat early to judge.

---

88.   Cox and Jacobson (fn. 60), p. 17.

89.   Jacobson (fn. 62), pp. 195-7. Consider especially this paragraph: "The existing evidence on how governmental policies about WHO are determined suggests that ministries of health or social welfare and foreign ministries are jointly involved, in varying combinations of strength. In general, ministries of health are very protective of their position as the dominant voice in what they consider to be technical issues. Since these ministries almost without exception provide the officials who head the delegations, they are in a strategic position to enforce their views. Indeed, since the head of the delegation might well be the minister of health, he might even determine policy on the spot. Foreign ministries, however, generally insist on having their way on matters like the membership of Communist China and the Republic of South Africa. In the case of most Western countries foreign ministries are also responsible for seeing that policies relating to basic budgetary matters are carried out."

The Normative Arenas

The multiplicity of normative arenas in which the future regulation of an international issue may be determined has a direct relationship to the technological phenomenon. In terms of the structure of the international normative process, several major trends pointing well into the future are easily observable: (1) due to the technical component of many normative issues, the actors have a greater choice of arenas within which the issues can be determined; (2) since technologies are particularistic, many technology-based issues require particular (i.e., functionally and/or geographically limited) solutions; (3) nation-states are improving their skills in handling the same issue in several normative arenas simultaneously; (4) the relative rapidity of technological developments makes actors resort to new, informal normative arenas for quick action.

A typology of normative arenas includes the following:

Class I—Universal

1. *Universal, structured, non-technical, norm-setting.* Usually issue- or area-oriented. Takes the form of global law-making conferences of the law-of-the-sea type. Normally preceded by a long preparatory phase also of considerable normative impact.

2. *Universal, structured, non-technical, norm-mapping.* Also issue- or area-oriented. Takes the form of specialized conferences or congresses typified by the 1972 Stockholm Conference on the Human Environment. Normally requires less preparation than category 1. Usually aims at general normative guidelines, or normative maps, rather than specific rules.

3. *Universal, semi-structured, non-technical, norm-mapping.* Typified by meetings of the U.N. General Assembly, its major committees, and similar bodies through which—by means of debates and/or resolutions—general normative guidelines are articulated.

4. *Universal, non-structured, non-technical, norm-setting or norm-mapping.* The generalized arena of state interaction giving rise to general customary rules or other types of *ius non scriptum.*

5. *Universal, structured, technical, norm-setting.* Refers primarily to normative as well as the more narrowly regulatory processes in specialized agencies, such as FAO, ITU, WHO; groups such as IOC; and to similar undertakings.

Class II—Regional

6-10. The second class of normative arenas includes basically the same five categories as above but on the regional level. There will be, of course, important variations in the use of these arenas: for instance, large-scale law-making conferences are probably much less frequent on the regional than on the global level.

Class III—Bilateral and Unilateral

11. *Bilateral, structured, norm-setting.* Bilateral and other small-scale arenas set up to arrive at a specific legal product, a treaty, or an explicit though unwritten agreement. Technical or non-technical. Bilateral treaty negotiations as well as proceedings before the International Court of Justice fall into this category.

12. *Bilateral, non-structured, norm-setting.* Interaction of two or very few actors leading to the formation of customary rules of behavior or other forms of mutual understandings and expectations with normative force.

13. *Unilateral, norm-mapping.* Unilateral acts, verbal or material, of international actors undertaken with the intention of creating an international

norm through a favorable response, acquiescence, or simply inability on the part of others to react. The 1945 U.S. Proclamation on the Continental Shelf or Canada's 1970 Arctic Waters Pollution Prevention Act are examples.

There are, of course, many other intermediate categories but the present listing should suffice for our purposes.

None of the normative arenas is a product of the technological age, except in the general sense in which international organizations and specialized agencies themselves are by-products of technological developments and of the technological spirit. What is new, however, and to at least some extent due to the technological phenomenon, is the way these arenas are being used.

First of all, there is an increased use of the structured universal arenas designed for norm-setting as well as norm-mapping. Two major forces drive this trend. One is what I have characterized elsewhere as scientific ethos,[90] the result of the fact-based recognition of the global interconnectedness of human and social activities and their consequences, and of the consequent demand that a social response, especially of the normative kind, match the comprehensiveness and scope of the issue. The policy-making processes for oceanic, environmental, and outer space affairs are replete with examples of the systemic, universalistic approach.[91] The second force bringing normative issues into the structured universal arenas is of a more political character: as an outcome of the continuous process of learning the ways of international diplomacy and the art of global bargaining, the third world countries tend to bring controversial issues into arenas within which they are relatively more influential. In the early stages of the seabed issue in the United Nations, the Soviet Union attempted to reroute the entire affair out of the General Assembly and into the cooler, more technical climate of IOC, and failed.[92] The smaller and developing countries resisted the pressure to keep the issue from falling victim to high-level expertise and a politically sterile area in which trade-offs and cross-issue bargains are difficult. But even when the issue was saved for the general Assembly, some diplomatic energy was still required to make sure that the seabed agenda item would be assigned to the First (Political) Committee rather than the Sixth (Legal) where, it was feared, it would receive a much more technical and legalistic treatment and possibly end up in the International Law Commission.[93]

The structured and semistructured universal arenas for normative action are indeed effective in generating broad normative maps of preferred international behavior. As if

---

90. Slouka (fn. 52), pp. 213-27.

91. E.g., Richard A. Falk's emphasis on the proper response to the ecological imperative: "From an ecological perspective, the political fragmentation of mankind into separately administered states makes no sense whatsoever. The basic ecological premise posits the wholeness and interconnectedness of things. Up until very recently, the scale of human life on the planet did not present any dangers to the system as a whole, but, more recently, technological developments, together with rapid population expansion, have removed this margin of safety and have started building up levels of pressure that threaten to disrupt the delicate balance of links in the cycle of life on earth. To moderate this pressure responses by man will be required to embrace the whole earth; there is need for central guidance of human activities in relation to natural surroundings." "Toward Equilibrium in the World Order System," Proceedings of the American Society of International Law, *American Journal of International Law*, Vol. 64, No. 4 (September 1970), pp. 217-218.

92. See statements at the United Nations by Soviet diplomats Mendelevich, Ananichev, and Malik, in the following U.N. documents: UNGA, 21st Session, *Official Records* (2nd Committee, 1060th Meeting, 7 November 1966); A/C.1/PV.1525 (10 November 1967), pp. 17-18; A/AC.135/SR.3 (2 March 1968), pp. 15-16; A/AC.135/SR.11 (20 June 1968), p. 8.

93. For more complete discussion see Slouka (fn. 49), p. 69.

compressing the generating process of customary law into the short period of a global debate with massive numbers of participants and with all action on the purely verbal level, the structured universal arenas often yield consensual forms of perhaps blurred but nevertheless recognizable contours. Minimally, the consensual process sets limits to state behavior. Before the 1967 Treaty on Principles Governing the Activities of States in the Exploration and Use of Outer Space was formulated, there already had been a broad consensus achieved through several years of debate and negotiations placing the outer space with all celestial bodies outside the scope of national appropriation by any means. Similarly, the first five years of the U.N. debate on the deep sea resources yielded a distinct consensus by which the deep ocean floor has been removed from the legal reach of exclusive national control.

However, the same normative arenas are singularly unproductive when it comes to the articulation and negotiation of specific legal rules of state conduct. Normative arenas with massive participation mostly require an inordinately long time to produce any norm,[94] and those that are produced are so highly diluted that they again serve more as general guidelines rather than clear prescriptions. The time lapse and the nonspecificity of the resulting norm may not be so crucial when the subject is, for instance, the definition of aggression—four decades or even half a century may make relatively little difference. Where technological issues are involved, however, time is of the essence; technological change is swift and the regulatory processes of the global community tend to lag more and more behind.

The trend of new issues being brought for normative action to the universal, structured arenas is therefore matched by the simultaneous tendency to resolve such issues at lower, more particular levels. While in 1970 the conference on the law of the sea was already being actively prepared, Canada resorted to what we have called the unilateral arena: by proclaiming its Arctic Waters Pollution Prevention Act it explicitly sought to avoid what was described as a dangerous delay which would result from handling the issue multilaterally.[95] Many such examples may be cited: unilateral action, after all, is still the dominant style in international policy-making. However, it is now being intensified by the growing gap between the rate of technological change and rate of the global response to it.

Other powerful factors leading toward particular normative solutions for global issues are the particularism of technology, the discernment of scientific knowledge, and the more systematically analytical style of political decision-making. The knowledge of the geographical and geological properties of the continental shelves adjacent to a number of countries in the mediterranean areas of most continents was one of the stimuli leading to the formulation of regional or bilateral continental shelf regimes—in the North Sea,

---

94.   According to my calculations the total normative process leading to the four major conventions produced by the 1958 Geneva Conference on the Law of the Sea required about two decades, if it is counted from the time the need for a new norm was first publicly recognized and acted upon by raising the issue in a normative arena, to the time the norm has achieved conventional legal form of a treaty in force. (This, of course, does not preclude the possibility that the normative process yielded specific customary or consensual rules or limited tacit agreements along the way.) If the contemporary efforts at regulating the deep ocean mining are taken to have started only in the 1966-67 period, better than a decade will have elapsed before a specific set of conventional norms is even formulated, with the entire ratification process still to come, an affair itself often requiring some five years or more.

95.   For citations to the statements of Prime Minister Trudeau and the Canadian Foreign Affairs Minister Mitchell Sharp to the effect that Canada had to act because an international regime would take years to establish, see Richard B. Bilder, "The Role of Unilateral State Action in Preventing International Environmental Injury" (University of Wisconsin 1973), p. 51.

the Adriatic, the Baltic, the Asian mediterranean seas, and probably still another one will emerge in the East China Sea as a consequence of the geological survey conducted in the area between Japan and Taiwan. The technical knowledge that oil spills in arctic zones are incomparably more harmful than in the tropics[96] points toward the requirement of discriminating norms more precisely fitting a given situation and the available technological responses.

A number of future situations where technological implications or scientific knowledge will push toward particular norms is already shaping in the wings of contemporary civilization. Different sets of norms may be needed for supersonic overflights of the North Atlantic than for other oceans due to different traffic densities. To tow an iceberg as a source of fresh water through the Pacific Ocean toward Los Angeles may have to be regulated very differently than if the iceberg should be brought through the Atlantic to England. Different dietary patterns require different tolerances for the use of pesticides in order not to exceed the acceptable limit, even if such an acceptable limit is agreed on internationally in some generalized instrument.

Again, normative particularism is not a new development in international law. In practice, states have always concluded treaties on a range of topics only with their neighbors, and entered into more distant or broadly multilateral legal relationships much less frequently.[97] However, the correct notion that advancing technology diminishes the importance of distance within the global system[98] describes only one side of the technological coin. The other depicts the fact that technological forces intensify the particularistic nature of the international normative process. Getting closer to other inhabitants of the global system also means seeing much more sharply the peculiarities of different areas and situation; where physical distances are reduced, conceptual, attitudinal, and policy distances may increase. The precision of science and the specificity of technology magnify the differences of natural conditions, the diversities of ideology and culture, and the inequalities of power.

On balance, the technological phenomenon tends to push normative issues not into one particular arena but into many of them simultaneously. The normative specificity required to control large-scale technologies and their impacts, and the potential of specific norms to discriminate between different systemic configurations of interests leaves to the universal arenas the role of normative map-makers whose task it is to define the broad outlines of issues and draw their political and legal boundaries. It is on the regional, bilateral and unilateral levels that actual operational norms are fashioned.

The multiplicity of law-making processes roughly corresponds to the basic trends in the development of international organization. There, too, the increasing activity and sometimes even cohesion of regional groupings coupled with their mutually contentious policies does not automatically presage the demise of the United Nations. These two worlds, the regional and the universal, are often quite discontinuous: they serve different functions through different facilities and the governments as well as other actors participating in them continue to act differently in their immediate neighborhoods, in their regional systems, and in the global system.

The proliferation of actors and of arenas in the international normative process are then two aspects of a broad trend with significant technological underpinnings: they lead toward a democratization of that process at least in the sense of improving the chances of

---

96. Oscar Schachter and Daniel Serwer, "Marine Pollution Problems and Remedies," *American Journal of International Law*, Vol. 65, No. 1 (January 1971), p. 89.

97. Fatouros (fn. 73), pp. 362-3.

98. Cf. Oran R. Young, "Political Discontinuities in the International System," *World Politics*, Vol. 20, No. 3 (April 1968), pp. 369-392.

all actors to act, and the chances of many to act effectively in defense of their interests. This, of course, does not as yet say anything about the costs of the democratizing trend.

Knowledge as Power in the Normative Process

The proliferating normative issues, actors, and arenas of the technological age form a complex of relationships bonded together and activated by the political skills of the participants in the normative process. How the participating actors manipulate that process, what sources of power they are capable of marshalling, and how effectively they use their capabilities determine the duration, place, and outcome of the interaction. The main general conclusions to be reached here are the following:

1. Technical knowledge will be increasingly a source of power in the international normative process.

2. The employment of technical knowledge as a source of power has formidable built-in restraints undercutting its actual potential as an instrument of policy.

3. While the material technology gap between global actors is growing, the transferability of technical knowledge for the purposes of diplomacy and bargaining may lead toward greater equalization of power in the normative arenas.

4. The trend toward greater equilibrium in the distribution of normative influence and the consequent necessity for large-scale compromises among actors will result in the diffusion of the normative process throughout a wide range of arenas, and in the rise of a multiplicity of diverse, pliable, and closely related international norms.

The employment of technical knowledge as a source of power in the global normative process is one of the most conspicuous contributions of the technological phenomenon to international law-making. Theoretically, political processing of technology-related issues in need of international regulation is controllable through techniques ranged along a continuum between two poles of power.

One pole is represented by overwhelming political and military power which enables one state to dictate the solution of the issue on its own terms. It is not entirely inconceivable that the United States and the Soviet Union may eventually throw their weight behind the demand for free navigation through international straits if other bargaining instruments fail. One the whole, however, the shift from an international normative process to an open power *diktat* is becoming an increasingly awkward, costly, and ineffective way of achieving a preferred order. Instead, states which can afford it tend to rely increasingly on a technological fait accompli. Remote sensing satellites (ERTS) offer a fairly close model. When the National Aeronautics and Space Administration sent the first ERTS up into outer space it also sent it into a relative legal vacuum as an instrument which may, orbit after orbit, carve out for itself the necessary norm permitting it to do legally what it was sent out to do in the first place.

The other pole is represented by overwhelming technological power used not to coerce other actors but to control the material environment, natural or man-made, a power enabling a state to erase a contentious issue by a technological fix. A dispute regarding the allocation of the radio spectrum or of the orbital paths for communication satellites may be resolved by a political agreement on a fair allocation of the given value. Or the issue may be resolved by a technological fix—a new technology capable of multiplying the number of allocable bands or spaces well beyond the need. A major roadblock on the way to the nuclear test-ban treaty was the U.S. demand for on-site inspections, a feature unacceptable to the Soviet Union. The issue has been considerably alleviated through a technological fix—a more effective monitoring system combined with better knowledge of the scientific circumstances of atomic tests made the on-site inspections less important.[99] The entire question of social fix (political, legal, economic, etc.) versus technological fix as two methods of dealing with international normative issues (there are no pure types of technological and social fixes), while largely outside the context of the present essay, is among the more important questions in need of full examination. A state may resort to a technological fix to halt, or to deflect the thrust of, an international normative activity it considers unfavorable. At the same time, technological fix may be included among the new managerial techniques used to avoid international conflict: while DDT controls may be negotiated politically, a substitute for DDT without the harmful effects of DDT may be a more effective way of settling the issue.

The two poles of political power and of technological power, manifested either through *diktat* or a technological fix, are indeed just extremities. The international normative process oriented to or affected by technological forces takes place between them and, ideally, around the center of the continuum. Political power has always been present in that process but had to be used within certain limits. Technological power, undoubtedly, also enters the process—how and under what constraints?

In the universal, structured, and technical arenas for normative action, technological superiority appears to be the dominant variable. In an agency such as IAEA, the major powers maintain regulatory controls within the well-established IAEA system of safeguards through their superior expertise.[100] A particularly illustrative example of one use of superior expertise in a technology-based normative process is provided by the experience of the 1963 Extraordinary Administrative Radio Conference considering problems of telecommunication in space as narrated by Jacobson:

> The United States spent two years preparing for the conference. Besides work by the government to prepare the United States position, major studies were undertaken by the RAND Corporation, Lockheed, General Electric, and others. At one point General Electric had a staff of more than two hundred working on its study. Prior to the conference the United States position was submitted to all of ITU's members; the United States government also conducted a number of bilateral and multilateral negotiations that resulted in some modifications of the American position. In view of this extensive preparation it is not surprising that the position taken by the United States was extremely influential, and that the United States was not at all disappointed with the outcome of the conference.

And Jacobson then generalizes:

> In the framing of norms, . . . influence goes to those states and private agencies that are technically prepared and that control the resources important in telecommunications, and extremely few meet these qualifications. Of course, these actors must be sensitive to the needs of others because they could always be voted down; but *there is no substitute for technical knowledge and control of the physical resources involved.*[101]

The employment of technological sinews in a bilateral normative activity is difficult to document—bilateral bargaining, particularly its preparatory phase, is not normally conducted within the public view and often defies attempts of researchers to penetrate

---

99. Good account of this process is in Harold K. Jacobson and Eric Stein, *Diplomats, Scientists, and Politicians: The United States and the Nuclear Test Ban Negotiations* (Ann Arbor: University of Michigan Press, 1966).

100. Scheinman (fn. 76), p. 237.

101. Jacobson (fn. 75), pp. 73, 74. Emphasis added.

into its policy-making stage. But it does seem reasonable to assume that, in a bilateral normative process between two actors on very different levels of technological development and faced by a technology-related issue, the advanced partner is likely to be at a distinct advantage. And this contrasts in many respects with the normative situation in universal, structured, and non-technical arenas characterized by: (1) a highly politicized setting permitting multiple trade-offs and cross-issue bargaining and (2) access by all participants to *denationalized* or *internationalized* sources of expertise.

States with adequate technical expertise and matching resources are again in an advantageous position. They can very easily show, with reference to any normative issue with a technological content of international dimensions, that a political and normative determination of the issue should rest on a full technological assessment of its implications, and they may then insist on the necessity to subject that issue to a few years of further study. This technique, designed to assert dominant influence over a normative issue, was adopted by the Soviet Union in the early phase of the seabed debate in the United Nations, with a call for a few more years of national deep sea exploration and evaluation of resources before tackling the issue normatively.[102] The Soviet policy was openly supported by the IOC spokesman addressing the General Assembly's First Committee.[103] The same technique of seeking normative influence through manipulation of knowledge is reflected in the use of experts and expert groups as legitimating devices whenever a scientific judgment is predictable and considered supportive of the preferred outcome.

Among the potentially significant elements giving an extra edge to the major advanced states participating in the universal normative arenas is the sheer mass of technical as well as bureaucratic professionals who can be mobilized into action––the Radio Conference just mentioned is illustrative of the possible scope of such an effort. However, at this very point one also may start noting the considerable constraints on the freedom of action experienced by the major advanced states in the universal normative arenas.

One such constraint is the relative difficulty with which a highly developed country, facing a rapidly politicized technology-related issue, can set its intricate policy-making and diplomatic apparatus into action. Technology-related issues of international dimensions are almost invariably complex issues. Consequently, the associated national policy-making process setting the chief normative goals involves a considerable number of interests within as well as outside the governmental structure. To sort out, synchronize, and eventually bring under one national policy direction this often amorphous mass of wants and needs, often each with its own source of particular expertise to help defend itself, is a time-consuming process which offers only two options: (1) the policy may be tightly coordinated through an institutionalized mechanism,[104] which leads to an inflexible negotiating posture with little room for bargaining during the normative process;[105] or (2) coordination remains loose, which means that the policy itself must be

---

102. See fn. 93.

103. It may be tempting to assume here that the confluence of the Soviet and IOC stands reflected the fact that at the time IOC executive leadership was in the hands of a Soviet national. However, as the preceding note and other evidence suggests, it is quite likely that the same position would have been taken had IOC been led by an American, French, or British oceanographer rather than Soviet.

104. For a proposal to create a separate agency in the United States capable of integrating policy across widely dispersed agency interests, one "technically within the Department of State but sufficiently independent to have its own budget and image" see Eugene B. Skolnikoff, "Policy Note: An "ACDA" for UN Policy," *International Organization*, Vol. 27, No. 1 (Winter 1973), p. 101.

105. For comments on the inflexibility of policies arrived at through a centralized system integrating

relatively soft with the result that it becomes very difficult to manipulate the available expertise to its full advantage—in diplomacy, technical and scientific knowledge is a precision tool which can be used effectively only when the policy goal is clearly set.

The sociotechnological complexity of many normative issues in the universal arenas also reduces the opportunity of less developed countries to pursue common policies. Either they develop bloc-wide stands and then lose negotiating flexibility, or else they have to rely on individual action. Yet, on balance, this point appears to favor the less developed states. Throughout the universal normative arenas, technical and nontechnical alike, the rule appears to be that the normative decision-makers representing the least developed states have the greatest freedom of negotiating action in relation to their government, while delegations such as those of the United States and the Soviet Union labor under the most rigid policy constraints. In general, the sociotechnological complexity of issues reduces either centralization or purposefulness.

The unwieldiness of the national policy-making phase of the normative process on the part of the advanced states opens up opportunities for weaker states to regain some negotiating equilibrium. We have already noted the potential role played in the universal normative arenas by technically trained international officials and consultants; they may act as brokers, as intermediaries, or as interpreters of technical data for those national delegations which do not have access to their own sources of expertise. A somewhat similar function of "science adviser" to less developed states is sometimes served indirectly by the delegates of smaller but advanced countries whose foreign policies permit or even require them to cross the North-South boundary; these delegates can provide less developed states with informed policy guidance. A general example is the foreign policy of Sweden embodying the Swedish aspiration to conduct a distinctive, activist policy in the international scene.[106] A more specific case comes from the stand of the Belgian delegate to the United Nations Seabed Committee, Roger Denorme, who explicitly argued against delaying the international normative efforts towards a seabed regime by waiting for further research to be first carried out.[107]

Looking into the future, a major question remains how fast and how extensively, if at all, the less developed countries participating in the universal normative arenas can learn to draw on international expertise and technical experience available to them in the institutional framework of the United Nations as well as outside it in the general

---

all intersecting interests see Chadwick F. Alger, "The United States in the United Nations," *International Organization*, Vol. 27, No. 1 (Winter 1973), p. 16.

106. Cf. *To Choose A Future*, report by the Swedish Royal Ministry for Foreign Affairs and the Secretariat for Future Studies (Stockholm, 1974), p. 81. For one of several specific examples of Swedish behavior in international normative arenas see in particular the records of the initial stages of the U.N. debate on the seabed in 1967-68 when Sweden, represented by Mrs. Alva Myrdal, was the most consistent and articulate defender of the Maltese proposal arguing in particular against the tendency to delay policy decisions by first accumulating further knowledge of the deep ocean resources. Docs. A/C.1/PV.1527 (14 November 1967), pp. 46-56. also PV.1542 (7 December 1967), pp. 22-26; and A/AC.135/1 (29 February 1968), pp. 19-21.

107. "The Ad Hoc Committee's report . . . reveals on practically every page our ignorance of the marine environment and of the processes explaining the natural phenomena which characterize it, and of the natural resources buried in the bedrock of the oceans. The need to fill the substantial gaps in our present knowledge by scientific research and exploration has been constantly emphasized. . . . Does this mean that the Committee is now entitled to wait for the result of this research before starting to carry out its mandate? Do not think that this is just a rhetorical question: on many occasions we have heard the argument that any commitment as regards a regime for the exploitation of undersea resources would be premature so long as their value and the techniques for exploiting them are not better known. This is why I consider it necessary to refute this argument." Doc. A/AC.135/SC.2/3 (12 March 1969), pp. 1-2.

technical and professional communities. This is not really a question of simply making more information more accessible to everyone.[108] The problem is rather one of selecting the appropriate items from the mountains of available data, and of learning how to use them effectively. This learning process may be helped along significantly through UNITAR's various training projects, especially if the UNITAR mandate could be strengthened and its operational base expanded[109] to correspond more nearly to the task at hand—the bridging of the gaps between preindustrial, industrial and postindustrial societies joined in a global normative activity.

As a source of power in international politics, scientific and technical knowledge has characteristics unlike those of material sources of national power: to be effective in policy processes, it must be shared with others beyond the national boundaries. This does signal a new phase in international affairs. In the past, the industrial states used their monopoly of power, without sharing it, to conquer and control huge parts of the world. Today, the material power of states is increasingly used not through the application of force but by exploiting the potential use of force. The shift from violence to deterrence is a shift from material to phenomenological evidence of power. Many modern weapons fulfill their roles not by being used but by being known (or thought) to exist. Scientific and technical knowledge must also be somehow demonstrated, or known, if it is to be used as a source of power in an international political process; but this automatically means a type of sharing it with others. Unlike weapons of war, scientific and technical knowledge utilized in a normative process is not used up. Unlike weapons of deterrence, it does not have its effectiveness worn out by overexposure. When employed internationally for however narrow a policy purpose, scientific and technical knowledge is being disseminated. Once a contentious issue related to scientific and technological progress has been internationally politicized, once it has become the stimulus for, as well as the subject of, an international normative process, the politically effective sharing of scientific and technical knowledge has begun.

On balance and in terms of the South-North axis of influence, the technological phenomenon helps toward further improvement[110] of the power equilibrium in universal normative arenas where the technologically weaker participants have access to technical knowledge as well as a recourse to trade-offs and cross-issue bargaining. It simultaneously tends toward still greater disequilibria in the normative process in technical and in subglobal, narrow arenas. However, since the growing influence of smaller and developing states includes the influence necessary to initiate and then sustain an international normative activity in the universal nontechnical arenas, the trend toward normative issues being dealt with on several levels simultaneously is likely to continue.

As to the distribution of influence between the state versus nonstate participants in the international normative process, the nonstate contribution in the form of transnational, individual, bureaucratic, and scientific and technical inputs is growing markedly

---

108.   On improved access to data as a way of increasing the participation in the normative processes by individuals from less developed areas, see Livingston (fn. 20), p. 71.

109.   Cf. Slouka (fn. 61), p. 34, for a listing of possible U.N. mechanisms serving as bridges between the sources of scientific data and the national delegations and providing for an effective, versatile, pluralistic information transfer process through which data can be distilled and softened to become pliable and more easily adapted to the various negotiating options.

110.   This refers, of course, to the fact that the influence of small and less developed states in international politics in general and in U.N. politics in particular is considerable and growing. An excellent study of this relationship between size and power, seeking to demonstrate that no clear correlation exists between wealth and military force and the ability to produce results, is Wayne A. Wilcox, "The Influence of Small States in a Changing World," Wilcox, ed. (fn. 71), pp. 80-87.

although in most instances the nonstate actors must still use the governmental mechanisms as the main vehicles to gain entry into the normative process.

The Normative Process And Product: A View From Technology

The inherent constraints of this study need to be restated. Although I tend to see technological change as being largely coterminous with the change in the nature of contemporary civilization and therefore as a preponderant influence on all normative activity, there are obviously other, nontechnological forces at work which may influence the international law-making process and product in ways we have not explored here. And that, of course, gives this study a heuristic complexion, however closely it may actually reflect the real-world pattern of relationships.[111]

The key words describing the impact of the technological phenomena on international law-making are stratification, diversification, pluralism, refinement, responsiveness, pliability, and continuous flux.

All signals from such limited observations as have been so far possible along the order-technology global interface tend to support the major conclusions others have arrived at by other means: (1) that the variety of quasi-normative (from the traditional point of view) forms and processes of order will be increasing, perhaps dramatically, with a corresponding increase of consensual as against contractual outcome; (2) that such nontraditional normative events will become more significant as the quest for universal formal rules becomes more difficult and protracted, with the further result that the normative dominance of the nation-state will be reduced and that of other actors will be enhanced; the state may be losing not authority, but elbow room and ability to act unaided.

The directions in which the technological phenomenon pushes the international law-making process may be depicted on a matrix setting forth several elements and attributes of normative activity in the form of continua connecting, in general terms, the world of politics with the world of law.[112] (Figure 4.1)

The continua span the full range of each of the elements of the normative process. The left hand pole in each case falls into what may be described as the political vortex: the interplay of sociopolitical forces, largely unguided by ultimate normative goals, reactive and dynamic. The right hand pole represents the traditional, solid, programmed law-making of the ideal legislative type. The international normative activity mostly takes place between the two poles. The conclusions of this study suggest that, on the whole, the technological phenomenon tends to lead the law-making process towards the left hand pole, into a progressively more intimate closeness of the social and political foundations of international law.

From this generalization, minor reservations regarding the effects on some of the elements are called for. There is no doubt, for instance, that the technological phenomenon has generated efforts toward preventive strategies: some objectives of the ongoing Law of the Sea Conference; the 1972 Conference on the Human Environment; the 1976

---

111.   A heuristic intent does not obviously exclude the possibility that the eventual explanation fully reflects the reality, just as the real-world theorists often end up designing heuristic constructs. Ernst B. Haas differentiates rather sharply between deterministic and heuristic constructs of systems theorists in "On Systems and International Regimes," *World Politics*, Vol. 27, No. 2 (January 1975), pp. 147-174, especially pp. 151-155.

112.   I wish to acknowledge my indebtedness to Gidon Gottlieb for the initial development of an early version of a similar matrix during the 1974 Law-making Conference at Princeton University's Center of International Studies. See also Gottlieb's much expanded rendition of that matrix elsewhere in this volume.

FIGURE 4.1

Elements of International Normative Activity:
A Matrix of Political-Legal Continua

Normative Elements	Socio-Political Realm	Legal Realm
	◄──────Technological Push───────	
strategies of normative activity	reactive; spontaneous	preventive; calculated
arenas	unstructured; the field of general interaction of socio-economic and political forces	law-making fora; conferences, formal exchanges
actors	mixed social forces—national, subnational, transnational, international; individuals	involved nation-states
time/density of normative activity	instantaneous; continuous	prearranged; low frequency
geopolitical scope	unilateral	universal
functional scope	issue-specific	comprehensive; systemic
product	consensus; non-articulated understanding	treaty; contract
control mechanism	technological fix	social fix

Conference on Human Settlements; U.N. debates regarding direct-broadcast satellites—all these and many other exchanges with regulatory intent have clearly been future oriented and intended to prevent potential conflict. Yet, even in these instances, as we have noted, the real normative action is still in the sociotechnical realm of day-to-day activity: the technological and political doers move faster and more resolutely than the institutionalized international law-makers. At best, there is a normative movement at two different levels: the preventive efforts seeking a formal articulation and acceptance of a global rule hopefully guide and civilize the contentious sociotechnological interactions.

In a most fundamental sense, then, the international normative process as observed under the impact of technological forces is becoming coterminous with its goal: order is served by the striving for it at all levels of international activity rather than by its finalization at the universal level. It is not only that technological particularism and the urgency it always carries lead toward a decentralized form of legal order by laying more naked its decentralized social, political, and economic substructure. The technological phenomenon also keeps normative activity perpetually in motion at the universal level where it may never result in specific rules and yet it may guide behavior, set boundaries to political interactions, generate expectations and reliances, and separate the feasible from the impossible. For analytical purposes, this may be seen as normative dualism, with one set of normative goals being achieved through one type of a process at the universal level, and another set reached through a different process below. But it is more realistic to view all this as one continuous, complete process in which the lower levels, bilateral, regional, technical, and functional, produce order, while the universal level gently, and sometimes not so gently, steers it toward greater justice.

Measuring Transformation in the Global Legal System

CHARLES W. KEGLEY, JR.

INTRODUCTION

The complexity of the processes by which laws are made in the global community presents many analytic obstacles. Any comprehensive assessment must take into account the interaction among a multitude of legal, social, psychological, economic, and political determinants.[1] Morever, inquiry also must confront the difficult problem of identifying the universe of legal norms and ascertaining the time of their formulation and acceptance,[2] a (practically intractable[3]) problem which has long preoccupied legal scholarship. Research problems are exacerbated because multiple sources of international legal rules, both formal and informal,[4] are recognized, and these sources are not accepted by all

The author is indebted to many people for their assistance in the preparation of this manuscript. In particular, I would like to thank William D. Coplin, Nicholas G. Onuf, Patrick J. McGowan, J. David Singer, Stephen Hibbard, Raymond Sexton, and Van Sturgeon for their helpful comments at various stages of the project. Professors Edward E. Azar and Margaret Ball and Mrs. Helen Philos are to be thanked for their help in facilitating the acquisition of international law treatises from the libraries of the University of North Carolina at Chapel Hill, Duke University, and the American Society of International Law, respectively. I would also like to thank the research associates of the Transnational Rules Indicators Project (TRIP), Professors Gregory A. Raymond (Boise State University), Kyngsook Choi (Sookmyun University, Seoul, Korea) and Barron Boyd (LeMoyne College) for their assistance in gathering data on which the study is based. Moreover, the institutional support of the Committee on Research and Productive Scholarship and the Institute of International Studies at the University of South Carolina is appreciatively acknowledged.

1. For discussions, see Wesley L. Gould and Michael Barkun, *International Law and the Social Sciences* (Princeton: Princeton University Press, 1970); and Ahmed Sheikh, *International Law and National Behavior* (New York: John Wiley and Sons, 1974).

2. Myres S. McDougal and Harold D. Lasswell, "The Identification and Appraisal of Diverse Systems of Public Order," *The American Journal of International Law*, Vol. 53, No. 1 (January 1959), pp. 1-29; Hersch Lauterpacht, "Codification and Development of International Law," in Leo Gross, ed., *International Law in the Twentieth Century* (New York: Appleton-Century-Crofts, 1969), pp. 47-74; R. Y. Jennings, "The Progressive Development of International Law and Its Codification," *British Year Book of International Law*. Vol. 24 (1947), pp. 301-329.

3. Because principles of international law are conventionally couched in a broad, abstract manner, and are imprecise, contradictory, and elastic, their identification and meaning is rendered difficult. As Laura Nader and Duane Metzger have noted, within a single society several legal systems may be operating, "complementing, supplementing, or conflicting with each other;" "Conflict Resolution in Two Mexican Communities," *American Anthropologist*, Vol. 65, No. 3 (June 1963) pp. 584-592. For discussions at the international level, see Richard A. Falk, *The Status of Law in International Society* (Princeton: Princeton University Press, 1970), pp. 15-17 et passim, and "The Adequacy of Contemporary International Law, Gaps in Legal Thinking," *Virginia Law Review*, Vol. 50, No. 2 (March 1964), pp. 231-265. For a further perceptive discussion, see Julius Stone, *The Quest for Survival* (Cambridge Harvard University Press, 1961).

4. See Onuf's essay in this volume for a discussion of this problem.

national members of the global system.[5] The lack of an intersubjective consensus as to whether these sources should be regarded as sources or merely evidence of international legal norms is a further complication.[6] As a consequence, it is not surprising to find conceptual, philosophical, and methodological diversity and disagreement in research on the process of law-making.

In order to facilitate research, it is advantageous to disaggregate the concept of international law-making and development into its basic components, and concentrate investigation on a few of its salient dimensions. A parsimonious treatment permits investigation to focus on particular features of the phenomena for which explanations are sought while holding constant those factors less amenable to analysis. This strategy postpones the attempt to construct a comprehensive model of the law-making process until the basic building blocks of such a theoretical system can be acquired through the less ambitious dissected approach.

This strategy requires the selection of some aspect of the law-making process which is at once amenable to systematic empirical observation and pertinent (causally related) to how legal norms are created and modified in the international system. One aspect of the law-making process which meets these criteria is the extent to which international norms relevant to the control of war are subject to long-term temporal variation. It is this empirical characteristic of the international legal order which the present study will address in order to suggest some propositions about the global rule-creation process.

The description of the global community's evolving legal posture toward war is recommended for several reasons. The management of violence is one of the few issue-areas in international law that enjoys a relative consensus on broad principle—an attribute which renders the identification of rule formation an objectively achievable task. The absence of intersocietal agreement in other areas of international law, exacerbated by the elasticity, obscurity, and ambiguity of most international norms,[7] precludes the possibility of ascertaining their formation in an objective fashion.

Attention to the development of legal rules for the control of inter-state war is also recommended because of the determinative role which conflict is presumed to play in the evolution of any legal system. The literature of historical sociology posits a strong correlation between the structure of a legal order and the underlying patterns of conflicting relationships among its members.[8] This view emphasizes the "central role of

---

5.   Sheikh (fn. 1), p. 328. See as well F. S. C. Northrop, *The Taming of Nations* (New York: Macmillan, 1952).

6.   Gould and Barkun (fn. 1), p. 176.

7.   See Lauterpacht (fn. 2); Falk, *The Status of Law in International Society* (fn. 3); and Adda B. Bozeman, *The Future of Law in a Multicultural World* (Princeton: Princeton University Press, 1971), for discussions of the consequences of the simultaneous presence of diverse cultural and legal orders for definitions of what rules exist. Efforts to authoritatively define the "sanctioned prescriptions for, or prohibitions against, others' behavior, belief, or feeling" are rendered difficult; Richard T. Morris, "A Typology of Norms," *American Sociological Review*, Vol. 21, No. 5 (October 1956), pp. 610-613. To dramatize the magnitude of the task of codifying legal norms in such a way as to organize, digest, collate, and eliminate obscure views and discrepancies, it is instructive to recall that Justin is reported to have compiled *Corpus Jusis Civilis* under ideal circumstances (i.e., conditions of systemic universality) only with an army of legal experts, after prolonged inquiry, and even at that time (527 A.D.) it was necessary to condense 2,000 books consisting of 3,000,000 lines to 150,000 lines.

8.   For early but lucid statements of the notion that the configuration of power relationships among the world's national actors influences the effectiveness of particular legal rules, see Morton A. Kaplan and Nicholas DeB. Katzenbach, *The Political Foundations of International Law* (New York, Wiley, 1961); and Morton A. Kaplan, *System and Process in International Politics* (New York, Wiley, 1957); for a review, see Falk (fn. 3), pp. 486-495.

violence" in the formation of a legal system and postulates that the use of violence is the "aspect of international relations that dominates;" thus, it is asserted that "those parts of international law that are most connected with the competition of states should be more important than the rules distant from the contest."[9] Scholars such as Aron, who argues that "the most distinguishing feature of international politics is the legitimacy of violence,"[10] and Kelsen, who contends that "punishment plays a far more important role than reward"[11] in influencing the relations of nations, are in accord with Morgenthau's[12] view that the behavior states engage in to attempt to coerce each other conditions the kind of legal order that will develop in the international community.

Is the level of conflict within a social system in fact related to the generation of new norms, the decay of preexisting ones, and the continuity of prevailing legal rules?[13] Indeed, is rule formation predicated on conflict, and legal innovation stimulated by the onset of violence?[14] Or, instead, as some believe,[15] is social equilibrium, in which consensus prevails and recourse to interstate violence is limited, a precondition for the development of legal norms and world order? Regardless of one's perspective on these issues, it would seem that bringing evidence to bear on them can shed light on the process by which legal rules are made and modified.

This reasoning recommends an approach to inquiry with the following features. First, for investigation of law-making in a decentralized environment, a macro level of analysis[16] befitting "the wide sweep of history"[17] and adopting an evolutionary time-frame of several centuries for the entire world[18] is called for. Focus on long-term secular trends enables the development and decay of particular legal norms to be traced, whereas a static description, which ignores the time dimension, precludes analysis of the *process* of rule formation, deterioration, and modification.[19] Since inter-temporal comparison of the global system as the primary unit-of-observation[20] provides the only meaningful way of

---

9. Stanley Hoffmann, *The State of War* (New York, Praeger, 1965), pp. viii, 128-129.

10. Raymond Aron, *Peace and War* (Garden City, N.Y.: Doubleday, 1966).

11. Hans Kelsen, *The Principles of International Law* (New York: Holt, Rinehart, 1952), p. 17.

12. Hans J. Morgenthau, *Politics Among Nations* (New York: Knopf, 3rd ed., 1961), pp. 275-311.

13. This was the view of Lewis A. Coser, *Continuities in the Study of Social Conflict* (New York: Free Press, 1967). See also Michael Barkun, "International Norms: An Interdisciplinary Approach," *Background*, Vol. 8, No. 2 (August 1964), pp. 121-130.

14. See Coser (fn. 13), p. 20; Kenneth Burke, *Permanence and Change* (New York: New Republic, 1936), p. 18.

15. Hans Speier, *Social Order and the Risks of War* (New York: George W. Stewart, 1952); Richard A. Falk, "Historical Tendencies, Modernizing and Revolutionary Nations, and the International Legal Order," in Saul H. Mendlovitz, ed., *Legal and Political Problems of World Order* (New York: The Fund for Education Concerning World Peace Through World Law, 1962), pp. 128-60.

16. J. David Singer, "The Level-of-Analysis Problem in International Relations," in Klaus Knorr and Sidney Verba, eds., *The International System: Theoretical Essays* (Princeton: Princeton University Press, 1961), pp. 77-92.

17. Lauterpacht (fn. 2), p. 77, argues that only the perspective of the long history of international law can provide the understanding necessary for inquiry.

18. Kenneth A. Dahlberg, "Environmental Studies: Some Problems and Priorities," *International Studies Notes*, Vol. 1, No. 2 (Summer 1974), p. 20. For a useful treatment of the concept of time, see Georges Gurvitch, *The Spectrum of Social Time* (Dordrecht: D. Reidel, 1969).

19. Gould and Barkun (fn. 1), pp. 176-224; James E. Harf and Charles W. Kegley, Jr., *Characteristics of International Systems, 1860-1970*, Consortium for International Studies Education (Pittsburgh: International Studies Association, 1979); Roderick Floud, *An Introduction to Quantitative Methods for Historians* (Princeton: Princeton University Press, 1973).

20. For a discussion of this term and what differentiates it from such related concepts as *unit-of-analysis* and *level-of-analysis*, see Patrick J. McGowan, "Meaningful Comparisons in the Study of Foreign Policy: A Methodological Discussion of Objectives, Techniques, and Research Findings," in Charles W. Kegley, Jr.,

detecting global rule change,[21] this would seem the best approach to pursuing Lauterpacht's suggestion[22] that the direction of evolution of international norms be investigated by study of long-term trends in international law. To study the process of law-making and legal development without reference to the temporal ordering of norms according to the time of their formation is sterile.

Second, analysis of the sources of global rule formation invites use of a systems theory framework.[23] Systems theory suggests that the factors most responsible for norm formation at the global level are those that serve to give definition to the international system in general. The global legal order, and changes in it, may be seen as dependent, at least in part, on changes in social and political conditions on the globe.[24] That is, norm revision is assumed to be stimulated primarily by fundamental changes in the structural attributes of the international system at large. This, indeed, will be a working hypothesis of the present study. If legal formation is a product of changes in the patterns of behavior practiced in international intercourse, as some research traditions assume, then behavior change and rule change may be intimately linked. An empirical association between the two is assumed, although the direction of causation and temporal ordering is problematic.[25] Some, such as Hoffmann,[26] see "rules *of* behavior" being converted, with time lags, into "rules *for* behavior." Others assume that legal change precedes and promotes behavioral change. A systems analysis permits a basis for testing these

---

and others, eds., *International Events and the Comparative Analysis of Foreign Policy* (Columbia: University of South Carolina Press, 1975), pp. 52-90; and Charles W. Kegley, Jr., "The Transformation of Inter-Bloc Relations," in Louis J. Mensonides and James A. Kuhlman, eds., *The Future of Inter-Bloc Relations in Europe* (New York: Praeger, 1974), pp. 3-27.

21.   James Ray and J. David Singer, "Aggregation and Inference: The Levels-of-Analysis Problem Revisited," paper presented at the 1973 Meeting of the International Studies Association.

22.   Lauterpacht (fn. 2), p. 77, urges examination of "the light which diplomatic history throws on the tendencies in international relations which constitute the setting and parts of the subject-matter of the law" and notes (p. 79) that "there is still no adequate history of the growth of international law as a world system which places in the perspective of their historical origin and development the contemporary problems of the law."

23.   For introductory statements, see Charles A. McClelland, *Theory and the International System* (New York: Macmillan, 1965); Ervin Laszlo, *Introduction to Systems Philosophy* (New York: Harper and Row, 1972); and Oran R. Young, *Systems of Political Science* (Englewood Cliffs: Prentice Hall, 1968).

24.   The literature on the relationship between international systems and international law is voluminous. Examples are Kaplan (fn. 8); Kaplan and Katzenbach (fn. 8); Stanley Hoffmann (fn. 9), pp. 88-133; Kenneth E. Boulding, "National Images and International Systems," in William D. Coplin and Charles W. Kegley, Jr., eds., *Analyzing International Relations: A Multimethod Introduction* (New York: Praeger, 1975), pp. 347-360; and Kjell Goldmann, "International Norms and Governmental Behaviour: A Model of Social Control, Applied to the International System," *Cooperation and Conflict*, Vol. 4, No. 3 (1969), pp. 162-204.

25.   While it may be argued that the relationship of the normative structure of international law to the social structure of the international system may be such that the former tends to influence the latter, the prevailing view in the literature depicts changes in international law taking place as a consequence of fundamental changes in the international system. Falk's comment (fn. 15, p. 134) is typical: "Any legal system is slow to change its rules to correspond to changes in its power structure, but the international system is peculiarly ill-adapted to accommodate the pressures of change." For other studies which follow this interpretation, see Gould and Barkun (fn. 1), pp. 100, 209; Kaplan and Katzenbach (fn. 8); Hoffmann, (fn. 9, p. 88); and William D. Coplin, International Law and Assumptions About the State System," in William D. Coplin and Charles W. Kegley, Jr., eds., *Analyzing International Relations* (New York: Praeger, 1975), pp. 270-280.

26.   Stanley Hoffmann, "International Law and the Control of Force," in Karl Deutsch and Stanley Hoffmann, eds., *The Relevance of International Law* (New York: Doubleday-Anchor, 1971), p. 35; Stanley Hoffmann, "The Study of International Law and the Theory of International Relations," in Gross, ed. (fn. 2), p. 156.

competing ideas, as shall be shown. This chapter will thus investigate law-making by observing historical changes in both state behavior and legal rules. In this manner the proposition that behavioral change leads to rule creation, and constitutes a source of international law, can be addressed.[27]

In short, the analysis of rule formation at the global level will be approached by investigating the relationship between systemic changes in interstate behavior, on the one hand, and changes in legal rules relevant to war and its control, on the other. This will afford the opportunity to inspect the impact of the former on the latter, and vice versa. And it will facilitate testing of the proposition that "the growth of international law [has come] to depend upon claims to regulate recourse to force."[28]

But before proceeding, some epistemological preliminaries are in order. The research strategy for empirically measuring temporal change in global norms must first be explicated. This then will permit diachronic transformations in those legal norms to be mapped, so that some inferences about the processes by which law-making unfolds can be drawn from this empirically derived evidence.

Rule Transformation and the International System: A Strategy of Inquiry

A conspicuous feature of contemporary research has been the prevalence of calls for the reintegration of the study of international law into that of international relations, and vice versa.[29] A related trend has been the growing frequency with which the methodologies of scientific inquiry are perceived to be applicable to the investigation of the international legal order.[30] In particular, it is increasingly proposed that legal scholarship advance beyond "the impressionism of earlier approaches" toward the empirical methods of behavioral research, including those quantitative techniques associated with the cliometric approach which employ measurement tools to study historical phenomena.[31] Such prescriptions are especially cogent and responsible when they recommend the

---

27.   This approach, it should be noted, conforms to the emphasis positivist theories place on customary international behavior as a source of international law. Kelsen's famous statement that "states ought to behave as they have customarily behaved" characterizes this interpretation of how laws are made in international society. The theory that the international system derives its legal rules from this source conforms to Hoebel's dictum "What the most do, others should do." E. Adamson Hoebel, *The Law of Primitive Man*, Cambridge: Harvard University Press, 1961.

28.   Falk (fn. 15), p. 133.

29.   Gould and Barkun (fn. 1); Skeikh (fn. 1); and Richard A. Falk, *Legal Order in a Violent World* (Princeton: Princeton University Press, 1968), pp. 8-31, are representative. Stanley Hoffmann has been particularly vehement on this point, arguing (fn. 9), p. 130, that "the task of social science at least consists in studying how people actually behave; it ought also to consist in studying how people think they should behave and what they try to institute and legislate to carry out their views. A social science that, under the name of behaviorism [sic] or whatever, neglected law as a form of social control would be poor indeed."

30.   Ibid. See as well Harold D. Lasswell and Richard Arens, "The Role of Sanction in Conflict Resolution," *Journal of Conflict Resolution*, Vol. 11, No. 1 (March 1967), 27; Vilhelm Aubert, "Courts and Conflict Resolution," *Journal of Conflict Resolution*, Vol. 11, No. 1 (March 1967), p. 50 et passim; Richard A. Falk, "New Approaches to the Study of International Law," in Morton A. Kaplan, ed., *New Approaches to International Relations* (New York: St. Martin's, 1968), pp. 357-380; Peter H. Rohn, *Institutions in Treaties: A Global Survey of Magnitudes and Trends from 1945 to 1965* (Syracuse: The Maxwell School of Syracuse University, 1970); William D. Coplin, "Current Studies in the Functions of International Law," in James A. Robinson, ed., *Political Science Annual*, Volume II (Indianapolis: Bobbs-Merrill, 1969), pp. 149-207; and Charles W. Kegley, Jr., "Measuring the Growth and Decay of Transnational Norms Relevant to the Control of Violence," paper presented at the 1974 Meeting of the American Political Science Association.

31.   Falk, *The Status of Law in International Society* (fn. 3), pp. 458-459. On cliometric approaches to the quantitative study of international law and international relations, see Floud (fn. 19) and Harf and Kegley (fn. 19).

combining of "traditional with modern methods of research and data collection."[32] Such calls are healthy because they contribute to the abatement of the antagonism dividing scientific and legal scholarship, and because they suggest ways in which verifiable knowledge regarding international legal norms might be acquired.

But these calls represent a research challenge as well. In order to respond to this challenge, the present study proposes to gather quantitative data measuring continuity and change in legal norms bearing on the regulation of war.

To assert that the international legal order is amenable to systematic observation is to contend that that order constitutes a social datum which can be treated as "an objective political concept," a view which Field[33] forcefully argued many years ago but which remains controversial despite supporting arguments by legal scholars (*e.g.,* McDougal and Feliciano[34] and Kelsen[35]) and political scientists (*e.g.,* Pye and Verba[36]). If, indeed, international legal norms are amenable to observation, then it is necessary to assume also that legal concepts are in principle measurable. Measurement is the *sine qua non* of scientific research. The symbolic nature of legal norms makes measurement of rules at the nominal level (classification of the presence or absence of specific legal categories) initially the most appropriate.[37]

Before turning to the implementation of this research design, some preliminary definitions are needed. First, what is meant by *global norms?* Given the attendant difficulties of devising a system for distinguishing legal from illegal forms of behavior,[38] and the impossibility of directly observing international laws in their complexity and totality,[39] it is advantageous epistemologically to jettison constitutive and composite definitions of transnational norms (which seek to demarcate the conduct proscribed by a legal order). Instead, definitions which depict norms according to the function(s) or task(s) they perform may be more useful. Here, if law is seen in its essence as crystallized public opinion,[40] then one of the basic functions of transnational legal norms is the communication and articulation of prevailing beliefs[41] regarding the nature of the global

---

32.   Falk (fn. 29), p. 26 *et passim.*

33.   G. Lowell Field, "Law as an Objective Political Concept," *American Political Science Review,* Vol. 43, No. 2 (April 1949), pp. 229-249.

34.   Myres S. McDougal and Florentino P. Feliciano, *Law and Minimum World Order* (New Haven: Yale University Press, 1961).

35.   Kelsen (fn. 11).

36.   Lucian W. Pye and Sidney Verba, *Political Culture and Political Development* (Princeton: Princeton University Press, 1965), pp. 512-560.

37.   Typology construction is conventionally considered to be the most appropriate first requisite in the scientific study of any phenomena, and is often conceived as a form of measurement itself. See Charles W. Kegley, Jr., *A General Empirical Typology of Foreign Policy Behavior,* Sage Professional Papers, International Studies Series, No. 02-014 (1973).

38.   See discussions in fns. 3 and 7. The difficulties with such definitional efforts are examined further in Charles W. Kegley, "Observations on Legal Vis-à-vis Moral Thought and Life," *The Personalist,* Vol. 51, No. 11 (Winter 1970), pp. 58-84.

39.   No complex phenomenon can be systematically observed in its entirety, so the researcher has no alternative but to select some aspect for examination at a time while ignoring others. Consequently, attempts to describe the "reality" of international law, whatever that may be, are precluded; only specific dimensions of that legal order can be described. For discussions of this fundamental epistemological point which stresses implications for research methodology, see James N. Rosenau, *The Scientific Study of Foreign Policy* (New York: Free Press, 1969), pp. 21-65; and Coplin and Kegley, eds. (fn. 24). esp. pp. 2-3 and pp. 414-415.

40.   This characterization is common. It might be more appropriate to think of global norms as *subjective culture,* or the international community's habitual way of perceiving the man-made component of its environment. For a discussion, see Harry C. Triandis, *The Analysis of Subjective Culture* (New York: Wiley-Interscience, 1972).

41.   This theme is developed most fully in William D. Coplin, *The Functions of International Law* (Chicago: Rand McNally, 1966), pp. 168-194. Coplin persuasively contends that international law is best

system and the appropriate behavior of members comprising it. That is, transnational legal rules serve the purpose of structuring[42] normative attitudes lodged in the collective beliefs of global society. This definition sees international legal rules fostering the creation of an image[43] of the global system, rather than identifying clear limits to permissible behavior or operating as a system of restraint. Global rules so defined are seen as contributing to the development of an international political *culture*,[44] inasmuch as they communicate symbolic representations of global society.[45]

Second, *international system* must be defined, since it is presumably in this milieu that international legal rules function. This term has been used since the beginning of scholarly interest with that aspect of man's behavior which transcends the geographic boundaries of sovereign territorial states. Let a commonsense definition be adopted. An international system shall be said to consist of the space and time which serve as the outside boundaries within which all public actors who engage in activities crossing state borders behave.[46] Although it is difficult to determine the precise date for the formation of the contemporary international system, we will follow others[47] who suggest that the present system of international law did not reveal its present shape until the Congress of Vienna concluded at the end of the Napoleonic Wars. Thus the temporal frame for this study will commence in 1815, a period of time sufficiently long to facilitate the search for continuity and change in legal rules.

A third problem concerns the methodological procedures by which reproducible

---

seen as contributing to "a climate of opinion on international relations." More specifically, international law is posited to communicate an awareness that there is community support for particular beliefs, to develop an international political culture articulating beliefs which members of the system hold about the proper relations of nations, and to foster the creation of an image of the global system.

42. For instance, Hoffmann, "International Law and the Control of Force," (fn. 26), p. 62, speaks of international law serving to structure expectations about anticipated behavior. As Gould and Barkun (fn. 1) describe this function: "International law provides a way of viewing events in the international arena. Its norms constitute a structure for processing information" (p. 121); "the concepts taken for granted in international law . . . are in fact symbolic representations for certain events and facts in the world of international relations. Law is a system of symbolic representation. . . . By functioning as a picture of the world—albeit a simplified one—a legal system of any kind performs more than coercive functions. First and foremost, to the extent we accept it, it gives us a grip of reality" (p. 127).

43. Ibid. See as well Kenneth E. Boulding, *The Image* (Ann Arbor: University of Michigan Press, 1956).

44. Coplin (fn. 41); Gould and Barkun (fn. 1). The idea that international law functions as a socializing agent in creating an international political culture is supported by recognition of the effect which (legal) language has on the formation of culture. By communicating values and describing the world with a common vocabulary, international legal terminology contributes to a common worldview and some minimum amount of shared culture. This proposition has been summarized as follows: "Some . . . have argued that the world of reality is given for us in the language that we use. There is a clear correlation between our reality and the concepts we use. In order to understand the world, we have to have concepts telling what belongs to its reality. . . . Observing the world necessarily implies a study of our ideas and concepts, and vice versa. Both reality and our concepts may change; but, when one of them changes, the other changes, too;" Erik Allardt, "Revolutionary Ideologies as Agents of Cultural and Structural Change," in Nancy Hammond, ed., *Social Science and the New Societies* (East Lansing: Michigan State University, 1973), p. 150. See as well Ernest Gellner, *Thought and Change* (London: Weidenfeld and Nicolson, 1964) pp. 153-157.

45. For an elaboration of this definition of transnational rules, see Charles W. Kegley, Jr., "Measuring the Growth and Decay of Transnational Norms of Relevant to the Control of Violence: A Prospectus for Research," *Denver Journal of International Law and Policy*, Vol. 5, No. 2 (Fall 1975), pp. 425-439.

46. See Harf and Kegley (fn. 19).

47. See Charles W. Kegley, Jr., and Eugene R. Wittkopf, *The Transformation of World Politics* (New York: St. Martin's, 1981) for a discussion of scholarly efforts to delineate the temporal boundaries of previous international systems. The periodization suggested here follows that of Clive Parry, "The Function of Law in the International Community," in Max Sørenson, ed., *Manual of Public International Law* (New York, St. Martin's, 1968), pp. 1-54. In addition, see fn. 59 for supporting references.

evidence of changes in legal rules can be generated. Publicly available source material needs to be identified and then systematically coded by operational procedures of classification and observation for conversion of such source information into quantitative data.[48]

Since one of the attributes of the international legal system is that its rules are not open to objective visual inspection, where might the researcher look in order to classify and monitor international norms? Hoffmann has implicitly proposed a possible solution: "The social scientist in search of models for the interpretation of world politics, whether he tries to use 'new' tools such as those provided by abstract systems analysis, or old concepts such as those of community and society, could do far worse than study the theories presented by writers on international law."[49] This proposal has been elaborated and specified by Gould and Barkun:

> Relatively little has been done to investigate how the normative statements of publicists enter international law, even though their writings have traditionally been cited as one of the sources of international law. . . . [But] in what ways was international law transformed to fit the world of 1945 and after instead of that of 1939 and before? Was it even transformed significantly. . . ? Even a comparison of textbooks of different periods might prove informative, providing the findings were tabulated and aggregated to present systematic evidence.[50]

These suggestions, echoed by others,[51] provide a reasonable solution. Evidence of those rules, and transformations in them, may be derived from what international jurists and publicists report about them in the international legal texts they publish. That is, authoritative classical legal texts may serve as a data source from which quantitative indicators of norm formation and change may be constructed. While such treatises may not reflect accurately whatever body of law may have been operative at a given time, the interpretations provided by these scholars provide an index of the perceived rules regarded as important at the point of observation. This approach is especially inviting in longitudinal explications where an extended temporal frame encourages the analyst to look at customary law (instead of just treaty law) as a measure of current law. If legal texts are treated as samples of opinions about the global community's working rules, then the accounts offered may serve as indicators of the transnational rules extant in particular temporal spans.

Such an approach to the measurement of rule change can be especially misleading[52] if textbook law is confused with the so-called living law, the "rules actually acknowledged, applied, and obeyed by states."[53] But the approach represents a reasonable—albeit imperfect—means of estimating the pace and type of rule modifications unfolding over time.

---

48. In principle, international norms, like any phenomena, are susceptible to quantitative and/or scientific treatment (Lasswell and Arens, fn. 30), especially if we accept Durkheim's belief that "moral facts are facts like any others; they consist of rules of action which can be recognized by some distinctive characteristics; thus, it must be possible to observe them, to describe and classify them." Cited in Maria Ossawska, *Social Determinants of Moral Ideas* (Philadelphia: University of Pennsylvania Press, 1970), p. 17.

49. Hoffmann (fn. 9), p. 132.

50. Gould and Barkun (fn. 1), pp. 184, 214.

51. Lauterpacht (fn. 2), p. 662 et passim.; Falk (fn. 29), pp. 26-27; and William D. Coplin, "Is International Law Relevant to International Politics?" paper presented at the 1969 Meeting of the American Political Science Association.

52. For warnings about the possible dangers of this approach, see Falk (fn. 29), p. 27; and Michael Barkun, *Law Without Sanctions* (New Haven: Yale University Press, 1968), p. 66.

53. Werner Levi, "International Law in a Multicultural World," *International Studies Quarterly*, Vol. 18, No. 4 (December 1974), p. 432.

To generate such a broad empirical base, the data gathered under the auspices of the Transnational Rules Indicators Project (TRIP)[54] have been utilized. The properties of that data set have been described elsewhere,[55] as has an account of the epistemological issues raised by this data gathering procedure.[56] Suffice it to point out here that the TRIP data uses thematic content analysis to probe and compare the textual material contained in 205 authoritative legal treatises.[57] The TRIP Coder's Manual[58] specifies the operational rules employed to scan these texts systematically for 185 variables. The treatment reported in this chapter is restricted to a subset of these variables, and to the writings of publicists published since 1815.

The Changing Character of War

Since the advent of the modern international system,[59] a central problem has been the status of war.[60] While the maintenance of order has been an enduring concern, attitudes about recourse to war, its legitimacy, and alternate approaches to its regulation have all undergone considerable change over time.[61] Policymakers have often sought legal controls for interstate disputes that could culminate in war; indeed, like any legal system, international law is aimed at the restriction of the unauthorized use of force.[62] But the extent to which law has been perceived as relevant to the regulation of interstate war has varied considerably across historical epochs.[63]

International law and interstate war may be closely linked.[64] Changes in the incidence of war may provoke changes in the importance attached to it by the

---

54. The operational procedures and philosophic underpinnings of the TRIP data are presented in Kegley (fn. 30), pp. 9-12, Kegley (fn. 45), and Gregory A. Raymond, "The Transnational Rules Indicators Project: An Interim Report," *International Studies Notes*, Vol 4, No. 1 (Spring 1977), pp. 12-16.

55. Kegley (fn. 30), pp. 9-16; Charles W. Kegley, Jr., and others, "The TRIP Data: A Description of the Variables," TRIP Technical Report 3, University of South Carolina (May 1974), and "TRIP Codesheet," TRIP Technical Report 2, University of South Carolina (May 1974), both mimeo.

56. For elaboration of TRIP's data-making procedures, see, in addition to references in preceding fn., Gregory A. Raymond, *Conflict Resolution and the Structure of the State System* (Montclair, N.J.: Allanheld, Osmun and Co., 1980), and *Arbitration, Military Capability and Major Power War, 1815-1914* (Carlisle Barracks, Pa.: U.S. Army War College, 1978).

57. For a complete listing of these 205 texts and the criteria which guided their selection for comparative coding, see Kegley (fn. 30), pp. 47-61.

58. Charles W. Kegley, Jr., Kyungsook Choi, and Gregory A. Raymond, "Coder's Manual for Transnational Rules Indicators Project," TRIP Technical Report 1, University of South Carolina (May 1974), mimeo.

59. For discussions emphasizing the Westphalian period as a turning point in international relations, see Leo Gross, "The Peace of Westphalia, 1648-1948," in Gross, ed. (fn. 2), pp. 25-46; and Richard A. Falk, "The Inter-Play of Westphalia and Charter Conceptions of the International Legal Order," in Richard A. Falk and Cyril E. Black, eds., *The Future of the International Legal Order, Vol. 1, Trends and Patterns* (Princeton: Princeton University Press, 1969).

60. William D. Coplin, *Introduction to International Politics* (Chicago: Rand McNally, 1974); Richard N. Rosecrance, *Action and Reaction in World Politics: International Systems In Perspective* (Boston: Little Brown, 1963).

61. Richard A. Falk, "World Law and Human Conflict," in Elton B. McNeil, ed., *The Nature of Human Conflict* (Englewood Cliffs: Prentice-Hall, 1965), p. 229; Quincy Wright, *A Study of War* (Chicago: University of Chicago Press, 1965), p. 173. As Wright has stated about this attribute of legal systems, "The normal end of law—the maintenance of order and justice—is hostile to violence."

62. The suggestion that "the true function of international law is not to regulate war, but to perfect the peaceful relations of states" reflects this attitude; James Brown Scott, *Law, The States, and the International Community* (New York: Columbia University Press, 1935), p. 101.

63. Wright (fn. 61), p. 173.

64. Morgenthau (fn. 12).

international legal culture.[65] War may act as an agent of transformation in both world politics and in international law. For these reasons, evidence about the changing frequency of war and its changing importance for international law may help to unravel the relationship between war and legal modification.

The changing incidence of interstate war is captured by data collected by the Correlates of War project at the University of Michigan.[66] Figure 5.1 records the distribution of wars over time, aggregated into seven chronologically ordered historical periods which conform to widely accepted transition points in history.[67] Absent from the trend data are the 1914–1918 and 1939–1945 periods, which involved nearly the entire world in violent conflict. These periods should be kept in mind in attempting to observe historical shifts, so that the impact which world war can exert on subsequent trends is not overlooked. Moreover, in interpreting this evidence it is important to note that each period does not span the same number of years and that the number of sovereign states comprising the international system has steadily increased (from 29 in 1815 to 149 in 1977). This latter feature of the time series is important because the number of wars can be hypothesized to be a function of the number of actors—the number of opportunities for contact among them will increase as the number of nations increases, and such contact is likely to stimulate increased occasions for conflict and war.

The data show war to be recurrent. But at most there is a moderate twenty-year periodicity in the amount of war underway, and the frequency of war is randomly distributed across time.[68]

Do changes in the frequency of war promote changes in global legal thinking, as many believe? To ascertain if war and subsequent legal change are correlated requires that the salience of war in the international legal culture be measured longitudinally, in order to determine if the importance attached to the laws of war in legal treatises has varied with systemic conditions. The linkage seems plausible, on the face of it; as Wright has noted, "What is the position of war in modern international law? No categorical answer can be given. International law is a dynamic system, and a careful examination of its sources . . . gives different answers if examined in the successive decades of the twentieth century."[69] To test for the presence of normative change, the TRIP data were employed to tap the salience of war as a normative area of concern. The following reasoning guides the measurement of this variable.

By tradition, international legal treatises have assumed that the law of war and the law of peace cover distinct phenomena,[70] and that law-relevant behavior in each domain falls into separate categories. Thus it is possible to dichotomize textbook opinion according to the importance legal scholars attribute to war vis-à-vis peaceful interstate intercourse.

---

65. Coplin (fn. 60).
66. The literature stemming from this project under the direction of J. David Singer is voluminous. See J. David Singer, ed., *The Correlates of War: II* (New York: The Free Press, 1980), pp. 323-328, for a complete bibliography. For a review, see Robert M. Rood and Charles W. Kegley, Jr., "Explaining War and Conflict: A Review of Contemporary Quantitative Studies," *Historical Methods Newsletter*, Vol. 7, No. 1 (December 1974), pp. 25-33.
67. See J. David Singer and Melvin Small, *The Wages of War, 1816-1965* (New York: John Wiley and Sons, 1972), for operational procedures employed to generate these data. See also Melvin Small and J. David Singer, "Conflict in the International System, 1816-1977," in Charles W. Kegley, Jr., and Patrick J. McGowan, eds., *Challenges to America* (Beverly Hills, Calif.: Sage Publications, 1979), pp. 89-116.
68. Ibid.
69. Wright (fn. 61), p. 183.
70. Myres S. McDougal and Florentino P. Feliciano, "The Initiation of Coercion: A Multi-Temporal Analysis," in Gross, ed. (fn. 2), p. 699.

FIGURE 5.1

Frequency of Wars Begun in Seven International Systems, 1816-1977

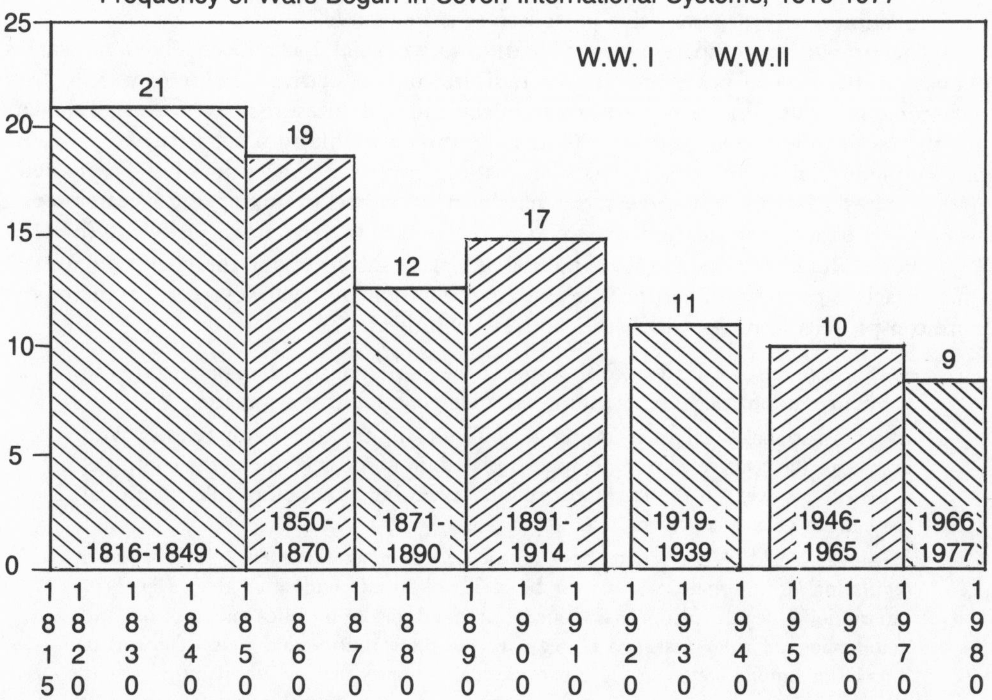

Source: Adapted from Melvin Small and J. David Singer, "Conflict in the International System, 1816-1977: Historical Trends and Policy Futures," in Charles W. Kegley, Jr. and Patrick J. McGowan (eds.), *Challenges to America* (Beverly Hills: Sage, 1979), p. 95.

On one extreme is the school of thought which sees war and its control as a peripheral issue. Representative of this opinion are those who contend that "the status of war is not equal to the status of peace,"[71] who assume "that peace is now the normal relation of states,"[72] and who conclude that "war . . . is a relatively infrequent abnormality and hardly seems to occupy a sufficiently important quantitative position in international relations to justify giving to the law of war much status."[73]

On the other extreme, however, are those who regard "the problem of the use and control of force today, as in the past, to be the central problem of international law" and who thus submit that "recent practice would appear to indicate that the situations in which the laws of war are considered applicable have expanded rather than contracted."[74] This

---

71. Richard J. Erickson, *International Law and the Revolutionary State* (New York: Oceana, 1972), p. 146.

72. George Grafton Wilson, *International Law* (New York: Silver, Bordett, 1901), p. 225.

73. Pitman B. Potter, *A Manual Digest of Common International Law* (New York: Harper and Brothers, 1932), p. 66. Concurrence with this image is also expressed by Amos Hershey, *The Essentials of International Public Law* (New York: Macmillan, 1927), p. 559.

74. Hans Kelsen, *Principles of International Law*, Second ed. revised and edited by Robert W. Tucker (New York: Holt, Rinehart, and Winston, 1966), v, p. 90.

position perceives conflict to be the dominant characteristic of international politics and assumes, à la Hobbes, that violence is the natural state governing relations among states. Preoccupation with war, from this perspective, is inevitable.

The proportionate space given in authoritative legal texts to the laws of war as opposed to the laws of peace provides an indicator of the relative salience of war in these dichotomous terms. Figure 5.2 summarizes the shift, as measured, over time. Calculating the mean ratio across successive periods permits a profile to be constructed. Because this chronological ordering suggests the possible presence of a cycle whose periodicity approximates 25 years, the time series has been smoothed by taking a 25-year moving average—a data transformation that renders the resultant trend more easily interpreted.

The resultant trend suggests a number of propositions about the changing importance attached to the problem of war and its regulation by legal observers. Some of the more conspicuous findings which the time series indicates are:

1. The salience of war, defined in terms of the proportionate attention allocated to it by international legal scholarship, has undergone substantial variation

2. Transnational legal rules manifest continuity in the nineteenth century with respect to the relatively strong emphasis placed on norms relevant to the control of violence; however, in the twentieth century declining attention to rules regarding the control of war is evident

3. Since World War I there has commenced a general tendency for the legal regulation of international war to be de-emphasized, and after that event the international legal culture has concentrated attention on the construction and maintenance of rules designed to regulate the more routine and peaceful forms of interaction among states. An alternate interpretation is that by "abolishing" war in 1928 and 1945, the international system was freed to concern itself with other norms

A potentially large number of factors may account for this observed transformation. The extent to which war is increasingly perceived as beyond legal influence may derive in part from the concomitant growth in the number of states in the international system and the corresponding decline in the cultural consensus and homogeneity of beliefs in the system. The growing sense of despair in legally addressing war may be attributable as well to the increasingly stratified, hierarchical international system (as economic and military capabilities have gradually been monopolized by a diminishing number of national actors). It may be suggested that the goal of legally regulating the behavior of such great powers under these conditions of systemic differentiation and fragmentation has tended to appear less and less feasible.

Another factor which may contribute to the diminishing salience of the legal control of war may be the transformation of modern weapons systems. Has growth of the destructive power of warfare technology so altered the nature of interstate warfare as to render traditional rules governing its conduct irrelevant, even obsolete? Have general rules been abrogated by changing global conditions? That the contemporary international political culture has yet to generate new norms relevant to the control of these new modes of destruction is a possibility.

A negative correlation between change in global circumstances (*i.e.*, the rising brutality of war) and global beliefs (*i.e.*, the salience of war) emerges:[75] the long-term increase in war's severity covaries temporally with a long-term declining trend in the

---

75. For several correlation coefficients among these variables (and others that will be mentioned below), see Charles W. Kegley and Gregory A. Raymond, "International Legal Norms and the Preservation of Peace, 1860-1964: Some Bivariate Relationships," paper presented at the 1980 Meeting of the

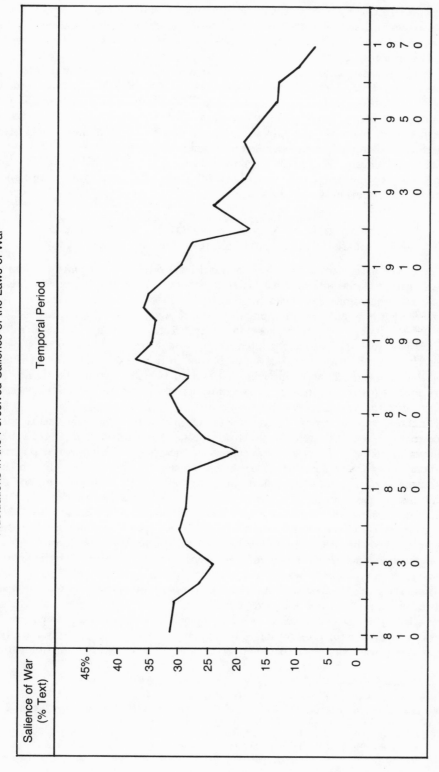

FIGURE 5.2

Fluctuations in the Perceived Salience of the Laws of War

salience of war. At first glance this is an unanticipated finding, given the expectation that increases in war's destructiveness would lead to a growth of normative attention to it. Note, however, that normative attention is defined here relatively in terms of war and peace. The immense growth in the volume of peaceful relations among states would compete with increasingly severe wars for attention in the necessarily limited space available to text writers. The strength of the association is moderately weak, suggesting that norm formation and abrogation may be affected by multiple changes in the environment in which law-making takes place. For whatever reasons, international normative opinion is increasingly allocating its attention to the formation of rules bearing on peaceful, not bellicose, intercourse between states.

But such propositions can be interpreted better in light of additional evidence about the temporal variation manifest in other legal rules. It is to the analysis of the trends in those rules that attention is now directed.

Controlling War: A Typology of Legal Procedures and Some Measures of Changes in Their Perceived Importance

The preceding has argued that international legal rules serve to convey assumptions about the nature of the international system; that legal norms are symbolic representations of, and expressions about, an international political culture; and that long-term shifts in the patterns of interaction among national actors affect the formation of legal norms and the process by which those norms are created. If changes in legal rules are precipitated by evolving patterns of interstate behavior, then insight into the process of the development of international law can be obtained by examining the behavior of nations that forms the basis of international custom (which in turn contributes to the "international legislative process").[76] How those actors deal with violence thus is seen as contributing to the process of law-creation.

The threat which war poses to the very existence of states (and today, mankind) may be expected to have accelerated the search for means to control it. The global system is "conditionally viable"[77] because the members of the system (nation-states) possess the capability to destroy one another; under these conditions the goal of bringing the use of force under control becomes paramount. Like any homeostatic social system, the global political culture has considered devising a number of regulative mechanisms through which violence stemming from competitive interaction might be diminished. A non-exhaustive typology of the principal conflict management procedures devised includes the following five categories: (1) the use of force itself; (2) supranational control; (3) coalition aggregation and treaty formation; (4) pacific means of dispute settlement; and (5) forcible methods short of war.

These categories require some brief elaboration. At the outset, to suggest that the international political culture recognizes the control of force by use of force is to suggest a contradiction in terms. Nevertheless, war between states has been legally tolerated,[78] and the use of violence for the preservation of the system has been perceived to be a legitimate goal. Waging war for peace has not been always seen as impermissible. In the

---

International Studies Association. See as well Charles W. Kegley and Gregory A. Raymond, "Fluctuations in Legal Norms and Arbitral Behavior, 1825-1970: Indicators of Major Power Conflict," paper presented at the 1979 World Congress of the International Political Science Association.

76. Coplin (fn. 30), p. 166.

77. Kenneth E. Boulding, *Conflict and Defense* (New York: Harper and Row, 1962).

78. Wright (fn. 61), pp. 173-202; Quincy Wright, *Contemporary International Law: A Balance Sheet* (New York: Random House, 1955), p. 13.

international legal culture, warfare has been rationalized as an instrument of justice,[79] as a means of coercing change,[80] and, most commonly, as a lawful act in support of the international legal order itself.[81] Hence conflict resolution through force has been intermittently tolerated and even encouraged at times throughout history. Accordingly, the preceding typology incorporates the use of force in order to acknowledge its historical legacy and to enable changes in this norm to be examined.

Supranational control refers to a theoretical tradition which views the competing territorially-based nation-state system as a source of war, and which recommends replacement of that system with a relatively consolidated, centralized federation of powers as a promising solution to the problem of war. As a general rule, subscribers to this view advocate maintaining global stability by placing states under the control of intergovernmental organizations.

Conflict management through alliance aggregation refers to the prescription that any threat of hegemony by force be met through the formation of counter-coalitions. The integrity of agreements to ally among states bears on systemic stability by enabling coalition creation and the successful operation of a balance of power.

Pacific means of dispute settlement is defined by jurisprudence as including a variety of procedures for the resolution of incompatible claims. Arbitration, adjudication, mediation, commissions of inquiry, good offices, and the like represent examples of this approach. The presumption is that disputes settled by these procedures will eliminate the temptation to use force of arms.

Finally, forcible methods short of war entail hostile actions to modify the behavior of an adversary to one's satisfaction, but not through violent coercion. Retortion and reprisals are basic examples; the former "consists of legal but deliberately unfriendly acts with a retaliatory or coercive purpose . . . [such as a] retaliatory increase in tariff rates against countries which discriminate against the products of a particular country," while the latter are "coercive measures taken by one state against another, without belligerent intent, in order to secure redress for, or to prevent recurrence of, acts or omissions which under international law constitute international 'delinquency.'"[82] Rupture of diplomatic relations, displays of military force, embargo, boycott, pacific blockade, and bombardment or military occupation of territory are also acts subsumed under this category in international law.

The relative emphasis placed on each of these procedures for controlling international violence has varied over time. Following the methodological precedent already established for measuring global value change with the TRIP data,[83] shifts in attitudes regarding the importance and efficacy of these norms may be charted. Each of these transnational norms will be examined in succession.

Conflict Management Through the Use of Force

How legal is the initiation of war for the redress of grievances? To what extent have rules in the international legal order condoned war as a permissible form of national behavior? Answers to these questions have been subject to long-term temporal variation;

---

79. Wright (fn. 61), p. 180.
80. Falk (fn. 29), p. 23.
81. Hedley Bull, "The Grotian Conception of International Society," in Herbert Butterfield and Martin Wight, eds., *Diplomatic Investigations* (Harvard: Cambridge University Press, 1968), p. 56.
82. Herbert Briggs, *The Law of Nations* (New York: Appleton-Century-Crofts, 1947), p. 682.
83. See above, especially p. 184 in this essay, for a discussion of the measurement procedures applied to the construction of the trend lines describing fluctuations in the salience of war.

moreover, within discrete periods observers disagree about whether war should be renounced and whether the resort to war should be regulated or restricted.

Opinions on the legality of war vary across a wide continuum. At one pole are those who think the system grants its national members, by virtue of their sovereign rights, wide latitude to engage in practically any form of aggressive behavior. Classical arguments of this type legalize the drive for power, rationalize territorial acquisition, and, in its extreme form, encourage war as a national policy under particular conditions.[84] Symptomatic of this once prevalent orientation[85] are the arguments of those who have contended that "every state has . . . a right to resort to force. . . . Every state is also entitled to judge for itself what . . . justifie[s] such a means of redress."[86] Representative as well of this perspective was the view that "did not deem international law violated when a state resorted to war for any reason it felt proper."[87] The slogans "defence by conquest" and "preventive attack" aptly characterize the approach. These opinions all reflect one view of international law, namely, that "paradoxical as it may seem, the fundamental conceptions of international law can best be understood if it is assumed that they maintain and support the rule of force."[88] In one way or another, the international legal culture has at various times perceived war as an acceptable means of self-help.

At the other pole are those who see international law as restricting absolutely the right of states to employ force as an instrument of political power. While a pacifist orientation has never dominated legal thought, recent decades have seen a rising tide of opinion and institutional developments directed against the unauthorized use of force. Potter took early note of this trend when in 1932 he observed that "there seems to be operating today a tendency to abolish certain rights formally recognized by international law such as the right to make war."[89]

An intermediate position between these two extremes has been prevalent throughout most of the history of the international system, and it takes a number of distinct forms. Some have emphasized war as a sanction crucial to the preservation of law in the system and have stressed the legality of war "as an instrument of international . . . policy."[90] Others, adhering to auto-limitation, consensual, or legal realist theories of jurisprudence, have viewed war as an undesirable but inevitable "consequence of the present structure of international relations."[91] A third variant of this position includes those who see international legal norms specifying limits of permissible state behavior in the conduct of

---

84. E.g., note the opinion of Suarez that "defensive war not only is permitted, but sometimes is even commanded." Cited in Scott (fn. 62), p. 289.

85. It is hardly an exaggeration to note that international law, particularly in its classical phase, invited violence by encouraging states to "arm for defense and kill for peace." The rules were designed to make killing more efficient rather than to eliminate it (for instance, international law provided statesmen with advice for war-making by outlawing the initiation of war during inclement seasons of the year; one text described war as a "gentleman's sport" and prescribed appropriate rules for killing). Moreover, much normative thinking was highly imaginative in devising justifications for aggression (recall Spinoza's famous metaphor about the sovereign natural right of big fish to devour the small, or Treitschke's declaration that "pacifists would mutilate human nature, but, fortunately, God would see that war returned to the earth again and again." As morally repugnant as these concepts are, their legacy and possible contemporary consequences for behavior should be considered.

86. Henry Wheaton, *Elements of International Law*, 3rd rev. ed. (Philadelphia: Lea and Blanchard, 1846), p. 339.

87. William Bishop, *International Law* (Boston: Little Brown, 1962), p. 755.

88. George W. Keeton and Georg Schwarzenberger, quoted but not cited in Falk (fn. 15), p. 151.

89. Potter (fn. 73), p. 339.

90. Kelsen (fn. 11), p. 43.

91. Charles DeVisscher, *Theory and Reality in Public International Law* (Princeton: Princeton University Press, 1957), p. 57; Kaplan and Katzenbach (fn. 8); Hoffmann (fn. 9).

hostilities but not in the initiation of hostilities.[92] Typical of this interpretation is the comment that "international law relates only to the methods that may or may not be used in a war that nations have chosen to begin."[93]

Figure 5.3 indexes the degree to which war has been perceived as a legitimate form of behavior across successive epochs. Legal observers' perceptions of the legality of war were coded on a four-category ordinal scale.[94] All opinions recorded in each 5-year period were then averaged to produce a composite score at 5-year intervals, and once again the data were transformed by computing a 25-year moving average.

Propositions about the nature of change in the global normative order are suggested by this evidence. By far the most conspicuous trend has been the gradual but steady decline in the international community's tolerance of war and concomitant rejection of the absolute prerogative of the state to employ force to achieve foreign policy objectives. This shift in value orientation is significant, for, as Falk has commented, "the willingness of nations to subscribe, even in principle, to the renunciation of their rights to use (except in self-defense) force is a significant step, an expression of willingness to move in one direction rather than another, and a disclosure of consensus on the most important aspect of political order in world affairs."[95] This transformation and others are summarized in the following observations:

> 1. A long-term secular trend toward the legal prohibition of war is evident; the use of force for the redress of grievances, once accepted by the majority of publicists, has given way to an era wherein the majority now reject the legality of the initiation of war.[96]

---

92. This position emphasizes the fact that in international law the "most frequently noted legal principles relate primarily to procedural matters;" William V. O'Brien, "The Law of War, Command Responsibility, and Vietnam," *Georgetown Law Journal*, Vol. 60, No. 3 (February 1972), p. 614. Those who interpret international law in these terms tend to see the objective of the international legal order to restrain in duration, method, and location the conduct of war, rather than to prevent its initiation. For a discussion, see Bull (fn. 81), pp. 51-73.

93. Elizabeth Read, *International Law and International Relations* (New York: The American Foundation, 1925), p. 151.

94. That is, each legal scholar's opinion was coded on an ordinal continuum from 1 ("war is best described as an acceptable tool of foreign policy") to 4 ("war is best described as an illegitimate tool for foreign policy"). Scaling and coding procedures of this and other variables are described in detail in the TRIP Coder's Manual (fn. 58).

95. Falk (fn. 61), pp. 233-234.

96. This evidence supports the general impression gleaned by students of the history of international law. The most important indicators of global rejection of violence and symptoms of legal development bearing on its prohibition include such international conventions as the Covenant of the League of Nations, the Kellogg-Briand Pact (1928), and the Charter of the United Nations. Articles 11 to 17 of the Covenant stipulate that in no case may a power resort to war until three months following a judicial determination by the League had elapsed. After nations had submitted their disputes to the arbitral tribunal of the League, the decision of the tribunal was to have been obligatory; thus states could not legally resort to force of arms (Art. 13) except for self-defense (Art. 16). The Kellogg-Briand Pact (General Treaty for the Renunciation of War as an Instrument of National Policy), *League of Nations Treaty Series*, Vol. 94 (1929), pp. 57-64, states that the signatories "condemn recourse to war for the solution of international controversies and renounce it as an instrument of national policy in their relations with one another." The Pact established for the first time the principle of the outlawry of all aggressive wars in an international convention. The most recent statement is the United Nations Charter. Article 2(4) declares: "All members shall refrain in their international relations from the threat or use of force against the territorial integrity or political independence of any state, or in any other manner inconsistent with the purposes of the United Nations." This, like the Kellogg-Briand Pact, is an unequivocal statement outlawing aggressive war as an instrument of national policy. Besides these international conventions, the war crimes trials further underline this position by giving it acceptance by an international court; for instance, the court at Nuremberg spoke of aggressive war as "the supreme international crime."

2. The general trend toward the delegitimation of war has accelerated most notably in the aftermath of increases in the frequency of *major* wars

3. Other things being equal, as the brutality of war has increased, the perceived legitimacy of war has declined

4. The scope and recurrence of war has not been strongly related to changes in its perceived legitimacy, other things being equal; war has become no more frequent, but toleration for it has diminished nonetheless

    4.1 The idea that the normal way of behaving tends to be interpreted as the proper way of behaving in the international political culture (following Kelsen's prescription that "states ought to behave as they have customarily behaved") is not valid with respect to the use of force: the incidence of war has not varied with the legitimacy of war. This suggests that regular behavior does not tend to become legal and that international law does not merely legitimate customary diplomatic practice, as frequently believed.

5. The salience of the laws of war is negatively correlated with their changing degree of permissibility; the delegitimation of war has been associated with a concomitant shift of international law's attention away from rules for war's control

    5.1 The importance of laws governing interstate aggression has declined as war has been interpreted as less legitimate

    5.2. As war increasingly has been perceived as less permissible, the scope of rules regulating the conduct of war subsequently has been reduced[97]

    It is tempting to account for the decline in the acceptability of the use of force by arguing, as Boulding does,[98] that images throughout the global system gradually have become more sophisticated and humanitarian through a macro learning process, wherein the costs associated with maintaining unsophisticated images exceeds benefits and are thus rejected.

    Alternatively, it is tempting to speculate that growing awareness of the horrors of modern warfare have stimulated norm transformation. According to this hypothesis, noted above, the perceived legitimacy of war has declined with each incremental increase in the magnitude and brutality of war. But the rejection of war cannot be related to changes in the incidence of war. Statistically the frequency of war has not varied with changing judgments about its legality. Instead, the acceptability of force declines in proportion to increases in the violence, and not the frequency, of modern warfare.

    But still other explanatory factors for this rule change might be cited as well. Certain dramatic events, such as the signing of the United Nations Charter with Article 2(4), for example, could be identified as catalysts to the rate of norm change. The demise of national chauvinism brought about by the growth of transnational travel and the development of cross-national transportation and communication,[99] or the growing interdependence of the global system in general (and consequent decline in the number of opportunities for potential adversarial interaction),[100] could also be contributing sources. So, too, could increased awareness of the conditions of balance-of-terror be a factor.

---

97. These findings suggest that legal rule decay is affected by normative tolerance for a mode of behavior; norms governing the conduct of war have tended to deteriorate as war has become less permissible. The converse of this suggests that legal development and law-making is precipitated by the acceptance of a particular form of behavior as legitimate. See also Kenneth E. Boulding, "The Learning of Peace," *International Studies Notes*, Vol. 1, No. 2 (Summer 1974), pp. 1-8.

98. Boulding (fn. 24).

99. Herbert C. Kelman, "International Exchanges: Some Contributions from Learning Theory," in Coplin and Kegley, eds. (fn. 24), pp. 205-218.

100. Karl W. Deutsch and J. David Singer, "Multipolar Power Systems and International Stability," in Coplin and Kegley, eds. (fn. 24), pp. 343-360.

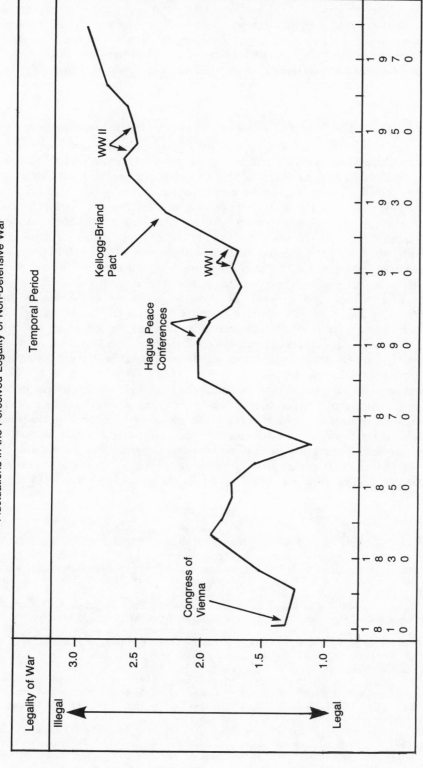

FIGURE 5.3

Fluctuations in the Perceived Legality of Non-Defensive War

Regardless of the causes of this norm transformation, the global community's prohibition of the absolute right of states to use military force to guard paramount national interests attests to the capacity of international laws to change. This change, unfolding slowly over many decades, shows that the global climate of normative opinion can undergo fundamental transformation in response to changing international circumstances.

Conflict Management Through Supranational Regulation

Since antiquity, some have believed that the formation of universal and/or regional organizations whose members consist of nation-states (intergovernmental organizations, or "IGOs") could contribute to peace. While to be sure such supranational institutions often perform functions fairly remote from the maintenance of global stability, world peace is generally a consideration of the architects of such institutions. As Inis L. Claude has commented: "In the realm of international organization, the essential criterion of legitimacy is relevance to the prevention of war; almost any multilateral program can be justified with, and hardly any can be justified without, the claim that it promises to promote conditions conducive to international peace."[102]

Generally, advocacy of supranational management of international affairs tends to carry with it a presumption in favor of a more centralized world society and a concomitant reduction in the power of nation-states.[103] The existence of a state system composed of autonomous territorial authorities is believed to contribute to "global inequalities, imperialism, wars and devastations;"[104] the cure is presumed to rest with the replacement of "nation-statism" with supranational institutions empowered to perform central guidance for the global system.

Such views enjoy a long history in international thought and represent a second prescription for the regulation of war.[105] These views are implicit in functional approaches to peace, in the international political integration literature, and in that body of scholarly writing emphasizing the mediation, socialization, collective security, preventive diplomacy, and peacekeeping functions of contemporary international institutions.[106]

Part of the reason for the growing attention given to the creation of global organizations stems from the dramatic increase in their numbers after 1815.[107] This

---

101.   J. David Singer and Michael Wallace, "International Organization and the Preservation of Peace, 1816-1964: Some Bivariate Relationships," *International Organization*, Vol. 24, No. 3 (Summer 1970), p. 520.

102.   Inis L. Claude, Jr., "Economic Development Aid and International Political Stability," in Robert W. Cox, ed., *The Politics of International Organizations* (New York: Praeger, 1970), p. 50, quoted ibid., p. 521.

103.   Richard A. Falk, "The International Law of Internal War," in James N. Rosenau, ed., *International Aspects of Civil Strife* (Princeton: Princeton University Press, 1964), p. 234 et passim.

104.   Edward E. Azar, "Notes on the Need for Better Sources of Indicators for Evaluating Foreign Policy and International Events Research," University of North Carolina, mimeo, February, 1975.

105.   Inis L. Claude, Jr., *Power and International Relations* (New York: Random House, 1962), and *Swords Into Plowshares* (New York: Random House, 1956).

106.   Ibid., Coplin (fn. 41), pp. 98-101, 105-167; Joseph S. Nye, *Peace in Parts* (Boston: Little Brown, 1971); Chadwick F. Alger, "Non-Resolution Consequences of the United Nations and Their Effect on International Conflict," in Coplin and Kegley, eds. (fn. 24), pp. 216-233; Donald McNemar, "The Future Role of International Institutions," in Black and Falk, eds., (fn. 59), Vol. IV, *The Structure of the International Environment* (1972), pp. 448-479; David Mitrany, *A Working Peace System* (Chicago: Quadrangle Books, 1966); and Ernst B. Haas, *Beyond the Nation-State* (Stanford, Calif.: Stanford University Press, 1964).

107.   Singer and Wallace (fn. 101); Michael Wallace and J. David Singer, "Intergovernmental Organization in the Global System, 1815-1964: A Quantitative Description," *International Organization*, Vol.

growth has stimulated much theoretical speculation about the consequences of that growth for the international system.[108] Figure 5.4 displays this trend quantitatively from the end of the Napoleonic Wars.

This trend has also affected international legal theory and stimulated changes in global opinions about supranational control of interstate war. Commenting on this revolution in beliefs, Skeikh has noted that "any theory of international relations that views the contemporary international system as the exclusive domain of nation-states, at the exclusion of . . . many international organizations, no longer reflects the realities of international life. It is a theory that has already been left behind in the history."[109]

This image has hardly prevailed in past epochs, however. Most normative character-izations of international society prescribed the preservation of the global system's decentralized or horizontal structure, advocated the perpetuation of state's foreign policy autonomy, and devised rules for maintenance of structural anarchy.[110] As Sohn reports, "In the textbooks on international law at the end of the 19th century, the phenomenon of international organization was not yet recognized, though several such organizations had flourished for many years."[111]

Changes in the extent to which international organizations are seen as relevant to war's regulation are detectable over time. Figure 5.5 traces transformations in global attitudes regarding this approach to peace as reflected in the changing treatments of this topic recorded in the writings of authoritative publicists.

The following propositions about norms bearing on conflict management through supranational regulation are especially noteworthy:

1. The percentage of textual space dealing with laws bearing on supranational actors in legal treatises has grown steadily since 1900

2. Falk's view[112] that international society is undergoing a fundamental long-term transition in the direction of non-territorial central guidance is supported by this quantitative evidence; since the First World War legal texts have stressed increas-ingly the importance of supranational organizations for the control of war

3. The growth of attention to and legal commentary about international organizations in law books correlates strongly with the growth in the number of international organizations in the system

4. Emphasis in legal treatises on international organizations has increased most dramatically in the aftermath of major wars

5. Contemporary emphasis on supranational institutions in legal texts represents a reassertion of a pattern of attention operative in the post-Vienna era of Metternich—a long-term cycle is evident

24, No. 2 (Spring 1970), pp. 239-287. Robert C. Angell, "An Analysis of Trends in International Organizations," *Peace Research Society (International) Papers*, Vol. 3 (1965), pp. 185-195; Paul Smoker, "Nation-State Escalation and International Integration," *Journal of Peace Research*, Vol. 4, No. 1 (1967), pp. 61-75; Charles W. Kogley, Jr., and Eugene Wittkopf, *World Politics: Trend and Transformation* (New York: St. Martin's, 1981), p. 105.

108.   For example, Charles W. Kegley, Jr., and J. Martin Rochester, "Assessing the Impact of Trends in the International System: The Growth of Intergovernmental Organizations," in Coplin and Kegley, eds. (fn. 24), pp. 401-412.

109.   Sheikh, (fn. 1), p. 62.

110.   McNemar (fn. 106); Coplin (fn. 25).

111.   Louis B. Sohn, "The Growth of the Science of International Organizations," in Deutsch and Hoffmann, eds. (fn. 26), pp. 328-353; see also Werner Levi, *Fundamentals of World Organization* (Minneapo-lis, 1950).

112.   See Richard A. Falk "A New Paradigm for International Legal Studies: Prospects and Proposals," *Yale Law Journal* Vol. 84, No. 5 (April 1975), pp. 975-1021.

FIGURE 5.4

The Number of International Governmental Organizations, 1815-1976

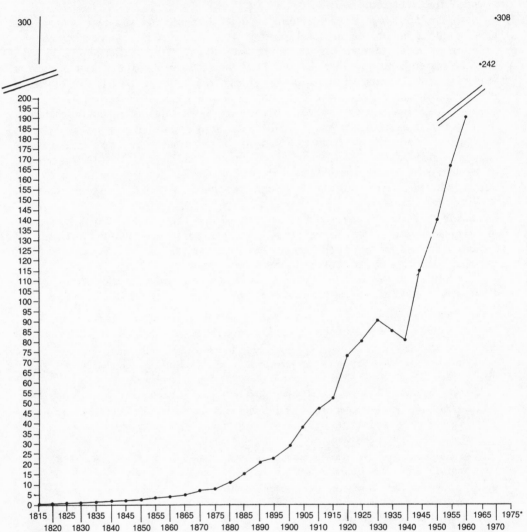

*Data are for 1976. Data derived as follows; for 1815-1960: Michael Wallace and J. David Singer, "Intergovernmental Organization in the Global System, 1815-1964: A Quantitative Description," *International Organization,* Vol. 24, No. 2 (Spring 1970), p. 277; for 1960-1976: *Yearbook of International Organizations* (Brussels: Union of International Associations, 1978), n.p.

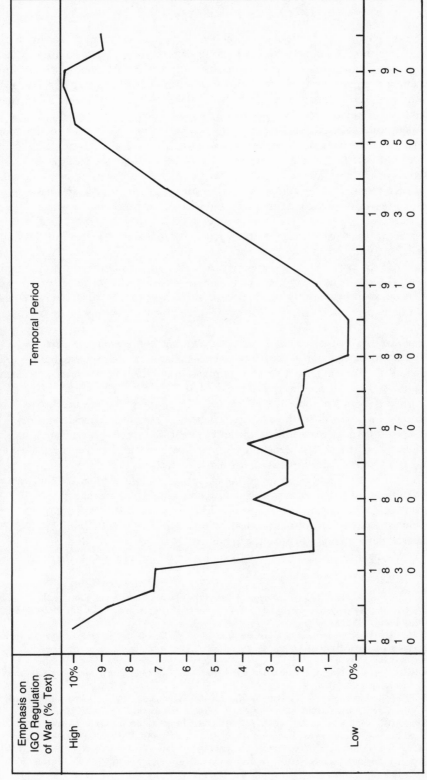

FIGURE 5.5

Fluctuations in the Perceived Importance of
Supranational Organizations in Legal Treatises

Conflict Management Through Coalition Formation

Since Thucydides, statesmen have regarded the formation of defensive alliances, cemented by treaty commitments, as a means of preserving global stability. Whether for the purpose of enhancing one's own power by alignment with another state to mutually deter outside aggression, or for the purpose of maintaining a balance of power to prevent the acquisition of preponderant power by a single state,[113] coalitions always have been perceived as important for the control of recourse to war.[114]

Many international legal rules relate in one fashion or another to the appropriate national behavior associated with alliance formation and the maintenance of a stable balance of power. For instance, treaty law stipulates rules for the creation and dissolution of alignments,[115] and international law has considered intervention for the restoration of the balance of power to be admissible.[116] Grotius suggested that states have the right to align themselves to participate in a struggle should war break out in which one party has a just cause.

International legal theory has been relatively consistent in stressing the importance of coalition formation to the preservation of peace, and in providing legal prescriptions for the successful operation of stable power balances through shifting alliance configurations. Much legal thought has been given over time to reflection about the "essential rules" that must be followed by states in order for alliance competition to culminate in equal power distributions precluding the acquisition of predominance by any actor or collection of actors.[117]

But far less consistent have been prescriptions concerning the perceived extent to which commitments and agreements between states to align have been regarded as binding. Rules for the formation and termination of alliance and treaty agreements have undergone substantial modification over the last 150 years. The degree to which alliance commitments between states have been seen as binding has covaried with, and been determined by, changes in the polarity structure of the international system,[118] that is, changes in the degree to which military power has been concentrated in polarized coalitions.[119] Often it has been argued that "the balance of power system necessitated flexibility in political alignments and meant that a state's enemy today might be its ally tomorrow;" this naturally led to norms accepting a loose definition of treaty commitments facilitating policy reversals. For instance, Gould notes that after 1777 "the oath dropped out of the picture. . . . Treaties either were binding or were not binding at all. The literature on the law of nations had been emphasizing the desirability, the necessity, and, particularly in the 18th century, the utility of good faith. Indeed, a considerable portion of the jurisprudence of the period was to revolve about the question of the

---

113. Ernst B. Haas, "The Balance of Power: Prescription, Concept, or Propaganda?" in Coplin and Kegley, eds. (fn. 24), pp. 312-333; Edward V. Gulick, *Europe's Classic Balance of Power* (Ithaca: Cornell University Press, 1955).

114. For a review and sampling of the literature on alliances, see Julian Friedman and others, ed., *Alliance in International Politics* (Boston: Allyn and Bacon, 1969).

115. Coplin (fn. 41).

116. Wesley L. Gould, *An Introduction to International Law* (New York: Harper and Brothers, 1957).

117. Kaplan (fn. 8).

118. J. David Singer and Melvin Small, "Alliance Aggregation and the Onset of War, 1815-1945," in J. David Singer, ed., *Quantitative International Politics* (New York: Free Press, 1968), pp. 247-286. See also Charles W. Kegley, Jr., and Gregory A. Raymond, "International Legal Norms and the Preservation of Peace, 1820-1964," *International Interactions*, Vol. 8, No. 3 (August 1981), pp. 171-187.

119. For a review of this concept which delineates its various definitions in the context of the scholarly literature, see Joseph L. Nogee, "Polarity: An Ambiguous Concept," *Orbis*, Vol. 28, No. 4 (Winter 1975), pp. 1193-1224.

binding nature of contracts and treaties."[120] Because the perceived degree to which treaties obligate may have changed through time, measurement of the extent to which this aspect of the global community's legal culture manifests transience or permanence can be illuminating.

To that end, attitudes may be characterized dichotomously in terms of two basic orientations which have prevailed at various times. On the one hand, there are those who adhere to the *pacta sunt servanda* principle that treaty commitments voluntarily entered into are binding and must be observed. Such a position rests on the assumption that relations between nations must be based on rules, that agreements once entered into should be honored, and that contractual coalitions must be considered relatively permanent arrangements. Those who stress this interpretation of coalition agreement generally express a desire for certainty, predictability, and order as a basis for the conduct of international relations.

On the other hand, the international legal culture recognizes a diametrically opposed conception, symbolized by the clause *rebus sic stantibus*, which claims, in its extreme interpretation, that states possess a sovereign right to unilaterally repudiate alliance obligations. Those adhering to this interpretation contend that a party to a contractual alliance may renounce its agreement by claiming that conditions have so changed from those operative at the time the treaty was made as to render the agreement obsolete and no longer obligatory.

To measure global norm change regarding coalition commitments on this dimension, legal observers' opinions in authoritative treatises about which principle was the more dominant at the time of writing were coded. These opinions in turn were aggregated and scaled[121] to profile transnational rule orientations and their change over time. The results are displayed in Figure 5.6 below.

This evidence suggests that the meaning of alliance commitments has undergone substantial change over the last 150 years. While there is an obvious long-term secular trend toward increases in the degree to which alliance agreements are perceived to be binding, there also appears to be some marked periodicities in the trend. Very roughly, one might interpret the evidence to indicate that *rebus sic stantibus* principles of treaty commitment prevailed from 1815 to 1860, and from 1875 to 1930, while in turn *pacta sunt servanda* conceptions were adhered to rather briefly in the previous century (1860-1875) and have steadily increased in emphasis since 1930. The shift in the latter period certainly conforms to the view that in the contemporary era obligations relating to alliances (e.g., NATO and the Warsaw Pact) have ceased to be flexible.

Although it is difficult to discern the most potent determinants of this trend, it is tempting to speculate about some of its consequences. For example, since some modicum of flexibility in alliance systems is crucial to the operation of a balance of power mechanism for the preservation of peace, the deterioration of that flexibility might be partly responsible for the contemporary obsolescence of balance of power on a global

---

120. Gould (fn. 116), p. 56.

121. The attitude disposition index was derived by (a) coding each author's conception of alliance commitments as either + or − depending on whether it conformed to a *pacta sunt servanda* or a *rebus sic stantibus* conception. Next a summary index for each five-year interval period was calculated by the formula

$(+) - (-) \div 100$ where $(+)$ = number of positive, binding conceptions, and
                 where $(-)$ = number of negative, flexible conceptions.

When attitudes are aggregated and scaled in this manner, the overall index at each point in time varies between an extreme of $+1.00$ (commitments are binding) to -1.00 (not binding), with 0.00 representing a neutral position. Again, the data were smoothed by taking 25-year moving averages of these scores.

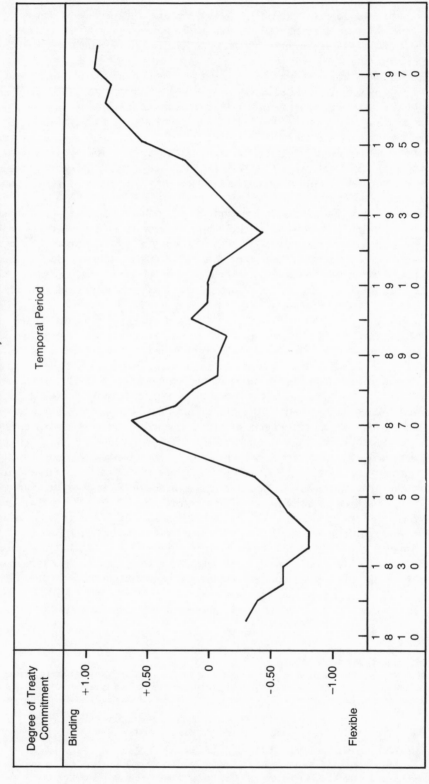

FIGURE 5.6

Transformations in the Perceived Flexibility of Alliance Commitments

scale. When coalition arrangements are binding, adjustments of power distributions through shifts in the composition of coalitions are precluded. Moreover, the observed trend toward binding commitments might account for the seeming paradox that alliance aggregation is negatively correlated with the incidence of war in the nineteenth century but positively correlated in the twentieth.[122] Such a proposition deserves careful future scrutiny.[123]

This trend has implications for global law-making. Since legal systems are contingent to some extent on the *pacta sunt servanda* principle for their existence, the trend suggests that the prospects for the creation of a world of law have been gradually enhanced since the first quarter of the present century. The international community has demonstrated a growing acceptance of the notion that formal, though political, agreements have legal meaning—an acceptance which indicates a growing willingness on the part of sovereign states to limit their freedom of choice as a matter of self-interest. While it would be reckless to contend that this trend may be partially responsible for the accelerated growth of treaty law, the trend provides a plausible explanation of contemporary legal development in this domain. Norm creation and rule maintenance, it may be assumed, are fostered by the stability of contractual agreements, whereas the absence of adherence to agreements promotes rule decay and termination.

Conflict Management Through Pacific Means of Dispute Settlement and Conflict Management Through Forcible Modes of Dispute Settlement by Methods Short of War

Although it has been asserted[124] that "the fundamental conceptions of international law can best be understood if it is assumed that they maintain and support the rule of force," and that, indeed, international law recognizes war as an extreme form of self-help for the redress of injuries, nonetheless the international legal culture has sought to reduce war's occurrence and severity. International law required states, for instance, to calibrate the amount of retaliatory force used in proportion to the offense committed. And it has been guided by the search for global order in its stress on at least two additional procedures for the promotion of peace: forcible dispute settlement short of war and pacific methods of conflict resolution. As sanctions, these three types of behavior for the redress of grievances may be arrayed on a hypothetical continuum reflecting the degree of force employed, with full scale war at one extreme and pacific settlement at the other.[125] However, they all represent types of behavior directed toward the same objectives, namely, conflict resolution and punishment for perceived injuries.[126]

A number of legal procedures may be subsumed under each of these non-forceful categories. Pacific methods include adjudication, judicial settlement, mediation, conciliation, negotiation, good offices, and commissions of inquiry.[127] Forcible methods short of

---

122. Singer and Small (fn. 118).

123. "Charles W. Kegley, Jr., and Gregory A. Raymond, "Alliances and War: A New Piece in an Old Puzzle," paper presented at 1980 Meeting of the Southern Political Science Association.

124. Keeton and Schwarzenberger (fn. 88).

125. To suggest that the "use of force short of war" represents an intermediate position between "warfare" and "pacific methods of dispute settlement" on such a continuum is not to contend that differences between them are equal (i.e., conform to an interval scale) or invariable. To some, for instance, "the use of force short of war in international relations is as much a danger as war itself;" Albert Hindmarch, *Force in Place* (Cambridge: Harvard University Press, 1933), p. 27.

126. See Gould (fn. 116), pp. 534-599, for an excellent conceptual and historical description of these legal procedures.

127. The following definitions convey the nature of these methods. *Arbitration* is a process by which the disputants agree to submit the issues in question to judges for decisions they agree to abide by.

war usually involve the use of some physical pressure for bargaining purposes, such as retortion and reprisals.[128] The rupture of diplomatic relations, nonrecognition, and imposition of tariffs and quotas are examples of the former method. Embargo, boycott, pacific blockade, military occupation of territory, and bombardment are examples of the latter.[129]

Given the relevance of changes in norms regarding[130] these substitutes for violent methods of dispute settlement for the creation of an international atmosphere conducive to the growth of world law, it is revealing to monitor over time the extent to which the international legal culture has regarded legal rules governing these devices to be important. To measure the temporal variance of the perceived importance of these methods, the proportionate attention given to them in legal treatises has been calculated.[131] The evidence is displayed below in Figures 5.7 and 5.8.

These time series suggest a number of hypotheses, described in the following summary:

Norms Relevant to Conflict Management Through Pacific Settlement:

1. The importance of pacific settlement is subject to both temporal variation and cyclical fluctuation

2. The perceived importance of pacific settlement has been greatest in the post-Napoleonic era and since 1930 (relative to the importance of other international legal issues)

3. The international legal culture was relatively inattentive to pacific settlement between 1830 and 1930

Adjudication applies when the court is a permanent one; thus adjudication takes place in a permanent international tribunal, such as the International Court of Justice. *Judicial settlement* means a settlement brought about by a properly constituted international court applying rules of law. *Mediation* consists of the direct participation of a third state in the negotiations between disputants, with the third state assigned to the task of making positive proposals in an effort to help disputants toward a solution of their differences. *Good offices* refers to the efforts of a third party to facilitate communication between the parties to a conflict, and to get them to agree to formal negotiations. *Conciliation* embodies an arrangement whereby a dispute is submitted to a commission which clarifies the facts and renders an advisory award or proposals for settlement without imposing any legal obligation to comply with such proposals. *Negotiation* is a process by which states undertake to adjust differences by an exchange *inter se* of their views. The *commission of inquiry* is employed in order to facilitate the solution of differences which diplomacy has not settled by elucidating the facts through investigations.

128. Briggs (fn. 82).

129. The distinction to be noted between retortion and reprisals is that the latter is designed to curb an illegal act and would itself be illegal were it not that a prior alleged illegality is thus being remedied, while the former is a legal but damaging act in retaliation for a similar act by another state. The common characteristic of each of these procedures for the control of international conflict is that while they may be forcible, they are authorized only for pacific purposes.

130. Several writers believe that forcible nonwar methods of dispute settlement are neither justified nor effective because they tend to impede further negotiation that might resolve the controversy and may create a deadlock that can be broken only with difficulty. Some suggest that Article 2 of the United Nations Charter might serve as a prohibition of acts of retortion that were disproportionate to the conduct against which the retortion was taken. Others argue that forcible nonwar methods are an appropriate means for the settlement of differences, although reprisals may give occasion for abuse in case of differences between a powerful and a weak state.

131. For these trends, the time series was constructed in the same manner as for Figure 5.2 (i.e., the mean percentage of text devoted to these separate procedures was calculated at 5-year intervals, and the trend line records a 25-year moving average of these scores in order to partially cancel out the effects of time and cyclical disturbances).

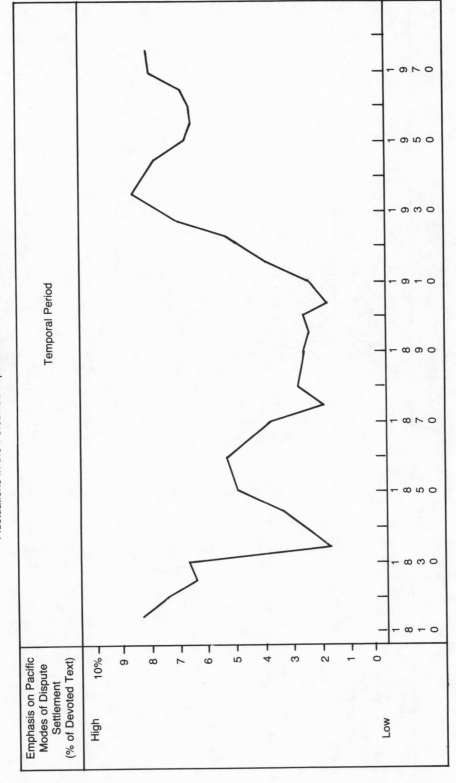

FIGURE 5.7

Fluctuations in the Perceived Importance of Pacific Settlement

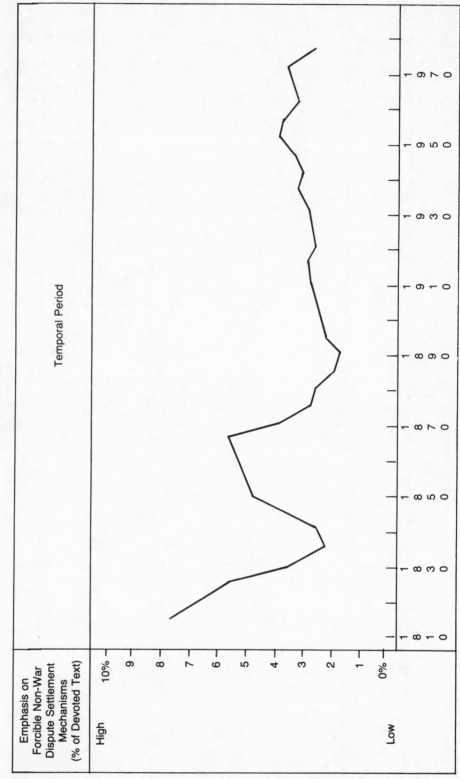

FIGURE 5.8

Fluctuations in the Perceived Importance of Forcible Conflict Settlement by Methods
Short of War

Norms Relevant to Conflict Management Through Forcible Methods Short of War:

1. Since approximately 1870 the importance of forcible conflict settlement by methods short of war has been moderate and relatively stable

2. The international legal culture placed relatively higher but widely fluctuating attention on forcible methods short of war in the 1815–1870 period

3. The perceived importance of these conflict regulation methods appears to have been influenced by technological developments and changes in the levels of interdependence in the system, since these factors have a direct bearing on the effectiveness of such methods as embargos and boycotts

An understanding of the determinants and consequences of variations in these time series necessitates the construction of rather complicated explanatory frameworks, an objective which exceeds the bounds of the present study. Inspection of changes reflected in textbook law, nevertheless, does suggest some additional insights into the process of legal development globally. The intercorrelations among these indicators reveal several patterns. Noteworthy, for instance, is the compelling inverse relationship emerging between the importance attributed by the international legal order to norms regarding self-help (*i.e.,* the legality of war initiation) and norms regarding pacific settlement. Among the ways in which the international legal order has changed during this century, one is in terms of a steady decline in the importance attributed to the laws of war, in association with a growth in the importance of pacific settlement. Also, as the importance of the laws of war has declined, the importance attributed to forcible measures short of war has gradually increased. While this upswing is not very great, it does give some backing to the idea that the primary reason for the development of forcible methods short of war was to provide an alternative to war as a mode of national redress.

And yet, when the meanings of correlations between and among these norm changes are considered closely, they indicate that relationships among legal changes are *not* directly linked. The formation of rules for conflict management is contingent upon neither the perceived importance of war nor war's perceived legality: both the development—and deterioration—of rules for pacific settlement and for forcible methods short of war appear to be unconnected to changes in either the frequency of or attitudes about the permissibility of war. On the contrary, norm formation and decay are not systematically related to, or contingent upon, changes in the behavior those norms address most specifically. Alternately stated, the extent to which some types of state behavior—such as war—are regarded as chronic or as permissible does not reliably predict rule creation or rule deterioration. Rather, the evidence suggests that the erosion of war's permissibility may lead, for instance, to the development of rules in some areas of conflict management (*e.g.,* pacific settlement) but not others (*e.g.,* non-forcible methods). The inference to be drawn from these observations is that the process of legal development is not even in all areas. Law-making may occur rather rapidly in a particular behavioral domain while legal development remains stagnant in a closely related area during the same period. Thus the data show growth of legal rules relevant to pacific settlement since 1900, while rules regarding the use of non-war force experienced relatively little evolution and expansion in this epoch. Law-making, in short, appears to progress in divergent directions in response to similar systemic developments.

RULE CHANGE IN THE INTERNATIONAL SYSTEM:
SOME CONCLUDING INTERPRETATIONS

The study of the processes leading to the formation of international legal rules is fraught with epistemological difficulties. Part of the reason for the primitive state of present knowledge regarding law-making in the global community is because "the study of the sources of international law has suffered from being primarily in the hands of scholars more interested in discovering the content of international legal norms than in studying the process of law-creation. As a result, the scholars have tended to be concerned only with authoritative sources that define the legal norms rather than with social and political processes surrounding the development of those authoritative sources."[132] Following this suggestion, the present study has attempted to investigate the development of international legal rules against the backdrop of historical sociopolitical trends occurring in a succession of historically discrete and identifiable international systems, each of which differs markedly from its predecessors.[133] Thus if transformations in international society affect the creation and evolution of legal norms, then "international law can be studied as a product of international systems as a repertory of normative theory about each one of them."[134] When international legal rules are thought of as psychocultural attributes of the international system, contributing to and reflecting a shared systemic consciousness about permissible national conduct, this approach to the analysis of norm transformation is particularly inviting.

In order to investigate the development of global legal rules and the modification of existing norms to fit new conditions in global society, attention was focused on those norms relevant to the control of war. Focus on this central but unique activity can be misleading,[135] but especially revealing of the law-creation process, since changes in the boundaries of warfare are capable of affecting the entire structure of the global legal system.[136]

Moreover, to probe the process of international legal development recommends examination of alternate legal media for conflict management. As Falk has commented, "Major changes in human affairs take place when there is a significant and effective shift in the locus of discretion with regard to the use of force."[137] Because "international law has evolved so significantly in the area of war and peace,"[138] a focus on the development of international legal rules in this area of norm evolution is especially attractive.

"The relevance of law to conflict," it may be submitted, "is a matter to be settled by systematic empirical inquiry,"[139] by evidence rather than mere assertion. Quantitative descriptions of rule change with respect to, and in response to, the advent of various types of international conflict can be inductively derived.[140] These descriptions raise a series of questions about the causes of rule formation, development, and modification.

Perhaps the most significant findings about the process of global norm creation,

---

132. Coplin (fn. 30), p. 164.

133. See, for example, Rosecrance (fn. 60) and Kaplan and Katzenbach (fn. 8) for defenses of this theoretical approach.

134. Hoffmann (fn. 9), p. 96.

135. Hoffmann (fn. 26), p. 65, has cautioned "what applies to the control of force does not obtain in other sectors of international behavior, where the development of international law can indeed proceed on the basis either of a stable reciprocity of state interests in certainty and security, or of a growing transnational society of individuals."

136. Kaplan and Katzenbach (fn. 8).

137. Falk (fn. 15), p. 148.

138. Richard A. Falk, *The Six Legal Dimensions of the Vietnam War*, Research Monograph No. 34, Center of International Studies, Princeton University (October 1968), p. 16.

139. Falk (fn. 29), p. 42.

140. The comments of Namenwirth and Lasswell on this point are worth noting: "For years the study of value change has been a central topic in intellectual, political, and social history. Unfortunately, speculating about causes and consequences of value change is far easier than determining accurately the magnitude and direction of such change; J. Zvi Namenwirth and Harold D. Lasswell, *The Changing Language of American Values*, Sage Professional Papers in Comparative Politics, No. 01-001 (1975), p. 5.

though certainly one of the least surprising, emerging from the evidence reported here is the extent to which rule modification resists rapid transformation. The normative structure of the international system is characterized by continuity and perseverance. Legal rules manifest a remarkable propensity for norm maintenance and endurance: many norms have a tendency to persist over time and to survive random or idiosyncratic systemic disruptions (*i.e.,* major events such as total wars on a global scale) or macrostructural adjustments (such as the universalization of the system's composition). Thus the empirical findings support those who emphasize the cultural persistence of the international legal order and who contend that once rules become part of the normative mainstream of the global system they tend to remain there over long periods of time. The evidence fits conventional impressions about the system: "All through the ages, international law keeps steadily its basic characteristics, notwithstanding the great changes that take place all over the world. This seems to be another strong proof that international law is an inherent corollary of civilization and invariably comes with any cultural development."[141] Or, alternately, "The rules of the game, embodied in international law, provide guidelines and controls for international relations. . . . The international legal order . . . rests on allegiance to shared myths. . . . The international system is the product of long historical experience. A sturdy understructure, well tested and built realistically by the trials and errors of history, will not be swept away by the turmoils of the twentieth century."[142]

A number of observations about law-formation and law modification follow from this attribute of the international legal order. First, the fact that international legal norms are stable does not mean that legal growth and development are precluded in particular sectors. The diminished tolerance of war and eventual abandonment of its legality by the system attests to the capacity of legal rules to undergo long-run transformation. Therefore, a feature of the international legal system worth appreciating is its ability to abrogate particular legal rules and to develop new ones in accordance with shifting systemic circumstances.

Second, this process of rule modification is clearly governed by evolution, not innovation. The "international legislative process"[143] is notoriously slow in generating new norms. The point, however, is that this process of law-making *is* occurring, however awkwardly and incrementally; to assume that the international legal order fails to legislate new rules[144] would be a misinterpretation.

Third, the duration of time required in the international legislative process for the creation and termination of legal rules is very long. While the duration varies according to the nature of the legal rule, most norm modifications necessitate decades. The time required for rule transformations ranges considerably. With respect to the legality of war, for instance, the step-by-step transition from an acceptance of the legitimacy of violence, through a period of limited tolerance, and to a final rejection of non-defense uses of force required approximately 150 years. Hence Boulding's contention[145] is supported that there is a "macro-learning" process at work in the international system which has led "within the last 200 years" to the emergence of "stable peace in segments of the international

141. Baron S. A. Korff, "An Introduction to the History of International Law," in Joel Larus, ed., *Comparative World Politics* (Belmont, Calif.: Wadsworth, 1964), p. 218.

142. McClelland (fn. 23), p. 46.

143. Coplin (fn. 30), p. 166.

144. The probability of making this fallacious assumption is increased if the analyst commits the error of observing legal development from a truncated time frame or static research design.

145. Boulding (fns. 24 and 98).

system."[146] The evidence generated here supports this view but cautions against optimism about the rate or permanence of learning on this scale. Apparently the learning process requires in excess of a century and may never be completed. The guidance offered by the lessons of history rarely goes uncontested for such extended periods. The slow pace of rule change in the international system presents yet another reason[147] why we should not be sanguine about "the prospects for the qualitative growth of a world legal order."[148]

Fourth, the varied rate of change of discrete bodies of global law suggests that it is dangerous to place historical eras into periods on the basis of observed fluctuations in a subset of norms. Changes in norms are neither sufficiently uniform nor cyclical to permit delineation of temporal boundaries of global normative systems. It would be arbitrary and misleading to posit dates for the termination of one legal system and the emergence of a new one. Historical epochs cannot be readily distinguished since the discontinuous growth and decay of norms renders few periods adequately homogeneous to be considered distinctive. Legal development is such that only particular sectors of legal rules manifest clear phase boundaries. Thus the pattern of legal development shows historical continuity in some areas of the law and discontinuity in others.[149] The prescriptions for future analysis of legal development are that it is dangerous to treat as recurrent in all systems those norms that may overlap temporally connected systems, and that a typological study of successive configurations of legal systems should be undertaken with extreme caution.[150]

A final observation about the consequences of norm persistence for global law-making relates to the relationship between concrete behavior and rule change. To what extent are diplomatic practice and rule change temporally associated? The impression gleaned from the evidence accumulated here suggests that behavioral change tends to precede legal change, that old legal doctrines tend to outlive the political system that precipitated and justified them, and that considerable portions of the body of international law lag behind fundamental changes in the international environment. If past behavior predicts future rules (*i.e.,* repeated behavior becomes obligatory), then it would appear that behavioral modification generates norm creation, legal transformation, and norm termination. And it suggests that transformations in the patterns of international custom can promote legal evolution and thereby serve as a catalytic source of legal development. In short, legal rules adapt and adjust in accordance with transitions in the political system of which they are a component. The potential presence of a time-lag effect in the international legal culture conforms with the general impression in the literature that legal adjustments follow behavioral changes.[151] "Cultural lag theory"[152]

---

146.   Kenneth E. Boulding, "The Learning and Reality-Testing Process in the International System," *Journal of International Affairs*, Vol. 21, No. 1 (1967), p. 14. See also his *Stable Peace* (Austin: University of Texas Press, 1978).

147.   Falk (fn. 29), p. 39, voices the sentiments of many when he contends that the prospects of international peace and the growth of world law are diminished because "the effective elites of major states are conflict-oriented and deferential to the habits of sovereignty."

148.   Ibid.

149.   This description conforms to Aron's impression (fn. 10, p. 330). Historical periods tend to suggest systems in the use of conflict which distinguish one from another; "Many philosophers or scholars," he argued, "would like to discover the law of these variations. It is tempting to imagine cycles, outcroppings, on the surface of history, of biological phenomena. None of the demonstrations which have been attempted seems convincing to me." For a recent analysis of this perspective, see Evan Luard, *Types of International Society* (New York: Free Press, 1976).

150.   For an excellent discussion of the analysis of such research problems, see Gordon Leff, *History and Social Theory* (Garden City: Doubleday-Anchor, 1971), pp. 117-137.

151.   Wright (fn. 61), pp. 35-36.

152.   See Richard P. Applebaum, *Theories of Social Change* (Chicago: Markham, 1970), esp. pp. 73-75, for a review of these theories.

suggests that the length of such lags is a good indicator of both the advent of conflict and the formation of new legal procedures to deal with that conflict.[153] Thus the existence and length of normative lags may be a crucial variable in the international legislative process, exerting a powerful impact on the development and decay of legal rules. Specifying precisely the causal impact of time-lag is problematical; Gould and Barkun provide us with perhaps the most useful statement of the problem by noting:

> a rule can persist long after it is required; it is a solution to problems which no longer exist. The extended time-lag between past rule and present reality has been all too common in contemporary international law, even though the lag may not be nearly as great as for private law. Yet it must also be observed that the total elimination of time-lag would produce even more disquieting results. If rules were totally responsive to behavior, they could serve no regulative function. The problem, then, is not one of eliminating the time-lag entirely, but of determining the *optimal* time-lag—short enough so that rules remain relevant, long enough to preserve continuity between past and present. In other words, law provides a range within which tolerable variations may occur. Efforts to reform, update, or modernize customary international law must consequently be directed at discovery of behavioral continuities, not at the fashionable inclusion of whatever happens to be current.[154]

The linkages between behavior change, rule transformation, and time-lags between the two, it may be submitted, go far in explaining variations in the process of international legal development. The process by which legal rules grow, change form, and undergo entropy is nonetheless complex. These complex connections are probably not the same for all, or even most, rules; we may need to construct different models of the law-making process for different components of the general body of law.

Mapping temporal variations in the growth and decay of international legal rules is one way to investigate processes leading to the creation of those norms. This concluding summary would not be complete without a consideration of the role which conflict plays in the process of norm formation in the international community, given the causal contribution to the development of international norms that warfare presumably exerts.

One compelling proposition suggested by the evidence is that war may operate as an agent of legal change. Transformations in some legal rules regulating war seem to be precipitated by social upheavals brought on by the outbreak of global war. Such events appear to stimulate the search for legal mechanisms designed to curtail their recurrence. The outbreak of conflict, it may thus be hypothesized, exerts pressure for legal creativity and innovation; conversely, the advent of global wars may serve to abrogate legal rules bearing on other control mechanisms (*e.g.,* coalition flexibility in the operation of a balance of power system). Recourse to war, in short, both generates new norms and terminates old ones. The immediate aftermath of world conflagrations appears to be especially auspicious for rule revision and innovation, although past experience in this respect is hardly uniform.

Another feature of normative change relates to the dynamic interplay among rules in the process of law-making, namely, the extent to which legal growth in one sector may be responsible for the erosion of rules in another. The evidence indicates that changes in legal rules do not adhere to a strictly linear trend and that cyclical patterns of growth and decay may covary negatively, positively, or share no systematic relationship. For example, the contemporary development of legal rules bearing on supranational regulation of

---

153. Ibid.
154. Gould and Barkun (fn. 1), p. 183.

violence has been simultaneous with (a) growth of pacific settlement and (b) relative decay of rules in the area of non-war methods of forcible conflict resolution. This observation encourages the speculation that rule-creation is dynamically related to the transformation of rules in other sectors of the legal system. Rule erosion in one segment of the law may precipitate rule-formation and rule-termination in other segments.

Another attribute of law-making which may be inferred from the data relates to the frequency of behavior and its perceived legality. The evidence reveals that the incidence of war is not related to its perceived permissibility. Repeated behavior has not become obligatory. And likewise, the efficacy of international law in deterring international violence is not supported. Hence, the stable incidence of the recourse to war cannot be attributed to legal constraints. It *can* be argued however, that the growth of opposition to war in the international legal culture is related to the severity of war, and that the former has led to that growth toward war's perceived illegitimacy. This point has been summarized by a student of international law in the following terms: "It would be foolish to suggest that international law is the main cause of the infrequency of wars; the destructiveness of modern war is a much more potent factor. The popular revulsion against the destructiveness of modern war gave rise to rules of law against the use of force; but those rules have in turn served to augment popular revulsion against war."[155] This suggests that the permissibility of a form of behavior in the legal culture is less related to the frequency of its occurrence than it is to its perceived acceptability and value. The brutality of contemporary war has done more to undermine its legality than has its incidence. When a legal norm becomes too costly to be maintained, does it therefore tend to be discarded?

The preceding characteristic might lead the theorist to conclude that the prohibition of a mode of activity would promote the erosion of the number of rules pertaining to that activity (according to the reasoning that "as war has been outlawed, rules for its regulation would in any case be unnecessary"[156]). Our evidence indicates, instead, that while the salience of beliefs regarding the control of war has declined with the prohibition of violence, particular segments of law underwent dramatic development as a consequence of war's prohibition. For instance, the decline in the perceived legality of war has been associated with a concomitant growth in legal rules of pacific settlement. Hence, while the evidence is far from unequivocal, it suggests that rule-creation may be stimulated by shifts toward the outlawing of some kind of activity.[157]

Finally, the impact of the changing incidence of war and legal norms bearing on its control can be assessed from another perspective: the consequent political and cultural atmosphere in which law-making takes place. Conflict, it is frequently noted, is capable of both destroying the social fabric of a community and of contributing to its integration and cohesion.[158] Where conflict has been especially intense (as during the most frigid periods of the cold war), norm stability has been threatened and the prospect of creating law through formal legislative channels has been diminished.[159] But conflict also serves to resolve divergent interests, to integrate nations, and to generate a consensus about issues

---

155. Michael Akehurst, *A Modern Introduction to International Law* (London: George Allen and Unwin, 1971), p. 321.

156. Terry Nardin, "The Laws of War and Moral Judgment," paper presented at the 1975 Meeting of the International Studies Association, p. 2.

157. The case of Prohibition in domestic law is instructive on the point. The advent of Prohibition encouraged the growth of laws designed to regulate the *distribution* of alcohol, whereas the repeal of this amendment stimulated the growth of rules regulating its *consumption*.

158. Coser (fn. 13).

159. Kaplan and Katzenbach (fn. 8), p. 347.

and their resolution.[160] Even the potential threat of conflict, such as that posed by contemporary war, can serve to bring about social cohesion and a sense of community. In a social system composed of sovereign national actors who possess the power to ignore all rules, this sense of community induced by the shared fear of violence can go far in producing consensus in the global community. Some modicum of consensus is a precondition for the growth of world law, for law-making in international relations must occur in a legal system based on voluntary consent. It may well be one of the ironies of history that the contemporary threat of global destruction which war poses in an increasingly interdependent and interactive world[161] may precipitate the birth of transnational attitudes[162] conducive to the development of international law and the creation of world law.

If this and the preceding hypotheses are valid, then two entwined conclusions are evident. First, the process of legal rule formation is potently affected by sociopolitical changes in the international system. And, second, the norm growth capable of eventually culminating in developed global law is contingent upon the continued evolution of those systemic political conditions. International law will not develop into world law until the global system makes the transition from an unorganized society to an organized community,[163] or when the prevailing "ordered anarchy"[164] of the present global system is replaced by a system with more effective law-making and law-enforcement institutions.

---

160.   For a review of these ideas, see Robert C. Angell, "The Sociology of Human Conflict," in Elton B. McNeil, ed., *The Nature of Human Conflict* (Englewood Cliffs: Prentice-Hall, 1965), pp. 91-115.

161.   For a complete discussion of these ideas, see Karl W. Deutsch, "The Probability of International Law," in Deutsch and Hoffmann, eds., (fn. 26), pp. 80-114.

162.   Elise Boulding, "The Measurement of Cultural Potentials for Transnationalism," paper presented at the 1972 Meeting of the International Studies Association.

163.   Lauterpacht (fn. 2), p. 80.

164.   Hedley Bull, *The Anarchical Society* (New York: Columbia University Press, 1977).

Books written under the auspices of the Center of International Studies, Princeton University

Books (available from publishers)

Gabriel A. Almond, *The Appeals of Communism* (Princeton University Press 1954)

William W. Kaufmann, ed., *Military Policy and National Security* (Princeton University Press 1956)

Klaus Knorr, *The War Potential of Nations* (Princeton University Press 1956)

Lucian W. Pye, *Guerrilla Communism in Malaya* (Princeton University Press 1956)

Charles De Visscher, *Theory and Reality in Public International Law, trans. by P.E. Corbett (Princeton University Press 1957; rev. ed. 1968)*

Bernard C. Cohen, *The Political Process and Foreign Policy: The Making of the Japanese Peace Settlement* (Princeton University Press 1957)

Myron Weiner, *Party Politics in India: The Development of a Multi-Party System* (Princeton University Press 1957)

Percy E. Corbett, *Law in Diplomacy* (Princeton University Press 1959)

Rolf Sannwald and Jacques Stohler, *Economic Integration: Theoretical Assumptions and Consequences of European Unification,* trans. by Herman Karreman (Princeton University Press 1959)

Klaus Knorr, ed., *NATO and American Security* (Princeton University Press 1959)

Gabriel A. Almond and James S. Coleman, eds., *The Politics of the Developing Areas* (Princeton University Press 1960)

Herman Kahn, *On Thermonuclear War* (Princeton University Press 1960)

Sidney Verba, *Small Groups and Political Behavior: A Study of Leadership* (Princeton University Press 1961)

Robert J. C. Butow, *Tojo and the Coming of the War* (Princeton University Press 1961)

Glenn H. Snyder, *Deterrence and Defense: Toward a Theory of National Security* (Princeton University Press 1961)

Klaus Knorr and Sidney Verba, eds., *The International System: Theoretical Essays* (Princeton University Press 1961)

Peter Paret and John W. Shy, *Guerrillas in the 1960's* (Praeger 1962)

George Modelski, *A Theory of Foreign Policy* (Praeger 1962)

Klaus Knorr and Thornton Read, eds., *Limited Strategic War* (Praeger 1963)

Frederick S. Dunn, *Peace-Making and the Settlement with Japan* (Princeton University Press 1963)

Arthur L. Burns and Nina Heathcote, *Peace-Keeping by United Nations Forces* (Praeger 1963)

Richard A. Falk, *Law, Morality, and War in the Contemporary World* (Praeger 1963)

James N. Rosenau, *National Leadership and Foreign Policy: A Case Study in the Mobilization of Public Support* (Princeton University Press 1963)

Gabriel A. Almond and Sidney Verba., *The Civic Culture: Political Attitudes and Democracy in Five Nations* (Princeton University Press 1963)

Bernard C. Cohen, *The Press and Foreign Policy* (Princeton University Press 1963)

Richard L. Sklar, *Nigerian Political Parties: Power in an Emergent African Nation* (Princeton University Press 1963)

Peter Paret, *French Revolutionary Warfare from Indochina to Algeria: The Analysis of a Political and Military Doctrine* (Praeger 1964)

Harry Eckstein, ed., *Internal War: Problems and Approaches* (Free Press 1964)

Cyril E. Black and Thomas P. Thornton, eds., *Communism and Revolution: The Strategic Uses of Political Violence* (Princeton University Press 1964)

Miriam Camps, *Britain and the European Community 1955–1963* (Princeton University Press 1964)

Thomas P. Thornton, ed., *The Third World in Soviet Perspective: Studies by Soviet Writers on the Developing Areas* (Princeton University Press 1964)

James N. Rosenau, ed., *International Aspects of Civil Strife* (Princeton University Press 1964)

Sidney I. Ploss, *Conflict and Decision-Making in Soviet Russia: A Case Study of Agricultural Policy, 1953–1963* (Princeton University Press 1965)

Richard A. Falk and Richard J. Barnet, eds., *Security in Disarmament* (Princeton University Press 1965)

Karl von Vorys, *Political Development in Pakistan* (Princeton University Press 1965)

Harold and Margaret Sprout, *The Ecological Perspective on Human Affairs, With Special Reference to International Politics* (Princeton University Press 1965)

Klaus Knorr, *On the Uses of Military Power in the Nuclear Age* (Princeton University Press 1966)

Harry Eckstein, *Division and Cohesion in Democracy: A Study of Norway* (Princeton University Press 1966)

Cyril E. Black, *The Dynamics of Modernization: A Study in Comparative History* (Harper and Row 1966)

Peter Kunstadter, ed., *Southeast Asian Tribes, Minorities, and Nations* (Princeton University Press 1967)

E. Victor Wolfenstein, *The Revolutionary Personality: Lenin, Trotsky, Gandhi* (Princeton University Press 1967)

Leon Gordenker, *The UN Secretary-General and the Maintenance of Peace* (Columbia University Press 1967)

Oran R. Young, *The Intermediaries: Third Parties in International Crises* (Princeton University Press 1967)

James N. Rosenau, ed., *Domestic Sources of Foreign Policy* (Free Press 1967)

Richard F. Hamilton, *Affluence and the French Worker in the Fourth Republic* (Princeton University Press 1967)

Linda B. Miller, *World Order and Local Disorder: The United Nations and Internal Conflicts* (Princeton University Press 1967)

Henry Bienen, *Tanzania: Party Transformation and Economic Development* (Princeton University Press 1967)

Wolfram F. Hanrieder, *West German Foreign Policy, 1949–1963: International Pressures and Domestic Response* (Stanford University Press 1967)

Richard H. Ullman, *Britain and the Russian Civil War: November 1918-February 1920* (Princeton University Press 1968)

Robert Gilpin, *France in the Age of the Scientific State* (Princeton University Press 1968)

William B. Bader, *The United States and the Spread of Nuclear Weapons* (Pegasus 1968)

Richard A. Falk, *Legal Order in a Violent World* (Princeton University Press 1968)

Cyril E. Black, Richard A. Falk, Klaus Knorr and Oran R. Young, *Neutralization and World Politics* (Princeton University Press 1968)

Oran R. Young, *The Politics of Force: Bargaining During International Crises* (Princeton University Press 1969)

Klaus Knorr and James N. Rosenau, eds., *Contending Approaches to International Politics* (Princeton University Press 1969)

James N. Rosenau, ed., *Linkage Politics: Essays on the Convergence of National and International Systems* (Free Press 1969)

John T. McAlister, Jr., *Viet Nam: The Origins of Revolution* (Knopf 1969)

Jean Edward Smith, *Germany Beyond the Wall: People, Politics and Prosperity* (Little, Brown 1969)

James Barros, *Betrayal from Within: Joseph Avenol, Secretary-General of the League of Nations, 1933–1940* (Yale University Press 1969)

Charles Hermann, *Crises in Foreign Policy: A Simulation Analysis* (Bobbs-Merrill 1969)

Robert C. Tucker, *The Marxian Revolutionary Idea: Essays on Marxist Thought and Its Impact on Radical Movements* (W. W. Norton 1969)

Harvey Waterman, *Political Change in Contemporary France: The Politics of an Industrial Democracy* (Charles E. Merrill 1969)

Cyril E. Black and Richard A. Falk, eds., *The Future of the International Legal Order*. Vol. I: *Trends and Pattern:* (Princeton University Press 1969)

Ted Robert Gurr, *Why Men Rebel* (Princeton University Press 1969)

C. Sylvester Whitaker, *The Politics of Tradition: Continuity and Change in Northern Nigeria 1946–1960* (Princeton University Press 1970)

Richard A. Falk, *The Status of Law in International Society* (Princeton University Press 1970)

Klaus Korr, *Military Power and Potential* (D. C. Heath 1970)

Cyril E. Black and Richard A. Falk, eds., *The Future of the International Legal Order*. Vol. II: *Wealth and Resources* (Princeton University Press 1970)

Leon Gordenker, ed., *The United Nations in International Politics* (Princeton University Press 1971)

Cyril E. Black and Richard A. Falk, eds., *The Future of the International Legal Order*. Vol. III: *Conflict Management* (Princeton University Press 1971)

Francine R. Frankel, *India's Green Revolution: Political Costs of Economic Growth* (Princeton University Press 1971)

Harold and Margaret Sprout, *Toward a Politics of the Planet Earth* (Van Nostrand Reinhold 1971)

Cyril E. Black and Richard A. Falk, eds., *The Future of the International Legal Order*. Vol. IV: *The Structure of the International Environment* (Princeton University Press 1972)

Gerald Garvey, *Energy, Ecology, Economy* (W. W. Norton 1972)

Richard Ullman, *The Anglo-Soviet Accord* (Princeton University Press 1973)

Klaus Knorr, *Power and Wealth: The Political Economy of International Power* (Basic Books 1973)

Anton Bebler, *Military Role in Africa: Dahomey, Ghana, Sierra Leone, and Mali* (Praeger Publishers 1973)

Robert C. Tucker, *Stalin as Revolutionary 1879–1929: A Study in History and Personality* (W. W. Norton 1973)

Edward L. Morse, *Foreign Policy and Interdependence in Gaullist France* (Princeton University Press 1973)

Henry Bienen, *Kenya: The Politics of Participation and Control* (Princeton University Press 1974)

Gregory J. Massell, *The Surrogate Proletariat: Moslem Women and Revolutionary Strategies in Soviet Central Asia, 1919–1929* (Princeton University Press 1974)

James N. Rosenau, *Citizenship Between Elections: An Inquiry Into the Mobilizable American* (Free Press 1974)

Ervin Laszlo, *A Strategy For the Future: The Systems Approach To World Order* (Braziller 1974)

John R. Vincent, *Nonintervention and International Order* (Princeton University Press 1974)

Jan H. Kalicki, *The Pattern of Sino-American Crises: Political-Military Interactions in the 1950s* (Cambridge University Press 1975)

Klaus Knorr, *The Power of Nations: The Political Economy of International Relations* (Basic Books Inc., 1975)

James P. Sewell, *UNESCO and World Politics: Engaging in International Relations* (Princeton University Press 1975)

Richard A. Falk, *A Global Approach to National Policy* (Harvard University Press 1975)

Harry Eckstein and Ted Robert Gurr, *Patterns of Authority: A Structural Basis for Political Inquiry* (John Wiley & Sons 1975)

Cyril E. Black, Marius B. Jansen, Herbert S. Levine, Marion J. Levy, Jr., Henry Rosovsky, Gilbert Rozman, Henry D. Smith, II, and S. Frederick Starr, *The Modernization of Japan and Russia* (Free Press 1975)

Leon Gordenker, *International Aid and National Decisions: Development Programs in Malawi, Tanzania, and Zambia* (Princeton University Press 1976)

Carl Von Clausewitz, *On War,* edited and translated by Michael Howard and Peter Paret (Princeton University Press 1976)

Gerald Garvey and Lou Ann Garvey, eds., *International Resource Flows* (Lexington Books, D. C. Heath 1977)

Walter F. Murphy and Joseph Tanenhaus, *Comparative Constitutional Law Cases and Commentaries* (St. Martin's Press 1977)

Gerald Garvey, *Nuclear Power and Social Planning: The City of the Second Sun* (Lexington Books, D. C. Heath 1977)

Richard E. Bissell, *Apartheid and International Organizations* (Westview Press 1977)

David P. Forsythe, *Humanitarian Politics: The International Committee of the Red Cross* (Johns Hopkins University Press 1977)

Paul E. Sigmund, *The Overthrow of Allende and the Politics of Chile, 1964–1976* (University of Pittsburgh Press 1977)

Henry S. Bienen, *Armies and Parties in Africa* (Holmes and Meier 1978)

Harold and Margaret Sprout, *The Context of Environmental Politics* (The University Press of Kentucky 1978)

Samuel S. Kim, *China, the United Nations, and World Order* (Princeton University Press 1979)

S. Basheer Ahmed, *Nuclear Fuel and Energy Policy,* (Lexington Books, D. C. Heath 1979)

Robert C. Johansen, *The National Interest and the Human Interest: An Analysis of U.S. Foreign Policy* (Princeton University Press 1980)

Richard A. Falk and Samuel S. Kim, eds., *The War System: An Interdisciplinary Approach* (Westview Press 1980)

James H. Billington, *Fire in the Minds of Men: Origins of the Revolutionary Faith* (Basic Books, Inc. 1980)

Bennett Ramberg, *Destruction of Nuclear Energy Facilities in War: The Problem and the Implications* (Lexington Books 1980)

Gregory T. Kruglak, *The Politics of United States Decision-Making in United Nations Specialized Agencies: The Case of the International Labor Organization* (University Press of America 1980)

James C. Hsiung and Samuel S. Kim, eds., *China in the Global Community* (Praeger Publishers 1980)

Douglas Kinnard, *The Secretary of Defense* (The University Press of Kentucky 1980)

Richard Falk, *Human Rights and State Sovereignty* (Holmes & Meier Publishers, Inc. 1981)

James H. Mittelman, *Underdevelopment and the Transition to Socialism: Mozambique and Tanzania* (Academic Press 1981)